Lecture Notes in Computer Science 1961

Edited by G. Goos, J. Hartmanis and J. van Leeuwen

Springer
Berlin
Heidelberg
New York
Barcelona
Hong Kong
London
Milan
Paris
Singapore
Tokyo

Jifeng He   Masahiko Sato (Eds.)

Advances in Computing Science – ASIAN 2000

6th Asian Computing Science Conference
Penang, Malaysia, November 25-27, 2000
Proceedings

 Springer

Series Editors

Gerhard Goos, Karlsruhe University, Germany
Juris Hartmanis, Cornell University, NY, USA
Jan van Leeuwen, Utrecht University, The Netherlands

Volume Editors

He Jifeng
United Nations University, International Institute for Software Technology
Casa Silva Mendes, Estrada do Engenheiro Trigo NO 4, Macau, China
E-mail: jifeng@iist.unu.edu

Masahiko Sato
Kyoto University, Graduate School of Informatics
Sakyo-ku, Kyoto 606-8501, Japan
E-mail: masahiko@kuis.kyoto-u.ac.jp

Cataloging-in-Publication Data applied for

Die Deutsche Bibliothek - CIP-Einheitsaufnahme

Advances in computing science - ASIAN 2000 : proceedings / 6th Asian
Computing Science Conference, Penang, Malaysia, November 25 - 27,
2000. Jifeng He ; Masahiko Sato (ed.). - Berlin ; Heidelberg ; New
York ; Barcelona ; Hong Kong ; London ; Milan ; Paris ; Singapore ;
Tokyo : Springer, 2000
    (Lecture notes in computer science ; Vol. 1961)
    ISBN 3-540-41428-2

CR Subject Classification (1998): F.4, F.3, I.2.3, C.2, F.2, F.1

ISSN 0302-9743
ISBN 3-540-41428-2 Springer-Verlag Berlin Heidelberg New York

Springer-Verlag Berlin Heidelberg New York
a member of BertelsmannSpringer Science+Business Media GmbH
© Springer-Verlag Berlin Heidelberg 2000
Printed in Germany

Typesetting: Camera-ready by author
Printed on acid-free paper   SPIN: 10781048   06/3142   5 4 3 2 1 0

Preface

The Asian Computing Science Conference (ASIAN) series was initiated in 1995 to provide a forum for researchers in computer science in Asia to meet and to promote interaction with researchers from other regions. The previous five conferences were held, respectively, in Bangkok, Singapore, Kathmandu, Manila, and Phuket. The proceedings were published in the Lecture Notes in Computer Science Series of Springer-Verlag.

This year's conference (ASIAN 2000) attracted 61 submissions from which 18 papers were selected through an electronic program committee (PC) meeting.

The themes for this year's conference are:

- Logics in Computer Science
- Data Mining
- Networks and Performance

The key note speaker for ASIAN 2000 is Jean Vuillemin (ENS, France) and the invited speakers are Ramamohanarao Kotagiri (U. Melbourne, Australia) and Alain Jean-Marie (LIRMM, France). We thank them for accepting our invitation.

This year's conference is sponsored by the Asian Institute of Technology (Thailand), INRIA (France), the National University of Singapore (Singapore), and UNU/IIST (Macau SAR, China). We thank all these institutions for their continued support of the ASIAN series.

This year's conference will be held in Penang, Malaysia. We are much obliged to Universiti Sains Malaysia and Penang State Government for providing the conference venue and to Dr. Abdullah Zawawi Haji Talib for making the local arrangements.

We also wish to thank the PC members and the large number of referees for the substantial work put in by them in assessing the submitted papers.

Finally, it is a pleasure to acknowledge the friendly and efficient support provided by Alfred Hofmann and his team at Springer-Verlag in bringing out this volume.

October 2000

He Jifeng
Masahiko Sato

Program Committee

Yuxi Fu (Shanghai Jiao Tong U., China)
Ian Graham (U. of Waikato, New Zealand)
He Jifeng (co-chair) (UNU/IIST, Macau SAR, China)
Alain Jean-Marie (LIRMM, France)
Kazunori Konishi (KDD, Japan)
Bing Liu (NUS, Singapore)
Zhen Liu (INRIA, France)
Ian Mason (U. of New England, Australia)
Yasuhiko Morimoto (IBM Tokyo, Japan)
Mitsu Okada (Keio U., Japan)
Luke Ong (Oxford U., UK)
Masahiko Sato (co-chair) (Kyoto U., Japan)
Kyuseok Shim (KAIST, Korea)

General Chair

Joxan Jaffar (National University of Singapore, Singapore)

Local Chair

Dr. Abdullah Zawawi Haji Talib (Universiti Sains Malaysia, Malaysia)

Steering Committee

Shigeki Goto (Waseda U., Japan)
Stephane Grumbach(INRIA, France)
Joxan Jaffar (NUS, Singapore)
Gilles Kahn (INRIA, France)
Kanchana Kanchanasut (AIT, Thailand)
R.K. Shyamasundar (TIFR Bombay, India)
Kazunori Ueda (Waseda U., Japan)
Zhou Chaochen (UNU/IIST, Macau SAR, China)

Referees

Yohji Akama	Kohei Honda	Yoshinari Kameda
Takeshi Fukuda	Wynne Hsu	Yukiyoshi Kameyama
Chris George	Dang Van Hung	Yoji Kishi
Andy Gordon	T. Ida	Yoshinori Kitatsuji
John Harrison	Takeuti Izumi	Naoki Kobayashi
Yuichiro Hei	Tomasz Janowski	Satoshi Konishi

Shinji Kono
Yiming Ma
M. Marin
Hirofumi Matsuzawa
Masaki Murakami
Yuko Murayama
Hiroshi Nakano
Susumu Nishimura
Hiroyuki Okano
M. Parigot

Franz Puntigam
Alexander Rabinovich
Chiaki Sakama
Etsuya Shibayama
Tetsuo Shibuya
Keizo Sugiyama
Taro Suzuki
Koichi Takahashi
Makoto Tatsuta
Atsushi Togashi

Yoshihito Toyama
Christian Urban
Osamu Watanabe
H. Wu
Xu Qiwen
Yiyuan Xia
Mitsuharu Yamamoto
Tetsushi Yamashita
Roland Yap

Table of Contents

Finite Digital Synchronous Circuits
Are Characterized by 2-Algebraic Truth Tables

Jean Vuillemin[1]

Ecole Normale Supérieure, 45 rue d'Ulm, 75230 Paris cedex 05, France.
Jean.Vuillemin@ens.fr

Abstract. A *digital* function maps sequences of binary *inputs*, into sequences of binary *outputs*. It is *causal* when the output at cycle N is a boolean function of the input, from cycles 0 through N.
A causal digital function f is characterized by its *truth table*, an infinite sequence of bits (F_N) which gathers all outputs for all inputs. It is identified to the power series $\sum F_N z^N$, with coefficients in the two elements field $\mathbf{F}_2$.

Theorem 1. *A digital function can be computed by a* finite digital synchronous circuit, *if and only if it is* causal, *and its truth table is an* algebraic number *over* $\mathbf{F}_2[z]$, *the field of polynomial fractions* (mod 2).

A data structure, *recursive sampling*, is introduced to provide a *canonical* representation, for each *finite causal* function f. It can be mapped, through finite algorithms, into a circuit $SDD(f)$, an automaton $SBA(f)$, and a polynomial $poly(f)$; each is *characteristic* of f. One can thus automatically synthesize a canonical circuit, or software code, for computing any *finite causal* function f, presented in some effective form. Through recursive sampling, one can verify, in finite time, the validity of any hardware circuit or software program for computing f.

1 Physical Deterministic Digital System

Consider a *discrete time digital system*: at each integer cycle N^1, the system receives input bits $x_N \in \mathbf{B} = \{0, 1\}$, and emits output bits $y_N \in \mathbf{B}$. The *function* f of this system, is to map *infinite* sequences of input bits $x = (x_N)$, into infinite sequences of output bits $y = f(x) = (y_N)$. Call *digital* such a function $f \in \mathbf{D} \mapsto \mathbf{D}$, where $\mathbf{D} = \mathbf{N} \mapsto \mathbf{B}$ is the set of infinite binary sequences. Our aim is to characterize which functions can be computed by deterministic digital *physical* systems, such as electronic circuits, and which *cannot*.

To simplify, we exclude *analog* [1], and *asynchronous* systems. As long as the function of such *exotic* systems remains deterministic, and digital, an equivalent system may be implemented through a *digital synchronous* electronic chip. The concept of *Digital Synchronous Circuit* **DSC**, provides a mathematical model for the *form* and *function* of this class of physical systems.

---

[1] Throughout this text, reserve the letter N to range over the natural numbers: $N \in \mathbf{N}$.

J. He and M. Sato (Eds.): ASIAN 2000, LNCS 1961, pp. 1–12, 2000.
© Springer-Verlag Berlin Heidelberg 2000

Established techniques exist to map finite **DSC** descriptions, into silicon chips [2]. With *reconfigurable systems* [3], the process can be fully automated: from a finite **DSC** representation for *mathematically* computing f, *compile* a binary configuration, and download into some *programmable* device, in order to *physically* compute f. Without further argument, admit here that the class of functions defined by *finite* **DSC** captures the proper mathematical concept, from the motivation question. No regard is given to size limitations, arising from technology, economics, or else.

- Physical circuits are constrained by *time causality*: output $y(t)$ at time t may only depend upon inputs $x(t')$, from the *past* $t' < t$.
- From their physical nature, electronic circuits must be *finite*.

Causality and finiteness are thus necessary conditions, for digital functions to be computable by deterministic *physical* devices. We show that they are sufficient, and characterize *finite causal* functions, in a constructive way.

1.1   Infinite SDD Procedure

A first answer to the motivating question is provided in [4], through an *infinite* construction, the *Synchronous Decision Diagrams* **SDD**.

Theorem 2 (Vuillemin [4]).

1. *To any causal function f, one can associate a canonical circuit $SDD(f) \in$ **DSC** for computing f.*
2. *Circuit $SDD(f)$ is finite, if and only if function f is computable by some finite system.*

Yet, the *infinite* **SDD** construction, relies on the ability to test for equality $g = h$ between digital functions g, h. This operation is *not computable* in general, even when g and h are both computable. Also, the definition of *"finiteness"* is not made explicit in Theorem 2, and the input to the *"procedure"* is ill-specified.

Such limitations are partly removed, by Berry [5] and Winkelman [6]: both base implementations of the **SDD** procedure, on representing digital functions by a *Finite State Machines* **FSM**.

2   Binary Algebra

Infinite binary sequences $\mathbf{D} \rightleftharpoons \mathbf{N} \mapsto \mathbf{B}$ have a rich mathematical structure. A digital sequence $a \in \mathbf{D}$ codes, in a unique way: the set $\{a\} = \{\mathbf{N} : a_\mathbf{N} = 1\}$ of integers; the formal power series $a(z) = \sum a_\mathbf{N} z^\mathbf{N}$; the 2-adic *"integer"* $a(2) = \sum a_\mathbf{N} z^\mathbf{N}$: $\mathbf{D} \rightleftharpoons \wp(\mathbf{N}) \rightleftharpoons \mathbf{F}_2(z) \rightleftharpoons \mathbf{Z}_2$. We identify all representations, and write (see [4]), for example:

$$(01) = \{1 + 2_\mathbf{N}\} = -\frac{2}{3} = z/(1 + z^2).$$

Binary Algebra imports all underlying operations, into a single structure:

$$\langle \mathbf{D}, \neg, \cup, \cap, z, z^-, \oplus, \otimes, +, -, \times, \uparrow, \downarrow \rangle.$$

1. $\langle \mathbf{D}, \neg, \cup, \cap \rangle$ is a *Boolean Algebra*, isomorphic to sets $\wp(\mathbf{N})$ of integers;
2. $\langle \mathbf{D}, z, \oplus, \otimes \rangle$ is a ring, isomorphic to the formal power series $\mathbf{F}_2(z)$;
3. $\langle \mathbf{D}, 0, 1, +, -, \times \rangle$ is a ring, isomorphic to the 2-adic integers $\mathbf{Z}_2$.

The *up-sampling* operator is noted $\uparrow x = x(z^2) = x \otimes x$. The *down-sampling* operator is noted $\downarrow x = \downarrow (x_\mathbf{N}) = (x_{2\mathbf{N}})$. See the related Noble identities, in the appendix.

In addition to the axiomatic relations implied by each of the three structures in $\mathbf{D}$, *hybrid* relations exist between the operators in Binary Algebra. Some are listed in the appendix. There are more: indeed, each arithmetical circuit implements some hybrid relation [4]. For example, base -2 coding, is defined by

$$\sum_{k \leq \mathbf{N}} x_k 2^k = \sum_{k \leq \mathbf{N}} y_k (-2)^k \pmod{2^\mathbf{N}}. \tag{1}$$

It is also known as Booth coding $y = \mathrm{booth}(x)$, Polish code (in [7]), and may be computed by the hybrid formula:

$$\mathrm{booth}(x) = (01) \oplus (x + (01)).$$

The infinite Binary Algebra $\mathbf{D} = \mathbf{Z}_2$, contains noteworthy sub-structures:

$$\mathbf{F}_2 \subset \mathbf{B}^\mathbf{N} \subset \mathbf{N} \subset \mathbf{Z} \subset \mathbf{P2} \subset \mathbf{P} \subset \mathbf{A}_2 \subset \mathbf{Z}_2 \subset \mathbf{Z}_2.$$

Here: $\mathbf{B}^\mathbf{N}$ are the finite sequences, $\mathbf{P}$ the *ultimately periodic* sequences, $\mathbf{P2}$ those of period length $2^\mathbf{N}$, $\mathbf{A}_2$ the 2-algebraic (definition 6), and $\mathbf{Z}_2$ the *computable* 2-adic integers. The appendix lists the closure properties of these sets, with respect to Binary Algebra operations.

3   Causal Function

Let $\|x\| \in \mathbf{Q}$ denote the *2-adic norm* of $x \in \mathbf{D}$: $\|0\| = 0$, $\|1 + zx\| = 1$, and $\|zx\| = \|x\|/2$. The *distance* $\|a - b\|$, between digital sequences $a, b \in \mathbf{D}$, is *ultra-metric*: $\|a + b\| \leq \max\{\|a\|, \|b\|\}$. Note that: $\|a - b\| = \|a \oplus b\|$.

Definition 1. *A digital function is* causal, *when the following (equivalent statements) hold:*

1. $\forall a, b \in \mathbf{D}: \|f(a) - f(b)\| \leq \|a - b\|$.
2. *Each output bit is a* Boolean function $f_\mathbf{N} \in \mathbf{B}^{\mathbf{N}+1} \mapsto \mathbf{B}$, *which exclusively depends on the first* $\mathbf{N} + 1$ *bits of input:*

$$y_\mathbf{N} = f_\mathbf{N}(x_0 \, x_1 \, \cdots \, x_{\mathbf{N}-1} \, x_\mathbf{N}) = f_\mathbf{N}(x),$$
$$y = (y_\mathbf{N}) = f(x) = (f_\mathbf{N}(x)) = \sum f_\mathbf{N}(x) z^\mathbf{N}.$$

The operators $\neg, \cap, \cup, \oplus, z, \otimes, \oslash, \uparrow, +, -, \times, /$ are *causal*. The *antiflop* z^- (defined by $y_\mathbf{N} = x_{\mathbf{N}+1}$), and down-sampling $\downarrow$ are *not causal*. We simply say *causal* f, when f is a *causal* digital function, with a single input x, and a single output $y = f(x)$; otherwise, we explicitly state the number of inputs, and outputs.

3.1 Truth Table

Definition 2. *The* truth table *of a causal function* $f(x) = (f_N(x))$, *combines the tables for each Boolean function* $f_N \in \mathbf{B}^{N+1} \mapsto \mathbf{B}$, *into a unique digital sequence* $truth(f) = F = (F_N) \in \mathbf{D}$, *defined by*

$$F_N = f_m(b_0 \, b_1 \cdots b_{m-1} \, b_m);$$

here: $m = \lfloor log_2(N+2) \rfloor - 1$, *and* $\sum_{k \leq m} b_k 2^k = N + 2 - 2^{m+1}$.

Proposition 1. *The truth table* $F = truth(f) \in \mathbf{D}$ *is a one-to-one digital code, for each causal function* $f = truth^-(F) \in \mathbf{D} \mapsto \mathbf{D}$.

Proposition 2. *For causal f and g:*
$$\begin{aligned} truth(\neg f) &= \neg truth(f), \\ truth(f \cup g) &= truth(f) \cup truth(g), \\ truth(f \cap g) &= truth(f) \cap truth(g), \\ truth(\widetilde{zf}) &= 1 + z \uparrow z \, truth(\widetilde{f}). \end{aligned}$$

3.2 Automatic Sequence

Although it is traditionally associated to a *finite* causal f, which is explicitly presented by a *finite state automaton*, the definition of an *automatic sequence* [9], may be extended to all causal functions, finite and infinite.

Definition 3. *The* automatic sequence $auto(f) = (a_N) \in \mathbf{D}$, *is associated to the causal function f, by:*

$$a_N = f_m(b_0 \, b_1 \cdots b_{m-1} \, b_m),$$

where $m = 0$ if $N = 0$, else $m = \lfloor log_2(N) \rfloor$, and $N = \sum_{k \leq m} b_k 2^k$.

In general, the value $y = (y_N) = f(x)$ of causal f, at $x = (x_N)$, *cannot* be reconstructed, from its automatic sequence $auto(f)$. Indeed, consider the causal: $firstbit(x) = x \cap 1$, and $zerotest(x) = \neg z^-(-x \oplus x)$. Both have the *same* automatic number: $auto(firstbit) = auto(zerotest) = 1(0)$. While $truth(firstbit) = 1$, we have $T = truth(zerotest) = 10100010000000100000000000000100 \cdots \neq 1$.

Proposition 3. *Let f be causal. The derived causal functions, $g(x) = f(\neg z \neg x)$ and $h(x) = zf(z^-x)$, are such that:*

$$\begin{aligned} auto(f) &= truth(g), \\ truth(f) &= z^{-2} auto(h). \end{aligned}$$

3.3 Time Reversal

Definition 4. *The* time reversed *function $\widetilde{f}$, is defined by*

$$\widetilde{f}(x) = \sum f_N(x_N \cdots x_0) z^N,$$

where the causal function f is given (definition 1) by:

$$f(x) = \sum f_N(x_0 \cdots x_N) z^N.$$

The *reversed* truth table $\text{truth}(\widetilde{f}) = (F_{\widetilde{\mathbf{N}}})$, is related to $\text{truth}(f) = (F_{\mathbf{N}})$ through:

$$\widetilde{\mathbf{N}} = (0\ 1\ 2\ 4\ 3\ 5\ 6\ 10\ 8\ 12\ 7\ 11\ 9\ 13\ 14\ 22 \cdots).$$

Let $\text{prefix}(f) = \{z^{-b}f(a + z^b x) : a, b \in \mathbf{N}, a < 2^b\}$, and $\text{suffix}(f) = \text{prefix}(\widetilde{f})$.

Proposition 4. *The class of causal functions is closed under composition, prefix, suffix, and time reversal operations.*

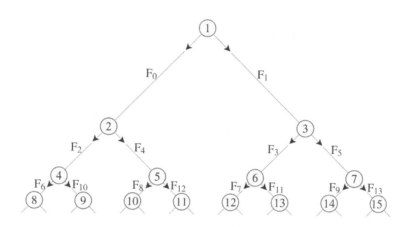

Fig. 1. Sequential Decision Tree, for the truth table $(F_{\mathbf{N}})$.

4 Universal Causal Machines

4.1 Sequential Decision Tree

Definition 5. *The* Sequential Decision Tree *$sdt(f)$, for computing causal f, is a complete infinite binary tree - fig. 1. A digital input $x \in \mathbf{D}$, specifies a unique path through the tree: start at the root, for cycle 0; at cycle $\mathbf{N}$, move down, to the left if $x_{\mathbf{N}} = 0$, right otherwise. Arcs in the tree are labeled, in hierarchical order, by bits from the time reversed $\text{truth}(\widetilde{f})$. Output $y = f(x)$, is the digital sequence of arc labels, along the path specified by input x.*

4.2 Sequential Multiplexer

A Digital Synchronous circuit **DSC** is obtained, by composing *primitive* components: the *register* **reg**, and Boolean (combinational, memoryless) operators. There is a restriction on composition: all *combinational* paths, through a chain

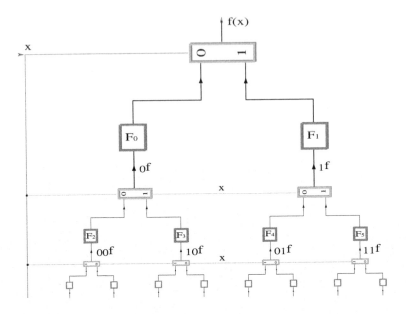

Fig. 2. Sequential multiplexer, for the truth table $(F_\mathbf{N})$.

of Boolean operators, must be *finite*. This implies that each feedback loop *must* contain, at least one memory element **reg** (positive feedback).

The operators $(\mathbf{reg}_0, \mathbf{reg}_1, \mathbf{mux})$ serve as a base, for the SDD procedure: registers $\mathbf{reg}_0(x) = \mathbf{reg}(x) = zx = 2x$, $\mathbf{reg}_1(x) = \neg z \neg x = 1 + 2x$, and multiplexer $\mathbf{mux}(c, b, a) = (c \cap b) + (\neg c \cap a) = c \cap (b \oplus a) \oplus a$.

The *sequential multiplexer* $SM(f)$, from [4], is shown in fig. 2. The registers in $SM(f)$, are labeled, 0 for $\mathbf{reg}_0$ and 1 for $\mathbf{reg}_1$, by truth(f), in *direct* order.

4.3 Share Common Expressions

The next step, in the infinite **SDD** construction [4], is to *share* all common sub-expressions, which appear in the process: the result is the *Sequential Decision Diagram* SDD(f), for *SM* - see fig. 4. Similarly, for *SDT*, we obtain the *Sequential Binary Automaton* SBA(f) - see fig. 3.

5   Finite Causal Function

The causal functions mentioned so far may all be realized by *finite* circuits, and finite state machines **FSM**, except for $\times$, $/$, $\otimes$, $\oslash$ and $\uparrow$, which are *infinite* [4].

Definition 6. *Digital sequence b is 2-algebraic, when $b(z) = \sum b_\mathbf{N} z^\mathbf{N}$ is algebraic over $\mathbf{F}_2(z)$. Let $\mathbf{A}_2$ denote the set of 2-algebraic sequences.*

$T(z) = \text{truth(zerotest)}$ is 2-algebraic, as root of: $1 + T + z^2 T^2 = 0 \pmod 2$.

Proposition 5. *Causal f is finite, if and only if the following equivalents hold:*

  a *f is computed by a finite circuit **DSC**;*
  b *f is computed by a finite state machine **FSM**;*
  c *prefix(f) is finite;*
  d *suffix(f) is finite;*
  e *truth(f) is 2-algebraic.*

Proof: The equivalence between (a) and (b) is well-known. The equivalence between (b), (c) and (d) follows from classical automata theory [7].

The equivalence between (d) and (e) is established, through a result in the theory of *automatic sequences*. Call *2-automatic*, a sequence $a \in \mathbf{D}$, such that $a = \text{auto}(f)$, for some **FSM** f.

Theorem 3 (Christol, Kamae, Mendès France, Rauzy [11]).
A digital sequence is 2-automatic, *if and only if it is* 2-algebraic.

Combine Theorem 3 with Proposition 3, to complete the proof of Proposition 5, hence that of Theorem 1. ∎

Proposition 6. *Finite causal functions, are closed, under composition, prefix, suffix, and time reversal.*

Theorem 4. *The class $\mathbf{A}_2$, of 2-algebraic sequences, is closed under:*

  1. *Boolean operations $\neg, \cup, \cap$, and shifts z, z^-;*
  2. *carry-free polynomial operations $\oplus, \otimes, \oslash$;*
  3. *up-sampling, down-sampling, and time reversal;*
  4. *application of any finite causal function, hence $+, -$.*

Proof: Boolean closure follows from Proposition 2. Polynomial manipulations show the closure under carry-free operations: $\oplus, \otimes, \uparrow$, and shifts. Item 3 follows from Theorem 6. A novel construction is given, for proving item 4. It implies, in particular, that $\mathbf{A}_2$ is closed under ordinary addition, and subtraction, *with* carries. We conjecture that $\mathbf{A}_2$ is also closed under multiplication $\times$, and division $/$. ∎

5.1 Transcendental Numbers

If one interprets a digital sequence $x = x(z) = x(2)$ in base $\frac{1}{2}$, rather than 2 or z, one gets a *real number*: $x(1/2) \in \mathbf{R}$. To each causal f, associate the real number $\text{real}(f) = \text{truth}(f)(1/2) \in \mathbf{R}$.

Theorem 5 (Loxton, van der Poorten [12]). *If $a(z) \in \mathbf{A}_2$ is 2-algebraic, then, either $a(\frac{1}{2}) \in \mathbf{Q}$ is rational, or it is* transcendental, *in the usual sense over* $\mathbf{Q}$.

As a consequence, $\text{real(zerotest)} = 1.2656860360875726\cdots$ is transcendental, over $\mathbf{Q}$. Similarly, for $\text{real(booth)} = 0.6010761186771489\cdots$.

Up-sampling $y = \uparrow x$ is causal, and $y_{\mathbf{N}} = f_{\mathbf{N}}(x_0 \cdots x_{\mathbf{N}})$ is the middle bit: $y_{2\mathbf{N}} = 0$, and $y_{2\mathbf{N}+1} = x_{\mathbf{N}}$. The *middle bit sequence* is the truth table $M = \text{truth}(\uparrow)$:
$M = 010000001100110000000000000000000011110000111100\cdots$. No finite circuit exists, to implement up-sampling [4]. It follows, from Theorem 1, that the middle bit series $M(z)$ is *transcendental* over $\mathbf{F}_2[z]$. Similarly for $\text{truth}(\otimes)$, and $\text{truth}(\times)$. It is not known, if $\text{real}(\uparrow) = 0.5062255860470657\cdots$ is *transcendental* over $\mathbf{Q}$, or not; similarly for $\text{real}(\otimes)$ and $\text{real}(\times)$.

6   Finite SDD Procedure

For f causal and finite, define $\text{size}(f)$ as the number of states, in the *minimal* **FSM** (see [7]), for computing f. For $F \in \mathbf{D}$, define $S = \text{sample}(F)$, as

$$S = \{F\} \cup (z^- \downarrow S) \cup (z^- \downarrow z^- S),$$

where the least fixed point $S \in \wp(\mathbf{D})$, is a set of digital sequences.

Theorem 6. *Each of the following (equivalent statements), provides a canonical representation for f finite causal, with $\text{size}(f) = n$, and $F = \text{truth}(f)$.*

1. *$\text{sample}(F)$ is finite, of size n.*
2. *$SBA(f)$ is the minimal **FSM** for computing f, with n states.*
3. *$SDD(\widetilde{f})$ is a finite **DSC** circuit, with n multiplexers, and at most $2n$ registers, $\mathbf{reg}_0$ or $\mathbf{reg}_1$.*
4. *$F = \text{truth}(f)$ is the unique 2-algebraic solution, to the system $\text{quadra}(f)$, made of n binary quadratic equations.*

This is established through an effective algorithm - *recursive sampling* - and data structure. In this extented abstract, we simply present the (computer generated) output from the procedure, for one example: Booth coding, as defined by (1), and where $\text{size(booth)} = 4$.

6.1   Recursive Sampling

For $f1 = \text{truth(booth)}$, compute $\text{sample}(f1) = \{f1, f2, f5, f11\}$:

$$f1 = 0100110011110000000011111111100000000111111111111\cdots$$
$$f2 = 0101100001111000011111111000000000000001111111\cdots$$
$$f5 = 1001100111100000000111111110000000011111111111111\cdots$$
$$f11 = 101100001111000011111111000000000000000011111111\cdots$$

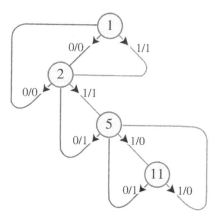

Fig. 3. The automaton SBA(booth), where $\text{booth}(x) = (01) \oplus (x + (01))$.

6.2 SBA Procedure

6.3 Characteristic Circuit Polynomial

A *binary quadratic equation* has the form: $f = a + bz + z^2 g^2 + z^3 h^2 \pmod 2$, for $a, b \in \mathbf{F}_2$, and $f, g, h \in \mathbf{D}$. Truth tables in $\text{sample}(\text{booth}) = \{f1, f2, f5, f11\}$ are related by the following system of *binary quadratic equations*:

$$f1 = z + z^2(1+z)f2^2,$$
$$f2 = z + z^2 f1^2 + z^3 f5^2,$$
$$f5 = 1 + z^2 f2^2 + z^3 f11^2,$$
$$f11 = 1 + z^2(1+z)f5^2.$$

Through *quadratic elimination*, derive $\text{quad}(F)$:

$$\text{quad}(\text{booth}) = a + bF + c \uparrow^2 F + d \uparrow^4 F \pmod 2,$$
$$a = z + z^2 + z^3 + z^8 + z^{16} + z^{28} + z^{32},$$
$$b = 1 + z + z^2 + z^3,$$
$$c = z^4(1 + z + z^2 + z^3 + z^4)^2,$$
$$d = z^{28}(1 + z + z^2 + z^3 + z^4)^4.$$

Through *algebraic simplifications*, obtain the irreducible *characteristic polynomial* poly(booth), of which $F = \text{truth}(\text{booth}) = f1$ is the only root:

$$F = z + z^4 + z^5 + z^4(1 + z + z^2 + z^3)F^4 \pmod 2.$$

A *decimal* expression for poly(booth): $F = 50 + 240 \uparrow^2 F$.

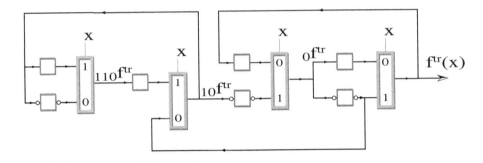

Fig. 4. The circuit SDD($\widetilde{\text{booth}}$).

6.4 SDD procedure

The circuit synthesized by the **SDD** procedure involves the *time reversed domain*. To keep the correspondence with Theorem 6.3, we show the circuit SDD($\widetilde{\text{booth}}$), in fig. 4. This circuit computes the function $\widetilde{\text{booth}}$, defined through time reversal in equation (1). For SDD(booth) $\rightleftharpoons$ SBA($\widetilde{\text{booth}}$), one finds 15 states.

7 Feed-forward Circuit

Proposition 7 (Feed-forward circuit). *The following are characteristic equivalents, for finite causal f to be free of* feed-back:

1. *SDD(f) is* acyclic;
2. *$F = truth(\widetilde{f}) \in \mathbf{P}2$ is ultimately periodic, with period length 2^b, for $b \in \mathbf{N}$;*
3. *$poly(\widetilde{f}) = a + (z^{2^b} - 1)F$, for $a \in \mathbf{N}$.*

Proposition 8 (Combinational circuit). *The following are characteristic equivalents, for finite causal f, with i inputs, to be* memoryless:

1. *SDD(f) contains no register;*
2. *size($\widetilde{f}$) = 1;*
3. *$F = truth(\widetilde{f}) \in \mathbf{P}2$ is periodic, i.e. $-1 \le F(2) \le 0$, with period length $2^{i'}$, for some integer $i' \le i$;*
4. *$poly(\widetilde{f}) = a + (z^{2^{i'}} - 1)F$, for some integer $a < 2^{2^{i'}}$.*

For Boolean functions, the **SDD** procedure is the same as the *Binary Decision Diagrams* **BDD** procedure, from [13].

8   Appendix

We use 14 operators, from Binary Algebra: 5 unary operations $\{\neg, z, z^-, \uparrow, \downarrow\}$, and 9 binary operations $\{\cup, \oplus, \cap, \otimes, \oslash, +, -, \times, /\}$. The binary operators are listed here in order of increasing syntactic precedence, so as to save parentheses.

- $\langle \mathbf{D}, (0), (1), \neg, \cup, \cap \rangle$ is a Boolean algebra;
  $\langle \mathbf{D}, (0), (1), \oplus, \cap \rangle$ is a Boolean ring: $a = a \cap a$, $0 = a \oplus a$ (see [8]).

- $$a = z^- z a,$$
  $$z z^- a = a \cap -2,$$
  $$\neg z^- a = z^- \neg a,$$
  $$\neg z a = 1 + z \neg a,$$
  $$z^-(a \odot b) = z^- a \odot z^- b, \text{ for } \odot \in \{\cup, \cap, \oplus\},$$
  $$z(a \odot b) = z a \odot z b, \text{ for } \odot \in \{\cup, \cap, \oplus, +, -\},$$
  $$z(a \odot b) = z a \odot b = a \odot z b, \text{ for } \odot \in \{\times, \otimes\},$$

- $\langle \mathbf{D}, 0, 1, \oplus, \oplus, \otimes \rangle$ is an *Integral Domain*, i.e. a commutative ring without divisor of 0. An element $a \in \mathbf{D}$ has a (polynomial) inverse $1 \oslash a$, such that $a \otimes (1 \oslash a) = a$, if and only if a is *odd* $(1 = a(0))$: $1 \oslash (1 + zb) = \bigoplus (zb)^{\mathbf{N}}$.
- $\langle \mathbf{D}, 0, 1, +, -, \times \rangle$ is an Integral Domain.

$$\neg a = -a - 1,$$
$$a + b = (a \cup b) + (a \cap b)$$
$$= (a \oplus b) + z(a \cap b),$$
$$a + b = a \cup b = a \oplus b \text{ iff } a \cap b = 0,$$
$$1/(1 - 2b) = \sum (2b)^{\mathbf{N}} = \prod (1 + (2b)^{\mathbf{N}}).$$

- $$\uparrow a = a(z^2) = a \otimes a,$$
  $$a = \downarrow \uparrow a,$$
  $$a = \uparrow \downarrow a + z \uparrow \downarrow z^- a,$$
  $$\neg \downarrow a = \downarrow \neg a,$$
  $$\neg \uparrow a = (01) \cup \uparrow \neg a,$$
  $$\downarrow z^2 a = z \downarrow a,$$
  $$\uparrow z a = z^2 \uparrow a,$$
  $$\downarrow (a \odot b) = \downarrow a \odot \downarrow b, \text{ for } \odot \in \{\cup, \cap, \oplus\},$$
  $$\uparrow (a \odot b) = \uparrow a \odot \uparrow b, \text{ for } \odot \in \{\cup, \cap, \oplus, \otimes, \oslash\}.$$

We list the known closure properties, for operators and sub-structures, in Binary Algebra.

- $\mathbf{F_2}^{\mathbf{N}}$ is closed, under $\{\neg, \cup, \oplus, \cap, z, \uparrow, \otimes, \oslash, +, -, \times, /\}$.
- $\mathbf{N}$ is closed, under $\{\cup, \oplus, \cap, z, z^-, \uparrow, \downarrow, \otimes, +, \times\}$.
- $\mathbf{Z}$ is closed, under $\{\neg, \cup, \oplus, \cap, z, z^-, \downarrow, +, -, \times\}$.
- $\mathbf{P2}$ is closed, under $\{\neg, \cup, \oplus, \cap, z, z^-, \uparrow, \downarrow, \otimes, +, -, \times\}$.
- $\mathbf{A_2}$ is closed under $\{\neg, \cup, \oplus, \cap, z, z^-, \uparrow, \downarrow, \otimes, \oslash, +, -\}$. The closure under carry-free product is shown in [14]. It is shown in [15] that $\mathbf{A_2}$ is not closed under multiplication $\times$ with carries.
- $\mathbf{P}$, $\mathbf{Z_2}$ and $\mathbf{Z_2}$ are closed, under all 14 operations.

References

1. C. Mead, *ANALOG VLSI AND NEURAL SYSTEMS*, Addison-Wesley, 1989.
2. N. Weste, K. Eshragian, *Principles of CMOS VLSI Design*, Addison-Wesley, 1985.
3. J. Vuillemin, P. Bertin , D. Roncin, M. Shand, H. Touati, P. Boucard *Programmable Active Memories: Reconfigurable Systems Come of Age*, IEEE Trans. on VLSI, Vol. 4, NO. 1, pp. 56-69, 1996.
4. J. Vuillemin, *On circuits and numbers*, *IEEE Trans. on Computers*, 43(8): pp. 868–879, 1994.
5. Gérard Berry, *private communication*, 1995.
6. Klaus Winkelman, *private communication*, 1996.
7. S. Eilenberg, *Automata, Languages, and Machines*, Academic Press, 1974.
8. W. J. Gilbert, *Modern Algebra with Applications*, A Wiley-Interscience publication, John Wiley & Sons, New York, 1976.
9. J. P. Allouche, *Automates finis en théorie des nombres*, in *Expositiones Mathematicae*, pp. 239–266, 5 (1987).
10. M. Mendès France, *Some applications of the theory of automata*, in *Prospects of Math. Sci.*, World Sci. Pub., pp. 127–144, 1988.
11. G. Christol, T. Kamae, M. Mendès France, G. Rauzy, *Suites algèbriques, automates et substitutions*, in *Bull. Soc. Math. France*, 108: pp. 401–419, 1980.
12. J.H. Loxton, A.J. van der Poorten, *Arithmetic properties of the solutions of a class of functional equations*, J. Reine Angew. Math., 330, pp. 159–172, 1982.
13. R. E. Bryant, *Graph-based Algorithms for Boolean Function Manipulation*, in *IEEE Trans. on Computers*, 35:8: pp. 677–691, 1986.
14. J.P. Allouche, J. Shallit, *The ring of k-regular sequences*, in *Theoret. Comput. Sci.*, 98 (1992) pp. 163–187.
15. S. Lehr, J. Shallit, J. Tromp, *On the vector space of the automatic reals*, in *Theoret. Comput. Sci.*, 163 (1996) pp. 193–210.

Performance Evaluation of Networks: New Problems and Challenges

Alain Jean-Marie[1]

Université de Montpellier 2, LIRMM, 161 Rue ADA, F-34392 Montpellier Cedex 5,
France, ajm@lirmm.fr,
WWW home page: http://www.lirmm.fr/~ajm

Abstract

The purpose of this talk is to give an introduction to the domain of *Performance Evaluation of Networks*, its methods and its practical results. The short tour will begin with the classical results and finish with some of the principal challenges faced by the theory today.

The concern about mathematically predicting the performance of communication systems is not new: the beginning of the theory is traditionally associated with the work of A.E. Erlang (1917) on the blocking probability for telephone trunk lines. The family of stochastic models used by him and his followers eventually led to *Queuing Theory*, a wealth of formulas and methods for computing throughputs, waiting times, occupation levels of resources and other performance measures.

From the point of view of networking, one of the main achievements of this theory is perhaps the family of *product form theorems* for networks of queues, obtained in the 70's. When they apply, these theorems allow reduce the analysis of a network to that of each of its elements in isolation. Among numerous possibilities, the results have been applied to the design of scheduling mechanisms for computers, to the problem of resource allocation, in particular the *optimal routing* in the then-emerging packet switching networks, and to the design of *window flow-control* mechanisms.

In the 80's, new problems appeared with the evolution of networking to higher speeds and to the *integration of the services* offered by classical telecommunications and computer networks. More stress was put on the necessity of an end-to-end "quality of service" (QoS), and "real-time" operation. In parallel, it was realized that the applications that were to use the networks (voice, video, data retrieving, distributed computing) generate a network traffic very different than the usual Poisson processes commonly assumed in the models. All this provoked the emergence of new concepts such as *traffic shaping*, and the *equivalent bandwidth* of complex sources. The importance of the *scheduling policy* for switching nodes in networks has been emphasized. Current research also tries to assess the importance of the *long range dependence* and fractal behavior of the traffic, which has been measured in local as well as in wide area networks.

J. He and M. Sato (Eds.): ASIAN 2000, LNCS 1961, pp. 13–14, 2000.
© Springer-Verlag Berlin Heidelberg 2000

Even more recently, the popularization of the Web has provoked a renewed interest in the analysis of the performances of the Internet, its protocols, its applications and its evolution. To name just some areas for research:

Internet performance & QoS. Flow control & congestion avoidance: TCP and its improvement. Reliable multicast. Feedback-less communication and forward error correction. Differential service. Traffic shaping, policing, pricing. Network interconnection and tunelling.

Web performance. Information transfer Protocols, HTTP 1.1 *vs* HTTP 1.2. Web server optimization: caching, multi-threading, mirroring.

Voice & Video. Network-conscious & adaptive compression and transmission. Dimensioning of buffers, playout. Real-time *vs* offline handling of video on demand.

The theoretical foundations of performance evaluation are currently receiving contribution from other fields of applied mathematics: statistics (time series analysis, parameter estimation), optimal control theory, game theory (fairness of resource sharing, individually *vs* socially optimal behavior).

Emerging Patterns and Classification

Jinyan Li[1], Kotagiri Ramamohanarao[1], and Guozhu Dong[2]

[1] Dept. of CSSE, The University of Melbourne, Vic. 3010, Australia.
{jyli, rao}@cs.mu.oz.au
[2] Dept. of CSE, Wright State University, Dayton OH 45435, USA.
gdong@cs.wright.edu

Abstract. In this work, we review an important kind of knowledge pattern, emerging patterns (EPs). Emerging patterns are associated with two data sets, and can be used to describe significant changes between the two data sets. To discover all EPs embedded in high-dimension and large-volume databases is a challenging problem due to the number of candidates. We describe a special type of EP, called jumping emerging patterns (JEPs) and review some properties of JEP spaces (the spaces of jumping emerging patterns). We describe efficient border-based algorithms to derive the boundary elements of JEP spaces. Moreover, we describe a new classifier, called DeEPs, which makes use of the discriminating power of emerging patterns. The experimental results show that the accuracy of DeEPs is much better than that of k-nearest neighbor and that of C5.0.

1 Introduction

We are now experiencing an era of data-explosion. Great advances in software and hardware engineering means that data are generated and collected at a tremendous rate and from a very wide variety of sources: including scientific domains (e.g., the human genome project), government organizations (e.g., census projects), and business corporations (e.g., supermarket transactions). With the major advances in the database and storage technology, it is easy for us to store vast amount of data in CD-ROMs, hard disks, and magnetic tapes, forming mountains of data [8]. The traditional statistical techniques, in analyzing data, rapidly break down as the volume and dimensionality of the data increase. Now, the question for us is how to efficiently discover "useful knowledge" from the mountains of data.

One solution to this problem is the use of *Knowledge Discovery in Databases* (KDD) techniques. Traditionally, KDD is defined as follows [8]:

Knowledge Discovery in Databases is the non-trivial process of identifying valid, novel, potentially useful, and ultimately understandable patterns in data.

The central term in this KDD definition is "patterns", constrained by some interesting properties such as validity, novelty, usefulness, and understandability. A crucial step in KDD processes is to identify "non-trivial" patterns. This important step is called *Data Mining*:

J. He and M. Sato (Eds.): ASIAN 2000, LNCS 1961, pp. 15–32, 2000.

Data Mining is a step in the KDD processes and consists of particular algorithms that, under some acceptable computational efficiency limitations, produces a particular enumeration of the required patterns.

In this work, we describe a new knowledge pattern, called **emerging pattern** (EP) [6], for KDD. Generally speaking, emerging patterns are associated with two data sets, and are used to describe significant changes (differences or trends) between these two data sets. In this work, we also propose data mining algorithms to efficiently discover and represent EPs. More importantly, to show the usefulness of the newly introduced patterns, we apply the ideas of emerging patterns to the problem of classification, and propose and develop accurate and scalable classifiers.

In the remainder of this paper, we begin by presenting a collection of preliminary definitions. We then in Section 3 describe two examples of emerging patterns. We formally define emerging patterns in Section 4. These definitions include general EPs, jumping emerging patterns, and strong emerging patterns. In Section 5, we explain how the concept of emerging patterns satisfies the properties of KDD patterns such as validity, novelty, potential usefulness, and understandability. In Section 6, we formally describe the space of jumping emerging patterns. An important property, convexity, of JEP spaces is reviewed, and the border-based algorithms which are used to discover the boundary elements of JEP spaces are also outlined in this section. To show the usefulness of EPs, we in Section 7 review a new classifier, DeEPs, by describing the basic idea behind in it and by providing its detailed performance. We present some related work in Section 8. We conclude this paper with a summary.

2 Preliminaries

In relational databases, the most elementary term is called an **attribute**. An attribute has its domain values. The values can be **discrete** (including **categorical**), or **continuous**. For example, colour can be an attribute in some database and the values for colour can be red, yellow, and blue. Another example is the attribute age which can have continuous values in the range of $[0, 150]$. We call the attribute-value pair an **item**. So, colour-red is an item. A set of items is simply called an **itemset**. We also define a set of items as a **transaction** or an **instance**. A **database**, or a **data set**, is defined as a set of transactions (instances). The **cardinality** or **volume** of a relational database $\mathcal{D} = \{T_1, T_2, \cdots, T_n\}$, denoted $|\mathcal{D}|$, is n, the number of instances in $\mathcal{D}$, treating $\mathcal{D}$ as a normal set. The **dimension** of $\mathcal{D}$ is the number of attributes used in $\mathcal{D}$.

Now, we present other basic definitions. We say that a transaction T **contains** an itemset X (or, X **occurs** in T) if $X \subseteq T$.

Definition 1. *Given a database $\mathcal{D}$ and an itemset X, the support of X in $\mathcal{D}$, denoted $supp_{\mathcal{D}}(X)$, is the percentage of transactions in $\mathcal{D}$ containing X. The count of X, denoted $count_{\mathcal{D}}(X)$, is the number of transactions in $\mathcal{D}$ containing X.*

The subscript $\mathcal{D}$ in both $supp_\mathcal{D}(X)$ and $count_\mathcal{D}(X)$ can be omitted if $\mathcal{D}$ is understood. Observe that

$$supp_\mathcal{D}(X) = \frac{count_\mathcal{D}(X)}{|\mathcal{D}|},$$

where $|\mathcal{D}|$ is the number of transactions in $\mathcal{D}$.

Definition 2. *Given a database $\mathcal{D}$ and a real number δ ($0 \le \delta \le 1$), an itemset X is defined as a large (or, frequent) itemset if $supp_\mathcal{D}(X) \ge \delta$.*

Emerging patterns are intended to capture trends over time and contrasts between classes. Assume that we are given an ordered pair of data sets $\mathcal{D}_1$ and $\mathcal{D}_2$. Let $supp_i(X)$ denote $supp_{\mathcal{D}_i}(X)$. The *growth rate* of an itemset X from $\mathcal{D}_1$ to $\mathcal{D}_2$ is defined as

$$\text{GROWTHRATE}_{\mathcal{D}_1 \to \mathcal{D}_2}(X) = \begin{cases} 0, & \text{if } supp_1(X) = 0 \text{ and } supp_2(X) = 0 \\ \infty, & \text{if } supp_1(X) = 0 \text{ and } supp_2(X) \ne 0 \\ \frac{supp_2(X)}{supp_1(X)}, & \text{otherwise} \end{cases}$$

This definition of growth rates is in terms of supports of itemsets. Alternatively, growth rates can be defined in terms of counts of itemsets. The counts-based growth rates are useful for directly calculating probabilities, especially for situations where the two data sets have very unbalanced population.

3   Two Examples of Emerging Patterns

Example 1. Millions of EPs were discovered in the mushroom data set (available from the UCI Machine Learning Repository [4]) when the minimum growth rate threshold was set as 2.5 [11]. The following are two typical EPs consisting of 3 items:

$$X = \{(\texttt{Odor = none}), (\texttt{Gill\_Size = broad}), (\texttt{Ring\_Number = one})\}$$

and

$$Y = \{(\texttt{Bruises = no}), (\texttt{Gill\_Spacing = close}), (\texttt{Veil\_Color = white})\}.$$

Their supports and growth rates are shown in Table 1. The EPs with very large growth rates are notable characteristics, differentiating edible and poisonous mushrooms.

Example 2. About 120 EP groups were discovered from the U.S. census PUMS database (available from www.census.gov) [6]; some of those EPs contain up to 13 items. They are derived from the population of Texas to that of Michigan using the minimum growth rate threshold 1.2. A typical one is: {Disabl1:2, Lang1:2, Means:1, Mobilili:2, Perscar:2, Rlabor:1, Travtim:[1..59], Work89:1}; the items relate to disability, language at home, means of transport, personal care, employment status, travel time to work, and working or not in 1989. Such EPs can describe differences of population characteristics amongst distinct social groups. Clearly, domain experts can analyze such EPs, and select the useful ones for further consideration in their specific applications.

Table 1. The supports and growth rates of two EPs.

EP	supp_in_poisonous	supp_in_edible	growth_rate
X	0%	63.9%	∞
Y	81.4%	3.8%	21.4

4   Definitions of Emerging Patterns

4.1   A Definition for General EPs

Having defined growth rates, emerging patterns are defined as follows.

Definition 3. *Given $\rho > 1$ as a growth rate threshold, an itemset X is called an ρ-emerging pattern from $\mathcal{D}_1$ to $\mathcal{D}_2$ if* GROWTHRATE$_{\mathcal{D}_1 \rightarrow \mathcal{D}_2}(X) \geq \rho$.

A ρ-emerging pattern is sometimes called ρ-EP briefly or simply EP when ρ is understood. "An EP from $\mathcal{D}_1$ to $\mathcal{D}_2$" is also sometimes stated as "An EP in (or of) $\mathcal{D}_2$" when $\mathcal{D}_1$ is understood. By the *support of an EP*, it is meant that its support in $\mathcal{D}_2$ is referred to.

Note that emerging patterns are closely associated with two data sets $\mathcal{D}_1$ and $\mathcal{D}_2$. In an interchangeable manner, the data set $\mathcal{D}_1$ will be called the *background* data set of the EPs, and $\mathcal{D}_2$ the *target* data set, particularly for the cases where data are time-ordered. For some other cases where data are class-related (e.g., poisonous class and edible class in the mushroom database), the data sets $\mathcal{D}_1$ is called *negative* class and $\mathcal{D}_2$ are called *positive* class.

Sample EPs were given in Section 3. For instance, the itemset Y in Example 1 is an EP from the edible-mushrooms data set to the poisonous-mushrooms data set with a growth rate of 21.4. For this particular EP, the edible mushrooms are considered as the negative class, the poisonous mushrooms are considered as positive, its support is 81.4%.

The growth rate of an EP measures the degree of changes in its supports, and it is of primary interest in our studies. The actual supports of EPs are only of secondary interest.

Given a growth rate threshold ρ and two data sets $\mathcal{D}_1$ and $\mathcal{D}_2$, the two supports of every emerging pattern from $\mathcal{D}_1$ to $\mathcal{D}_2$ can be described by Figure 1. In this support plane, the horizontal axis measures the support of every itemset in the target data set $\mathcal{D}_2$; the vertical axis measures the support in the background data set $\mathcal{D}_1$. So, for each emerging pattern X from $\mathcal{D}_1$ to $\mathcal{D}_2$, the point $(supp_2(X), supp_1(X))$ must be enclosed by the triangle $\triangle ABC$. As discussed in [6], it is very difficult to discover all emerging patterns embedded in two dense high dimensional data sets.

4.2   Definitions for More Specific EPs

Two special types of emerging patterns are introduced in this section. The first type are the EPs with the growth rate of ∞, specifically called **jumping emerg-**

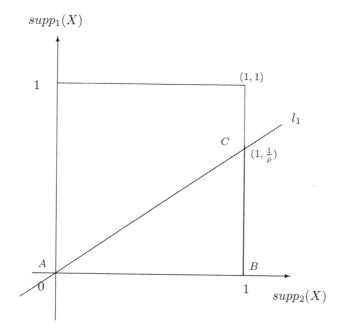

Fig. 1. The support plane.

ing patterns. The second type are those EPs satisfying the *subset-closure* property, called **strong emerging patterns**. Formally,

Definition 4. *A jumping emerging pattern (JEP) from $\mathcal{D}_1$ to $\mathcal{D}_2$ is defined as an emerging pattern from $\mathcal{D}_1$ to $\mathcal{D}_2$ with the growth rate of ∞.*

The itemset X in Example 1 is a JEP of the edible-mushroom data set, since it occurs in this data set with a support of 63.9% but it has 0% support (it does not occur) in the poisonous-mushroom data set. In other words, this pattern dominates in edible mushrooms. However, it does not occur in any poisonous instances. As all jumping emerging patterns have their supports increase in the background data set from 0% support to a none-zero supports in the target data set, our intuition leads us to add the "jumping" prefix to our traditional EPs to name JEPs.

For any jumping emerging pattern X of $\mathcal{D}_2$, the point $(supp_2(X), supp_1(X))$ must lie on the horizontal axis in Figure 1. This is simply because $supp_1(X) = 0$.

Emerging patterns do not always have the *subset-closure* property [6]. (A collection $\mathcal{C}$ of sets is said to have the subset-closure property if and only if all subsets of any set X ($X \in \mathcal{C}$) belong to $\mathcal{C}$.) Therefore, a proper subset of a known EP is not necessarily an emerging pattern. The notion of *strong emerging patterns* is proposed to describe the emerging patterns satisfying the subset-closure property. Formally,

Definition 5. *For a given growth rate threshold ρ, an emerging pattern is defined to be a strong emerging pattern if all of its nonempty subsets are also EPs.*

The problem of efficiently mining strong emerging patterns is fundamentally similar to the problem of mining *frequent itemsets* [1]. Approaches to efficiently mining frequent itemsets include APRIORI [2] and MAX-MINER[3].

5   Emerging Patterns: A Type of KDD Pattern

Emerging patterns satisfy the following properties.

- **Validity** — The discovered patterns should be valid on new data with *some* degree of certainty: In our experiments, we found that most of the EPs remain EPs after the previous databases are updated by adding a small percentage of new data. We also found that there exist some EPs that tend to remain EPs, with high degree of certainty, even when a large percentage of new data are incorporated into the previously processed data. These facts imply that we can capture some nature of the systems by using the concept of EPs. Hence, EPs are a type of valid knowledge pattern.
- **Novelty**: Sometimes, EPs are long, which might be never discovered by the traditional statistical methods. These astonishingly long patterns are providing new insights into previously "well" understood problems.
- **Potential Usefulness**: Emerging patterns can describe trends in any two non-overlapping temporal data sets and describe significant differences in any two spatial data sets. Clearly, the discovered EPs can be used for predicting business market trends, for identifying hidden causes to some specific diseases among different racial groups, for hand-writing characters recognition, and for differentiating *positive* instances and *negative* instances (e.g., edible or poisonous, win or fail, healthy or sick).
- **Understandability**: Emerging patterns are basically conjunctions of simple conditions. For example, the pattern

$$\{(\text{Odor} = \text{none}), (\text{Gill\_size} = \text{broad}), (\text{Ring\_number} = \text{one})\}$$

consisting of three simple conditions, is an EP in the mushroom database [4]. Two facts concerning this pattern are:
  1. Given a mushroom, if its `Odor` is `none` *and* its `Gill_size` is `broad` *and* its `Ring_number` is `one`, then this mushroom must be edible rather than poisonous.
  2. About 63.9% of edible mushrooms have the above physical characteristics. But, no single poisonous mushroom satisfies those three characteristics.

Clearly, this pattern gives a difference description between edible and poisonous mushrooms. It can be seen that EPs are easily understandable due to the lack of complexity involved in their interpretation.

In the subsequent sections, we describe some properties of the space of jumping emerging patterns, and describe the usefulness of EPs in constructing our newly proposed **DeEPs** classifier [10].

6   The Space of Jumping Emerging Patterns

Since jumping emerging patterns are special EPs, with the specification that their supports in one data set are zero but non-zero in the other data set, we are able to use this constraint to efficiently discover all jumping emerging patterns.

In Section 2, we have presented some basic definitions such as attributes, itemsets, supports, large itemsets, and instances. Here, we require further basic definitions for us to describe JEP spaces. These definitions mainly include **specific itemsets**, **general itemsets**, **maximal itemsets**, and **minimal itemsets**.

Definition 6. *Given two itemsets I_1 and I_2, itemset I_1 is more general than itemset I_2 if $I_1 \subset I_2$; it is also said that I_2 is more specific than I_1.*

For example, the set $\{1, 2\}$ is more general than the set $\{1, 2, 3, 4\}$. In other words, the set $\{1, 2, 3, 4\}$ is more specific than $\{1, 2\}$.

Definition 7. *Given a collection C of itemsets, an itemset $X \in C$ is defined as maximal in C if there is no proper superset of X in C. Similarly, an itemset $Y \in C$ is defined as minimal in C if there is no proper subset of Y in C*

For example, for the collection of $\{\{1\}, \{2\}, \{1, 2\}, \{1, 2, 3\}, \{1, 2, 4\}\}$, a maximal itemset in this collection is $\{1, 2, 3\}$ and a minimal itemset is $\{1\}$.

For a given collection of itemsets, observe that its maximal itemsets are equivalently the **most specific** elements in it; its minimal itemsets are equivalently the **most general** elements in it.

For an arbitrary set S, recall that $|S|$ represents the cardinality (or length) of S, namely, the number of the elements in S. Therefore, the most specific elements in a collection always have the largest cardinality among the elements.

6.1   JEP Spaces and Convexity

Suppose we are given a set of positive and negative instances. By gathering together all individual jumping emerging patterns and viewing them as a whole, this collection itself creates a new property in addition to the sharp discriminating power held in its every elements. This collection is called a JEP space, and the property is called convexity. Formally,

Definition 8. *Given a set $\mathcal{D}_p$ of positive instances and a set $\mathcal{D}_n$ of negative instances, the JEP space with respect to $\mathcal{D}_p$ and $\mathcal{D}_n$ is defined as the set of all the JEPs from $\mathcal{D}_n$ to $\mathcal{D}_p$.*

"A JEP from $\mathcal{D}_n$ to $\mathcal{D}_p$" is sometimes referred to as "A JEP with respect to $\mathcal{D}_p$ and $\mathcal{D}_n$". Recall that an itemset X is considered to *occur* in a data set $\mathcal{D}$ if and only if one or more instances in $\mathcal{D}$ contain this itemset, namely, $supp_{\mathcal{D}}(X) > 0$. So, a JEP space can be stated as a collection in which each element only occurs in $\mathcal{D}_p$ but not in $\mathcal{D}_n$.

Note that JEP space is significantly different from version space [14,15] because of different consistency restrictions on their elements with the data. In our framework, version spaces are defined as follows:

Definition 9. *Given a set $\mathcal{D}_p$ of positive instances and a set $\mathcal{D}_n$ of negative instances, the version space with respect to $\mathcal{D}_p$ and $\mathcal{D}_n$ is the set of all the itemsets whose supports in $\mathcal{D}_p$ are 100% and whose supports in $\mathcal{D}_n$ are 0%.*

Consequently, each element in a version space must occur (or be contained) in every positive instance and no negative instance (under the partial order of set-containment). This condition is much stricter than that of JEPs. In practice, for example, the data sets in the UCI Machine Learning Repository (Blake & Murphy, 1998) always produce empty version spaces rather than those discussed in (Hirsh, 1994; Mitchell, 1982) which contain large, even sometimes infinite, number of elements. With a weaker consistency restriction, JEP space becomes more useful in practice.

We now show two examples.

Table 2. Weather conditions and *SaturdayMorningSport*.

Instance	OUTLOOK	TEMPERATURE	HUMIDITY	WINDY	*SaturdayMorningSport*
1	rain	mild	high	false	Yes
2	rain	mild	normal	false	Yes
3	sunny	hot	high	false	No
4	sunny	hot	high	true	No

Example 3. Table 2 contains four training instances, each represented by four attributes: OUTLOOK, TEMPERATURE, HUMIDITY, and WINDY. The positive instances are those where the weather conditions are good (Yes) for *Saturday-MorningSport*, and the negative instances are those where the weather conditions are not good (No). For this data set, the version space consists of the following six itemsets: $\{rain\}$, $\{mild\}$, $\{rain, mild\}$, $\{rain, false\}$, $\{mild, false\}$, $\{rain, mild, false\}$. (The attribute names are omitted in the itemsets if they are understood.) Note that these itemsets occur in the positive class with 100% support but they do not occur in the negative class at all.

Example 4. Continuing with Table 2, the JEP space with respect to those four instances consists of the following itemsets: $\{r\}$, $\{m\}$, $\{r, m\}$, $\{r, high\}$, $\{r, f\}$, $\{m, high\}$, $\{m, f\}$, $\{r, m, high\}$, $\{r, m, f\}$, $\{m, high, f\}$, $\{r, high, f\}$, $\{r, m, high, f\}$, $\{r, n\}$, $\{m, n\}$, $\{r, m, n\}$, $\{m, n, f\}$, $\{r, n, f\}$, and $\{r, m, n, f\}$. (For convenience, we use the first letter of the attribute values to represent those values when there is no confusion.)

Because of different consistency restrictions on the elements within the training data, the sizes of version space and JEP space are quite different as shown in Example 3 and Exampl 4. For the same training data, the JEP space always contains the elements covered by the version space.

One may argue that the supports of *most* JEPs are too small to be useful. Fortunately, our border-based algorithms can efficiently derive the most general JEPs, namely those with the largest supports, and use them to form one bound of the "border" representation of JEP spaces. So, if the smaller support JEPs are not interesting, then the boundary JEPs can be focused. Moreover, the non-boundary JEPs can be easily generated from the boundary elements. The supports of the most general JEPs can reach 60% or even 70% in some data sets such as the mushroom and nursery data sets. Generally the support level of the most general JEPs discovered in our experiments is in the range of 10% – 20%.

The size of JEP spaces can be large. For instance, the JEP space in Example 4 contains 18 itemsets. In another example the JEP space of the mushroom data [4] contains up to 10^8 itemsets. To enumerate all these itemsets is prohibitively expensive. Interestingly, JEP spaces evince a property called *convexity* [9] or *interval closure* [6]. By exploiting this property, JEP spaces can be succinctly represented by the most general and the most specific elements among them.

Definition 10. *[9,6] A collection $\mathcal{C}$ of sets is said to be a convex space if, for all X, Y and Z, the conditions $X \subseteq Y \subseteq Z$ and $X, Z \in \mathcal{C}$ imply that $Y \in \mathcal{C}$.*

If a collection is a convex space, we say it holds convexity or it is interval closed.

Example 5. All of the sets $\{1\}$, $\{1, 2\}$, $\{1, 3\}$, $\{1, 4\}$, $\{1, 2, 3\}$, and $\{1, 2, 4\}$ form a convex space. The set $\mathcal{L}$ of all the most general elements in this space is $\{\{1\}\}$; the set $\mathcal{R}$ of all the most specific elements in this space is $\{\{1, 2, 3\}, \{1, 2, 4\}\}$. All the other elements can be considered "between" $\mathcal{L}$ and $\mathcal{R}$.

Theorem 1. *Given a set $\mathcal{D}_p$ of positive instances and a set $\mathcal{D}_n$ of negative instances, the JEP space with respect to $\mathcal{D}_p$ and $\mathcal{D}_n$ is a convex space.*

Using this property, JEP spaces can be represented and bounded by two sets like the sets $\mathcal{L}$ and $\mathcal{R}$ in Example 5 — $\mathcal{L}$ and $\mathcal{R}$ play the boundary role.

With the $\mathcal{L}$-and-$\mathcal{R}$ representation, all the other JEPs in a JEP space can be generated and recognized by examining its bounds. We next formalize the two boundary sets by using the concept of *borders*.

6.2   Using Borders to Represent JEP Spaces

A border is a structure, consisting of two bounds. A simple example might be $<\{\{a\}, \{b\}\}, \{\{a, b, c\}, \{b, d\}\}>$, which represents all those sets which are supersets of $\{a\}$ or $\{b\}$ and subsets of $\{a, b, c\}$ or $\{b, d\}$. Formally,

Definition 11. *[6] An ordered pair $<\mathcal{L}, \mathcal{R}>$ is called a border, $\mathcal{L}$ the left bound of this border and $\mathcal{R}$ the right bound, if (i) each one of $\mathcal{L}$ and $\mathcal{R}$ is an anti-chain — a collection of sets in which any two elements X and Y satisfy $X \not\subseteq Y$ and $Y \not\subseteq X$, (ii) each element of $\mathcal{L}$ is a subset of some element in $\mathcal{R}$ and each element of $\mathcal{R}$ is a superset of some element in $\mathcal{L}$. The collection of sets* *represented by, or the set interval of, a border* $<\mathcal{L}, \mathcal{R}>$ *consists of those itemsets which are supersets of some element in* $\mathcal{L}$ *but subsets of some element in* $\mathcal{R}$. *This collection is denoted* $[\mathcal{L}, \mathcal{R}] = \{Y \mid \exists X \in \mathcal{L}, \exists Z \in \mathcal{R} \text{ such that } X \subseteq Y \subseteq Z\}$. *The collection* $[\mathcal{L}, \mathcal{R}]$ *is said to have* $<\mathcal{L}, \mathcal{R}>$ *as border.*

There is a one-to-one correspondence between borders and convex spaces.

Proposition 1. *Each convex space* $\mathcal{C}$ *has a unique border* $<\mathcal{L}, \mathcal{R}>$, *where* $\mathcal{L}$ *is the collection of the most general sets in* $\mathcal{C}$ *and* $\mathcal{R}$ *is the collection of the most specific sets in* $\mathcal{C}$.

In summary, it can be seen that

- Given a border $<\mathcal{L}, \mathcal{R}>$, then its corresponding collection $[\mathcal{L}, \mathcal{R}]$ is a convex space.
- Given a convex space, then it can be represented by a unique border.

Example 6. The JEP space in Example 4 can be represented by the border

$$<\{\{r\}, \{m\}\}, \{\{r, m, high, f\}, \{r, m, n, f\}\}>.$$

Its left bound is $\{\{r\}, \{m\}\}$ and its right bound is $\{\{r, m, high, f\}, \{r, m, n, f\}\}$. This border represents all the sets which are supersets of $\{r\}$ or $\{m\}$ and subsets of $\{r, m, high, f\}$ or $\{r, m, n, f\}$. This border is a concise representation because it uses only four sets to represent 18 sets.

We next describe two further types of convex spaces in addition to JEP spaces which are frequently used in data mining tasks. The two types are **large spaces** and **small spaces**. Given a data set $\mathcal{D}$ and a support threshold δ, the collection of all the large itemsets is called a large space; the collection of all the itemsets whose supports are smaller than the threshold δ is called a small space. According to Proposition 1, there exists a unique border for any large space or any small space. The left bound of any large space is $\{\emptyset\}$, and the right bound is the set of the maximal large itemsets. The MAX-MINER algorithm [3] can be used to discover the maximal large itemsets with respect to a support threshold in a data set.

In the following subsection, we describe **horizontal spaces**, a special type of large space. Horizontal spaces are useful for us in rewriting and computing JEP spaces.

6.3   Using Horizontal Spaces to Rewrite and Compute JEP Spaces

Given a data set $\mathcal{D}$, all **non-zero support** itemsets X, namely, $supp_{\mathcal{D}}(X) \neq 0$, form a convex space. This is mainly due to the fact that any subset of a non-zero support itemset has a non-zero support. This convex space is specifically called a **horizontal space**. Horizontal spaces can be used to *exclude* those itemsets Y which do not occur in $\mathcal{D}$, namely $supp_{\mathcal{D}}(Y) = 0$. As each horizontal space is convex, it can be represented by a border. This border is specifically called a

horizontal border. The left bound of this border is $\{\emptyset\}$ and the right bound $\mathcal{R}$ is the set of the most specific non-zero support itemsets. The right bound $\mathcal{R}$ can be viewed as a horizontal line which separates all non-zero support itemsets from those zero support itemsets.

In our framework, the most specific non-zero support itemsets are those instances in a data set $\mathcal{D}$, assuming there are no duplicate instances in this data set. This is due to the fact that all instances have the same cardinality and there are no duplicates in the data, and thus the data set itself is an anti-chain collection.

We can use horizontal spaces for computing JEP spaces.

Proposition 2. *Given a set $\mathcal{D}_p$ of positive instances and a set $\mathcal{D}_n$ of negative instances, then the JEP space with respect to $\mathcal{D}_p$ and $\mathcal{D}_n$ is*

$$[\{\emptyset\}, \mathcal{R}_p] - [\{\emptyset\}, \mathcal{R}_n]$$

where, $[\{\emptyset\}, \mathcal{R}_p]$ is the horizontal space of $\mathcal{D}_p$ and $[\{\emptyset\}, \mathcal{R}_n]$ is the horizontal space of $\mathcal{D}_n$.

Proof. By definition, all elements of a JEP space must occur in the positive data set but not in the negative data set. So, subtracting all non-zero support itemsets in $\mathcal{D}_n$ from all non-zero support itemsets in $\mathcal{D}_p$ produces all the JEPs.

Therefore, the JEP space with respect to $\mathcal{D}_p$ and $\mathcal{D}_n$ can be "represented" by the two horizontal borders of the two data sets. The border of this JEP space can be efficiently derived by using border-based algorithms (Dong & Li, 1999). This idea also constructs a foundation for maintaining JEP spaces efficiently [12].

6.4   Border-based Algorithms for Efficiently Discovering JEPs

We need three algorithms HORIZON-MINER, BORDER-DIFF, and JEPPRODUCER to efficiently discover the border of the JEP space with respect to a set $\mathcal{D}_p$ of positive instances and a set $\mathcal{D}_n$ of negative instances. The first algorithm HORIZON-MINER is used to derive the horizontal border of $\mathcal{D}_p$ or of $\mathcal{D}_n$. With these two discovered horizontal borders as arguments, JEPPRODUCER outputs a border as a concise representation of the JEP space. BORDER-DIFF is a core subroutine in JEPPRODUCER.

The details of these algorithms are omitted here. Readers are referred to [6], [11], and [12] for further details.

7   Instance-based Classification by EPs

An important characteristic of emerging patterns is their strong usefulness. In this section, we describe a new instance-based classifier, called **DeEPs** (short for **De**cision making by **E**merging **P**atterns), to show the usefulness of emerging patterns in solving classification problems.

The DeEPs classifier has considerable advantages with regard to accuracy, overall speed, and dimensional scalability over other EP-based classifiers such as CAEP [7] and the JEP-Classifier [11], because of its efficient new methods of selecting sharp and relevant EPs, its new ways of aggregating the discriminating power of individual EPs, and most importantly its use of instance-based approach which creates a remarkable reduction on both the volume and the dimension of the training data.

7.1   Overview of DeEPs

Given two classes of data $\mathcal{D}_1$ and $\mathcal{D}_2$ and a testing instance T, the central idea underpinning DeEPs is to discover those subsets of T which are emerging patterns between $\mathcal{D}_1$ and $\mathcal{D}_2$, and then use the supports of the discovered EPs for prediction. We use the following example to illustrate DeEPs.

Example 7. Table 3 [16] contains a training set, for predicting whether the weather is good for some "Saturday morning" activity. The instances, each described by four attributes, are divided into two classes: class $\mathcal{P}$ and class $\mathcal{N}$.

Table 3. Weather conditions and Saturday Morning activity.

Class $\mathcal{P}$ (suitable for activity)				Class $\mathcal{N}$ (not suitable)			
outlook	temperature	humidity	windy	outlook	temperature	humidity	windy
overcast	hot	high	false	sunny	hot	high	false
rain	mild	high	false	sunny	hot	high	true
rain	cool	normal	false	rain	cool	normal	true
overcast	cool	normal	true	sunny	mild	high	false
sunny	cool	normal	false	rain	mild	high	true
rain	mild	normal	false				
sunny	mild	normal	true				
overcast	mild	high	true				
overcast	hot	normal	false				

Now, given the testing instance $T=\{sunny, mild, high, true\}$, which class label should it take? Initially, DeEPs calculates the supports (in both classes) of the proper subsets of T in its first step. The proper subsets of T and their supports are organized as the following three groups:

1. those that only occur in Class $\mathcal{N}$ but not in Class $\mathcal{P}$:

Subset of T	Support in Class $\mathcal{P}$ ($supp_\mathcal{P}$)	$supp_\mathcal{N}$
{sunny,high}	0	60%
{sunny,mild,high}	0	20%
{sunny,high,true}	0	20%

2. *those that only occur in Class $\mathcal{P}$ but not in Class $\mathcal{N}$:*

Subset of T	$supp_{\mathcal{P}}$	$supp_{\mathcal{N}}$
{sunny,mild,true}	11%	0

3. *those that occur in both classes:*

Subset of T	$supp_{\mathcal{P}}$	$supp_{\mathcal{N}}$
∅	100%	100%
{mild}	44%	40%
{sunny}	22%	60%
{high}	33%	80%
{true}	33%	60%
{sunny,mild}	11%	20%

Subset of T	$supp_{\mathcal{P}}$	$supp_{\mathcal{N}}$
{mild,high}	22%	40%
{sunny,true}	11%	20%
{high,true}	11%	40%
{mild,true}	11%	20%
{mild,high,true}	11%	20%

Obviously, the first group of subsets — which are indeed EPs of Class $\mathcal{N}$ as they do not appear in Class $\mathcal{P}$ at all — favours the prediction that T should be classified as Class $\mathcal{N}$. However, the second group of subsets gives us a contrasting indication that T should be classified as Class $\mathcal{P}$, although this indication is not as strong as that of the first group. The third group also strongly suggests that we should favour Class $\mathcal{N}$ as T's label, although the pattern {mild} contradicts this mildly. Using these EPs in a *collective* way, not separately, DeEPs would decide that T's label is Class $\mathcal{N}$ since the "aggregation" of EPs occurring in Class $\mathcal{N}$ is much stronger than that in Class $\mathcal{P}$.

In practice, an instance may contain many (e.g., 100 or more) attributes. To examine all subsets and discover the relevant EPs contained in such instances by naive enumeration is too expensive (e.g., checking 2^{100} or more sets). We make DeEPs efficient and scalable for high dimensional data by the following data reduction and concise data-representation techniques.

- We reduce the training data sets firstly by removing those items that do not occur in the testing instance and then by selecting the **maximal** ones from the processed training instances. This data reduction process makes the training data **sparser** in both horizontal and vertical directions.
- We use borders, two-bound structures like $<\mathcal{L}, \mathcal{R}>$, to succinctly represent all EPs contained in a testing instance.
- We select boundary EPs (typically small in number, e.g., 81 in mushroom) for DeEPs' decision making.

Detailed discussions and illustrations of these points are given in [10]. Table 4 illustrates the first stage of the sparsifying effect on both the volume and dimension of $\mathcal{D}_{\mathcal{P}}$ and $\mathcal{D}_{\mathcal{N}}$, by removing all items that do not occur in T. Observe that the transformed $\mathcal{D}_{\mathcal{P}}$ and $\mathcal{D}_{\mathcal{N}}$ are sparse, whereas the original $\mathcal{D}_{\mathcal{P}}$ and $\mathcal{D}_{\mathcal{N}}$ are *dense* since there is a value for each attribute of each instance.

For continuous attributes, we describe a new method, called **neighborhood-based intersection**. This allows DeEPs to determine which continuous attribute values are relevant to a given testing instance, without the need to pre-discretize data. More details can be found in [6].

Table 4. Reduced training data after removing items irrelevant to the instance {sunny, mild, high, true}. A "*" indicates that an item is discarded. There are only two maximal itemsets in the Reduced Class $\mathcal{P}$ (namely {$sunny, mild, true$} and {$mild, high, true$}) and only 3 maximal itemsets in the Reduced Class $\mathcal{N}$.

Reduced Class $\mathcal{P}$				Reduced Class $\mathcal{N}$			
outlook	temperature	humidity	windy	outlook	temperature	humidity	windy
*	*	high	*	sunny	*	high	*
*'	mild	high	*	sunny	*	high	true
*	*	*	*	*	*	*	true
*	*	*	true	sunny	mild	high	*
sunny	*	*	*	*	mild	high	true
*	mild	*	*				
sunny	mild	*	true				
*	mild	high	true				
*	*	*	*				

7.2   Performance Evaluation: Accuracy, Speed, and Scalability

We now present experimental results to mainly demonstrate the accuracy of DeEPs. We have run DeEPs on 40 data sets which are taken from the UCI Machine Learning Repository [4]. The accuracy results were obtained using the *stratified* ten-fold cross-validation methodology (CV-10), where each fold has the same class distribution as the original data. These experiments were carried out on a 500MHz PentiumIII PC, with 512M bytes of RAM.

We first compare DeEPs with k-nearest neighbor (k-NN) [5] as it is also an instance-based classifier and it has received extensive research since its conception in 1951. As traditionally, we set k as 3. We also compare DeEPs with C5.0 [Release 1.12], a commercial version of C4.5 [17]. We report our experimental results in Table 5. The testing accuracies of DeEPs, k-nearest neighbor, and C5.0 are achieved under the condition that they use the same data for their training and the same data for their testing. We list the names of the data sets in Column 1 of Table 5, and their properties in Column 2. Columns 3 and 4 show the CV-10 average accuracy of DeEPs, when the neighborhood factor α is fixed as 12 for all data sets, and respectively when α is dynamically selected within each data set. (see [10] for how to select α.) We list the accuracies of k-nearest neighbor and C5.0 respectively in Column 5 and Column 6. Column 7 and Column 8 respectively show the average time used by DeEPs and k-nearest neighbor to test one instance.

Firstly, for the mushroom data set, DeEPs, k-NN, and C5.0 can all achieve 100% testing accuracy. For the remaining data sets, we highlight some interesting points.

1. DeEPs versus k-NN.
   - Both DeEPs and k-NN perform equally accurately on soybean-small (100%) and on iris (96%).
   - DeEPs wins on 26 data sets; k-NN wins on 11 data sets. We conclude that the accuracy of DeEPs is generally better than that of k-NN.
   - The speed of DeEPs is about 1.5 times slower than k-NN does. The main reason is that DeEPs needs to conduct border operations.
2. DeEPs versus C5.0.
   - DeEPs wins on 25 data sets; C5.0 wins on 14 data sets. Therefore, DeEPs is generally much more accurate than C5.0.
   - DeEPs is much slower than C5.0. However, DeEPs takes an instance-based learning strategy.
3. DeEPs, k-NN, and C5.0.
   - DeEPs wins on 20 data sets; k-NN wins on 7 data sets; C5.0 wins on 14 data sets.

An important conclusion we can reach here is that DeEPs is an accurate instance-based classifier. Its accuracy is generally better than that of the state-of-the-art classifiers such as C4.5 and k-nearest neighbor. However, the speed of DeEPs requires great improvement to compete well with other classifiers. This problem constitutes our future research topic.

The primary metric for evaluating classifier performance is classification accuracy. We have already shown DeEPs is an accurate classifier and it is generally better than the other classifiers. Our experimental results have also shown that the decision speed of DeEPs is fast, and it has a noticeable scalability over the number of training instances.

8 Related Works

In previous works, we proposed two eager learning classifiers by making use of the discriminating power of emerging patterns. One is called CAEP [7], and the other the JEP-Classifier [11]. Both of these have a learning phase which is used to generate a collection of emerging patterns, and a testing phase. Usually the size of the collection of the discovered EPs is large, and a large proportion of these EPs are never used to test any instances. The learning phase usually takes a significant amount of time. On the other hand, the testing phase is very fast.

How to maintain a system in response to minor data changes is an important problem. The problem of incrementally maintaining JEP spaces has been well solved in [12]. The proposed algorithms can handle a wide range of data changes including insertion of new instances, deletion of instances, insertion of new attributes, and deletion of attributes.

Top rules are the association rules which have the 100% confidence. In [13], we proposed a technique, which is fundamentally different from the traditional approaches, to discover all top rules. The top rules are concisely represented by means of JEP spaces regardless of their supports. The advantage of our method is that it can discover very low support top rules.

9 Conclusions

In this paper, we have reviewed the concept of emerging patterns. Emerging patterns can capture emerging trends in business data and sharp contrasts in classes. Emerging patterns satisfy the properties of validity, novelty, potential usefulness, and understandability. We have described a special type of EP, jumping emerging patterns. JEP spaces have been shown to have the property of convexity. Based on this property, JEP spaces can be concisely represented by boundary elements which can be efficiently derived by our border-based algorithms. We have described an EP-based classifier, DeEPs. The DeEPs classifier takes an instance-based learning strategy. The reported experimental results have shown that its accuracy is better than that of k-nearest neighbor and C5.0.

References

1. R. Agrawal, T. Imielinski, and A. Swami. Mining association rules between sets of items in large databases. In *Proceedings of the 1993 ACM-SIGMOD International Conference on Management of Data*, pages 207–216, Washington, D.C., May 1993. ACM Press.

2. R. Agrawal and R. Srikant. Fast algorithms for mining association rules. In *Proceedings of the Twentieth International Conference on Very Large Data Bases*, pages 487–499, Santiago, Chile, September 1994.

3. Roberto J. Bayardo. Efficiently mining long patterns from databases. In *Proceedings of the 1998 ACM-SIGMOD International Conference on Management of Data*, pages 85–93. ACM Press, 1998.

4. C.L. Blake and P.M. Murphy. The UCI machine learning repository. [http://www.cs.uci.edu/~mlearn/MLRepository.html]. In *Irvine, CA: University of California, Department of Information and Computer Science*, 1998.

5. T. M. Cover and P. E. Hart. Nearest neighbor pattern classification. *IEEE Transactions on Information Theory*, 13:21–27, 1967.

6. Guozhu Dong and Jinyan Li. Efficient mining of emerging patterns: Discovering trends and differences. In *Proceedings of the Fifth ACM SIGKDD International Conference on Knowledge Discovery and Data Mining*, pages 43–52, San Diego, CA, 1999. ACM Press.

7. Guozhu Dong, Xiuzhen Zhang, Limsoon Wong, and Jinyan Li. CAEP: Classification by aggregating emerging patterns. In *Proceedings of the Second International Conference on Discovery Science, Tokyo, Japan*, pages 30–42. Springer-Verlag, December 1999.

8. U. M. Fayyad, G. Piatetsky-Shapiro, and P. Smyth. From data mining to knowledge discovery: An overview. In U.M. Fayyad, G. Piatetsky-Shapiro, P. Smyth, and R. Uthurusamy, editors, *Advances in Knowledge Discovery and Data Mining*, pages 1–34. AAAI/MIT Press, 1996.

9. Carl A. Gunter, Teow-Hin Ngair, and Devika Subramanian. The common order-theoretic structure of version spaces and ATMS's. In *Artificial Intelligence*, volume 95 of *2*, pages 357–407, 1997.

10. Jinyan Li, Guozhu Dong, and Kotagiri Ramamohanarao. Instance-based classification by emerging patterns. In *Proceedings of the Fourth European Conference on Principles and Practice of Knowledge Discovery in Databases*, page in press, Lyon, France, September 2000. Springer-Verlag.

11. Jinyan Li, Guozhu Dong, and Kotagiri Ramamohanarao. Making use of the most expressive jumping emerging patterns for classification. In *Proceedings of the Fourth Pacific-Asia Conference on Knowledge Discovery and Data Mining. An expanded version of the paper was accepted by Knowledge and Information Systems: An International Journal*, pages 220–232, Kyoto, Japan, April 2000. Springer-Verlag.

12. Jinyan Li, Kotagiri Ramamohanarao, and Guozhu Dong. The space of jumping emerging patterns and its incremental maintenance algorithms. In *Proceedings of the Seventeenth International Conference on Machine Learning, Stanford, CA, USA*, pages 551–558, San Francisco, June 2000. Morgan Kaufmann.

13. Jinyan Li, Xiuzhen Zhang, Guozhu Dong, Kotagiri Ramamohanarao, and Qun Sun. Efficient mining of high confidence association rules without support thresholds. In *Proceedings of the Third European Conference on Principles and Practice of Knowledge Discovery in Databases*, pages 406–411, Prague, Czech Republic, September 1999. Springer-Verlag.

14. T. M. Mitchell. Version spaces: A candidate elimination approach to rule learning. In *Proceedings of the Fifth International Joint Conference on Artificial Intelligence*, pages 305–310, Cambridge, MA, 1977.

15. T.M. Mitchell. Generalization as search. *Artificial Intelligence*, 18:203–226, 1982.

16. J. R. Quinlan. Induction of decision trees. *Machine Learning*, 1:81–106, 1986.

17. J. R. Quinlan. *C4.5: Programs for Machine Learning*. Morgan Kaufmann, San Mateo, CA, 1993.

Table 5. Accuracy of DeEPs in comparison to those of k-nearest neighbor and C5.0.

Data sets	inst, attri classes	DeEPs $\alpha = 12$	$dynamical\ \alpha$	k-NN $k = 3$	C5.0	time (s.) DeEPs	time (s.) k-NN
australia	690, 14, 2	84.78	88.41* (5)	66.69	**85.94**	0.054	0.036
breast-w	699, 10, 2	96.42	96.42 (12)	**96.85**	95.43	0.055	0.036
census	30162, 16, 2	**85.93**	85.93* (12)	75.12	85.80	2.081	1.441
chess	3196, 36, 2	97.81	97.81	96.75	**99.45**	0.472	0.145
cleve	303, 13, 2	**81.17**	84.21* (15)	62.64	77.16	0.032	0.019
diabete	768, 8, 2	**76.82**	76.82* (12)	69.14	73.03	0.051	0.039
flare	1066,10,2	**83.50**	83.50	81.62	82.74	0.028	0.016
german	1000, 20, 2	**74.40**	74.40 (12)	63.1	71.3	0.207	0.061
heart	270, 13, 2	**81.11**	82.22 (15)	64.07	77.06	0.025	0.013
hepatitis	155, 19, 2	**81.18**	82.52 (11)	70.29	74.70	0.018	0.011
letter-r	20000, 16, 26	93.60	93.60* (12)	**95.58**	88.06	3.267	1.730
lymph	148, 18, 4	**75.42**	75.42 (10)	74.79	74.86	0.019	0.010
pima	768, 8, 2	**76.82**	77.08* (14)	69.14	73.03	0.051	0.038
satimage	6435, 36, 6	88.47	88.47* (12)	**91.11**	86.74	2.821	1.259
segment	2310, 19, 7	94.98	95.97* (5)	95.58	**97.28**	0.382	0.365
shuttle-s	5800, 9, 7	97.02	99.62* (1)	99.54	**99.65**	0.438	0.295
splice	3175, 60, 3	69.71	69.71	70.03	**94.20**	0.893	0.248
vehicle	846, 18, 4	70.95	74.56* (15)	65.25	**73.68**	0.134	0.089
voting	433, 16, 2	95.17	95.17	92.42	**97.00**	0.025	0.012
waveform	5000, 21, 3	**84.36**	84.36* (12)	80.86	76.5	2.522	0.654
yeast	1484, 8, 10	**59.78**	60.24* (10)	54.39	56.14	0.096	0.075
anneal	998, 38, 6	**94.41**	95.01 (6)	89.70	93.59	0.122	0.084
auto	205, 25, 7	67.65	72.68 (3.5)	40.86	**83.18**	0.045	0.032
crx	690, 15, 2	84.18	88.11* (3.5)	66.64	83.91	0.055	0.038
glass	214, 9, 7	58.49	67.39 (10)	67.70	**70.01**	0.021	0.017
horse	368, 28, 2	84.21	85.31* (3.5)	66.31	**84.81**	0.052	0.024
hypo	3163, 25, 2	97.19	98.26 (5)	98.26	**99.32**	0.275	0.186
ionosph	351, 34, 2	86.23	91.24 (5)	83.96	**91.92**	0.147	0.100
iris	150, 4, 3	**96.00**	96.67* (10)	**96.00**	94.00	0.007	0.006
labor	57, 16, 2	87.67	87.67* (10)	**93.00**	83.99	0.009	0.008
mushroom	8124, 22, 2	**100.0**	100.0	**100.0**	**100.0**	0.436	0.257
nursery	12960, 8, 5	**99.04**	99.04	98.37	97.06	0.290	0.212
pendigits	10992, 16, 10	98.21	98.44 (18)	**99.35**	96.67	1.912	0.981
sick	4744, 29, 2	94.03	96.63 (5)	93.00	**98.78**	0.284	0.189
sonar	208, 60, 2	**84.16**	86.97* (11)	82.69	70.20	0.193	0.114
soybean-s	47, 34, 4	**100.0**	100.0* (10)	**100.0**	98.00	0.022	0.017
soybean-l	683, 35, 19	90.08	90.08	91.52	**92.96**	0.072	0.051
t-t-t	958, 9, 2	**99.06**	99.06	98.65	86.01	0.032	0.013
wine	178, 13, 3	**95.58**	96.08* (11)	72.94	93.35	0.028	0.019
zoo	101, 16, 7	**97.19**	97.19	93.93	91.26	0.007	0.005

IPv6 Performance Analysis on FreeBSD Workstation Using Simple Applications

K.Ettikan and V.Ganapathy

Faculty of Information Technology
Multimedia University (MMU)
Jalan Multimedia, 63100 Cyberjaya
Selangor, Malaysia.
email : ettikan@mmu.edu.my

Abstract. The twenty five year- old Internet Protocol (IP) or known as IPv4, has its own history in connecting the world for information exchange. Its' new successor, IPv6 with promising functionality and capability is being designed to replace the predecessor. This paper analyses the performance of the new IP compared to old IP on dual stack implementation of KAME [7] FreeBSD [9] using ping and FTP application. Packet transmission time as been taken as the measurement metric. Test results of experiment shows that IPv6 performance is inferior to IPv4 and does not conform with the theoretical results.

1 Introduction

The twenty-five year- old Internet Protocol (IP) or known as IPv4, has its own history in connecting the world for information exchange. However the need for larger address space, simple routing capability, scalability, security, easier network configuration and management, QoS (Quality of Service), mobility and multicasting forced IETF to design it's successor, IPv6 [1,2]. Eventhough work on design and implementation of IPv6 has started since year 1992, it has not been widely accepted by the world community. It is expected that by year 2008, for with current rate of IP address allocation, IPv4 will see address depletion [3]. So, transition from IPv4 to IPv6 is inevitable even address shortage problem can be minimized by adopting temporary techniques such as Network Address Translation (NAT), IP Masquerade and Dynamic Host Configuration Protocol (DHCP).

However the transition from existing IPv4 to new IPv6 will be a gradual process as planed by the IETF IPng Work Group. This step is necessary to guarantee that the transition process does not interrupt the entire Internet activities. Besides, it also ensures financial and time flexibility for organization to upgrade and replace the relevant applications and equipment. Existence of IPv4 entities in the IPv6 Internet or IPv6 entities in IPv4 Internet will a common phenomena for at-least few years before complete replacement of IPv4 takes place. Dual stack implementation, which supports

J. He and M. Sato (Eds.): ASIAN 2000, LNCS 1961, pp. 33-42, 2000.

both version of IP, will be used together with native IPv4 and native IPv6 nodes in the Internet during this period.

IPv6 generally has been accepted as the next generation protocol, which solves many of today networks' constraints and problems with improvement in performance [4]. It is important to examine the performance of the promising IPv6 as native and also as dual stack host. The papers' objective is to analyze and study the performance of IPv6 using ping and FTP applications on FreeBSD implementation.

2 IPv6 Features

Version	Traffic Class	Flow Label	
Payload Length		Next Header	Hop Limit
Source Address			
Destination Address			

Fig. 1. IPv6 Header

The new design of the IPv6 header format [2] with fewer fields compared to IPv4 is aimed to increase the speed at which the packets travel through the router. Unnecessary fields which are not examined by the router along the path but, required by the sending and receiving nodes are placed in between the IPv6 header and transport layer header. Besides simplifying the header this reduces router's computational workload and speeds up the packet delivery. Additional optional header are also easier to be added, making IPv6 more flexible than IPv4. Since the IPv6 header has fixed length, processing is also simplified.

IPv6 does not fragment packets as they are routed unlike IPv4. Transmission's paths Maximum Transmission Unit (MTU) will be discovered before packets being transported on different network layers. This means packet fragmentation and reassembly are done exclusively in the communicating hosts, reducing the workload of the routers. It is expected, by completion of IPv6 deployment over the Internet, Internet will have networks with MTU not smaller than 576 bytes.

The present IP requires checksum calculation within IP packets, and therefore their computation at each routing step. This computation be done for every packet and total expenditure of involved computing resources and checksumming in the Internet which carries trillions of packet is significance. In IPv6 the checksum operation has been eliminated and done by other layers in ensuring accurate packet delivery.

The use of flow labels in IPv6 will further optimize IPv6 performance. The flow source specification in the Flow Label field will have labels of any special service requirements from the router along the path, such as priority, delay or bandwidth. All the packets of that particular flow will carry same information in the field, enabling request for a service type in the intermediate routes, thereby minimizing the necessary computation to deliver each packet. Multicast function in IPv6, which replaces broadcast, allows nodes to discover the participating group of a group communication via neighbor discovery and Internet Control Message Protocol (ICMPv6) messages reduces unnecessary packet examination by routers. All these features were not possible in IPv4 Internet.

IPv6 address assignment is more efficient and conforms to the hierarchical structure of the Internet compared to IPv4. Concept of CIDR (Classless Inter Domain Routing) has been adopted in formulating the addressing structure, which allows address aggregation with the provider based address format. Addresses had two main portions, which are routing and interface identifiers. The routing identifiers have been further divided to subfields, denoting registries, providers, sub-subscribers and subnets. Route aggregation will limit the router table explosion problem and makes routing even simpler. It is an exciting exercise to evaluate and analyze the multi-feature Internet Protocol for it's performance with above mentioned criterions.

3 Challenges

Eventhough IPv6 promises many advanced features in the transition period, it will face many challenges, which will effect the overall performance. Dual protocol stacks configuration will be a common in all exchange points, at least for few years. Before switching completely from native IPv4 to IPv6, clients, servers and routers will be running both IPv4 and IPv6 protocols. This dual stack mechanism will compromise IPv6 performance. Figure 2 depicts the general protocol layers for dual IP.

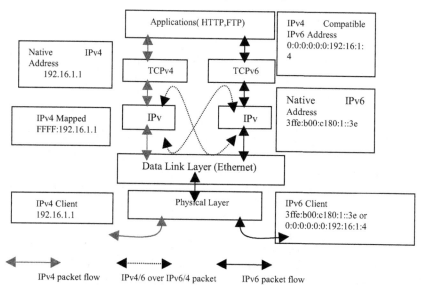

Fig. 2. General Protocol Layers for Dual IP Stacks.

Besides that IETF plans to adopt tunneling as another transition technique to migrate to IPv6. This technique allows native IPv6 notes or islands to communicate in IPv4 ocean, where all the interconnecting nodes are running IPv4. The vice-versa communication is also possible where IPv4 packets tunneled through IPv6 infrastructure. Communicating nodes packet will be encapsulated by the packet carrying IP as their payload. On the other end of communication receiver will decapsulate the packet before processing the actual packet. Figure 3 shows the encapsulation and decapsulation process for both IPs. Most of the inter-network connections in IPv6 test-bed, 6bone are connected via tunneling technique. Tunneling will cause overhead since header of either IP will reduces the actual payload of the packet.

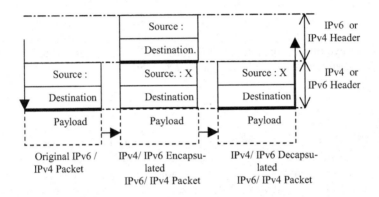

Fig. 3. Encapsulation and Decapsulation IPv4 and IPv6 packtes.

Besides the above-mentioned factors, inter-operability incompatibility between multiple vendors' equipment will cause additional problem on the performance and delays the process of IPv6 deployment over the Internet. Independent bodies such as TAHI [12] are carried out conformance tests to ensure the IPv6 nodes are compatible.

Translation, which covers Network Address Translation & Port Translation, Protocol Translation and Application Proxies is another method that has been adopted by IETF to allow inter-protocol communication. IP translation [5] for IPv4/IPv6 and ICMPv4/ICMPv6 has been carried out and the result is encouraging. In this technique IP header fields are either directly copied, translated or eliminated to suite the version of the IP. However information loss is unavoidable and increase of header length also experienced during the header translation [5].

In this paper we will discuss the performance of IPv6 on Ethernet network layer for KAME [7] FreeBSD [9] dual stack implementation as in the following section. Previous work [6] on this issue was not concluded with concrete results due to dynamism in implementation of the KAME FreeBSD dual stack. In this paper a stable version of IPv6 stack implementation has been adopted for performance analysis.

4 Experiment

We adopt the dual IP stack, FreeBSD with KAME IPv6 patch, [8] the famous, stable and up-to-date IPv6 implementation. Tests were conducted using KAME FreeBSD FTP and Ping applications that runs on reliable TCP layer and ICMP messages. FTP measurement was done for only data connection [6]. Two sets of network configuration, namely On-Link and Off-Link have been set-up to conduct the experiments. Off-link configuration allows data transfer between workstations without the presence of router. While on-link tests have routers in-between the workstations.

The on-link test is significance to test the impact of checksum operation removal in IPv6 compared to IPv4 at routers. Besides that, effect of simplified header fields to the data transfer also can be analyzed by the on-link tests. The above are the two specific features that we would like to investigate in the experiment configuration. As shown in Figure 2, FTP and Ping file/message transfer will take place between the two test workstations. The packets will be transferred according to the configuration of layers that shown in Figure 2. The only difference between TCP or UDP implementation in KAME [8] for IPv6 and IPv4 is the address length, which is 128bits compared to 32 bits in IPv4. We assume that the implementation of the stack is identical between IPv4 and IPv6 for KAME in FreeBSD. The only major difference between them is IPv6 [2] implementation.

Ping and FTP tests were carried out in our experiment for both on-link and off-link configuration for IPv4 and IPv6. TAHI group upon our request conducted the off-link FTP test 1 and we conducted the other two tests. Ping test for off-link was not conducted. The ping and FTP (including server and client)[6] applications for IPv4 that used in our experiment were from FreeBSD, as for IPv6, from KAME patch for FreeBSD.

Table 1. List of tests in the experiment

Tests IP ver.	Ping (On link)	FTP (On link and Off link)
IPv4	FreeBSD	FreeBSD
IPv6	FreeBSD/ KAME patch	FreeBSD/ KAME patch

4.1 Off-Link Configuration

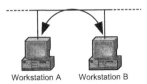

Workstation A   Workstation B

Fig. 4. Off-Link FreeBSD with Kame patch dual Stack network configuration

Figure 4 shows two workstations have been interconnected via Ethernet LAN directly and attached to the same segment. The link speed is 100 Mbps and both workstations run on Pentium II processor at 350 MHz with 64MB memory. Ping application for both versions of IP has been tested for the above setup. As for FTP test, TAHI group has been contacted for confirmation of the performance problem and they have carried out the experiment [12][1].

4.2 On-Link Configuration

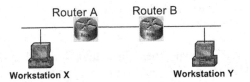

Fig. 5. On-Link FreeBSD with Kame patch dual Stack network configuration for workstations and also routers

Figure 5 shows, the two workstations have been interconnected via two FreeBSD routers with KAME patch. All the routers and workstations for above setup run on FreeBSD and KAME patch for IPv6. The workstation configuration is attached in Appendix A.

---

[1] The FTP experiment has been conducted by TAHI group upon the author's request since they perform conformance and interoperability test for all IPv6 products and implementation. Experiment results viewable at http://www.tahi.org.

5 Results and Analysis

The present implementation of KAME IPv6 dual stack implementation has modification to the TCP layer, where the address size has been changed from 32 bit to 128 bits and checksum calculation has been disabled at IP layer. Besides that, simplified IP header and no further fragmentation of packets done in IPv6 since the Ethernet layer with MTU 1500 bytes. We would like to investigate the impact of IPv6 characteristics on application layer based on these above factors.

Table 2. Ethernet packet size breakdown

Ethernet MTU (including header)		1514 bytes
Ethernet header		14 bytes
Ethernet Payload		1500 bytes
	IPv4 (bytes)	**IPv6 (bytes)**
IP Header	20	40
IP Payload	1480	1460
TCP Header	20	20
TCP Payload	1460	1440
Options	xxxx	xxxx
Actual Payload	yyyy	yyyy

Table 2 shows the packet composition which, is carried across the network on the Ethernet medium. The actual TCP payload for IPv4 is 1460 and IPv6 is 1440. It is expected with reduction of TCP payload in IPv6 as 20 bytes or 1.37 %, the performance should also degrade by 1.37 %. Richard Draves and el. [10] reported 2 % of performance degradation on their implementation of IPv6 for NT system, which is tolarable. However another performance evaluation [11] for MBONE multicast tools on IPv6 shows the performance reduction is more than expected.

5.1 Off Link Test

The test shows average 4-5% deterioration in overall performance for the ping test between two off-link workstation. Figure 6 shows the measured result.

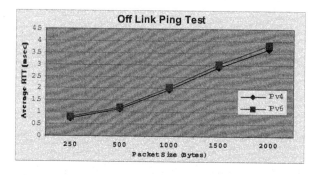

Fig. 6. Off-link Ping test result

Off-link FTP test [12] was conducted by TAHI group. They setup four different environment, namely native IPv4, only IPv4 on dual stack, IPv4 on dual stack with IPv6 and IPv6 on dual stack with IPv4 for the test [12]. The transmission time is shown in Figure 7[2]. FTP tests shows similar performance deterioration for IPv6 compared to IPv4 as the file size gets larger.

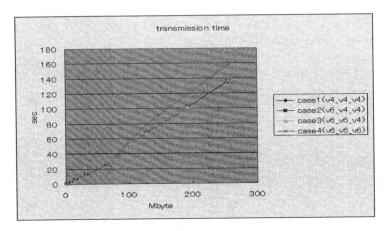

Fig. 7[2]. Transmission time for Off-link FTP test results (please refer Appendix B for better figure)

5.2 On-link Test

The on-link test results show similar behavior of IPv6 performance as the off-link test. The presents of the router does not influence the time taken to transfer the files across the network. Transmission of IPv6 encapsulated IPv4 has degraded performance, as IPv6. While IPv4 encapsulated IPv6 packets does not show much difference compared to IPv4 since the transport mechanism is still IPv4.

---

[2] The transmission diagram has been extracted from tahi project homepage with their permission.

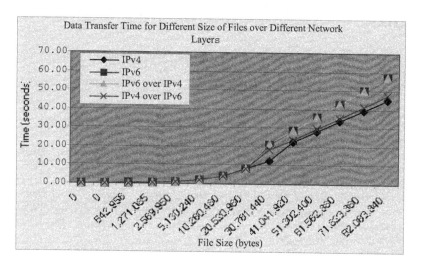

Fig. 8. On-link FTP test result

6 Conclusion and Future Work

IPv6 has degraded performance compared to IPv4 for the files that has been transferred and also for the ICMP packets in Ping test. Eventhough the expected performance deterioration was ~1.5%, but in actual implementation it is more than 5% in average. Besides that for file transfers, as the file size increases the performance of IPv6 further deteriorates as shown in Figure 7 and Figure 8.

The results show IPv6 performance is not better than IPv4, instead worst than IPv4 and expected result. Further analysis of the codes is necessary to clarify the real constraint of IPv6 performance and fine tuning need to be done.

The performance analysis is ongoing activity in our lab. There are some suspected reasons for the performance degradation in IPv6. In the test we assume that FreeBSD for IPv4 and IPv6 KAME patch for FreeBSD is similar except the IPv6 implementation. Besides that TCP and ICMPv6 implementation has been assumed to work well. Currently we are conducting tests to verify all the implementations that may effect the test results with help of the KAME group. Code analysis for the dual stack is necessary to find out the reasons for the deterioration and also for further enhancement. In our future paper we expect to justify the performance degradation with improvements for it.

IPv6 promises many advance features, therefore proper implementation is necessary to this new protocol. During the transition period users should be convinced that this migration is towards a better IP. Until the stable and fine-tunned version of IP is available, users will be skeptical and resist migrating to the newer version of IP.

References

1. Steve King, Ruth Fax, Dimitry Haskin, Wenken Ling, Tom Meehan, Robert Fink, Charles E.Perkins " The Case for IPv6, draft-ietf-iab-case-for-ipv6-05.txt, Oct 1999
2. R.Hinden, S.Geering, "Internet Protocol Version 6 (IPv6) Specification, Internet Draft, Nov. 1997
3. F.Solensky, "IPv4 Address Lifetime Expectations", in IPng: Internet Protocol Next Generation (S.Bradner, A.Mankin, ed), Addison Wesley, 1996
4. Marcus Goncalves and Kitty Niles, "IPv6 Networks",MacGraw Hill, 1998
5. Marc E.Fiuczynski, Vincent K.Lam and Brian N.Bershad, "The Design and Implementation of an IPv6/IPv4 Network Address and Protocol Translator", Proceedings of the 1998 USENIX Technical Conference, June 1998
6. Ettikan Kandasamy Karuppiah, Gopi Kurup and Takefumi Yamazaki, "Application Performance Analysis in Transition Mechanism from IPv4 to IPv6" Proceedings IWS2000, Tsukuba, Japan, Feb. 15-17,2000
7. KAME Project, http://www.kame.net
8. KAME Implementation, "KAME-STABLE-20000428", http://www.kame.net.
9. FreeBSD, http://www.freebsd.org
10. Richard P.Draves, Allison Mankin and Brian D.Zill, "Implentating IPv6 for Windows NT", Proceedings of the 2nd USENIX Windows NT Symposium, Seattle, WA, August 3-4,1998
11. Behcet Sarikaya, "Performance of Mbone Tools on IPv6 Using MGEN", February 24, 2000, http://www.u-aizu.ac.jp/~sarikaya/fukazawa.thesis.ps.gz
12. TAHI Project, http://www.tahi.org

Acknowledgement

Special thanks to Minoru Teraoka and other TAHI group members for implementing the off-link conformance test, which is available at their site http://www.tahi.org. Their kind input and assistance very much appreciated.

Performance of Location Caching Scheme to Support Call Locality in Wireless Networks

DongChun Lee[1], JeomGoo Kim[2], and JooSeok Song[3]

[1] Dept. of Computer Science, Howon Univ., South Korea
ldch@sunny.howon.ac.kr
[2] Dept. of Computer Science, Namseoul Univ., Korea
[3] Dept. of Computer Science, Yonsei Univ., South Korea

Abstract. To support call locality (CL) in wireless networks, we locate the cache in local signaling transfer point (LSTP) level. The terminal registration area (RA) crossings within the LSTP area do not generate the home location register (HLR) traffic. The RAs in LSTP area are grouped statically. It is to remove the signaling overhead and to mitigate the RSTP bottleneck in dynamic grouping. The idea behind LSTP level caching is to decrease the inconsistency ratio (ICR) with static RA grouping. Our scheme solves the HLR bottleneck problem due to the terminal' frequent RA crossings.

1 Introduction

The mobility management schemes are based on Interim Standard-41 (IS-41) and Global System for Mobile Communication (GSM) standard. Those schemes use the two level hierarchies composed of home location register (HLR) and visitor location register (VLR) [2,9]. Whenever a terminal crosses a RA or a call originate, HLR should be updated or queried. Frequent DB accesses and message transfers may cause the HLR bottleneck and degrade the system performance. To access the DBs and transmit the signaling messages frequently cause the HLR bottleneck and load the wireless network [1]. There are several schemes to solve the problems in standard scheme [5,6,7,8].

In Local Anchor (LA) scheme, it is method that it permits one of VLRs to local anchor and replaces a HLR to VLR rolling of local anchor in location registration. This has the merits of reducing registration cost but location-tracking cost increases as through local anchor on location tracking.

In Forwarding Pointer (FP) scheme, whenever RA is changed, it does not register to HLR but proceeds by creating the forwarding pointer from the previous VLR of RA. Thus location registration does not access into HLR and the cost reduces for registration. However, in location request, the cost can increases because of finding location of terminal depending on step of forwarding pointer.

To support the CL, our scheme locates the cache in local signaling transfer point (LSTP) level and groups the RAs of which their serving mobile switching centers (MSCs) are connected to LSTP, which is depicted in Fig. 1.

J. He and M. Sato (Eds.): ASIAN 2000, LNCS 1961, pp. 43–57, 2000.

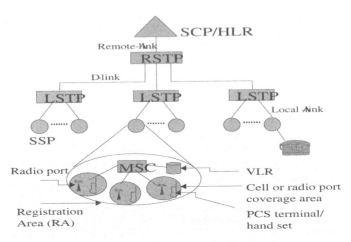

Fig.1.Conceptual System Architecture

In wireless network environments, one of the distinct characteristics of call patterns is the CL. The CL is related to the regional distribution with which the caller's request calls to a given callee. The concept is conspicuous when the callee is moving out his home area temporally. The call pattern has importance in the mobility management scheme. Using the conceptual call pattern, we estimate the region from which a lot of calls to a given user originate. We define the regional scope as the degree of call locality. The degree of CL for each user is different but we can limit the scope to the regional area approximately. The degree is said to be high when a lot of calls is generated from a few RAs to a given terminal. Generally, it is reasonable to assume the degree to be low enough to the extent that the domain of calling region covers the callee's working area and its neighboring RAs.

Applying the CL to tracking a call in an efficient manner, we can decrease the signaling traffic load greatly. It implies that the HLR query traffic caused whenever a call originates is reduced to some extent by applying the cache. The key idea behind applying the cache is to make the cached information be referred frequently and maintain the consistency to some extent. The consistency problem is issued in improving the performance.

Our scheme is to present the improved caching scheme to support the CL and to quantify its benefits compared to other schemes. In this paper, we compare the performance in our scheme to previous schemes.

2   Proposed Scheme

We define the LSTP area as the one composed of the RAs which the corresponding MSCs serve. Then we statically group the VLRs in LSTP area in order to maintain the consistency rate high. Even though it is impossible to maintain the consistency at all times as the computer system does, we can effectively keep it high to some extents by grouping method. The cache is used to reduce the call-tracking load and make the fast call setup possible. It is also possible to group RAs dynamically regardless of the LSTP area. Let define post VLR, P_{VLR} which keeps the callee's current location information as long as the callee moves within its LSTP area. Suppose that the P_{VLR} and the VLR which serves the callee's RA are related to the physically different LSTPs. In this case, we should tolerate the signaling overhead even though the caller and callee belong to same dynamic group. A lot of signaling messages for registering a location and tracking a call is transmitted via RSTP instead of LSTP. If the cost of transmitting the signaling messages via RSTP is large enough compared to LSTP, dynamic grouping method may degrade the performance although it solves the Ping-Pong effect. Furthermore, it is critical in case that RSTP is bottlenecked.

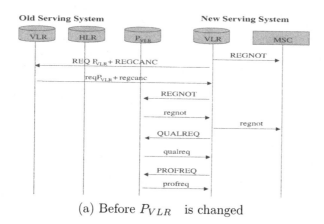

(a) Before P_{VLR} is changed

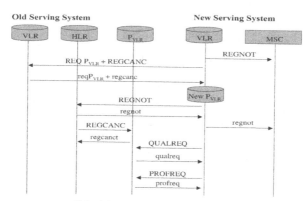

(b) After P_{VLR} is changed

Fig. 2.Location registration in LSTP level caching scheme

If a call originates and the entry of the callee's location exists in LSTP level cache, it is delivered to the P_{VLR}. We note that we don't have to consider where the callee is currently. It is because the P_{VLR} keeps the callee's current location as long as the callee moves within its LSTP area. Without the terminal movements into a new LSTP area, there is no HLR registration. Fig. 2 shows the message flow due to the location registration according to the status of P_{VLR} change.

In our scheme, the location information of terminals is stored in the cache in LSTP level, where the number of call requests to those terminals are over threshold (K). The number of call requests are counted in the P_{VLR} or the VLR which serves the callee's RA. If we take the small K, there are a lot of the entries in cache but the possibility that the cached information and the callee's current location are inconsistent is increased. It is because of the terminals of which call-to-mobility ratios (CMRs) are very low. To the contrary, if we take the large K, the number of terminals of which location information is referred is decreased but the consistency is maintained high. As for the hierarchical level in which the cache is located, the MSC level is not desirous considering the general call patterns. It is effective only for the users of which working and resident areas are regionally very limited, i.e., one or two RAs. When a call is tracked using the cached information, the most important thing is how to maintain the ICR low to some extent that the tracking using the cache is cost effective compared to otherwise. In our scheme, the terminals with high rate of call request regardless of the RA crossings within LSTP area are stored in cache. As for the cached terminal, it is questionable to separate the terminals by CMR. Suppose that the terminal A receive only one call and cross a RA only one time and the terminal B receive a lot of calls (n) and cross the RAs n times. Then the CMRs of two terminals are same but it is desirous that the location information of terminal B is stored in the cache. As for caching effect, the improvement of the performance depends on the reference rate of the user location information more than the number of entries in cache, i.e., the cache size. The object of locating cache in LSTP level is to extend the domain of the region in which the callee's location information is referred for a lot of calls.

The algorithm to track a call using the redial and LSTP level caches is shown below.

```
    LSTP_Cache_Tracking ()

    {Call to mobile user is detected at local switch;

    If callee is in its RA then

    Return;

    Redial_Cache ( );
    /*optional*/

    If there is an entry for callee in LSTP_Cache then
    /*cache hit*/
```

```
{Query corresponding PVLR specified in cache entry;

    If there exists the entry for callee in PVLR then

    Callee VLR, V maintained in PVLR returns callee's
location info. to calling switch;
    else
/*inconsistent state*/

    Switch which serves PVLR  continues Basic_Tracking ( );
    }
  else
/*cache miss*/

continue Basic_Tracking ();
                    /* Basic_Tracking () is used in IS-41 */

}
```

Using the above algorithms, we support the locality shown in user's general call behavior. The tracking steps are depicted in Fig. 3.

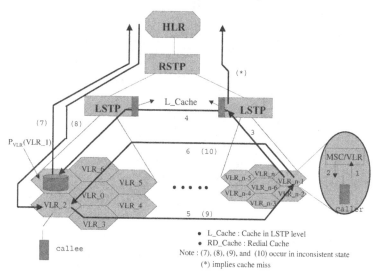

Fig3.Call tracking in LSTP level caching scheme

In Fig.3, we describes the call tracking steps in detail.

(1)Call originates → VLR
    If callee is in its RA then (2)
(2)Return

(3)If callee is found in RD_Cache entry, then (5)
    Else (4)
(4)If callee is found in L_Cache, then (5)
    Else (9)
(5)Query PVLR
(6)If callee exists in PVLR entry, then(7)
    Else(8)
(7)VLR_{callee} return the routing info. To MSC_{callee}
(8)Execute the IS-41call tracking mechanism (step 9 is initiated)
(9)Query HLR
(10)Query PVLR to which HLR points for callee's current location
    info.
(11)VLR_{callee} to which PVLR points returns the routing info. To
    MSC_callee

3   Performance Analysis

For numerical analysis, we adopt hexagon model as geometrical RA model. Generally, it is assumed that a VLR serves one RA.

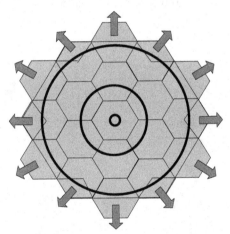

Fig.4.RA model with hexagon structure

As shown in Fig. 4, RAs in LSTP area can be grouped. For example, there are 7 RAs in circle 1 area and 19 RAs in circle 2 area. The terminals in RAs inside circle n area still exist in circle n area after their first RA crossings. That is, the terminals inside circle area cannot cross their LSTP area when they cross the RA one time. While the terminals in RAs which meet the line of the circle can move out from their LSTP area. We can simply calculate the number of moving out terminals. Intuitively, the terminals in arrow marked areas move out in Fig. 4. Using the number of outside edges in arrow marked polygon, we can compute the number of terminals which move out from the LSTP area as follows.

$$\left(\frac{Total No. of outside edges in a row marked polygons}{No. of edges of hexagon \times No. of RAs in LST Pare}\right) \quad (1)$$

$$\times NO. of terminals in LST Parea$$

In Fig. 4, the number of terminals which move out from LSTP area is the terminal in LSTP area x 5/19. The number of VLRs in LSTP area represented as circle n is generalized as follows.

$$No. of VLRs in LST Parea = 1 + 3n(n+1) \quad (where \quad n = 1, 2, \ldots) \quad (2)$$

The rate of terminals which move out from LSTP area can be generalized as follows.

$$R_{move\_out, No. of VLRs in LStparea} =$$

$$((6x2^{n-1})/2)/No. of VLRs \quad in LST Parea \quad (where \quad n = 1, 2, \ldots) \quad (3)$$

The RA is said to be locally related when they belong to the same LSTP area and remotely related when the one of them belongs to the different LSTP area. The terminal's RA crossings should be classified according to the local and remote relations in the following schemes.

1. LA scheme
   - Relation of LA serving RA and callee's last visiting RA
   - Relation of callee's last visiting RA and callee's current RA
2. FP scheme
   - Relation of RA (where T = 0) and next visiting RA (where T = 1)
   - Relations of intermediate RAs in moving route of the terminal
   - Relation of previous RA (where T = n - 1) and callee's current RA
     (Supposed that callee is currently located in the RA where T = n)
3. Proposed scheme
   - Relation of PVLR serving RA and callee's last visiting RA
   - Relation of RA where callee's last visiting RA and callee's current RA

We define the probabilities that a terminal moves within the LSTP area and crosses the LSTP area as P (local) and P (remote), respectively. The above relations are determined according to the terminal's moving patterns.

$$P(local) = R_{move\_in, No. of VLRs in LST Parea}$$

$$P(remote) = R_{move\_out, No. of VLRs in LST Parea} \quad (4)$$

P(local) and P (remote) are varied according to the number of VLRs in LSTP area. Consider the terminals n time RA changes, where the number of RAs in LSTP area is 7. If a terminal moves into a new LSTP area in n^{th} movement, the terminal is located in one of outside RAs - 6 RAs - of the new LSTP area. Therefore, when the terminal moves $(n+1)^{th}$ times, two probabilities, $R_{move\_in,No.of VLRsinLSTParea}$ and $R_{move\_out,No.of VLRsinLSTParea}$ are both 3/6. If the terminals $(n+1)^{th}$ movement occurs within the LSTP area, the probabilities of terminals $(n+2)^{th}$ movement are the two probabilities are 4/7, 3/7 , respectively. Otherwise, the terminal moves into a new LSTP area again. The two probabilities are both 3/6.

3.1   Location registration cost

If a terminal moves within the LSTP area - in case of the local relation -, the PVLR is updated and the entry in old VLR is cancelled. If a terminal moves into the RA in a new LSTP area, the HLR is updated. And then the entries in old PVLR and old VLR are cancelled. We define the signaling costs (SCs) as follows.

```
SC1: Cost of transmitting a message from one VLR to another VLR
     through HLR
SC2: Cost of transmitting a message from one VLR to another VLR
     through RSTP
SC3: Cost of transmitting a message from one VLR to another VLR
     through LSTP
```

We evaluate the performance according to the relative values of SC1, SC2, and SC3 which need for location registration. Generally, we can assume SC3 SC2 < SC1 or SC3 SC2 << SC1. Even though the absolute values can not determined, the difference of relative values can be computed.

Case 1: SC3 < SC2 < SC1
Case 2: SC3, SC2 << SC1
Case 3:SC3 << SC2,SC1
Case 4: SC3, SC2 < SC1

The registration cost for LSTP level caching scheme is computed as follows.

$$C\_LSTPlevelcaching, Loc.Reg = R\_move\_in,NO.of \quad VLRs \quad in \quad LSTP$$
$$area \times (2 \times 2SC3) +$$

$$R_{move\_out,No.of VLRsinLSTParea} \times 2(SC1 + SC3) \qquad (5)$$

The registration cost set (RCS) consists of SC1, SC2, and SC3. We note that the larger RCS number in following figures is, the relative value difference of SC2 and SC3 to SC1 is smaller. It is applied to above 4 cases. In Fig. 5, registration cost is reduced according to the number of the VLRs in LSTP area. In case that terminals average speed is fixed and $R_{move\_out,No.of VLRsinLSTParea}$ is less, the HLR access cost is reduced. Therefore, the more VLRs in the LSTP area are, the performance is improved result.

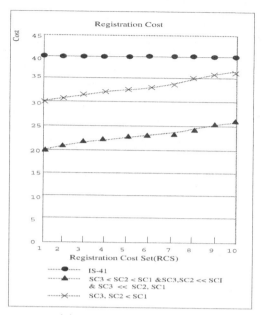

(a) 7 VLRs in LSTP area

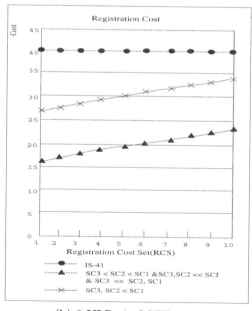

(b) 9 VLRs in LSTP area

Fig. 5.Registration cost comparison

As you see in equation (5), the registration cost is independent of SC2. We assume that SC3 in case 4 is greater than those in other cases. With a common SC1, the performances in case 1, 2, and 3 are better compared to that in case 4.

The difference between Fig. 5 (a) and (b) results from the reduced HLR access traffic according to the VLRs in LSTP area.

Fig. 6 (a) shows that LSTP level caching scheme shows the better results compare to LA scheme in case of $1/M\_no. >= 0.5$ where M_no is the number of terminal RA crossings before call request. The more VLRs are in LSTP area, the smaller $1/M\_no$ can be taken for similar performances in two schemes. This implies that the performance in LSTP level caching scheme with large number of VLRs is prepositional to the effectiveness in aspect of registration cost when LA scheme is applied in terminals high mobility environments.

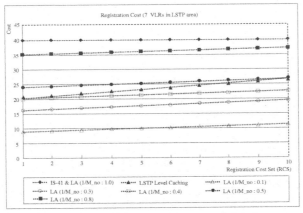

(a) LSTP level caching scheme vs. LA scheme

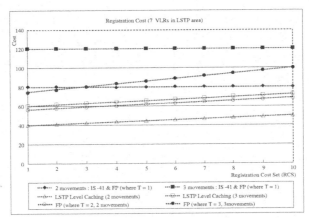

(b) LSTP level caching scheme vs. FP scheme

Fig. 6.Registration cost comparison

Compared to FP scheme in which T is 2, 3, respectively, LSTP level caching scheme shows the better results in both cases. It is mainly caused by degenerating all VLRs in terminals moving route when T is reset in FP scheme. In case of 2 movements in Fig. 6 (b), the performance in T = 1 is better than the one in T = 3 when RCS 3~10 are applied. We anticipate that the registration cost for FP scheme is decreased during terminals (T - 1) RA crossings but increased suddenly when terminals T^{th} RA crossing compared to other schemes. This effect becomes greater with larger T.

3.2   Call tracking cost

We define the rate of the cached terminals of which the number of call_count is over threshold (K) in P_{VLR} as $R_{no.ofCachedTRs}$ · If there exists an entry in LSTP level cache for the subsequent requested call, the corresponding P_{VLR}, is queried. If not, HLR is queried and the pointed VLR in HLR entry is queried subsequently. A call is said to originate locally if the caller and callee is located in same LSTP area. Otherwise, it is said to originate remotely. In call tracking, we consider those two call types and classify each call type into two cases of consistent call and inconsistent one. We define ICR, which is the ratio that the cached information and the entry in PVLR are inconsistent. Therefore, ICR is the ratio of the number of terminals which move out from their LSTP area to the number of terminals in LSTP area to which calls are requested. Described simply, it is the rate of terminals which move out from their LSTP area if the calls are requested to all terminals in LSTP area. ICR is written as follows.

$$ICR = (P_{move\_out,LSTParea} \times R_{reg,VLR})$$

$$(R_{callOrig.jhr/Tr} \times (No.ofTerminals/VLR)) \tag{6}$$

In equation (6), $R_{reg.,VLR}$ is directly proportional to the terminals average speed. If terminals average speed is fixed, then the more calls originate, the less ICR is. The call tracking cost is influenced by the number of VLRs in LSTP area, the terminals moving speed, the call origination rate, and cache reference rate. In other words, the caching effect is dependent on HR in LSTP level cache and the ICR in callee's LSTP area. We mentioned above that the call relations between caller and callee should be considered. According to the relations, the message-transmitting route via LSTP or RSTP is determined. The followings are the generalized tracking costs according to the call relations.

– Tracking cost when caller and callee are locally related:

$$C_{LSTPlevelcaching,CallTracking} = (1 - R_{NO.ofcachedTRs})$$

$$C_{IS-41,CallTracking} + R_{No.ofcachedTRs}$$

$$[HR \times \{(1 - ICR) \times 2SC3 + ICR \times 2(SC1 + SC3)\}+$$

$$(1 - HR) \times 2SCI] + C_{cache} \tag{7}$$

– Tracking cost when caller and callee are remotely related:

$$C_{LSTPlevelcaching.CallTracking} = (1 - R_{No.ofcachedTRs})$$

$$C_{IS-41,CallTracking} + R_{No.ofCachedTRs}$$

$$[HR\{(1 - ICR) \times 2SC2 + ICR \times 2(SC1 + SC2)\}+$$

$$(1 - HR) \times 2SC1 + C_{cache} \tag{8}$$

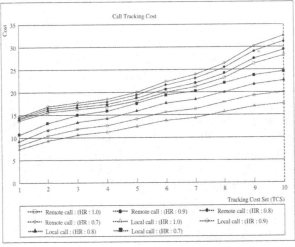

(a) SC3, SC2 < SC1

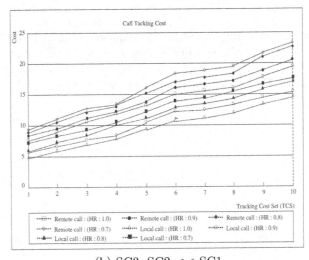

(b) SC3, SC2 << SC1

Fig.7. TCS classification (9 VLRs in LSTP area)

The tracking cost is reduced according to the number of the VLRs in LSTP area. It implies that the more VLRs in LSTP area are, the lower

$R_{move\_out, No.ofVLRsinLSTParea}$ is and the lower ICR is subsequently. The performance is dependent on the ICR as well as the HR and the influence of terminals moving speed on ICR. Like RCS in section 3.1, the larger tracking cost set (TCS) number is, the relative value difference of SC2 and SC3 to SC1 is smaller. Unlike the registration cost, SC2 has influence on the tracking cost. The influence of SC2 varies according to the rate of the remote calls to the total ones. If the difference between SC2 and SC3 is very small, we don't have to classify the local and remote calls. The reduced traffic in Fig. 7 (b) results from relatively smaller SC2 and SC3 than those in (a). The performances in cases of local call and remote call are shown separately. Note that the call relation should be considered separately. The degree of the call locality is related to the size of area in which the calls generate to a terminal. Considering the geographical region to which caller and callee belong, the caller's moving speed heavily affects the call relation but little affects call locality when the cache is in LSTP level. With the LSTP level caching, we can get over the limit of the degree of call locality. If so, the reference rate of the callee's location information is increased.

3.3   Traffic comparison

In performance evaluation, the rate of the local calls is assumed as 0.7. As we simulated with various rates, there were slight changes in the results. In fact, the performance is mainly dependent on SC1 instead of SC2 or SC3. If the value difference between SC2 and SC3 is not great, we can regard them as the same cost terms. If the HR is less in local and remote calls, the relative portion of SC1 to SC2 and SC3 in tracking a call is increased. In case of cache miss, we submit to the call tracking mechanism in IS-41 scheme.

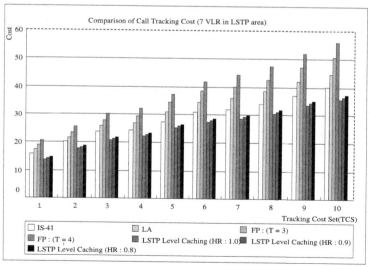

Fig. 8. Tracking cost comparison (where SC3, SC2 << SC1)

In Fig. 8, the costs are decreased in order as FP > LA > IS-41 > LSTP level caching. LA scheme has one more traverse to track a call compared to IS-41 scheme. The difference between two costs in FP scheme is due to one more traverse via LSTP or RSTP. Additionally, the cost for one more traverse varies according to the local or remote relation between callee's RA and the previous RA in tracking route. T should be taken considering cost effectiveness in call tracking and the degeneration overhead together. If T is too large, we should tolerate the setup delay too. Although the registration costs in LA and FP schemes vary according to $"M\_no."$, T, respectively, those two schemes are cost effective compared to IS-41 scheme. However, as for tracking cost, those two schemes degrade the performance due to the inherent additional traverses and degeneration overhead. The larger the relative value difference of SC2 and SC3 to SC1 is, the performance in LSTP level caching scheme is improved result compared to those in other schemes. In the environment with high call origination rate, LA and FP schemes degrade the performance and delay the setup time. Therefore, those schemes should be adopted considering the trade-off between the registration cost and call tracking one.

4   Conclusions

Previous schemes are to decrease the registration cost due to terminals RA crossing or the call tracking cost due to the call origination [2,5,6,7,8]. In those schemes, however, the trade-off between the registration cost and call tracking cost is an issue. Although a few schemes try to reduce the signaling traffic due to tracking calls, many schemes mainly focused on reducing the signaling traffic due to the location registration. We propose a solution to improve the performance in previous schemes including IS-41 and GSM standard. Our scheme is mainly focused on supporting the CL efficiently. The object that we locate the cache in LSTP level is to reuse the location information of the callee to which there are lots of call requests and furthermore to increase the reference rate. In addition, the RAs in LSTP area are grouped statically to decrease the ICR and mitigate the traffic bottleneck in HLR and RSTP, and also decrease the signaling traffic caused by terminals frequent RA crossings. As a result of cost evaluation, the more the VLRs in LSTP area are and the higher the call origination rate is, the performance is improved result. The terminals frequent RA crossings compared to the previous schemes including IS-41 and GSM standard much less affect our scheme.

References

1. Andrew D.Malyan,L.J.Ng,V. C.M. Leung, and Robert W. Donaldson," Network Architecture and Signaling for Wireless Personal Communications", IEEE JSAC., Vol. 11, No. 6, pp. 830-840, Aug. 1993.
2. EIA/TIA," Cellular Radiotelecommunications Intersystem Operations: Automatic Roaming", Technical Report IS-41 (Revision B), EIA/TIA, July 1991.

3. G.P. Pollini and D.J.Goodman, "Signaling System Performance Evaluation for Personal Communications", IEEE Trans. on Veh. Tech., May 1994.
4. Ian F. Aky ld z, Janise McNair, Joseph Ho, H Seiyo Uzunalio lu, and Wenye Wang," Mobility Management in Current and Future Communications Networks", IEEE Network Mag., Vol. 12, No. 4, pp. 39-49, July/Aug., 1998.
5. J.S.M. Ho and I.F.Akyildiz," Local Anchor scheme for Reducing Location Tracking Cost in PCNs", ACM MOBICOM'95, (1995)
6. J.Z. Wang, "A Fully Distributed Location Registration Strategy for Universal Personal Communication Systems", IEEE JSAC., Vol. 11, No. 6, pp. 850-860, August 1993.
7. R. Jain and Y.B Lin, "A Caching Strategy to Reduce Network Impacts of PCS", IEEE JSAC., Vol. 12, No. 8, pp. 1434-1444, Oct. 1994.
8. R. Jain and Y.B.Lin," An Auxiliary User Location Strategy Employing Forwarding Pointers to Reduce Network Impacts of PCS", IEEE ICC'95, (1995)
9. S. Mohan and R. Jain, "Two User Location Strategies for Personal Communications Services", IEEE Personal Comm. Mag., Vol. 1, No.1, pp. 42-50, First Quarter, 1994.
10. SeungJoon Park, DongChun Lee, and JooSeok Song, "Querying User Location Using Call Locality Relation in Hierarchically Distributed Structure", IEEE GLOBECOM'97, (1997) pp. 699-703.

A Practical Parity Scheme for Tolerating Triple Disk Failures in RAID Architectures

Chong-Won Park[1] and Young-Yearl Han[2]

[1] Electronics and Telecommunications Research Institute,
161 Kajong-dong, Yusong-gu, Taejon, 305-350 KOREA
cwpark@etri.re.kr
[2] Division of Electrical and Computer Engineering, Hanyang University,
17 Haengdang-dong, Seongdong-ku, Seoul, 133-791 KOREA
yyhan@email.hanyang.ac.kr

Abstract. Although theoretical methods were proposed for tolerating multiple disk failures, their complexities are too high to be practically applicable. In this paper, we proposed a practical parity scheme for tolerating simultaneous triple disk failures in RAID architectures. We first formalized the problems with matrix operations. Our scheme is practical in the sense that it employs three redundant disks for tolerating triple disk failures. Furthermore, it requires simple arithmetic computations only, and it can easily be implemented on current RAID controllers.

1 Introduction

Computers are changing rapidly in terms of its application areas and the performance level. Even two or three year old computers are becoming obsolete in the worst case for the customer's point of view. Meanwhile, the I/O systems and the storage systems are lagging behind the performance increase of the processors. As the gap between the performance of processors and I/O systems are becoming large, the performance of a computer system will eventually be limited by the performance of I/O[1],[2]. Therefore, it is important to balance the I/O performance and the capability of storage systems with the processing power in order to improve the overall performance of a computer system.

Improving I/O performance[2],[3],[4], known as data clustering and disk striping in disk array systems, has been one of the main research topics for computer architects in recent years. Disk array systems utilize the parallelism among many disks in a system. Furthermore, we need more disks for storing new forms of data like audio, video and fax. However, incorporating such a large number of disks into a system makes the disk system vulnerable to failure than a single disk case[3]. Hence, designing a disk array system which can keep data correct while tolerating disk failures is essential.

Patterson et al.[3] have proposed Redundant Array of Inexpensive Disks (RAID). They defined five different levels of RAID structures(RAID level 1~5) depending on the data and parity placement scheme. Basically RAID tolerates only one disk failure, data may be lost when two or more disks fail.

J. He and M. Sato (Eds.): ASIAN 2000, LNCS 1961, pp. 58–68, 2000.

Although error-correcting scheme such as Hamming and Reed-Solomon codes[5] were used to tolerate multiple disk failures, its implementation detail was extremely complex. Thus, it would be desirable to have codes doing relatively simple operations, such as exclusive-ORs or simple arithmetic calculations. Some convolutional type codes[6] were also used for tolerating disk failures. When the error correcting capacity of the code is broken, however, there happens infinite error propagation. Therefore, we need a block type code having simple operations.

Theoretically, such coding scheme was proposed in [7],[8],[9] and later was generalized in [10] for multiple erasures, where an erasure is an error whose location is known. However, one problem remains. The encoding or decoding scheme is very complex[11]. Although multiple erasure correcting scheme was implement practically in [12],[13], it could tolerate only double failures.

These days, there is a growing demand in high reliable storage systems for user data, RAID has to be extended to recover data when two or more disks fail. Hence, in order to satisfy the requirement, we need a practical scheme to tolerate more disk failures.

In this paper, we proposed a practical scheme for tolerating triple disk failures in RAID architectures. We first formalized the problems with matrix operations. Our scheme is practical in the sense that it employs three redundant disks for tolerating single, double and triple disk failures simultaneously. We present a simple encoding procedure that is based on exclusive-OR operations and independent parities. Therefore, our encoding scheme has no recursion such as convolutional type codes. We also present a practical decoding procedure for tolerating triple erasures as well as single and double errors.

The paper is organized as follows. In the next section, we describe the encoding procedure used in our scheme. In Section 3, we present the corresponding decoding procedure. Then, we consider the implementing our scheme on standard RAID controller in Section 4. Finally, we present some concluding remarks in Section 5.

2   Encoding

For the purpose of explanation, the following assumptions are made. First, we assume that there are $m+3$ disks with the information stored in the first m disks while the redundant data are stored in the last three disks. We also assume that m, the number of information disks, is a prime number. However, if we want to store an arbitrary(not necessarily prime) number of disks, we can take the next prime number following this arbitrary number and assume that the extra disks have no information. This means that all the information bits are 0. These disks are not actually used, there are only for computation.

Our procedure works for disks with arbitrary capacity by treating each block of $m-1$ symbols separately. For simplicity, in some of our examples, we will assume that each symbol is a bit. In some applications, a symbol may be as big as a 512 byte disk sector. It is not required to assume that the symbols are binary.

Based on the assumptions, the problem of tolerating triple disk failures can be described as follows. First, consider an $(m-1) \times (m+3)$ array, where m is a prime number. And, symbol $a_{i,j}$, $0 \le i \le m-2$, $0 \le j \le m+2$, is the ith symbol in the jth disk. For some applications, a column of array may be regarded as a disk and a symbol as a disk sector. The last three disks m, $m+1$, and $m+2$ are the disks with the redundant information.

We consider the notation that $\langle n \rangle_m = j$ is if and only if $j \equiv n(mod\ m)$ and $0 \le j \le m-1$. For instance, $\langle 7 \rangle_5 = 2$ and $\langle -2 \rangle_5 = 3$.

In addition, $A = \overset{m}{\underset{t=l}{\oplus}} a_{n,t}$ means $A = a_{n,l} \oplus a_{n,l+1} \oplus a_{n,l+2} \oplus \cdots \oplus a_{n,m}$ and $\oplus$ represents modular addition.

We also assume that there is an imaginary 0 row after the last, such as $a_{m-1,j} = 0$, $0 \le j \le m-1$, which consider that the array is now an $m \times (m+2)$ array.

Then, for each l, $0 \le l \le m-2$, the redundant symbols are computed as follows:

$$a_{l,m} = \overset{m-1}{\underset{t=0}{\oplus}} a_{l,t} \tag{1}$$

$$a_{l,m+1} = \overset{m-1}{\underset{t=0}{\oplus}} a_{\langle l-t \rangle_m,t} \tag{2}$$

$$a_{l,m+2} = \overset{m-1}{\underset{t=0}{\oplus}} a_{\langle -2(l-t) \rangle_m,t} \tag{3}$$

Equations (1), (2) and (3) define the encoding procedure. We have three types of redundancy: one for the horizontal redundancy and two for the vertical redundancies. Disk m is simply the exclusive-OR of disks 0, 1,$\cdots$, $m-1$. Its contents are exactly the same as those of the parity. Disk $(m+1)$ carries the vertical redundancy according to (2) and disk $(m+2)$ carries another vertical redundancy according to (3).

Let us look closely at equations (1), (2) and (3). We know that the horizontal redundancy is a simple parity of row symbol disks. Also, the first vertical redundancy is the parity of column symbol disks which is the modular addition of one cyclic shift of the 1st row, two cyclic shifts of the 2nd row, three cyclic shifts of the 3rd row,$\cdots$, and $(m-1)$ cyclic shifts of the $(m-1)$th row. The second vertical redundancy is the parity of column symbol disks which is the modular addition of two cyclic shifts of the 1st row, 4 cyclic shifts of the 2nd row, 6 cyclic shifts of the 3rd row,$\cdots$, and $2 \times (m-1)$ cyclic shifts of the $(m-1)$th row. The $(m-1) \times (m+3)$ array defined above can recover the information lost in any of the three columns.

We can show the encoding procedure by figures at $m=5$ for example. We will show how to make the horizontal redundancy in Fig. 1, the first vertical redundancy in Fig. 2, and the second vertical redundancy in Fig. 3.

$D_{0,0}$	$D_{0,1}$	$D_{0,2}$	$D_{0,3}$	$D_{0,4}$	P_0		
$D_{1,0}$	$D_{1,1}$	$D_{1,2}$	$D_{1,3}$	$D_{1,4}$	P_1		
$D_{2,0}$	$D_{2,1}$	$D_{2,2}$	$D_{2,3}$	$D_{2,4}$	P_2		
$D_{3,0}$	$D_{3,1}$	$D_{3,2}$	$D_{3,3}$	$D_{3,4}$	P_3		
$D_{4,0}$	$D_{4,1}$	$D_{4,2}$	$D_{4,3}$	$D_{4,4}$	P_4		

Fig. 1. Calculation of horizontal parity

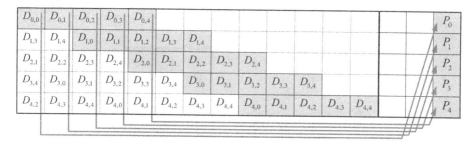

$D_{0,0}$	$D_{0,1}$	$D_{0,2}$	$D_{0,3}$	$D_{0,4}$					P_0	
$D_{1,4}$	$D_{1,0}$	$D_{1,1}$	$D_{1,2}$	$D_{1,3}$	$D_{1,4}$				P_1	
$D_{2,3}$	$D_{2,4}$	$D_{2,0}$	$D_{2,1}$	$D_{2,2}$	$D_{2,3}$	$D_{2,4}$			P_2	
$D_{3,2}$	$D_{3,3}$	$D_{3,4}$	$D_{3,0}$	$D_{3,1}$	$D_{3,2}$	$D_{3,3}$	$D_{3,4}$		P_3	
$D_{4,1}$	$D_{4,2}$	$D_{4,3}$	$D_{4,4}$	$D_{4,0}$	$D_{4,1}$	$D_{4,2}$	$D_{4,3}$	$D_{4,4}$	P_4	

Fig. 2. Calculation of the 1st vertical parity

$D_{0,0}$	$D_{0,1}$	$D_{0,2}$	$D_{0,3}$	$D_{0,4}$									P_0
$D_{1,3}$	$D_{1,4}$	$D_{1,0}$	$D_{1,1}$	$D_{1,2}$	$D_{1,3}$	$D_{1,4}$							P_1
$D_{2,1}$	$D_{2,2}$	$D_{2,3}$	$D_{2,4}$	$D_{2,0}$	$D_{2,1}$	$D_{2,2}$	$D_{2,3}$	$D_{2,4}$					P_2
$D_{3,4}$	$D_{3,0}$	$D_{3,1}$	$D_{3,2}$	$D_{3,3}$	$D_{3,4}$	$D_{3,0}$	$D_{3,1}$	$D_{3,2}$	$D_{3,3}$	$D_{3,4}$			P_3
$D_{4,2}$	$D_{4,3}$	$D_{4,4}$	$D_{4,0}$	$D_{4,1}$	$D_{4,2}$	$D_{4,3}$	$D_{4,4}$	$D_{4,0}$	$D_{4,1}$	$D_{4,2}$	$D_{4,3}$	$D_{4,4}$	P_4

Fig. 3. Calculation of the 2nd vertical parity

As we can see, our encoding procedure is very simple and the circuits implementing (1), (2) and (3) are straightforward. More generally, we can implement (1), (2) and (3) in software with exclusive-OR hardware of the current RAID controllers.

The following example illustrates the encoding procedure for $m = 5$.

Example 1: Let m=5, and let the symbols be denoted by $a_{i,j}$, $0 \leq i \leq 3$, $0 \leq j \leq 7$. The redundant symbols are in column 5, 6 and 7. A practical implementation of this example considers 8 disks numbered 0 to 7, each disk has 4 disk sectors. The data sectors are on disks numbered 0, 1, 2, 3 and 4, and the redundant disk sectors are on disks numbered 5, 6 and 7. Then, according to (1), (2) and (3), the redundant symbols are computed as follows:

$$a_{l,5} = a_{l,0} \oplus a_{l,1} \oplus a_{l,2} \oplus a_{l,3} \oplus a_{l,4}, 0 \le l \le 3$$
$$a_{0,6} = a_{0,0} \oplus a_{3,2} \oplus a_{2,3} \oplus a_{l,4}$$
$$a_{1,6} = a_{1,0} \oplus a_{0,1} \oplus a_{3,3} \oplus a_{2,4}$$
$$a_{2,6} = a_{2,0} \oplus a_{1,1} \oplus a_{0,2} \oplus a_{3,4}$$
$$a_{3,6} = a_{3,0} \oplus a_{2,1} \oplus a_{1,2} \oplus a_{0,3}$$
$$a_{0,7} = a_{0,0} \oplus a_{2,1} \oplus a_{1,3} \oplus a_{3,4}$$
$$a_{1,7} = a_{3,0} \oplus a_{0,1} \oplus a_{2,2} \oplus a_{1,4}$$
$$a_{2,7} = a_{1,0} \oplus a_{3,1} \oplus a_{0,2} \oplus a_{2,3}$$
$$a_{3,7} = a_{1,1} \oplus a_{3,2} \oplus a_{0,3} \oplus a_{2,4}$$

For instance, assume that we want to encode the 5 columns shown in Fig. 4.

1	0	1	1	0			
0	1	1	0	0			
1	1	0	0	0			
0	1	0	1	1			

Fig. 4. An example of 4 × 5 array for encoding.

We have filled up the last three columns with encoded symbols. The encoding procedure computes the following array shown in Fig. 5.

1	0	1	1	0	1	1	1
0	1	1	0	0	0	1	0
1	1	0	0	0	0	0	0
0	1	0	1	1	1	1	0

Fig. 5. Encoding result of Fig. 1.

The Proposed encoding scheme satisfies the following theorems for computation amount and memory space requirement.

Theorem 1: *Given m information disks, redundant data for tolerating triple disk failures can be computed in $O(m^2)$ time by using our encoding procedure.*

Proof: Equations (1), (2), and (3) require $O(m)$ time, and each equation should be executed for m times. Therefore, the total time for encoding is $O(m^2)$.

Corollary 1: *Given m information disks, redundant data for tolerating triple disk failures can be computed in $O(m^2)$ space by using our encoding procedure.*

Proof: Additional memory space requirement is determined by the size of the matrix, $(m-1) \times (m+3)$. Thus, the memory space requirement for the encoding procedure is bounded by $O(m^2)$.

3   Decoding

The essential part of our scheme is the decoding algorithm for triple erasures. Our algorithm can be implemented either in software or in hardware, depending on the application. It will be executed when a disk fails, when two disks fail simultaneously, or when three disks fail simultaneously. We assume an $(m-1)(m+3)$ array for decod-ing shown in Fig. 6. In the following, we present the algorithm which in effect corrects triple erasures.

$a_{0,0}$	$a_{0,1}$	...	$a_{0,i}$	...	$a_{0,j}$	...	$a_{0,k}$	...	$a_{0,m-1}$	$a_{0,m}$	$a_{0,m+1}$	$a_{0,m+2}$
$a_{1,0}$	$a_{1,1}$	...	$a_{1,i}$	...	$a_{1,j}$	...	$a_{1,k}$	...	$a_{1,m-1}$	$a_{1,m}$	$a_{1,m+1}$	$a_{1,m+2}$
$a_{2,0}$	$a_{2,1}$	...	$a_{2,i}$	...	$a_{2,j}$	...	$a_{2,k}$	...	$a_{2,m-1}$	$a_{2,m}$	$a_{2,m+1}$	$a_{2,m+2}$
...	...	...	...	...	...	...	...	...	...	...	...	...
$a_{m-2,0}$	$a_{m-2,1}$	...	$a_{m-2,i}$	...	$a_{m-2,j}$	...	$a_{m-2,k}$	...	$a_{m-2,m-1}$	$a_{m-2,m}$	$a_{m-2,m+1}$	$a_{m-2,m+2}$

Fig. 6. An $(m-1) \times (m+3)$ array for decoding

We assume that columns (disk) i, j and k have failed, where $i < j < k$. Then, we can compute the number of $(m-1) \times 3$ equations by equation (1), (2) and (3). We have $(m-1) \times 3$ unknown values and $(m-1) \times 3$ independent equations such as (4), (5) and (6). Thus, we can get the solutions by applying the matrix equation[14].

$$
\begin{aligned}
&a_{0,0} \oplus a_{0,1} \oplus a_{0,2} \oplus \cdots \oplus a_{0,i} \oplus \cdots \oplus a_{0,j} \oplus \cdots \oplus a_{0,k} \oplus \cdots \oplus a_{0,m-1} = a_{0,m} \\
&a_{1,0} \oplus a_{1,1} \oplus a_{1,2} \oplus \cdots \oplus a_{1,i} \oplus \cdots \oplus a_{1,j} \oplus \cdots \oplus a_{1,k} \oplus \cdots \oplus a_{1,m-1} = a_{1,m} \\
&a_{2,0} \oplus a_{2,1} \oplus a_{2,2} \oplus \cdots \oplus a_{2,i} \oplus \cdots \oplus a_{2,j} \oplus \cdots \oplus a_{2,k} \oplus \cdots \oplus a_{2,m-1} = a_{2,m} \\
&\qquad\vdots \qquad\qquad\qquad \vdots \qquad\qquad\qquad \vdots \\
&a_{m-2,0} \oplus a_{m-2,1} \oplus a_{m-2,2} \oplus \cdots \oplus a_{m-2,i} \oplus \cdots \oplus a_{m-2,j} \oplus \cdots \oplus a_{m-2,k} \oplus \\
&\qquad\qquad\qquad\qquad\qquad\qquad \cdots \oplus a_{m-2,m-1} = a_{m-2,m}
\end{aligned} \tag{4}
$$

$$
\begin{aligned}
&a_{0,0} \oplus a_{m-1,1} \oplus a_{m-2,2} \oplus \cdots \oplus a_{\langle -i \rangle_m, i} \oplus \cdots \oplus a_{\langle -j \rangle_m, j} \oplus \cdots \oplus a_{m-k,k} \oplus \cdots \\
&\qquad\qquad\qquad\qquad\qquad\qquad\qquad \oplus a_{1,m-1} = a_{0,m+1} \\
&a_{1,0} \oplus a_{0,1} \oplus a_{m-1,2} \oplus \cdots \oplus a_{\langle 1-i \rangle_m, i} \oplus \cdots \oplus a_{\langle 1-j \rangle_m, j} \oplus \cdots \oplus a_{\langle 1-k \rangle_m, k} \oplus \cdots \\
&\qquad\qquad\qquad\qquad\qquad\qquad\qquad \oplus a_{2,m-1} = a_{1,m} \\
&a_{2,0} \oplus a_{1,1} \oplus a_{0,2} \oplus \cdots \oplus a_{\langle 2-i \rangle_m, i} \oplus \cdots \oplus a_{\langle 2-j \rangle_m, j} \oplus \cdots \oplus a_{\langle 2-k \rangle_m, k} \oplus \cdots \\
&\qquad\qquad\qquad\qquad\qquad\qquad\qquad \oplus a_{3,m-1} = a_{2,m+1} \\
&\qquad\vdots \qquad\qquad\qquad \vdots \qquad\qquad\qquad \vdots \\
&a_{m-2,0} \oplus a_{m-2,1} \oplus a_{m-2,2} \oplus \cdots \oplus a_{\langle m-2-i \rangle_m, i} \oplus \cdots \oplus a_{\langle m-2-j \rangle_m, j} \oplus \cdots \oplus a_{\langle m-2-k \rangle_m, k} \oplus \\
&\qquad\qquad\qquad\qquad\qquad\qquad\qquad \cdots \oplus a_{0,m-1} = a_{m-2,m+1}
\end{aligned} \tag{5}
$$

$$a_{0,0} \oplus a_{2,1} \oplus a_{4,2} \oplus \cdots \oplus a_{\langle 2i \rangle_m, i} \oplus \cdots \oplus a_{\langle 2j \rangle_m, j} \oplus \cdots \oplus a_{\langle 2k \rangle_m, k} \oplus \cdots \oplus a_{\langle 2(m-1) \rangle_m, m-1}$$
$$= a_{0,m+2}$$

$$a_{\langle -2 \rangle_m, 0} \oplus a_{0,1} \oplus a_{2,2} \oplus \cdots \oplus a_{\langle 2(i-1) \rangle_m, i} \oplus \cdots \oplus a_{\langle 2(j-1) \rangle_m, j} \oplus \cdots \oplus a_{\langle 2(k-1) \rangle_m, k}$$
$$\oplus \cdots \oplus a_{\langle 2(m-2) \rangle_m, m-1} = a_{1,m+2}$$

$$a_{\langle -4 \rangle_m, 0} \oplus a_{\langle -2 \rangle_m, 1} \oplus a_{0,2} \oplus \cdots \oplus a_{\langle 2(i-2) \rangle_m, i} \oplus \cdots \oplus a_{\langle 2(j-2) \rangle_m, j} \oplus \cdots \oplus a_{\langle 2(k-2) \rangle_m, k} \quad (6)$$
$$\oplus \cdots \oplus a_{\langle 2(m-3) \rangle_m, m-1} = a_{2,m+2}$$

$$\vdots \qquad\qquad \vdots \qquad\qquad \vdots$$

$$a_{4,0} \oplus a_{6,1} \oplus a_{8,2} \oplus \cdots \oplus a_{\langle 2(i+2) \rangle_m, i} \oplus \cdots \oplus a_{\langle 2(j+2) \rangle_m, j} \oplus \cdots \oplus a_{\langle 2(k+2) \rangle_m, k} \oplus \cdots$$
$$\oplus a_{2,m-1} = a_{m-2,m+2}$$

We can form $[\Phi]$ by equations (4), (5) and (6), and a matrix equation (7) as follows. Then, we can make matrix $[\Phi]$ of (7) to identity matrix $[I]$, thus presenting matrix $[\Omega]$ of (8) be the values of unknown symbols.

$$\begin{bmatrix} \Phi \end{bmatrix} \begin{bmatrix} a_{0,i} \\ a_{1,i} \\ \vdots \\ a_{n-2,i} \\ a_{0,j} \\ a_{1,j} \\ \vdots \\ a_{n-2,j} \\ a_{0,k} \\ a_{1,k} \\ \vdots \\ a_{n-2,k} \end{bmatrix} = \begin{bmatrix} \Psi \end{bmatrix} \quad (7) \qquad \begin{bmatrix} I \end{bmatrix} \begin{bmatrix} a_{0,i} \\ a_{1,i} \\ \vdots \\ a_{n-2,i} \\ a_{0,j} \\ a_{1,j} \\ \vdots \\ a_{n-2,j} \\ a_{0,k} \\ a_{1,k} \\ \vdots \\ a_{n-2,k} \end{bmatrix} = \begin{bmatrix} \Omega \end{bmatrix} \quad (8)$$

The following example illustrates the decoding procedure for m=5.

Example 2: We assume that $m = 5$, as in Example 1. Also, we assume the following array where columns 1, 3 and 4, represented as symbol $\times$ have been erased shown in Fig. 7.

1	X	1	X	X	1	1	1
0	X	1	X	X	0	1	0
1	X	0	X	X	0	0	0
0	X	0	X	X	1	1	0

Fig. 7. An example of 3 disks erases.

We can make the following 12 equations from (1), (2) and (3):

$$
\begin{array}{lll}
1 = 1 \oplus a_{0,1} \oplus 1 \oplus a_{0,3} \oplus a_{0,4} & 1 = 1 \oplus 0 \oplus a_{2,3} \oplus a_{1,4} & 1 = 1 \oplus a_{2,1} \oplus a_{1,3} \oplus a_{3,4} \\
0 = 0 \oplus a_{1,1} \oplus 1 \oplus a_{1,3} \oplus a_{1,4} & 1 = 0 \oplus a_{0,1} \oplus a_{3,3} \oplus a_{2,4} & 0 = 0 \oplus a_{0,1} \oplus 0 \oplus a_{1,4} \quad (9) \\
0 = 1 \oplus a_{2,1} \oplus 0 \oplus a_{2,3} \oplus a_{2,4} & 0 = 1 \oplus a_{1,1} \oplus 1 \oplus a_{3,4} & 0 = 0 \oplus a_{3,1} \oplus 1 \oplus a_{2,3} \\
1 = 0 \oplus a_{3,1} \oplus 0 \oplus a_{3,3} \oplus a_{3,4} & 1 = 0 \oplus a_{2,1} \oplus 1 \oplus a_{0,3} & 0 = a_{1,1} \oplus 0 \oplus a_{0,3} \oplus a_{2,4}
\end{array}
$$

Then, we have 12 unknown symbols, and also have 12 equations. Thus, we can make the following matrix equation (10) from (9). The equation (10) can be written as (11).

$$
\begin{bmatrix}
1 & 1 & 1 & 0 & 0 & 0 & 0 & 0 & 0 & 0 & 0 & 0 \\
0 & 0 & 0 & 1 & 1 & 1 & 0 & 0 & 0 & 0 & 0 & 0 \\
0 & 0 & 0 & 0 & 0 & 0 & 1 & 1 & 1 & 0 & 0 & 0 \\
0 & 0 & 0 & 0 & 0 & 0 & 0 & 0 & 0 & 1 & 1 & 1 \\
0 & 0 & 0 & 0 & 0 & 1 & 0 & 1 & 0 & 0 & 0 & 0 \\
1 & 0 & 0 & 0 & 0 & 0 & 0 & 0 & 1 & 0 & 1 & 0 \\
0 & 0 & 0 & 1 & 0 & 0 & 0 & 0 & 0 & 0 & 0 & 1 \\
0 & 1 & 0 & 0 & 0 & 0 & 1 & 0 & 0 & 0 & 0 & 0 \\
0 & 0 & 0 & 0 & 1 & 0 & 1 & 0 & 0 & 0 & 0 & 1 \\
1 & 0 & 0 & 0 & 0 & 1 & 0 & 0 & 0 & 0 & 0 & 0 \\
0 & 0 & 0 & 0 & 0 & 0 & 0 & 1 & 0 & 1 & 0 & 0 \\
0 & 1 & 0 & 1 & 0 & 0 & 0 & 0 & 1 & 0 & 0 & 0
\end{bmatrix}
\begin{bmatrix}
a_{0,1} \\ a_{1,3} \\ a_{0,4} \\ a_{1,1} \\ a_{1,3} \\ a_{1,4} \\ a_{2,1} \\ a_{2,3} \\ a_{2,4} \\ a_{3,1} \\ a_{3,3} \\ a_{3,4}
\end{bmatrix}
=
\begin{bmatrix}
1 \\ 1 \\ 1 \\ 1 \\ 0 \\ 1 \\ 0 \\ 0 \\ 0 \\ 0 \\ 1 \\ 0
\end{bmatrix}
(10)
$$

$$
\begin{bmatrix}
1 & 0 & 0 & 0 & 0 & 0 & 0 & 0 & 0 & 0 & 0 & 0 \\
0 & 1 & 0 & 0 & 0 & 0 & 0 & 0 & 0 & 0 & 0 & 0 \\
0 & 0 & 1 & 0 & 0 & 0 & 0 & 0 & 0 & 0 & 0 & 0 \\
0 & 0 & 0 & 1 & 0 & 0 & 0 & 0 & 0 & 0 & 0 & 0 \\
0 & 0 & 0 & 0 & 1 & 0 & 0 & 0 & 0 & 0 & 0 & 0 \\
0 & 0 & 0 & 0 & 0 & 1 & 0 & 0 & 0 & 0 & 0 & 0 \\
0 & 0 & 0 & 0 & 0 & 0 & 1 & 0 & 0 & 0 & 0 & 0 \\
0 & 0 & 0 & 0 & 0 & 0 & 0 & 1 & 0 & 0 & 0 & 0 \\
0 & 0 & 0 & 0 & 0 & 0 & 0 & 0 & 1 & 0 & 0 & 0 \\
0 & 0 & 0 & 0 & 0 & 0 & 0 & 0 & 0 & 1 & 0 & 0 \\
0 & 0 & 0 & 0 & 0 & 0 & 0 & 0 & 0 & 0 & 1 & 0 \\
0 & 0 & 0 & 0 & 0 & 0 & 0 & 0 & 0 & 0 & 0 & 1
\end{bmatrix}
\begin{bmatrix}
a_{0,1} \\ a_{1,3} \\ a_{0,4} \\ a_{1,1} \\ a_{1,3} \\ a_{1,4} \\ a_{2,1} \\ a_{2,3} \\ a_{2,4} \\ a_{3,1} \\ a_{3,3} \\ a_{3,4}
\end{bmatrix}
=
\begin{bmatrix}
0 \\ 1 \\ 0 \\ 1 \\ 0 \\ 0 \\ 1 \\ 0 \\ 0 \\ 1 \\ 1 \\ 1
\end{bmatrix}
(11)
$$

So we can solve the unknown symbols from (11). Finally, the reconstructed array is shown in Fig. 8.

1	0	1	1	0	1	1	1
0	1	1	0	0	0	1	0
1	1	0	0	0	0	0	0
0	1	0	1	1	1	1	0

Fig. 8. Reconstruction of 3 disks erases.

We can also reconstruct the single and double disks failures by (4) through (8). In those cases, we only care less unknown values of $(m - 2)$ or $2 \times (m - 2)$.

Additionally, we can consider the following special cases for the positions of failed disks. In these cases, we can reduce the computation by applying encoding procedure instead of matrix operations for decoding.

Triple disk failures are considered.

- $m \leq i$, j, $k \leq m+2$: all of the redundant disks have failed. We can reconstruct disk m using (1), disk $m+1$ using (2), and disk $m+2$ using (3). In other word, the reconstruction is the same as encoding.
- $i<m$ and $m+1 \leq j, k \leq m+2$: one information disk and two vertical redundant disks have failed. We can reconstruct the information disk by equation (1), and the redundant disks by (2) and (3).

Double disk failures are considered.

- $m+1 \leq i$, $j \leq m+2$: vertical redundant disks have failed. We can reconstruct disk $m+1$ using (2) and disk $m+2$ using (3). In other word, the reconstruction is the same as encoding.
- $i=m$ and $m+1 \leq j \leq m+2$: one horizontal redundant disk and one vertical redundant disk have failed. We can reconstruct the horizontal redundant disk by equation (1), and the redundant disks by (2) or (3).
- $i<m$ and $m+1 \leq j \leq m+2$: one information disk and one vertical redundant disk have failed. We can reconstruct the horizontal redundant disk by equation (2) or (3).

Finally, single disk failure is considered.

- $m \leq i \leq m+2$: one redundant disk has failed. We can reconstruct disk m using (1), disk $m+1$ using (2), or disk $m+2$ using (3). In other word, the reconstruction is the same as encoding.

- $i<m$: one information disk has failed. We can reconstruct the information disk by equation (1).

The proposed decoding scheme satisfies the following theorems for computation amount and memory space requirement.

Theorem 2: *Given m information disks, triple disk failures can be recovered in $O(m^3)$ time by using our decoding procedure.*

Proof: Equation (8) can be solved in $O(m^3)$ time. Therefore, the total time for decoding is $O(m^3)$.

Corollary 2: *Given m information disks, triple disk failures can be recovered in $O(m^2)$ space by using our decoding procedure.*

Proof: Additional memory space requirement is determined by the size of $(m-1) \times (m+3)$ matrix. Thus, the memory space requirement for the decoding procedure is bounded by $O(m^2)$.

4   Implementing on standard RAID controller

The configuration of standard RAID system consists of the disk pool and the RAID controller such as Fig. 9. The RAID controller includes driver software and the parity controller for parity management, and the RAID controller can be implemented by software or hardware.

For implementing our scheme, we need to change the parity control algorithm such as in Fig. 10. Normally, the parity controller implements XOR function in hardware and calculation function in software, so we can implement our scheme on the calculation function in software without hardware change.

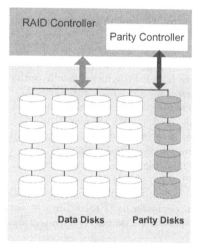

Fig. 9. Configuration of standard RAID system

Fig. 10. Configuration of proposed algorithm implemented in standard RAID controller

5   Concluding Remarks

In this paper, we presented a practical scheme for tolerating simultaneous triple disk failures in RAID architectures. We first formalized the problem by using matrix operations. Then we showed the encoding and the decoding schemes in detail. The scheme requires simple arithmetic computations and can be easily implemented on standard RAID controllers without any hardware change. The proposed scheme can be computed in $O(m^3)$ time, whereas the theoretical approach requires $O(m^4)$ time.

The symbols can be any size, from bit to multiple sectors. In some previous methods, convolutional type codes were used and an error in decoding propagated indefinitely. However, our scheme employs block type codes, which do not cause this problem.

Although we illustrated the RAID architectures in this paper as an example of target applications, our encoding/decoding scheme can also be used in multiple track recording applications, such as magnetic recording.

References

1. Randy H. Katz, Garth A. Gibson and David A. Patterson: Disk system architectures for high performance computing. Proceedings of the IEEE, vol.77, no.12. (1989) 1842-1858

2. L. Narasimha Reddy and Prithviraj Banerjee: An evaluation of multiple-disk I/O systems. IEEE Transactions on Computers, vol.38, no.12. (1989) 1680-1690

3. D. Patterson, G. Gibson, and R. Katz: A case for redundant arrays of inexpensive disks(RAID). Proceedings of the ACM SIGMOD International Conference on Manage-ment of Data (1988) 109-116,

4. K. Salem and H. Garcia-Molina: Disk striping. Proceedings of the International Confer-ence of Data Engineering (1986) 336-342

5. Shu Lin and Daniel J. Costello Jr.: Error Control Coding: Fundamentals and Applica-tions. Prentice Hall, New Jersey (1983)

6. T. Fuja, C. Heegard, and M. Blaum: Cross parity check convolutional codes. IEEE Transactions on Information Theory, vol.35, no.6. (1989) 1264-1276

7. M. Blaum, J. Bruck, and A. Vardy: MDS array codes with independent parity symbols. IEEE Transactions on Information Theory, vol.42, no.2. (1996) 529-542

8. Keren and S. Litsyn: A class of array codes correcting multiple column erasures. IEEE Transactions on Information Theory, vol.43, no.6. (1997) 1843-1851

9. M. Blaum, J. Bruck, and A. Vardy: Binary codes with large symbols. Proceedings of IEEE International Symposium on Information Theory. (1994) 508

10. M. Blaum and R. Roth: New array codes for multiple phased burst correction. IEEE Transactions on Information Theory, vol.39, no.1. (1993) 66-77

11. G. Alvarez, W. Burkhard, and F. Cristian: Tolerating multiple failures in RAID architec-tures with optimal storage and uniform declustering. Proceedings of the 24th Annual ACM/IEEE International Symposium on Computer Architecture. (1997) 62-72

12. M. Blaum, J. Brady, J. Bruck, and J. Menon: EVENODD: an efficient scheme for tolerat-ing double disk failures in RAID architectures. IEEE Transactions on Computers, vol.44, no.2. (1995) 192-202

13. C. Park: Efficient placement of parity and data to tolerate two disk failures in disk array systems. IEEE Transactions on Parallel and Distributed Systems, Vol.6, No.11. (1995) 1177-1184

14. Eric W. Weisstein: Concise Encyclopedia of Mathematics(CD-ROM). CRC Press (1998)

15. D. Patterson, P. Chen, G. Gibson, and R. Katz: Introduction to redundant arrays of inex-pensive disks(RAID). Proceedings of COMPCON Spring '89. (1989) 112-117

16. W. Nurkhard and J. Menon: Disk array storage system reliability. Proceedings of the Twenty-third International Symposium on Fault-Tolerant Computing. (1993) 432-441

17. W. Courtright II., G. Gibson, M. Holland, and J. Zelenka: A structured approach to re-dundant disk array implementation. Proceedings of IEEE International Computer Per-formance and Dependability Symposium. (1996) 11-20

Genetic Algorithm for Extended Cell Assignment Problem in Wireless ATM Network

Der-Rong Din[1], Shian–Shyong Tseng[2], and Mon-Fong Jiang[3]

[1] Department of Computer and Information Science
National Chiao-Tung University
Hsinchu 300, Taiwan R.O.C.
deron@aho.cis.nctu.edu.tw

[2] To whom all correspondences should be addressed
Department of Computer and Information Science
National Chiao-Tung University
Hsinchu 300, Taiwan R.O.C.
sstseng@cis.nctu.edu.tw
FAX: 886–35–721490

[3] Department of Computer and Information Science
National Chiao-Tung University
Hsinchu 300, Taiwan R.O.C.
jmf@eknow.com.tw

Abstract. In this paper, we investigate the *extended cell assignment problem* which optimally assigns new and split cells in *PCS (Personal Communication Service)* to switches in a wireless ATM network. Given cells and switches in an ATM network (whose locations are fixed and known), the problem is assigning cells to switches in an optimum manner. We would like to do the assignment in as attempt to minimize a cost criterion. The cost has two components: one is the cost of handoffs that involve two switches, and the other is the cost of *cabling*. This problem is modeled as a complex integer programming problem and finding an optimal solution to this problem is *NP-complete*. A stochastic search method, based on a genetic approach is proposed to solve this problem. Simulation results show that genetic algorithm is robust for this problem.

Keywords: wireless ATM, genetic algorithms, design of algorithm, assignment problem.

1 Introduction.

The rapid worldwide growth of digital wireless communication services motivates a new generation of mobile switching networks to serve as infrastructure for such services. Mobile network being deployed in the next few years should be capable of smooth migration to future broadband services based on high-speed wireless access technologies, such as *wireless asynchronous transfer* mode *(ATM)*[1]. The architecture shown in Fig. 1 was presented in [1]. In this architecture, the base

J. He and M. Sato (Eds.): ASIAN 2000, LNCS 1961, pp. 69–87, 2000.
© Springer-Verlag Berlin Heidelberg 2000

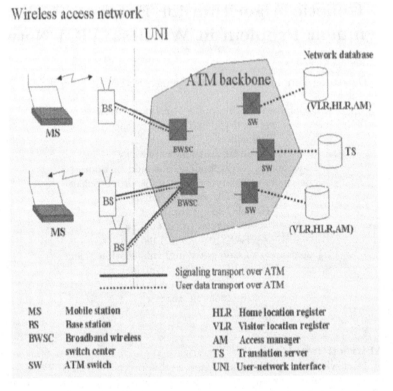

Fig. 1. Architecture of wireless ATM PCS.

station controllers (BSCs) are omitted, and the base stations (BSs or cells) are directly connected to the ATM switches. The mobility functions supported by the BSCs will be moved to the BSs and/or the ATM switches. In this paper, we address the problem that is currently faced by designers of mobile communication service and in the future, it is likely to be faced by designers of personal communication service (PCS).

In the designing process of wireless ATM system, telephone company first estimated the usage of the mobile users and divided the global service area into many coverage areas. Second, the cellular system, base stations are constructed and connected to the switches in ATM network to form the topology of wireless ATM. But this topology may be out of date, since more and more users may use the PCS communication system. Some areas, which have not been covered in the originally designing plan may have mobile users to traverse on. The services requirement of some areas which covered by original cells may be increased and the capacities of the original cells may be exceeded. Though, the wireless ATM system must be extended such that the system can provide higher quantity of services to the mobile users. Two methods can be used to extend the capacities of system and provide higher quantity of services. The first one is: several cells

Fig. 2. Cell splitting.

or base-stations (BSs) are built and added to the system such that the non-covered areas in the original wireless ATM network can be cover. The other is: in the cellular radio extending process, the capacity of a system may be increased by reducing the size of the cells so that the total number of channels available per unit area is increased. In practice, this is achieved by the process of *cell splitting*[6], where new base stations are established at specific points in the cellular pattern, reducing the cell size by a factor of 2 or more as shown in Fig. 2.

In this paper, we are given a two-level wireless ATM network as shown in Fig. 3. In the PCS network, cells are divided into two sets, one is the set of cells, which are built originally, and each cell in this set has been assigned to a switch in ATM network (*e.g.*, cells c_1, c_2 are assigned to switch s_2, and cells c_3, c_4, and c_5 are assigned to switch s_4 in Fig. 3). The other is the set of cells, which are newly added (*e.g.*, c_6, c_7, c_8) or established by cell splitting (*e.g.*, c_9, c_{10}, c_{11}, c_{12}, c_{13}, and c_{14}). Moreover, the locations of cells and switches are fixed and known. To simplify the discussion, we assumed that the number of cells and switches are fixed. The problem is to assign new and split cells to switches of the ATM network in an optimum manner. We would like to do the assignment in as attempt to minimize a cost criterion. The cost has two components: one is the cost of handoffs that involve two switches and the other is the cost of *cabling* (or *trucking*)[3][4][5].

Consider the example shown in Fig. 4, where cells A and B are connected to switch s_1, and cells C and D are connected to switch s_2. If the subscriber moves from cell B to cell A, switch s_1 will perform a handoff for this call. This handoff is relatively simple and does not involve any location update in the databases that record the position of the subscriber. The handoff also does not involve any network entity other than switch s_1. Now let support that the subscriber moves from cell B to cell C. Then the handoff involves the execution of a fairly complicated protocol between switches s_1 and s_2. In addition, the location of the subscriber in the databases has to be updated. There are two types of

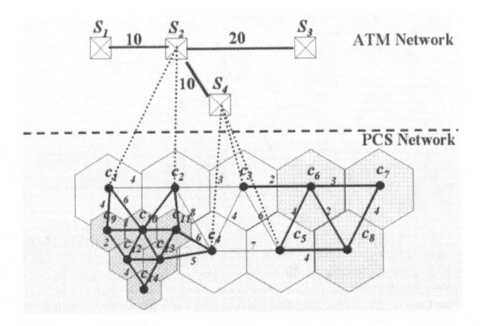

Fig. 3. Two-level wireless ATM network

handoffs: one involves only one switch and the other involves two switches. The handoffs that occur between two cells connected to different switches consume much more network resources (therefore, are much more costly) than those between cells connected to the same switch[3][4][5]. Based on the discussion given in the previous paragraph, we assume that the cost of handoffs involving only one switch is negligible. Through this paper, we assume each cell to be connected to only one switch.

In [5], Merchant and Sengupta had considered the *cell assignment problem* which assign cells to switches in PCS network, and they formulated the problem and proposed a heuristic algorithm to solve it such that the total cost can be minimized. The total cost consists of cabling cost and location update cost. The location update cost considered in [5] which only depends on the frequency of handoff between two switches is not realistic. Since the switch of ATM backbone is widely spread, the communication cost between two switches should be considered in calculating the location update cost. In [3][4], the model was extended to solve the problem that grouped cells into LAs and assign LAs to switches of ATM network in an optimum manner by considering the communication cost between two switches. A three phases heuristic algorithm and two genetic algorithms are proposed to solve assignment problem, respectively. In this paper, we follow the objective function which was formulated in [3] and [4] and solve the problem of assigning new and split cells to the switches of ATM network such that the total cost can be minimized; this problem is defined as *extended cell assignment problem*.

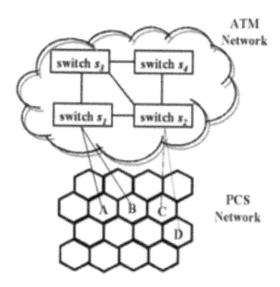

Fig. 4. Handoff from B to C is more expensive from B to A

It is easy to see that finding an optimal solution to this problem is NP-complete, and that, an exact search for optimal solutions is impractical due to exponential growth in execution time. Moreover, traditional heuristic methods and greedy approaches should trap in local optima. Genetic algorithms (GA) have been touted as a class of general-purpose search strategies that strike a reasonable balance between explorations and exploitation. Genetic algorithms proposed by Richardson et al.[7], and Davis[2] have been constructed as robust stochastic search algorithms for various optimization problems. GA searches by exploiting information sampled from different regions of the solution space. The combination of crossover and mutations helps GA escape from local optima. These properties of GA provide a good global search methodology for the two-level wireless ATM network design problem. In this paper, we propose a genetic algorithm for optimal design the two-level wireless ATM network problem.

The organization of this paper is as follows. In Section 2, we formally define the problem. The background of Genetic Algorithms is described in Section 3. In Section 4, we describe our genetic algorithm for the extended cells assignment problem. In Section 5, we give our experimental results. Finally, a conclusion is given in Section 6.

2   Problem Formulation.

Let $CG(C,L)$ be the PCS network, where C is a finite set of cells with $|C| = n$ and L is the set of edges such that $L \subseteq C \times C$. We assume that $C^{new} \cup C^{old} = C$, $C^{new} \cap C^{old} = \emptyset$, C^{new} be the set of new and split cells where $|C^{new}| = n'$, cells in C^{new} have not yet been assigned to switches of ATM and C^{old} be the set of original cells where $|C^{old}| = n - n'$. Without loss of generality, we assume that cells in C^{old} and C^{new} are indexed from 1 to $n - n'$ and $n - n' + 1$ to n, respectively. If cells c_i and c_j in C are assigned to different switches, then a handoff cost is incurred. Let f_{ij} be the frequency of handoff per unit time that occurs between cells c_i and c_j, $(i, j = 1, ..., n)$ and is fixed and known. We assume that all edges in CG are undirected and weighted; and assume cells c_i and c_j in C are connected by an edge $(c_i, c_j) \in L$ with weight w_{ij}, where $w_{ij} = f_{ij} + f_{ji}$, $w_{ij} = w_{ji}$, and $w_{ii} = 0$[3][4]. Let $G(S, E)$ be the ATM network, where S is the set of switches with $|S| = m$, $E \subseteq S \times S$ is the set of edges, s_k, s_l in S and (s_k, s_l) in E and G is connected. We assume that the locations of cells and switches are fixed and known. The topology of ATM network $G(S, E)$ is also fixed and known. Let (X_{s_k}, Y_{s_k}) be the coordinate of switch s_k, $k = 1, 2, ..., m$, (X_{c_i}, Y_{c_j}) be the coordinate of cell c_i, $i = 1, .2, ..., n$; and d_{kl} be the minimal communication cost between the switches s_k and s_l. Let l_{ik} be the cost of cabling per unit time and between cell c_i switch s_k, $(i = 1, ..., n; k = 1, ..., m)$ and assume l_{ik} is the function of Euclidean distance between cell c_i and switch s_k, that is,

$$l_{ik} = \sqrt{(X_{c_i} - X_{s_k})^2 + (Y_{c_i} - Y_{s_k})^2}. \tag{1}$$

Assume the number of calls that can be handled by each cell per unit time is equal to 1. Let Cap_k be the number of remained cells that can be assigned to switch s_k. Our objective is to assign cells in C^{new} to switches so as to minimize (total cost) the sum of cabling cost and handoffs cost per unit time of whole system.

To formulate this problem, let us define the following variables. Let $x_{ik} = 1$ if cell $c_i \in C$ is assigned to switch s_k; $x_{ik} = 0$, otherwise. Since each cell should be assigned to only one switch, we have the constraint $\sum_{k=1}^{m} x_{ik} = 1$, for $i = 1, .., n$. Further, the constraint on the call handling capacity is

$$\sum_{i=n-n'+1}^{n} x_{ik} \leq Cap_k, k = 1, ..., m. \tag{2}$$

Also, the sum of cabling costs is

$$\sum_{i=1}^{n} \sum_{k=1}^{m} l_{ik} x_{ik}. \tag{3}$$

To formulate handoff cost, variables $z_{ijk} = x_{ik} x_{jk}$, for $i, j, = 1, ..., n$ and $k = 1, ..., m$ are defined in [5]. Thus, z_{ijk} equals 1 if both cells c_i and c_j are connected to a common switch k; otherwise it is zero. Further, let

$$y_{ij} = \sum_{k=1}^{m} z_{ijk}, i, j = 1, ..., n \tag{4}$$

Thus, y_{ij} takes a value of 1 if both cells c_i and c_j are connected to a common switch and 0 otherwise. With this definition, it is easy to see that the cost of handoffs per unit time is given by [3][4]

$$\sum_{i=1}^{n}\sum_{j=1}^{n}\sum_{k=1}^{m}\sum_{l=1}^{m} w_{ij}(1 - y_{ij})x_{ik}x_{jl}d_{kl} \tag{5}$$

This, together with our earlier statement about the sum of cabling costs, gives us the objective function[3][4]:

$$minimize: \sum_{i=1}^{n}\sum_{k=1}^{m} l_{ik}x_{ik} + \alpha \sum_{i=1}^{n}\sum_{j=1}^{n}\sum_{k=1}^{m}\sum_{l=1}^{m} w_{ij}(1 - y_{ij})x_{ik}x_{jl}d_{kl} \tag{6}$$

where α is the ratio of the cost between cabling and handoff costs.

The following assumptions will be satisfied:

(1) We assume that the number of cells in C^{new} is less or equal to $\sum_{k=1}^{m} CAP_k$. That is, there is no need for adding new switches into the ATM network.

(2) The structures and locations of ATM network and PCS network are fixed and known.

(3) Each cell in PCS network will be directly assigned and connected to only one switch in ATM network.

(4) To simplify the discussion, we assumed that $Cap_k > 0$, for $k = 1, ..., m$.

Example 1. Consider the graph shown in Fig. 3. There are 14 cells in CG and they should be assigned to 4 switches in S. In CG, cells are divided into two sets, one is the set C^{old} of cells which are built originally and have been assigned to a switch in ATM network (e.g., $\{c_1, c_2, c_3, c_5\}$ in Fig. 3); the other is the set C^{new} of cells which are new cells (e.g., $\{c_6, c_7, c_8\}$) or split cell (e.g., $\{c_9, c_{10}, c_{11}, c_{12}, c_{13}, c_{14}\}$). The weight of edge between two cells is the frequency of handoffs per unit time that occur between them. Four switches are positioned at the center of the cell: c_1, c_2, c_4, and c_6.

3   Background of Genetic Algorithms.

The *Genetic Algorithm (GA)* was developed by John Holland at the University of Michigan[7]. Genetic Algorithms are search techniques for global optimization in a complex search space. As the name suggests, GA employs the concepts of natural selection and genetic. Using past information, GA directs the search with expected improved performance. The concept of GA is based on the theory of adoption in natural and artificial systems[7]. In artificial adaptive systems, adaptation starts with an initial set of structures (possible solutions). These initial structures are modified according to the performance of their solution by using an adaptive plan to improve the performance of these structures. It has been proved by Holland that repeatedly applying this adaptive plan to input structures results in optimal or near optimal solutions [7]. The traditional methods of optimization and search do not fare well over a broad spectrum of problem domains[2]. Some are limited in scope because they employ local search techniques (e.g., calculus based methods). Others, such as enumerative schemes, are not efficient when the practical search space is too large.

3.1   Concept of GA

The search space in GA is composed of possible solutions to the problem. A solution in the search space is represented by a sequence of $0s$ and $1s$. This solution string is referred as a chromosome in the search space. Each chromosome has an associated objective function called the *fitness*. A good chromosome is the one that has a high/low fitness value, depending upon the nature of the problem (maximization/minimization). The strength of a chromosome is represented by its *fitness value*. Fitness values indicate which chromosomes are to be carried to the next generation. A set of chromosomes and associated fitness values is called the *population*. This population at a given stage of GA is referred to as a *generation*. The general GA proceeds as follows:

Genetic Algorithm()

Begin

Initialize population;

while (not terminal condition) do

Begin

choose parents from population; /* Selection */

construct offspring by combining parents; /* Crossover */

optimize (offspring); /* Mutation */

if suited (offspring) then

replace worst fit (population) with better offspring;

/*Survival of the fittest */

End;

End.

There are three main processes in the while loop for GA:

(1) The process of selecting good strings from the current generation to be carried to the next generation. This process is called *selection/reproduction*.

(2) The process of shuffling two randomly selected strings to generate new offspring is called *crossover*. Sometimes, one or more bits of a chromosome are complemented to generate a new offspring. This process of complementation is called *mutation*.

(3) The process of replacing the worst performing chromosomes based on the fitness value.

The population size is finite in each generation of GA, which implies that only relatively fit chromosomes in generation (i) will be carried to the next generation ($i + 1$). The power of GA comes from the fact that the algorithm terminates rapidly to an optimal or near optimal solution. The iterative process terminates when the solution reaches the optimum value. The three genetic operators, namely, selection, crossover and mutation, are discussed in the next section.

3.2   Selection / Reproduction

Since the population size in each generation is limited, only a finite number of good chromosomes will be copied in the *mating pool* depending on the fitness value. Chromosomes with higher fitness values contribute more copies to the mating pool than do those with lower fitness values. This can be achieved by assigning proportionately a higher probability of copying a chromosome that has a higher fitness value[2]. Selection/reproduction uses the fitness values of the chromosome obtained after evaluating the objective function. It uses a biased roulette wheel[2] to select chromosomes, which are to be taken in the mating pool. It ensures that highly fit chromosomes (with high fitness value) will have a higher number of offspring in the mating pool. Each chromosome (i) in the current generation is allotted a roulette wheel slot sized in proportion (p_i) to its fitness value. This proportion p_i can be defined as follows. Let Of_i be the actual fitness value of a chromosome (i) in generation (j) of g chromosomes, $Sum_j = \sum_{i=1}^{g} Of_i$ be the sum of the fitness values of all the chromosomes in generation j, and let $p_i = Of_i/Sum_j$.

When the roulette wheel is spun, there is a greater chance that a better chromosome will be copied into the mating pool because a good chromosome occupies a larger area on the roulette wheel.

3.3   Crossover

This phase involves two steps: first, from the mating pool, two chromosomes are selected at random for mating, and second, crossover site c is selected uniformly at random in the interval $[1, n]$. Two new chromosomes, called *offspring*, are then obtained by swapping all the characters between positions $c + 1$ and n. This can be shown using two chromosomes, say P and Q. each of length $n = 6$ bit positions

chromosome P: 111|000;
chromosome Q: 000|111.

Let the crossover site be 3. Two substrings between 4 and 6 are swapped, and two substrings between 1 and 3 remain unchanged; then, the two offspring can be obtained as follows:

chromosome R: 111|111;
chromosome S: 000|000.

3.4   Mutation

Combining the reproduction and crossover operations may sometimes result in losing potentially useful information in the chromosome. To overcome this problem, mutation is introduced. It is implemented by complementing a bit (0 to 1 and vice versa) at random. This ensures that good chromosomes will not be permanently lost.

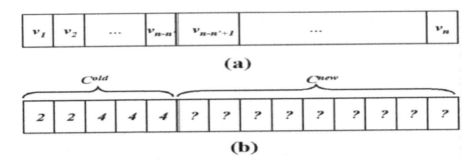

Fig. 5. (a) Cell–oriented representation of chromosome structure. (b) Cell–oriented representation of Example 1.

4   Genetic Algorithm for Cells Extended Assignment Problem.

In this section, we discuss the details of GA developed to solve the problem of optimum assignment of cells in PCSs to switches in the ATM network. The development of GA requires: (1) a chromosomal coding scheme, (2) a chromosome adjustment procedure, (3) a genetic crossover operator, (4) mutation operators, (5) a fitness function definition, (6) a replacement strategy, and (7) termination rules.

4.1   Chromosomal coding

Since our problem involves representing connections between cells and switches, we employ a coding scheme that use positive integer numbers. Cells are labeled from one to n (the total number of cells), and switches are labeled from one to m (the total number of switches). The *cell–oriented representation* of chromosome structure is shown in Fig. 5(a), where the ith cell belongs to the $v_i th$ switch. Without loss of generality, we assume that cells in C^{old} are indexed from 1 to $n - n'$ and cells in C^{new} are indexed from $n - n' + 1$ to n. For example, the chromosome of the example shown in Fig. 3 is shown in Fig. 5(b). It is worth noting that, the cell-oriented representation of chromosome structure can be divided into two sets, the first set of cells which represents the assignment of cells in C^{old} is fixed in running of GA. It is worth noting that the first set of cells can be ignored since it is unchanged during experiments. For the reason of easily understanding, the fixed set of cells is still kept in chromosome in the reset of this paper.

4.2   Chromosome Adjustment Procedure

Since the initial population of our solution method is random generated and the operator of GA sometimes generates a chromosome which does not represent a feasible assignment. This event is adjusted by means of the chromosome adjustment procedure described below: Let n_k be the number of cells assigned to switch s_k; three types of switches are defined:

(1) *over-switch*: if $n_k > Cap_k$;

(2) *saturated-switch*: if $n_k = Cap_k$;

(3) *poor–switch*: if $n_k < Cap_k$.

Switches are grouped into sets S_{over}, S_{sat}, and S_{poor} for over-switch, saturated-switch and poor-switch, respectively. To change infeasible chromosomes into feasible ones, chromosome adjustment procedure is repeatedly used to reassign the cells from over-switches to poor-switches until all over-switches become saturated-switches.

We have following algorithm:

Algorithm: Chromosome Adjustment Procedure.

Step   1: Switches are grouped into sets S_{over}, S_{sat}, and S_{poor} according to the number of cells being assigned to it; without loss of generality, switches are renumbered such that $n_k \geq n_{k+1}$, $k = 1, ..., m - 1$.

Step   2: Construct a set SP (switch pool) of number of switches by putting Cap_k-n_k "k" into SP, if $n_k < Cap_k$, for $k = 1, 2, ..., m$.

Step   3: Randomly generate a number as the adjustment point z in $[n - n' + 1, n]$, while S_{over} is nonempty do Step 4.

Step   4: If $l = v_z \in S_{over}$, then randomly select and remove a number (say k) from SP; reassign cell c_z to switch s_k, i.e., set the value of v_z to k; decrease the n_l by 1; if $n_l = Cap_l$ then move switch s_l from S_{over} to S_{sat}. Otherwise, increase z by 1, if $z > n$ then $z = n - n' + 1$.

Example: For the example shown in Fig. 3, we assume $Cap_k = 4$, for $k = 1, 2, ..., m$. The running results by applied chromosome adjustment procedure to this example is shown as follows:

Before adjustment: Chromosome is generated as:

$$2\ 2\ 4\ 4\ 4 \parallel 1\ 1\ 2\ 1\ 3\ 1\ 1\ 1\ 4$$

After running steps 1 and 2, we have: $S_{over} = \{1\}$, $S_{sat} = \{4\}$, and $S_{poor} = \{2, 3\}$. Since $n_3 = 1 < Cap_3$ and $n_2 = 3 < Cap_2$, three "3" and one "2" are put in SP, respectively; thus, $SP = \{2, 3, 3, 3\}$. Moreover,

switch number	1	2	3	4
# of cells being assigned (n_k)	6	3	1	4

When running Step 4, assume z= 11 is randomly generated. Since $v_z \in S_{over}$, cell c_{11} is assigned to switch s_3 which is random selected from SP. We have

$$2\ 2\ 4\ 4\ 4 \parallel 1\ 1\ 2\ 1\ 3\ 3\ 1\ 1\ 4$$

and

switch number	1	2	3	4
# of cells being assigned (n_k)	5	3	2	4

By repeatedly executing the Step 4, assume 3 is randomly selected from SP for cell c_{12}. Finally, the chromosome is changed to

$$2\ 2\ 4\ 4\ 4 \parallel 1\ 1\ 2\ 1\ 3\ 3\ \mathbf{3}\ 1\ 4$$

and

switch number	1	2	3	4
# of cells be assigned (n_k)	4	3	3	4

4.3   Genetic crossover operator

Two types of genetic operators were used to develop this algorithm:

(1) *single point crossover*,

(2) *cell-exchanging operator*.

The single point crossover is randomly selecting two chromosomes (say P_1 and P_2) for crossover from previous generations and then by using a random number generator, an integer value i is generated in the range $[n - n', n - 1]$. This number is used as the crossover site. To create new offspring, the single point crossover consists of two stages: first, all characters between i and n of two parents are swapped and temporal chromosomes C_1 and C_2 are generated. Then, chromosome adjustment procedure is to applied temporal chromosomes and modifies chromosomes to feasible chromosomes.

The following example provides the detailed description of single point crossover operation: (Assume crossover site $i = 9$), parent P_1:

$$2\ 2\ 4\ 4\ 4 \parallel 1\ 1\ 2 \mid 1\ 3\ 3\ 3\ 1\ 4,$$

parent P_2:

$$2\ 2\ 4\ 4\ 4 \parallel 3\ 3\ 3 \mid 1\ 4\ 1\ 1\ 2\ 1.$$

First, two substrings between 9 and 14 are swapped, we have: temporal chromosome C_1:

$$2\ 2\ 4\ 4\ 4 \parallel 1\ 1\ 2 \mid 1\ 4\ 1\ 1\ 2\ 1,$$

temporal chromosome C_2:

$$2\ 2\ 4\ 4\ 4 \parallel 3\ 3\ 3 \mid 1\ 3\ 3\ 3\ 1\ 4.$$

Then, the Chromosome Adjustment Procedure is applied to change temporal chromosomes C_1 and C_2, to O_1 and O_2 as follows: (assume adjustment points are 10 and 13 for C_1 and C_2, respectively.) offspring O_1:

$$2\ 2\ 4\ 4\ 4 \parallel 1\ 1\ 2 \mid 1\ 4\ \mathbf{3}\ \mathbf{3}\ 2\ 1,$$

offspring O_2: (assume "1" and "2" are selected from SP for c_6, c_7, respectively)

$$2\ 2\ 4\ 4\ 4 \parallel \mathbf{1}\ \mathbf{2}\ 3 \mid 1\ 3\ 3\ 3\ 1\ 4.$$

In cell-exchanging operator, two cells in C^{new} of a chromosome are randomly selected, and the assigned switches of two cells are exchanged.

For example, before exchanging, we have:

$$2\ 2\ 4\ 4\ 4\ \|\ 1\ 1\ \mathbf{2}\ 1\ 3\ 3\ \mathbf{3}\ 2\ 4.$$

(Assume that the two cells c_8 and c_{11} are selected.) After exchanging:

$$2\ 2\ 4\ 4\ 4\ \|\ 1\ 1\ \mathbf{3}\ 1\ 3\ \mathbf{2}\ 3\ 2\ 4.$$

4.4   Mutations and Heuristic Mutations

Six types of mutations used to develop of this algorithm and the active probabilities of mutations are the same.

(1) *Traditional Mutation* (**TM**): randomly select a cell of vector v_i, where i in $[n - n' + 1, n]$ and transform to a random number between 1 to m. After the transformation, the chromosome may became a infeasible one, thus, the Chromosome Adjustment Procedure must be applied to the chromosome.

(2) *Multiple Cells Mutation* (**MCM**): randomly select two random numbers k, l between 1 and m, transform the value of cells which value is k to l and l to k. The following example provides the detailed description of multiple cells mutation: (assume random number $k = 3$ and $l = 2$) before mutating, we have

$$2\ 2\ 4\ 4\ 4\ \|\ 1\ 1\ 3\ 1\ 3\ 2\ 3\ 1\ 4.$$

After mutating, we have

$$2\ 2\ 4\ 4\ 4\ \|\ 1\ 1\ \mathbf{2}\ 1\ \mathbf{2}\ \mathbf{3}\ \mathbf{2}\ 1\ 4.$$

After the transformation, the chromosome may become an infeasible one; thus, the Chromosome Adjustment Procedure must be applied to the chromosome, (assume adjustment point is 11) we have

$$2\ 2\ 4\ 4\ 4\ \|\ 1\ 1\ 2\ 1\ 2\ 3\ \mathbf{3}\ 1\ 4.$$

(3) *Heaviest Weight First Preference* (**HWFP**)[3]: Since the handoff cost involving only one switch is negligible, two cells can be assigned to the same switch so as to reduce the handoff cost between these cells. Two cells with higher weight w_{ij} should have a higher probability of being assigned to the same switch. Thus, if we consider two connected cells c_i and $c_j \in C$, then the probability of mutation from v_i of cell c_i to the value v_j of cell c_j is as follows:

$$P_{(i,j)} = \frac{w_{ij}}{\sum_{i=1}^{n} \sum_{j=1}^{degree(c_i)} w_{ij}},$$

where $degree(c_i)$ is the number of cells connected to cell c_i in CG.

(4) *Minimal Cabling Cost First Preference* (**MCCFP**)[3]: To reduce the cabling costs between cells and switches, we prefer to assign each cell to the nearer switch rather than the farther one. Cell c_i and switch s_k with lower

cabling cost l_{ik} should result in higher probability that c_i will be assigned to s_k. Thus, if we consider the randomly selected cell c_i, then the probability of mutation from v_i of cell c_i to the value v_k is :

$$P_{(i,k)} = \frac{L_{max} - l_{ik}}{\sum_{l=1}^{m}(L_{max} - l_{il})},$$

where $L_{max} = \max_{l=1}^{m}\{l_{il}\}$.

(5) *Minimal Fixed Handoff Cost First Preference* (**MFHCFP**): Given m sets of cells $P = \{P_l\}$, $l = 1,2,...,m$, we assume $P_1 \cup P_2 \cup ... \cup P_m = C^{old}$ and $P_i \cap P_j = \phi$, where $i \neq j$. For example, in Fig. 3, $P_2 = \{c_1, c_2\}$, $P_4 = \{c_3, c_4, c_5\}$, $P_3 = P_1 = \emptyset$. Without loss of generality, we assume that the cell in set P_j is assigned to switch s_j, $j = 1,..,m$. Let $sid(c_i) = l$, if c_i in P_l where l is called the sid of cell c_i. Let $LUCS(i,l) = \sum_{\forall c_j \in P_l} w_{ij}$.

For example, since $c_1 \in P_2$ and $c_2 \in P_2$, thus $sid(c_1) = sid(c_2) = 2$, $LUCS(2,2) = \sum_{\forall c_j \in P_2} w_{2j} = w_{21} = 4$, $LUCS(2,4) = \sum_{\forall c_j \in P_4} w_{2j} = w_{23} + w_{24} + w_{25} = 3 + 8 + 0 = 11$. $D(2,4) = LUCS(2,4) - LUCS(2,2) = 11 - 4 = 7$.

To evaluate the effect of cell c_i in C^{new} being assigned to switch s_k, we must compute the cabling cost and location update cost derived from this event. By the definition described above, the cabling cost is l_{ik}. The location update cost has two components, one is the location update cost between cell in C^{new} and cell in C^{old}; the other is the location update cost of two cells in C^{new}. Since the cell in C^{old} has been assigned to switch in ATM, if c_i in C^{new} is assigned to s_k, the location update cost between cell c_i in C^{new} and cell c_j in C^{old} is fixed and can be computed by

$$A_{ik} = \alpha \sum_{\forall s_l \in S, l \neq k} (LUCS(i,l) \cdot d_{kl}), (i = n-n'+1, n-n'+2, ..., n; k = 1, 2, ..., m).$$

For the example shown in Fig. 3, if c_6 is assigned to s_3 and $\alpha = 1$, then $A_{63} = LUCS(6,1) \times d_{31} + LUCS(6,2) \times d_{32} + LUCS(6,4) \times d_{34} = 0 \times 30 + 0 \times 20 + (2+4) \times 30 = 180$.

Thus, consider cell $c_i \in C^{new}$, the probability of mutation from $sid(c_i)$ to k is

$$P_{(i,k)} = \frac{A_{max} - A_{ik}}{\sum_{l=1}^{m}(A_{max} - A_{il})},$$

where $A_{max} = \max_{l=1}^{m}\{A_{il}\}$.

(6) *Minimal Estimated Handoff Cost First Preference* (**MEHCFP**): Since cells in C^{new} have not yet been assigned to switches, the location update cost of two cells $\in C^{new}$ cannot have a determinative formula to compute. To estimate the location update cost between $c_i \in C_{new}$ and the other cell in C^{new}, let $avgDIST_k = \sum_{l=1}^{m} d_{kl}/(m - 1)$ be the average distance between switch s_k and the other switch, $avgLU_i = \sum_{j=1}^{n'} w_{ij}/n$ be the average location update cost between c_i and the other cell c_j in C^{new}. It is worth noting that if two cells be assigned to the same switch then the handoff cost between two cells is ignored. If cell c_i in C^{new} is assigned to switch s_k and the capacity of switch s_k is

Cap_k, i.e., if all cells are assigned to switches, then at most $n' - CAP_k$ cells may be computed the location update cost with cell c_i which assigned to s_k. Let $NL_i = \sum_{\forall c_j \in C^{new}, i \neq j} w_{ij} \neq 0$ be the number of cells in C^{new} which the frequency of handoff between c_i and c_j is not zero. The total location update cost between c_i which assigned to s_k and cells assigned to another switches can be estimated by

$$B_{ik} = \{ \begin{matrix} \alpha \times (n' - CAP_k) \times avgLU_i \times avgDIST_k, & if Cap_k \leq NL_i \\ 0 & otherwise \end{matrix}$$

If $Cap_k > NL_i$, then NL_i cells can be assigned to same switch s_k, that is, B_{ik} is set to 0.

For example, if $c_6 \in C^{new}$ is assigned to switch s_3 in Fig. 3, then $avgDIST_3 = 23.33$, $avgLU_6 = (w_{67} + w_{68})/9 = 0.556$. Assume $Cap_3 = 2$, at most 7 cells in C^{new} may be computed the location update cost with cell c_i. Thus, $B_{63} = \alpha \times 7 \times 0.556 \times 23.33 = 90.728$.

Thus, consider cell $c_i \in C^{new}$, the probability of mutation from vih to k is

$$P_{(i,k)} = \frac{B_{max} - B_{ik}}{\sum_{l=1}^{m} (B_{max} - B_{il})},$$

where $B_{max} = \max_{l=1}^{m} \{B_{ik}\}$.

4.5   Fitness function definition

Generally, genetic algorithms use fitness functions to map objectives to costs to achieve the goal of an optimally designed two-level wireless ATM network. If cell c_i is assigned to switch s_k, then v_i in the chromosome is set to k. Let $d_{(v_i, v_j)}$ be the minimal communication cost between switches s_k and s_l in G. An objective function value is associated with each chromosome, which is the same as the fitness measure. We use the following objective function:

$$minimize \sum_{i=1}^{n} l_{iv_i} + \alpha \sum_{i=1}^{n} \sum_{j=1}^{n} w_{ij} d_{(v_i, v_j)}.$$

4.6   Replacement strategy

This subsection discusses a method used to create a new generation after crossover and mutation is carried out on the chromosomes of the previous generation. Several replacement strategies have been proposed in the literature, and a good discussion can be found in [2]. The most common strategies probabilistically replace the poorest performing chromosomes in the previous generation. The *elitist strategy* appends the best performing chromosome of a previous generation to the current population and thereby ensures that the chromosome with the best objective function value always survives to the next generation. The algorithm developed here combines do both the concepts maintained above. Each offspring generated after crossover is added to the new generation if it has a better objective function value than both of its parents. If the objective function value of an offspring is better than that of only one of the parents, then we select a chromosome randomly from the better parent and the offspring. If the offspring is worse than both parents then each of the parents is selected at random for the next generation. This ensures that the best chromosome is carried to the next generation, while the worst is not carried to the succeeding generations.

4.7   Termination rules

Execution of GA can be terminated using any one of the following rules:
R1: when the average and maximum fitness values exceed a predetermined threshold;
R2: when the average and maximum fitness values of strings in a generation become the same; or
R3: when the number of generations exceeds an upper bound specified by the user.

The best value for a given problem can be obtained from a GA when the algorithm is terminated using R2[2] .

5   Experimental Results.

In order to evaluate its performance, we have implemented the algorithm and applied it to solve problems that were randomly generated. The results of these experiments are reported below. In all the experiments, the implementation language was conducted in C, and all experiments were run on a Windows NT with a Pentium II 450MHZ CPU and 256MB RAM. We simulated a hexagonal system in which the cells were configured as an H-mesh. The handoff frequency f_{ij} for each border was generated from a normal random number with mean 100 and variance 20. The performance of the algorithm was evaluated based on the speed of improving the fitness of its solution and based on its complexity. The time complexity of our genetic algorithm is $O((n^2 + m^2)n_p g)$, where, g is is the maximum number of generations, and n_p is the population size of the generation. To examine the effect of the mutation probability of genetic algorithms, we set $n = 500$, $n' = 3n/4$, $m = 50$, $Cap = 50$, $\alpha = 1$, population size (popsize) $= 50$, crossover probability (P_c)=1.0, maximum number of generations =1000, and mutation probability is selected from {0.001, 0.005, 0.01, 0.02, 0.05, 0.1, 0.2, 0.5}. The experimental results were shown in Fig. 6. We found that when the mutation probability is small (0.001) or large (0.5), the total cost starts to improve later and may get trapped in a local minimum. We find that in general, a moderate value of the mutation probability leads to the best performance.

To examine the effect of the population size, we set $n = 500$, $n' = 3n/4$, $m = 50$, $Cap = 50$, $\alpha = 5$, mutation probability (P_m) =0.05, maximum number of generations =1000, and population size varied from 20 to 100 (with gap 20).

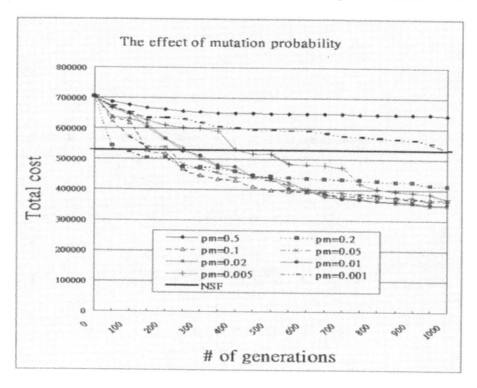

Fig. 6. The effect of the mutation probability with $n = 500$.

We find that population size should be kept high (80 or 100) in order to get good performance of the algorithm.

To examine the performance of algorithm, we simply constructed an algorithm named NSF(Nearest Switch First)[4], which is a two-phase heuristic algorithm. In the first phase of NSF, cells are assigned to the switch that is nearest. If the nearest switch is full, then another near switch is tried. In the second phase, two cells, which are assigned to different switches with the greatest reduced total cost, are selected and exchanged; this process is repeatedly used to reduced the total cost until the total cost cannot be reduced. Figures 6 and 7 also show the comparing results of algorithms in $n = 500$. Observe the results of GA in Fig. 6 and Fig. 7, in first 200 generations, the total cost rapidly decreases. After running 1000 generations, the improvement ($\frac{NSF-GA}{GA}$) is near 34.6%.

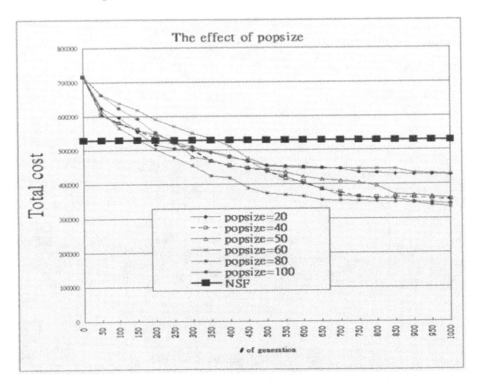

Fig. 7. The effect of the population size with $n = 500$.

6   Conclusions.

In this paper, we investigate the *cells extended assignment problem* which optimum assignment new added and split cells in *PCS (Personal Communication Service)* to switches in a wireless ATM network. This problem is currently faced by designers of mobile communication service and in the future, it is likely to be faced by designers of personal communication service (PCS). Since more and more users may use the PCS communication system. Some areas, which have not been covered in the originally designing plan may have mobile users to traverse on. The services requirement of some areas which covered by original cells may be increased and the capacities of the original cells may be exceeded. Though, the wireless ATM system must be extended such that the system can provide higher quantity of services to the mobile users. Two methods can be used to extend the capacities of system and provide higher quantity of services. The first one is: several cells or base-stations (BSs) are built and added to the system such that the non-covered areas in the original wireless ATM network can be cover. The other is: in the cellular radio extending process, the capacity of a system may be increased by reducing the size of the cells so that the total number of channels available per unit area is increased. In practice, this is achieved by the process of *cell splitting*[6].

Since finding an optimal solution of extended cell assignment is NP-Complete, a stochastic search method based on a genetic approach is proposed to solve it. Simulation results showed that genetic algorithm is robust for this problem. In our methods, cell-oriented representation is used to represent the cell assignment; three general genetic operators - selection, crossover, and mutation - were employed. Chromosome adjustment method is proposed to adjust chromosome to represent a feasible solution and find the fitness of chromosome. Two types of operator (single point crossover and cell-exchanging) and six types of mutation (TM, MCM, HWFP, MCCFP, MFHCFP, and MEMCFP) are employed in our method. Experimental results indicate that the algorithm run efficiently. The total cost of GA rapidly decrease in first 200 generations and get better performance than NSF algorithm.

7   Acknowledgment.

This work was supported in part by MOE program of Excellence Research under Grant 89-E-FA04-1-4.

References

1. M. Cheng, S. Rajagopalan, L. F. Chang, G. P. Pollini, and M. Barton, "PCS Mobility Support over Fixed ATM Networks," *IEEE Communication Magazine*, Nov. 1997, pp. 82–91.
2. Davis, L. (ed) (1991) *Handbook of Genetic Algorithms.* Van Nostrand Reinhold, New York NY. U. S. A.
3. Der–Rong Din and S. S. Tseng, "Genetic Algorithms for Optimal design of two–level wireless ATM network," Technical Report, Department of Computer Science, NCTU, TR-WATM-9902 Taiwan, R.O.C, 1999 or http://aho.cis.nctu.edu.tw/~deron/; to appear in *Proceeding of NSC*.
4. Der-Rong Din and S. S. Tseng, "Heuristic Algorithm for Optimal design of two-level wireless ATM network, "Technical Report, Department of Computer Science, NCTU, TR-WATM-9901 Taiwan, R.O.C, 1999 or http://aho.cis.nctu.edu.tw/~deron/; to appear in *JISE*.
5. A. Merchant and B. Sengupta, "Assignment of Cells to Switches in PCS Networks", *IEEE/ACM Trans. on Networking*, Vol. 3, no. 5, 1995, pp. 521-526.
6. R. C. V. Macario, Cellular Radio. McGraw-Hill, New York (1993).
7. Richardson, J. T. M. R. Palmer, G. L. Liepins, and M. Hilliard, (1989) Some guidelines for genetic algorithms with penalty functions. In Proceedings of the 3rd International Conference on Genetic Algorithms (Edited by J. D. Schaffer). George Mason University.

Spatial Congruence
for Ambients Is Decidable

Silvano Dal Zilio

Microsoft Research

Abstract. The ambient calculus of Cardelli and Gordon is a process calculus for describing mobile computation where processes may reside within a hierarchy of locations, called ambients. The dynamic semantics of this calculus is presented in a chemical style that allows for a compact and simple formulation. In this semantics, an equivalence relation, called spatial congruence, is defined on the top of an unlabelled transition system.
We show that it is decidable to check whether two ambient calculus processes are spatially congruent or not. This result is based on a natural and intuitive interpretation of ambient processes as edge-labelled unordered trees, which allows us to concentrate on the subtle interaction between two key operators of the ambient calculus, namely restriction, that accounts for the dynamic generation of new location names, and replication, used to encode recursion. The result of our study is the definition of an algorithm to decide spatial congruence and a definition of a normal form for processes that is useful in the proof of important equivalence laws.

1 Introduction

Algebraic frameworks, of which process algebras are one of the most prominent examples, have proved to be a valuable mathematical tool to reason about the behaviour of distributed and communicating systems. Recently, Cardelli and Gordon have proposed a new process algebra, the ambient calculus [3], for describing systems with mobile computations.

In the ambient calculus, processes may reside within a hierarchy of locations, called *ambients*. Each location is a cluster of processes and sub-ambients that can move as a group.

Ambients provide an interesting abstraction that combines, within the same theoretical framework, three essential notions: *mobile computation, site* and *mobility*. Mobile computations are computations that can dynamically change the place where they are executed and are continuously active before and after movement, like it is the case with agents. Sites are the location where these computations happen, like processors or routers. Finally, mobility represents a modification in the sites topology that occurs, for instance, with mobile or temporarily disconnected computers, and in the crossing of administrative boundary, like applets crossing a firewall.

J. He and M. Sato (Eds.): ASIAN 2000, LNCS 1961, pp. 88–103, 2000.

Inspired by Berry's and Boudol's Chemical Abstract Machine model [2] and Milner's "chemical" presentation of the π-calculus [13], the dynamic semantics of the ambient calculus is based on a *spatial congruence* relation, denoted $\equiv$, on which the reduction system is based. Spatial congruence identifies processes up to elementary spatial rearrangements and allows a simple and compact presentation of the reduction rules in which the sub-processes having to interact – the redexes in λ-calculus terminology – appear in contiguous position.

This paper reports a proof that spatial congruence, one of the simplest and most basic equivalence between processes, is decidable. That is, the problem of checking whether two processes are spatially congruent, or not, is decidable.

To prove the decidability of spatial congruence, we use a natural and intuitive interpretation of ambient processes as edge-labelled unordered trees. This allows us to concentrate on the subtle interaction between restriction and replication, two key operators of the ambient calculus. Roughly speaking, restriction accounts for the dynamic generation of fresh location names and replication is used to encode recursive behaviours.

The result of our study is twofold. First, we define an effective decision procedure to test spatial congruence. This procedure is based on basic algorithmic on trees and can be easily implemented. Second, we define a normal form for processes and a proof method that demonstrate useful in the proof of important equivalence laws.

The decidability result presented in this paper is useful in many respects. Since spatial congruence plays a central role in the definition of the operational semantics, any attempt to provide a mechanical proof of semantics-based properties will rely on a formal study of spatial congruence and an implementation of a test for equivalence of processes. Interesting examples of semantical properties include proof of equivalences or validity of program transformations.

Another application of our result is the study of the *modal logic for ambients* [4], where spatial congruence is used in the definition of the satisfaction relation. The decidability of spatial congruence is essential in the proof that model checking, for a particular subset of the logic, is decidable.

The outline of the remainder of this paper is as follows. Section 2 introduces the syntax of the ambient calculus and the definition of spatial congruence, and Section 3 defines an interpretation of processes as a certain kind of edge-labelled trees, called *spatial trees*. Section 4 studies a very simple notion of equivalence between spatial trees. We prove that this equivalence is decidable and we define a procedure to test the equivalence of spatial trees. This result relies on the existence of a computable normal form. In Section 5, we relate spatial trees to processes and tree equivalence to spatial congruence. Then, by transferring the results obtained on spatial trees, we prove the decidability of spatial congruence. Before concluding, we use our results to prove some interesting equivalence laws. Complete definition of the calculus and omitted proofs may be found in a long version of this paper [6].

2   The Ambient Calculus

The following tables summarize the syntax of processes and the definition of spatial congruence. For the sake of simplicity, we consider a minimal version of the untyped ambient calculus that includes only mobility primitives, as defined in [3], Section 2. In the extended version of this paper [6], we show that the results and algorithms presented here can be smoothly extended to the full ambient calculus.

The operators of the ambient calculus can be separated into two categories: *spatial constructs*, which describe the "spatial configuration" of processes, and *temporal constructs*, which describe their, possible, dynamic behaviours.

Spatial constructs are composed of restriction, void, composition and replication, which are commonly found in process calculi, and include an original constructor, $n[P]$, called an ambient. In the minimal ambient calculus, temporal constructs are only composed of actions, $act\,n.P$, where n is an *ambient name* and P is a process. In the full ambient calculus, temporal constructs also include the input and output operators defined in [3], which are missing from our presentation. As pointed out in [4], this separation is similar to the distinction between static and dynamic constructs made in CCS [12].

Capabilities and processes:

$act\,n ::=$	capability
$in\,n$	can enter n
$out\,n$	can exit n
$open\,n$	can open n
$P, Q, R ::=$	processes
$(\nu n)P$	restriction
$\mathbf{0}$	void
$P \mid Q$	composition
$!P$	replication
$n[P]$	ambient
$act\,n.P$	action

In a restriction, $(\nu n)P$, the name n is bound with scope P. The set of free names occurring in a process P, written $fn(P)$ is defined as follows, where restriction is the only binders. We identify processes up to consistent renaming of bound names.

Free names, $fn(P)$, of process P:

$fn((\nu n)P) \triangleq fn(P) \setminus \{n\}$	$fn(\mathbf{0}) \triangleq \varnothing$
$fn(P \mid Q) \triangleq fn(P) \cup fn(Q)$	$fn(!P) \triangleq fn(P)$
$fn(n[P]) \triangleq \{n\} \cup fn(P)$	$fn(act\,n.P) \triangleq \{n\} \cup fn(P)$

The rules defining spatial congruence can also be separated in different categories. The first two categories of rule state that it is an equivalence relation and a congruence. The third category states that parallel composition is an associative and commutative operator with identity element **0**. Another category specifies properties of replicated processes, $!P$, which acts like an infinite parallel composition of replicas of P. The last category describes scoping rules for the restriction operator, $(\nu n)P$, used to model the dynamic generation of new ambient names.

Spatial congruence: $P \equiv Q$

$P \equiv P$	(Struct Refl)
$Q \equiv P \Rightarrow P \equiv Q$	(Struct Symm)
$P \equiv Q, Q \equiv R \Rightarrow P \equiv R$	(Struct Trans)
$P \equiv Q \Rightarrow (\nu n)P \equiv (\nu n)Q$	(Struct Res)
$P \equiv Q \Rightarrow (P \mid R) \equiv (Q \mid R)$	(Struct Par)
$P \equiv Q \Rightarrow !P \equiv !Q$	(Struct Repl)
$P \equiv Q \Rightarrow n[P] \equiv n[Q]$	(Struct Amb)
$P \equiv Q \Rightarrow act\, n.P \equiv act\, n.Q$	(Struct Action)
$P \mid Q \equiv Q \mid P$	(Struct Par Comm)
$(P \mid Q) \mid R \equiv P \mid (Q \mid R)$	(Struct Par Assoc)
$P \mid \mathbf{0} \equiv P$	(Struct Par Zero)
$!(P \mid Q) \equiv !P \mid !Q$	(Struct Repl Par)
$!\mathbf{0} \equiv \mathbf{0}$	(Struct Repl Zero)
$!P \equiv P \mid !P$	(Struct Repl Copy)
$!P \equiv !!P$	(Struct Repl Repl)
$(\nu n)(\nu m)P \equiv (\nu m)(\nu n)P$	(Struct Res Res)
$(\nu n)\mathbf{0} \equiv \mathbf{0}$	(Struct Res Zero)
$n \notin fn(P) \Rightarrow (\nu n)(P \mid Q) \equiv P \mid (\nu n)Q$	(Struct Res Par)
$n \neq m \Rightarrow (\nu n)m[P] \equiv m[(\nu n)P]$	(Struct Res Amb)
$n \neq m \Rightarrow (\nu n)act\, m.P \equiv act\, m.(\nu n)P$	(Struct Res Action)

Almost every rule in the spatial congruence definition has an equivalent in the corresponding π-calculus equivalence, called *structural congruence*. The most significant differences lies in the axioms for replication, (Struct Repl Par) and (Struct Repl Repl), that are missing in the traditional definition of structural congruence [13]. As a matter of fact, these axioms are also missing in the seminal presentation of the ambient calculus [3], where the relation $\equiv$ is also called structural congruence. These differences have motivated our change in terminology.

Intuitively, the structural congruence relation of the π and ambient calculi should be decidable relations. But the author is not aware of any proof that structural congruence is decidable (or undecidable!) and these results seem very difficult to obtain.

The rules added to spatial congruence are similar to the rules proposed in [7,8] to extend the standard definition of structural congruence in the π-calculus. In these papers, the authors proved that the resulting equivalence is decidable. Another related work is [10], where Hirschkoff independently proposed a similar extension to structural congruence and proved the decidability result using a more algorithmic approach. We go back to these results in Section 7, where we review related works.

Since the definition of the operational semantics is not needed in our study, we omit the definition of the reduction relation from the presentation. The reader interested in a thorough introduction to the ambient calculus is referred to [3].

3   Spatial Trees

We define an interpretation of spatial processes as a certain kind of edge-labelled unordered trees, which we name *spatial trees*. A spatial tree will represent the hierarchy defined by ambients nesting, using the traditional notion of hierarchy defined by sub-trees. In our intuition, *edges* stands for ambients and are tagged with an ambient name, *nesting* stands for ambient encapsulation and, following our analogy, parallel composition of processes naturally arises as trees sharing the same root. Since it is not possible to define a process containing an unbounded number of nested ambients, we will only consider finite-depth trees.

For convenience, and to avoid confusion, we use a distinct category of names, called *markers*, to model restricted ambient names. Markers are ranged over by $x, y, \ldots$ We use η to denote a name, n, or a marker, x. We use $K, L, \ldots$ to denote sets of names, and $X, Y, Z \ldots$ for sets of markers.

A *multiplicity*, μ, is either 1 or ∞. A *cone*, C, is either the empty vector, written ϵ, an action: $\mu act\, \eta.T$, or an edge: $\mu\eta[T]$ or $!X.T$, where T is a spatial tree and X is a non-empty set of markers.

A *spatial tree* is a finite vector of cones, $C_1 + \cdots + C_k$, also written $\sum_{i\in 1..k} C_i$. The $+$ operator is commutative and associative, with identity element ϵ; spatial trees are identified up to these equations.

Cones and spatial trees:

$\mu ::=$	multiplicity
$\quad 1$	single
$\quad \infty$	infinite
$C ::=$	cone
$\quad \epsilon$	empty vector
$\quad \mu act\, \eta.T$	action
$\quad \mu\eta[T]$	edge tagged η
$\quad !X.T$	replicated edge with markers X
$S, T ::=$	spatial trees
$\quad C_1 + \cdots + C_k$	vector of cones

Cones are a special type of spatial trees. The cone $!X.T$ represents an infinite copy of the tree T such that, in each copy, the elements of X are replaced with fresh markers. In an edge, $!\mathsf{X}.T$, the markers in X are bound with scope T. Spatial trees are identified up to consistent renaming of bound markers.

Free markers, $fm(T)$, of tree T:

$$
\begin{array}{ll}
fm(\epsilon) \triangleq \varnothing & fm(!\mathsf{X}.T) \triangleq fm(T) \setminus \mathsf{X} \\
fm(\mu n[T]) \triangleq fm(T) & fm(\mu act\, n.T) \triangleq fm(T) \\
fm(\mu\mathsf{x}[T]) \triangleq fm(T) \cup \{\mathsf{x}\} & fm(\mu act\, \mathsf{x}.T) \triangleq fm(T) \cup \{\mathsf{x}\} \\
fm(S + T) \triangleq fm(S) \cup fm(T) &
\end{array}
$$

We write $T\{n\leftarrow\mathsf{x}\}$ for the capture-avoiding substitution of the marker x for each occurrences of the name n in the tree T. For convenience, we extend the replication constructor, $!\mathsf{X}.T$, to the empty set of markers as follows:

$$
\begin{array}{l}
!\varnothing.\epsilon \triangleq \epsilon \\
!\varnothing.\mu act\, \eta.T \triangleq \infty act\, \eta.T \\
!\varnothing.\mu\eta[T] \triangleq \infty\eta[T] \\
!\varnothing.!\mathsf{X}.T \triangleq !\mathsf{X}.T \\
!\varnothing.(S + T) \triangleq !\varnothing.S + !\varnothing.T
\end{array}
$$

Proposition 3.1. *We have $!\varnothing.!\varnothing.T = !\varnothing.T$.*

Since we have a notion of free and bound markers, we can define a notion of connected tree, that is, tree whose sub-trees share mutual markers.

Connected trees:

A tree $\sum_{i\in 1..p} C_i$ is connected if and only if there are no partitions of $1..p$ into two non-empty subsets, I, J, such that $fm(\sum_{i\in I} C_i) \cap fm(\sum_{i\in J} C_j) = \varnothing$.

Using this definition, we can compute for each tree the (unique) set of its connected sub-trees as follows. For all tree $T \triangleq \sum_{i\in 1..p} C_i$ we can construct a graph as follows.

(1) Let $\mathcal{N}$ be the set of cones $\{C_1, \ldots, C_p\}$.
(2) Let $\mathcal{G}$ be the graph with nodes in $\mathcal{N}$ and edges between nodes that have at least one common free marker.
(3) Compute the connected components of the graph $\mathcal{G}$, say $\mathcal{G}_1, \ldots, \mathcal{G}_k$.

The connected parts of T, written $conn(T)$, is the set $\{T_1, \ldots, T_k\}$ such that for all $i \in 1..k$ the spatial tree T_i is the vector of the cones included in $\mathcal{G}_i$. Basic properties of the connected components of a spatial tree are:

Proposition 3.2. *If $\{T_1, \ldots, T_p\}$ is the set of connected components, $conn(T)$, of a tree T then $T = T_1 + \cdots + T_p$, and for each $j \in 1..p$ the tree T_j is connected.*

4   Equality of Spatial Trees

We define a reduction relation between trees, $X \vdash S \rightarrow T$, parameterised by a set of markers, X, called the *effect* of the reduction. This reduction relation captures the essential intuitions of the equivalence between edge-labelled trees and every rule in its definition corresponds to basic axioms of spatial congruence. For instance, rule (Red Zero) implies that "empty cones can be forgotten" and corresponds to rule (Struct Par Zero) of structural congruence. Likewise, rule (Red Add Edge) implies that "two infinite copies of a sub-tree can be replaced by only one copy" and corresponds to rule (Struct Repl Copy). We also define the equivalence induced by $\rightarrow$, in almost the same way the λ-calculus reduction relation induces β-equivalence.

In this section, we prove that every spatial tree can be factorised to an irreducible form, also called a *normal form*, which is not related to the reduction sequence used to compute it. Normal forms provide us with a unique representative for each tree and, more significantly, allow us to define a formal procedure to test the equivalence of trees, a key result in the proof of the decidability of spatial congruence.

Reduction: $X \vdash S \rightarrow T$

(Red Zero)   (Red Add Edge)

$$\varnothing \vdash T + \epsilon \rightarrow T \qquad \varnothing \vdash \infty \eta[T] + \mu \eta[T] \rightarrow \infty \eta[T]$$

(Red Add Action)

$$\varnothing \vdash \infty act\, \eta.T + \mu act\, \eta.T \rightarrow \infty act\, \eta.T$$

(Red Add Repl)   (Red Copy)

$$\varnothing \vdash !X.T + !X.T \rightarrow !X.T \qquad X \vdash !X.T + T \rightarrow !X.T$$

(Red Sub)   (Red Repl)

$$\frac{X \vdash T \rightarrow S \qquad X \subseteq Y}{Y \vdash T \rightarrow S} \qquad \frac{X \vdash T \rightarrow S \qquad (Z = Y \cap fm(S))}{X \setminus Y \vdash !Y.T \rightarrow !Z.S}$$

(Red η)   (Red +)

$$\frac{X \vdash T \rightarrow S \qquad (\eta \notin X)}{X \vdash \mu \eta[T] \rightarrow \mu \eta[S]} \qquad \frac{X \vdash T \rightarrow S \qquad (fm(R) \cap X = \varnothing)}{X \vdash T + R \rightarrow S + R}$$

(Red Action)

$$\frac{X \vdash T \rightarrow S}{X \vdash \mu act\, \eta.T \rightarrow \mu act\, \eta.S}$$

The rules for reduction can be separated in two categories. Rules (Red Zero) to (Red Copy) that involve two cones, or *critical pairs*, of which only (Red Copy) can extend the effect. Rules (Red Repl) to (Red Action), the *structural rules*, which states that the relation $\to$ is compositional.

In a reduction, $\mathsf{X} \vdash S \to T$, the effect X records the markers that must not appear free in the result of the reduction.

We can derive an equivalent of rules (Red Add Repl), (Red Copy) and (Red Repl), for the special case where the set X is empty.

- $\varnothing \vdash\; !\varnothing.T + !\varnothing.T \to^* !\varnothing.T.$
- $\varnothing \vdash\; !\varnothing.T + T \to^* !\varnothing.T.$
- If $\varnothing \vdash T \to S$ then $\varnothing \vdash\; !\varnothing.T \to^* !\varnothing.S.$

Next, we define the equivalence relation on spatial trees induced by $\to$.

Equivalence relation between trees: $S \sim_\mathsf{X} T$ **and** $S \approx T$

The relation $\sim_\mathsf{X}$ is the smallest reflexive, symmetric and transitive relation such that if $\mathsf{X} \vdash S \to T$ then $S \sim_\mathsf{X} T$. The relation $\approx$ is such that $S \approx T$ if and only if there exist two finite injective mappings, σ_1, σ_2, and a set of markers X such that $dom(\sigma_1) = fm(S)$ and $dom(\sigma_2) = fm(T)$ and $S\sigma_1 \sim_\mathsf{X} T\sigma_2$.

From the structural rules of $\to$, it is trivial to show that $\sim_\mathsf{X}$ is a congruence and that if $\mathsf{Y} \subseteq \mathsf{X}$ then $\sim_\mathsf{Y} \subseteq \sim_\mathsf{X} \subseteq \approx$. Basic properties of $\approx$ are:

Proposition 4.1. *The relation $\approx$ satisfies the congruence properties, that is, if $(fm(S) \cup fm(T)) \cap fm(R) = \varnothing$ and $S \approx T$ then $S + R \approx T + R$; if $S \approx T$ then $\mu n[S] \approx \mu n[T]$; if $S \approx T$ then $\mu act\, \eta.S \approx \mu act\, \eta.T$.*

We prove that the reduction relation on spatial trees is locally confluent.

Lemma 4.2. *If $\mathsf{X}_1 \vdash T \to T_1$ and $\mathsf{X}_2 \vdash T \to T_2$ then there exists a tree S such that $\mathsf{X}_1 \cup \mathsf{X}_2 \vdash T_1 \to^* S$ and $\mathsf{X}_1 \cup \mathsf{X}_2 \vdash T_2 \to^* S$.*

Proof. By induction on the derivation of $\mathsf{X}_1 \vdash T \to T_1$. For the sake of brevity, we only consider the cases in which the two reductions originate from critical pairs that share a common cone. The complete proof can be found in [6].

In the particular case considered here, the tree T must be a composition, $R_1 + C + R_2 + T'$, where $\mathsf{X}_i \vdash R_i + C \to S_i$ and $T_i = S_i + R_j + T'$ for each $i \in \{1, 2\}$ and $i \neq j$. These must have been derived from (Red +) and therefore we have the side condition $(\star)$ $fm(R_2 + T') \cap \mathsf{X}_1 = fm(R_1 + T') \cap \mathsf{X}_2 = \varnothing$.

The proof follows by a case analysis on the rules used to derive the two reductions $\mathsf{X}_1 \vdash R_1 + C \to S_1$ and $\mathsf{X}_2 \vdash R_2 + C \to S_2$.

(Red Zero)-(Red Zero) Then $C = \epsilon$ and $T_1 = T_2 = R_1 + R_2 + S$. Trivial.

(Red Add Edge)-(Red Add Edge) Then $R_1 = \mu_1\eta[R]$, $R_2 = \mu_2\eta[R]$, $S_1 = S_2 = \infty\eta[R]$ and C is a cone $\mu\eta[R]$ for some multiplicities μ_1, μ_2, μ such that $\infty \in \{\mu, \mu_i\}$ for each $i \in \{1, 2\}$. Trivial. Case (Red Add Repl)-(Red Add Repl) is similar.

(Red Add Edge)-(Red Copy) Then C is an edge $\mu\eta[R]$ and it must be the case that $R_1 = \mu_1\eta[R]$ and $R_2 = !\mathsf{X}.\mu\eta[R]$, where μ or μ_1 is an infinite multiplicity and $\mathsf{X} \subseteq \mathsf{X}_2$. This case is impossible since (Red Copy) implies that $fm(\eta(R_1)) \cap \mathsf{X}_2 \neq \varnothing$, which conflicts with the side condition $(\star)$. Case (Red Copy)-(Red Add Edge) is similar.

(Red Add Repl)-(Red Copy) Then $T = R + !\mathsf{X}.R + !\mathsf{X}.R + T'$ and $S_1 = R + !\mathsf{X}.R$ and $S_2 = !\mathsf{X}.R + !\mathsf{X}.R$, where $\mathsf{X}_1 = \varnothing$ and $\mathsf{X}_2 = \mathsf{X}$. By (Red Copy) and (Red +), we have that $\mathsf{X} \vdash T_1 \to !\mathsf{X}.R + T'$. By (Red Add Repl) and (Red +), $\varnothing \vdash T_2 \to !\mathsf{X}.R + T'$, as required.

(Red Copy)-(Red Copy) Then $C = !\mathsf{X}.R$ for some tree R and sets of markers X, such that $R_1\{\mathsf{X}{\leftarrow}\mathsf{X}_1\} = R_2\{\mathsf{X}{\leftarrow}\mathsf{X}_2\} = R$ and $(\mathsf{X}_1 \cup \mathsf{X}_2) \cap fm(T') = \varnothing$. By (Red Copy) and (Red +), we get that $\mathsf{X}_2 \vdash T_1 \to !\mathsf{X}.R + T'$ and $\mathsf{X}_1 \vdash T_2 \to !\mathsf{X}.R + T'$, as required. $\square$

Since it can be proved that the reduction relation is decreasing, in the sense that the number of symbols in the definition of a tree decreases after a reduction, there can only be a finite number of reductions from any tree and we have:

Theorem 4.3. *The relation* $\to$ *is strongly normalizing and confluent.*

We can define an algorithm to decide the equivalence of spatial trees based on this result. To decide if $S_1 \sim_\mathsf{X} S_2$, you compute the normal form of S_1 and S_2, that is, the spatial trees S_1', S_2' such that $\mathsf{X} \vdash S_i \to^* S_i'$ and S_i' is irreducible for each $i \in 1..2$. By Theorem 4.3, these trees exist and can be computed using a finite number of reductions. Then, you verify whether the normal forms are equal.

Theorem 4.4. *The equivalences* $\sim_\mathsf{X}$ *and* $\approx$ *are decidable.*

Proof. To decide if $S_1 \sim_\mathsf{X} S_2$, you compute the normal form of S_1 and S_2, that is, the spatial trees S_1', S_2' such that $\mathsf{X} \vdash S_i \to^* S_i'$ and S_i' is irreducible for each $i \in 1..2$. By Theorem 4.3, these trees exist and can be computed using a finite number of reductions. Then, you verify whether the normal forms are equal. This amount to test the equality of trees up to the renaming of bound markers and the associativity-commutativity of $+$. Since this is a decidable problem, we get that $\sim_\mathsf{X}$ is decidable.

To decide if $S_1 \approx S_2$, you test whether $S_1\sigma_1 \sim_\mathsf{X} S_2\sigma_2$ for each finite injective mapping σ_1, σ_2 and for each set X such that such that $dom(\sigma_1) = fm(S_1)$ and $dom(\sigma_2) = fm(S_2)$ and $\mathsf{X} \subseteq fm(S_1\sigma_1) \cup fm(S_2\sigma_2)$. It is sufficient to consider mappings σ_1, σ_2 that have their image in a fresh set of markers that has the cardinality of $fm(S_1) \cup fm(S_2)$. Since the sets $fm(S_2)$ and $fm(S_1)$ are finite, and since $\sim_\mathsf{X}$ is decidable, we get that $\approx$ is decidable. $\square$

Using the strong normalization property, we can define a notion of *normal form* for trees. For all spatial trees T, there is a tree T' such that $T \approx T'$ and:

$$T' \stackrel{\Delta}{=} \sum_{i_1 \in I_1} \mu_{i_1}\eta_{i_1}[T_{i_1}] + \sum_{i_2 \in I_2} !\mathsf{X}_{i_2}.T_{i_2} + \sum_{i_3 \in I_3} \mu_{i_3}\, act\, n_{i_3}.T_{i_3} \qquad (4.1)$$

Where (1) I_1, I_2 and I_3 are finite and pairwise disjoint sets of indices; (2) for all indices $i \in \bigcup_{j \in 1..3} I_j$, the tree T_j is in normal form; (3) for all $i, j \in I_1$, if $\eta_i = \eta_j$ then $T_i \not\sim_{\varnothing} T_j$ or $\mu_i = \mu_j = 1$; and (4) for all $i, j \in I_2$, if $!\mathsf{X}_i.T_i \sim_{\varnothing} !\mathsf{X}_j.T_j$ then $i = j$.

It is worth mentioning that, contrary to a typical situation with normal forms found in other theoretical frameworks, the normal form given in (4.1) is syntactically smaller than the spatial trees associated with it.

5   Relation Between Trees and Processes

We define the tree semantics of processes, that is, a mapping from ambient processes to spatial trees, and we relate spatial congruence with the equivalence on spatial trees. Then, by transferring the decidability result obtained in the previous section, we infer the decidability of spatial congruence. This semantics extends a similar definition given in an extended version of [4] for a calculus without name restriction.

In the definition of the tree semantics of processes, we use a new operation on trees called *exponentiation*, $exp(T)$, obtained as the outcome of replicating every connected part of T. More formally, the exponentiation of a tree T, is the composition $!\mathsf{X}_1.T_1 + \cdots + !\mathsf{X}_p.T_p$ where $\{T_1, \ldots, T_p\} = conn(T)$ are the connected parts of T and $\mathsf{X}_i = fm(T_i)$ for each $i \in 1..p$.

Tree semantics:

$$[\![\mathbf{0}]\!] \triangleq \epsilon \qquad\qquad\qquad\qquad\qquad\qquad\qquad\qquad\qquad\text{(Zero)}$$
$$[\![act\,\eta.P]\!] \triangleq 1\,act\,\eta.[\![P]\!] \qquad\qquad\qquad\qquad\qquad\qquad\text{(Action)}$$
$$[\![n[P]]\!] \triangleq 1n[[\![P]\!]] \qquad\qquad\qquad\qquad\qquad\qquad\qquad\text{(Amb)}$$
$$[\![!P]\!] \triangleq exp([\![P]\!]) \qquad\qquad\qquad\qquad\qquad\qquad\qquad\text{(Repl)}$$
$$fm([\![P]\!]) \cap fm([\![Q]\!]) = \varnothing \;\Rightarrow\; [\![P \mid Q]\!] \triangleq [\![P]\!] + [\![Q]\!] \qquad\text{(Par)}$$
$$\mathsf{x} \notin fm([\![P]\!]) \;\Rightarrow\; [\![(\nu n)P]\!] \triangleq [\![P]\!]\{n \leftarrow \mathsf{x}\} \qquad\qquad\text{(Res)}$$

In the same way tree composition, $S + T$, corresponds to parallel composition for processes, exponentiation is the analogue of replication, Furthermore, it is possible to prove properties of this derived operator corresponding to rules (Struct Repl), (Struct Repl Par), (Struct Repl Repl) and (Struct Repl Copy) respectively.

Proposition 5.1.

(1) *If* $S \approx T$ *then* $exp(S) \approx exp(T)$.
(2) *If* $fm(S) \cap fm(T) = \varnothing$ *then* $exp(S + T) \approx exp(S) + exp(T)$.
(3) *The function* $exp(.)$ *is idempotent:* $exp(exp(T)) = exp(T)$.
(4) *For all spatial trees* T *we have* $exp(T) + T \approx exp(T)$.

Using these properties, it is easy to prove that the axiomatisation of spatial congruence is sound.

Lemma 5.2. *If $P \equiv Q$ then $[P] \approx [Q]$.*

Next, we prove the completeness of our axiomatisation. We start by defining an inverse mapping from trees to processes.

Process semantics of trees:

$([\epsilon]) \triangleq \mathbf{0}$	(Empty)
$([1\, act\, n.T]) \triangleq act\, n.([T])$	(Action 1)
$([\infty\, act\, n.T]) \triangleq !act\, n.([T])$	(Action ∞)
$([1n[T]]) \triangleq n[([T])]$	(Edge 1)
$([\infty n[T]]) \triangleq !n[([T])]$	(Edge ∞)
$([!\{x_1,\ldots,x_p\}.T]) \triangleq !(\nu n_1)\ldots(\nu n_p)([T\{x_1 \leftarrow n_1\}\ldots\{x_p \leftarrow n_p\}])$	(Repl)
where $\{n_1,\ldots,n_p\}$ is a set of pairwise distinct names not free in $([T])$.	
$([S+T]) \triangleq ([S]) \mid ([T])$	(Sum)

The composition of the two interpretations $([.])$ and $[.]$ differs from the identity over processes. For instance, we have $([[(\nu u)\mathbf{0}]]) = ([[\mathbf{0}]])$. Nonetheless, we can draw a simple relation between a process and the meaning of its interpretation. See Proposition 5.3 (2) below.

Let the *meaning* of a tree T, written $mean(T)$, be the process $(\nu K)([T\sigma])$, where σ is a bijection from $fm(T)$ to a set of fresh names and K is $\sigma(fm(T))$, the image of σ. Properties of $mean(.)$ are:

Proposition 5.3. (1) *If $S \approx T$ then $mean(S) \equiv mean(T)$ and* (2) *for all processes P we have $mean([P]) \equiv P$.*

Let P and Q be two processes such that $[P] \approx [Q]$. By Proposition 5.3 (1), $mean([P]) \equiv mean([Q])$. By Proposition 5.3 (2), $P \equiv mean([P])$ and $Q \equiv mean([Q])$. Hence, by transitivity of spatial congruence, $P \equiv Q$. This proves that our interpretation of processes as spatial trees is *complete*, that is:

Lemma 5.4. *If $[P] \approx [Q]$ then $P \equiv Q$.*

Lemmas 5.2 and 5.4 state a full abstraction result between ambient processes and spatial trees with respect to the equivalences $\equiv$ and $\approx$ respectively. Therefore, every problem in the ambient calculus can be expressed in terms of problem on spatial trees. For instance, to decide whether $P \equiv Q$, a possible method is to compute $[P]$ and $[Q]$ and to verify if they are equivalent. By Theorem 4.4, this problem is decidable. It follows that:

Theorem 5.5. *The relation $\equiv$ is decidable.*

Using our interpretation of processes as spatial trees, we obtain another result for free. Indeed, through Lemma 5.4 and the normal form for spatial trees given in Section 4, we obtain a normal form for ambient processes that is unique up to very simple spatial transformations, that is, commutativity-associativity of the parallel composition and the reordering of restrictions. If L is a finite set of names $\{n_1, \ldots, n_p\}$, we write $(\nu L)P$ for the process $(\nu n_1) \ldots (\nu n_p)P$. For all processes P, there is a process P' such that $P \equiv P'$ and:

$$P' \triangleq (\nu L)(\prod_{i_1 \in I_1} n_{i_1}[Q_{i_1}] \mid \prod_{i_2 \in I_2} !n_{i_2}[Q_{i_2}] \mid \prod_{i_3 \in I_3} !(\nu L_{i_3})Q_{i_3} \qquad (5.1)$$
$$\mid \prod_{i_4 \in I_4} act\, n_{i_4}.Q_{i_4} \mid \prod_{i_5 \in I_5} !act\, n_{i_5}.Q_{i_5})$$

Where (1) the set of indices $I_1, \ldots, I_5$ are finite and pairwise disjoint; (2) for all $i \in \bigcup_{j \in 1..5} I_j$, the processes Q_j are in normal form; (3) for all $i \in I_1, j \in I_2$, if $n_i = n_j$ then $Q_i \not\equiv Q_j$; (4) for all $i, j \in I_3$, if $(\nu L_i)Q_i \equiv (\nu L_j)Q_j$ then $i = j$.

6   Applications

We can apply the results given in this paper to prove interesting equivalence laws like, for example, the one listed in Lemma 6.1 below. The laws examined in this section are particularly interesting because they are, at the same time, very useful in the formal study of the ambient calculus, and very difficult to prove directly, that is, for example, using an induction on derivations of the form $P \equiv Q$.

In the particular example of Lemma 6.1, we study three equivalence laws extracted from the presentation of Cardelli's and Gordon's modal logic for ambients [4], a logic used to describe properties of processes. These laws are essential to prove the soundness of several axioms of the logic.

An interesting fact is that we follow a similar proof technique in each case. We start by using the full abstraction result obtained in Section 5 to restate the problem in terms of equivalence between spatial trees, then, we prove the desired equivalence by exhibiting a property invariant by the reduction relation over trees.

Lemma 6.1.

(1) If $P \mid Q \equiv \mathbf{0}$ then $P \equiv \mathbf{0}$ and $Q \equiv \mathbf{0}$.
(2) If $n[P] \equiv Q \mid R$ then either $Q \equiv n[P]$ and $R \equiv \mathbf{0}$, or $Q \equiv \mathbf{0}$ and $R \equiv n[P]$.
(3) If $m[P] \equiv n[Q]$ then $m = n$ and $P \equiv Q$.

Proof. We only sketch the proof for case (1). Proofs for the other cases are similar and can be found in [6].

By the full abstraction result stated in Section 5, this problem is equivalent to prove that for every spatial trees, S, T, if $S + T \approx \epsilon$ then $S \approx \epsilon$ and $T \approx \epsilon$. By Theorem 4.3, since ϵ is an irreducible spatial tree with no free markers, this is also equivalent to prove that if $S + T \to^* \epsilon$ then $S \to^* \epsilon$ and $T \to^* \epsilon$.

The proposition follows by showing that for any finite set of cones, $(C_i)_{i \in I}$, if $\mathsf{X} \vdash \sum_{i \in I} C_i \to^* \epsilon$ then $\mathsf{X} \vdash C_i \to^* \epsilon$ for all $i \in I$. This can be proved by an easy induction on the derivation of $\mathsf{X} \vdash \sum_{i \in I} C_i \to^* \epsilon$.

Now, assume $P \mid Q \equiv \mathbf{0}$. By Lemma 5.2, $[\![P]\!] + [\![Q]\!] \approx \epsilon$. Hence, there exists a set X such that $[\![P]\!] + [\![Q]\!] \sim_\mathsf{X} \epsilon$. By Lemma 4.2, and since ϵ is an irreducible spatial trees, we get that $X \vdash [\![P]\!] + [\![Q]\!] \to^* \epsilon$, and therefore, $X \vdash [\![P]\!] \to^* \epsilon$ and $X \vdash [\![Q]\!] \to^* \epsilon$. Hence, $[\![P]\!] \approx \epsilon$ and $[\![Q]\!] \approx \epsilon$. By Lemma 5.4, $P \equiv Q \equiv \mathbf{0}$. □

Next, we prove three equivalence laws that validate the distribution of name restriction over void, ambient, and parallel composition. These laws play an essential role in the definition of axioms for an extension of the ambient modal logics with an operator for name restriction [5].

Lemma 6.2.

(1) If $(\nu n)P \equiv \mathbf{0}$ then $P \equiv \mathbf{0}$
(2) If $(\nu n)P \equiv m[Q]$ then there exists R such that $P \equiv m[R]$ and $Q \equiv (\nu n)R$.
(3) If $(\nu n)P \equiv Q \mid R$ then there exist two processes, P_1, P_2, such that $P \equiv P_1 \mid P_2$, and $Q \equiv (\nu n)P_1$, and $R \equiv (\nu n)P_2$.

Proof. Proof of (1) is similar to the proof of Lemma 6.1 (1) sketched above. In particular, we use the property that for any finite set of cones, $(C_i)_{i \in I}$, if $X \vdash \sum_{i \in I} C_i \to^* \epsilon$ then $X \vdash C_i \to^* \epsilon$ for all $i \in I$.

For (2), assume $(\nu n)P \equiv m[Q]$. By Lemma 5.2, $[\![(\nu n)P]\!] \approx [\![m[Q]]\!]$. Therefore, for every fresh marker, x, we have $[\![P]\!]\{n \leftarrow x\} \approx 1m[\![Q]\!]$. By definition of $\approx$, there exist two finite injective mappings, σ_1, σ_2 and a set X such that $[\![P]\!]\sigma_1\{n \leftarrow y\} \sim_x 1m[\![Q]\!]\sigma_2]$ where $y = \sigma_1(x)$. Let S be the normal form of $[\![P]\!]\sigma_1$. Therefore, $S \approx [\![P]\!]\sigma_1 \sim_y 1m[\![Q]\!]\sigma_2\{y \leftarrow n\}]$. Since S is in normal form, it must be the case that $S = 1m[T]$ for some tree T such that $T \approx [\![Q]\!]\sigma_2\{y \leftarrow n\}$. Let R be the process $mean(T)$. Then, $[\![m[R]]\!] \approx S \approx [\![P]\!]$ and, by Lemma 5.4, $m[R] \equiv P$. Moreover, $[\![(\nu n)R]\!] \approx T\{n \leftarrow y\} \approx [\![Q]\!]$. By Lemma 5.4, $(\nu n)R \equiv Q$, as required.

For (3), Assume $(\nu n)P \equiv Q \mid R$. By Lemma 5.2, $[\![Q \mid R]\!] \approx [\![(\nu n)P]\!]$. Therefore, for every fresh marker, x, we have $[\![Q]\!] + [\![R]\!] \approx [\![P]\!]\{n \leftarrow x\}$, where $fm([\![Q]\!]) \cap fm([\![R]\!]) = \varnothing$. By definition, there exist two finite injective mappings, σ_1, σ_2 and a set X such that $[\![Q]\!]\sigma_1 + [\![R]\!]\sigma_1 \sim_x [\![P]\!]\sigma_2\{n \leftarrow y\}$, where $y = \sigma_2(x)$.

Let S, T and O be the normal forms of $[\![Q]\!]\sigma_1$, $[\![R]\!]\sigma_1$ and $[\![P]\!]\sigma_2$ respectively. Hence, $S + T \sim_Y O\{n \leftarrow y\}$ for some set of markers Y such that $X \subseteq Y$ and with the side condition: $fm(S) \cap fm(T) = \varnothing$. Assume $\sum_{i \in 1..p} C_i$ is the, common, normal form of $S + T$ and $O\{n \leftarrow y\}$. Since S, T and O are normal forms, there exist three families of spatial trees in normal form, $(S_i)_{i \in 1..p}$, $(T_i)_{i \in 1..p}$, and $(O_i)_{i \in 1..p}$, such that:

(1) $S = \sum_{i \in 1..p} S_i$ and $T = \sum_{i \in 1..p} T_i$ and $O = \sum_{i \in 1..p} O_i$.
(2) $S_i + T_i \sim_Y O_i\{n \leftarrow y\}$ for each $i \in 1..p$.
(3) $Y \vdash S_i + T_i \to^* C_i$ and $Y \vdash O_i\{n \leftarrow y\} \to^* C_i$ for each $i \in 1..p$.

The proof follows by constructing the spatial trees corresponding to the processes P_1, P_2. We proceed by defining two families of trees, $(S_i')_{i \in 1..p}$ and $(T_i')_{i \in 1..p}$, and proving that $O_i \sim_Y (S_i' + T_i')$, and $S_i \sim_Y S_i'\{n \leftarrow y\}$, and $T_i \sim_Y T_i'\{n \leftarrow y\}$ for each $i \in 1..p$. The trees S_i' and T_i' are defined by case analysis on the definition of C_i.

(Empty) Then $C_i = \epsilon$. Since S, T and O are in normal form, it must be the case that $S_i = T_i = O_i = \epsilon$. Let $S_i' = T_i' = \epsilon$. Trivial.

(Action) Then $C_i = \mu act\, \eta.S'$. Since O_i is in normal form, it must be the case that $O_i\{n\leftarrow y\} = \mu act\, \eta.S'$. Let $S_i' = S_i\{y\leftarrow n\}$ and $T_i' = T_i\{y\leftarrow n\}$. Trivial. We follow the same definition for the cases where C_i is an edge.

(Repl) Then $C_i = !Y'.T'$. Since O_i is in normal form, it must be the case that $O_i\{n\leftarrow y\} = !Y'.T'' + T'''$ and $T' \sim_{Y\cup Y'} T''$. Since S_i and T_i are in normal form and $fm(S_i) \cap fm(T_i) = \varnothing$, it must be the case that either (1) $S_i \sim_Y C_i$ or (2) $T_i \sim_Y C_i$. Assume we are in case (1). Let $S_i' = (S_i + T''')\{y\leftarrow n\}$ and $T_i' = T_i\{y\leftarrow n\}$. Then $S_i'\{n\leftarrow y\} \sim_Y C_i + T''' \sim_Y C_i \sim_Y S_i$, and $(S_i' + T_i') = (S_i + T_i + T''')\{y\leftarrow n\} \sim_Y (C_i + T''')\{y\leftarrow n\} \sim_Y O_i$, as required.

An easy induction on the definition of $\sum_{i\in1..p} C_i$ proves that $\sum_{i\in1..p} S_i \sim_Y \sum_{i\in1..p} S_i'\{n\leftarrow y\}$, and $\sum_{i\in1..p} T_i \sim_Y \sum_{i\in1..p} T_i'\{n\leftarrow y\}$, and $O \sim_Y \sum_{i\in1..p}(S_i' + T_i')$. Let P_1 and P_2 be the processes $mean(\sum_{i\in1..p} S_i')$ and $mean(\sum_{i\in1..p} T_i')$ respectively. Hence, $[\![P]\!] \approx O \sim_Y [\![P_1]\!] + [\![P_2]\!]$ and, by Lemma 5.4, $P \equiv P_1 \mid P_2$. Moreover, $[\![(\nu n)P_1]\!] \approx \sum_{i\in1..p} S_i \approx [\![Q]\!]$ and $[\![(\nu n)P_2]\!] \approx \sum_{i\in1..p} T_i \approx [\![R]\!]$. By Lemma 5.4, $(\nu n)P_1 \equiv Q$ and $(\nu n)P_2 \equiv R$, as required. $\qquad\square$

Given three processes, P, Q and R, such that $(\nu n)P \equiv Q \mid R$, we define a *solution* of Lemma 6.2 (3) to be a couple (P_1, P_2) such that $P \equiv P_1 \mid P_2$, $Q \equiv (\nu n)P_1$, and $R \equiv (\nu n)P_2$. For example, the next equations give a solution to a non-trivial instance of (3) obtained by following the steps described in the proof of Lemma 6.2.

$$(\nu n)\underbrace{(!(\nu n)n[\mathbf{0}] \mid n[\mathbf{0}])}_{P} \equiv \underbrace{!(\nu n)n[\mathbf{0}]}_{Q} \mid \underbrace{!(\nu n)n[\mathbf{0}]}_{R}$$

$$\equiv (\nu n)\underbrace{(!(\nu n)n[\mathbf{0}] \mid n[\mathbf{0}])}_{P_1} \mid (\nu n)\underbrace{!(\nu n)n[\mathbf{0}]}_{P_2}$$

It is not clear how to prove Lemma 6.2 (3) without using spatial trees as an intermediate representation, and it is even less clear how to obtain solutions for this law. Therefore, it is interesting to note that, following the constructive approach taken in this paper, our proof not only demonstrates that there is always a solution, but also describes an algorithm to compute it.

7 Discussion

We propose an algorithmic method to decide whether two ambient processes are spatially congruent, or not. This method is based on an intuitive interpretation of processes as edge-labelled trees, and a strongly normalizing rewriting system.

The definitions and proof techniques defined in this paper can easily be transposed to other process calculi equipped with a chemical semantics, such as the π-calculus for instance, and natural candidates for comparison are [7] and [10]. Other examples of calculi amenable for the same study include the spi-calculus of Abadi and Gordon [1] and some process calculi of concurrent objects, like TyCo [14] and **concς** [9].

Our definition of spatial congruence is very similar to the definition of the π-calculus equivalence given in [7]. Hence, we obtain a new proof of decidability for structural congruence. A major difference with Engelfriet's and Geselma's work is that we propose a more direct approach, and define an algorithm to decide the equivalence of processes.

In the work of Hirschkoff [10], the decidability of structural congruence is proved using a rewriting system, as it is the case in this paper. There are two main differences with Hirschkoff's approach. First, we use an intermediate data structure, the spatial trees, which eliminate the need to explicitly manipulate the associative and commutative parallel composition operator. Second, we use an exponentiation function in the interpretation of processes. These two differences should result in a more efficient algorithm. Another distinguishing feature of our work is the definition of an effective technique for proving equivalence laws.

The results obtained in this paper are interesting because they lay the formal basis for the development of an algorithm to check spatial congruence. Such automatic tool for testing the equivalence of processes is a necessary component in machine-based verification of properties of the ambient calculus. A benefit of the algorithm obtained with our approach, which has been successfully implemented by Romain Kervarc and Daniel Hirschkoff [11], is that it is based on well-studied algorithmic over trees, such as associative-commutative tree unification.

Another interest of our study is given in Section 6, where we apply our theoretical framework to the proof of equivalence laws used in the definition of Cardelli's and Gordon's modal logic for mobile ambients [4,5].

References

1. Martìn Abadi and Andrew D. Gordon. A calculus for cryptographic protocols: the spi calculus. *Information and Computation*, 148:1–70, 1999.
2. Gérard Berry and Gérard Boudol. The chemical abstract machine. *Theoretical Computer Science*, 96:217–248, 1992.
3. Luca Cardelli and Andrew D. Gordon. Mobile ambients. In *Proceedings of FoS-SaCS '98*, volume 1378 of *LNCS*, pp. 140–155, 1998.
4. Luca Cardelli and Andrew D. Gordon. Anytime, anywhere: Modal logics for mobile ambients. In *Proceedings of POPL '00*, pp. 365–377, 2000.
5. Luca Cardelli and Andrew D. Gordon. Logical properties of name restriction. unpublished notes, 2000.
6. Silvano Dal Zilio. Spatial congruence for the ambients is decidable. Technical Report MSR-TR-2000-41, Microsoft Research, May 2000.
7. J. Engelfriet and T. Geselma. Multisets and structural congruence of the pi-calculus with replication. *Theoretical Computer Science*, 211(1-2):311–337, Jan. 1999.
8. J. Engelfriet and T. Geselma. Structural congruence in the pi-calculus with potential replication. Technical Report 00-02, Leiden Institute of Advanced Computer Science, Jan. 2000.
9. Andrew D. Gordon and Paul D. Hankin. A concurrent object calculus: reduction and typing. In *Proceedings of HLCL '98*, Elsevier ENTCS, 1998.

10. Daniel Hirschkoff. *Mise en oeuvre de preuves de bisimulation*. PhD thesis, École Nationale des Ponts et Chaussées, 1999.
11. Daniel Hirschkoff and Romain Kervarc. Implementation of an algorithm to decide spatial congruence for ambients. LIP, École Normale Supérieure de Lyon, August 2000.
12. Robin Milner. Flow graphs and flow algebras. *Journal of the ACM*, 26(4):794–818, Oct. 1979.
13. Robin Milner. *Communicating and Mobile Systems: the Pi-Calculus*. Cambridge University Press, 2000.
14. Vasco T. Vasconcelos. Typed concurrent objects. In *Proceedings of ECOOP '94*, volume 821 of *LNCS*, pages 100–117, 1994.

A Spatio-temporal Representation Scheme for Modeling Moving Objects in Video Data

Choon-Bo Shim and Jae-Woo Chang

Dept. of Computer Engineering, Chonbuk National University
Chonju, Chonbuk 560-756, South Korea

Abstract. The trajectory of moving objects in video data plays an important role in video indexing for content-based retrieval. In this paper, we propose a new spatio-temporal representation scheme for modeling moving objects' trajectories in video data. In order to support content-based retrieval on video data very well, our representation scheme considers the moving distance of an object during a given time interval as well as its temporal and spatial relations. Based on our representation scheme, we present two similarity measures for both the trajectory of a single moving object and those of multiple moving objects, which provide ranking for the retrieved video results. Finally, we show from our experiment that our representation scheme achieves about 10-20% higher precision while it holds about the same recall, compared with its competitors, such as Li's and Shan's schemes.

1 Introduction

Multimedia database systems have recently become a critical research area of computer systems because so many applications are required to deal with multimedia data such as image, audio and video. These applications include digital libraries, advertisements, video on demand (VOD), digital broadcasting, cyber museum, and electronic commerce. Because they generally handle a very large number of multimedia data, it is necessary to support content-based retrieval on multimedia data themselves[WN1][PH1][JS1][TG1][VE1]. In video data, the trajectory of a moving object plays an important role in video indexing for content-based retrieval. The trajectory can be represented as a spatio-temporal relationship between moving objects, including both their spatial and temporal properties[NF1][SA1][HS1][GD1][AM1]. User queries based on the spatio-temporal relationship are as follows: "*Finds all objects whose motion trajectory is similar to the trajectory shown in a user interface.*" or "*Finds all shots with such a scene as two cars approach to each other.*"

To handle the queries, there have been many studies on temporal relationship and spatial relationship between moving objects in video data. The studies on the temporal relationship are based on thirteen temporal relations proposed by Allen[JF1] while those on the spatial relationship[SQ1] [JY1] are based on topological and directional relations using spatial coordinates. While most of the studies have concentrated on spatio-temporal relationships between moving

J. He and M. Sato (Eds.): ASIAN 2000, LNCS 1961, pp. 104–118, 2000.

objects, they did not consider their moving distance during a given time interval. For modeling moving objects' trajectories in video data, it is necessary to consider their moving distance as well as their spatio-temporal relationships so as to support content-based retrieval on video data very well. For example, in case of soccer game video data, it is very important to decide whether the trajectory of a soccer ball belongs to "a long pass" or "a short pass". This can be determined by using the moving distance of the ball in a given time interval, rather than using the direction of it.

In this paper, we propose a new spatio-temporal representation scheme for modeling moving objects' trajectories in video data. In order to support content-based retrieval on video data very well, our representation scheme considers the moving distance of an object during a given time interval as well as its temporal and spatial relations. Based on our representation scheme, we present two similarity measures for both a single moving object's and multiple moving objects' trajectories, called SDST (Similarity measure based on moving Distance for Single object's Trajectories) and SDMT (Similarity measure based on moving Distance for Multiple objects' Trajectories).

This paper is organized as follows. In Section 2, we introduce related work in the area of content-based video retrieval using spatio-temporal relationships. In Section 3, we propose a new spatio-temporal representation scheme for modeling moving objects' trajectories. In Section 4, we describe new similarity measure algorithms to calculate the similarity between a user query and moving objects in video databases. In Section 5, we compare the performance of our scheme with those of the Li's and Shan's schemes. Finally, we draw our conclusions and suggest future work in Section 6.

2   Related Work

There have been some researches on content-based video retrieval using spatio-temporal relationships in video data. First, when assuming a moving object is a salient one moving over time, Li et al.[JM1][JM2] represented the trajectory of a moving object as eight directions, such as North(NT), Northwest(NW), Northeast(NE), West(WT), Southwest(SW), East(ET), Southeast(SE), and Southwest(SW). They represented as (S_i, d_i, I_i) the trajectory of a moving object A over a given time interval I_i where S_i is the displacement of A and d_i is a direction. They also represented as $A(\alpha, \beta, I_k)B$ the spatio-temporal relationships between moving objects A and B over time interval I_k. Here α is one of eight topological relationships: Disjoint(DJ), Touch(TC), Equal(EQ), Inside(IN), Coverd_by(CB), Contains(CT), Covers(CV), Overlap(OL). β is the directional relationship between moving objects A and B. Therefore, the spatio-temporal relationships between moving objects A and B can be represented as a list of motions, like $A[(\alpha_1, \beta_1, I_1), (\alpha_2, \beta_2, I_2), ...,(\alpha_n, \beta_n, I_n)]B$. Based on the representations for moving objects' trajectories, they present a similarity measures to computes the similarity of spatio-temporal relationships between two moving object. Let $\{M_1, M_2, ..., M_m\}$ (m $\geq$ 1) be the trajectory of moving

Table 1. Distances of directional relations

	NT	NW	NE	WT	SW	ET	SE	ST
NT	0	1	1	2	3	2	3	4
NW	1	0	2	1	2	3	4	3
NE	1	2	0	3	4	1	2	3
WT	2	1	3	0	1	4	3	2
SW	3	2	4	1	0	3	2	1
ET	2	3	1	4	3	0	1	2
SE	3	4	2	3	2	1	0	1
ST	4	3	3	2	1	2	1	0

Table 2. Distances of topological relations

	DJ	TC	EQ	IN	CB	CT	CV	OL
DJ	0	1	6	4	5	4	5	4
TC	1	0	5	5	4	5	4	3
EQ	6	5	0	4	3	4	3	6
IN	4	5	4	0	1	6	7	4
CB	5	4	3	1	0	7	6	3
CT	4	5	4	6	7	0	1	4
CV	5	4	3	7	6	1	0	3
OL	4	3	6	4	3	4	3	0

object A, $\{N_1, N_2, ..., N_n\}$ be the trajectory of moving object B, and m ≤ n. The similarity measure between the trajectory of object A and that of object B, TrajSim(A, B), is computed by using the similarity distances of directional(Table 1) and topologicla relations (Table 2) as follows:

$$minDiff(A, B) = MIN\{\sum_{i=1}^{m} distance(M_i, N_{i+j})\} \qquad (\forall j, 0 \le j \le n - m)$$

$$TrajSim(A, B) = \frac{maxDiff(A, B) - minDiff(A, B)}{maxDiff(A, B)}$$

Here, minDiff(A, B) and maxDiff(A, B) are the smallest distance between A and B and the largest distance, respectively. When the moving direction of A is opposite to that of B in all the comparisons, maxDiff(A, B) = 4*m where the maximum number of comparing motions is m. Also, it considered only directional relationship to compute the similarity of a single object's trajectory between video and query.

Secondly, Shan and Lee[MS1] introduced similarity retrieval algorithms for both a single moving object's and multiple moving objects' trajectories in order to support content-based video retrieval. For retrieval based on the single moving object's trajectory, they represented the trajectory of a moving object as a sequence of segments, each being expressed as the slope ranging from 0 to 360 degree. For the single moving object's trajectory, they proposed two algorithms to measure the similarity between a query trajectory and moving objects' trajectories in video data by using only directional property, i.e., OCM(Optimal Consecutive Mapping) and OCMR(Optimal Consecutive Mapping with Replication). In order to represent the multiple moving object' trajectories, they simply used the 2D string scheme proposed by Chang[SQ1]. So, the multiple moving objects' trajectories consist of a set of symbol objects, each being represented as a 2D string. However, in the 2D-string scheme, it is difficult to express the spatio-temporal relationships between moving objects precisely.

3   New Spatio-temporal Representation Scheme

Both Li's and Shan's schemes concentrated on spatio-temporal relationships between moving objects, but they did not consider their moving distance during a given time interval. In order to support content-based retrieval on video data very well, it is necessary to consider the moving distance of objects in the video data as well as their spatio-temporal relationships. For this, we propose a new spatio-temporal representation scheme for modeling moving objects in video data which considers their moving distance during a given time interval as well as their temporal and spatial relations. In order to approximate the position of an object, we use MBR (Minimum Bounding Rectangle). We define a moving object as one whose position is changed over a given time interval and (x_i, y_i) as the center point of object A in XY-coordinates. So, the trajectory of the moving object A is represented as $[(x_0, y_0, t_0), (x_1, y_1, t_1),..., (x_n, y_n, t_n)]$ at time t_0, $t_0, ..., t_0$. We define I_i as the difference between a start frame and a finish frame in a set of consecutive video frames. Here, I_i means a time interval between time t_{i-1} and time t_i, $[t_{i-1}, t_i]$ as shown in Fig.1. First, the single moving object's trajectory is defined as follows.

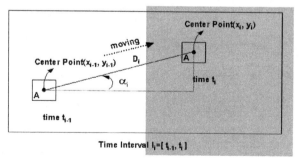

Fig. 1. MBR representation of moving object

Definition 1. *Let the motion (M_i) of a moving object A over time interval I_i be (α_i, D_i, I_i). Here, α_i is a direction being made from A at time t_{i-1} to A at time t_i, which is represented by the real angle ranging from 0 to 360 degree. D_i is the* *relative moving distance (0 to 100) of A over I_i, which is computed as dividing the sum of moving distance between I_1 and I_n by the moving distance during I_i and multiplying by 100. For a given order list of time intervals $[I_1, I_2,..., I_n]$, the trajectory of a single moving object A can be described by a list of motions $[M_1, M_2,... , M_m]$, i.e.*

$$[(\alpha_i, D_1, I_1), (\alpha_2, D_2, I_2), ... , ((n, D_n, I_n)]$$

Example 1. Fig. 2(a) shows a trajectory of object A. The trajectory for a single moving object A consists of a sequence of motions which is expressed by $[(0^o, 15, I1), (90^o, 15, I2), (40^o, 23, I3), (300^o, 32, I4), (0^o, 15, I5)]$ as shown in Fig. 2(b).

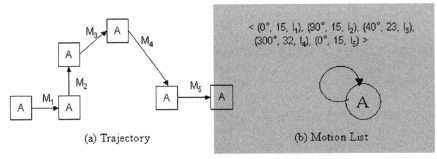

(a) Trajectory   (b) Motion List

Fig. 2.Trajectory and motion list of an object A

In order to describe the spatial relationships between multiple moving objects, we define seven topological operators being constructed from SMR scheme proposed by Chang[JY1], like Faraway(FA), Disjoint(DJ), Meet(ME), Overlap(OL), Is_included_by(CL), Include(IN), Same(SA). Fig. 3(a) depicts the seven topological operators for a single dimension. Thus, topological relations on X-axis are shown in Fig. 3 $R_i{}^{AB}$ is a topological operator between two objects A and B on i-axis as shown in Table 3.

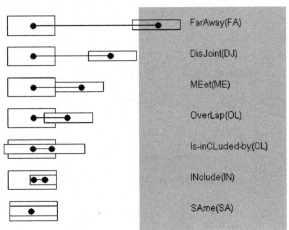

Fig. 3. Seven topological operators on X-axis

Table 3. Spatial relation on XY-coordinates

	FA	DJ	ME	OL	CL	IN	SA
FA	FA	FA	FA	FA	FA	FA	FA
DJ	FA	DJ	DJ	DJ	DJ	DJ	DJ
ME	FA	DJ	ME	ME	ME	ME	ME
OL	FA	DJ	ME	OL	OL	OL	OL
CL	FA	DJ	ME	OL	CL	OL	CL
IN	FA	DJ	ME	OL	OL	IN	IN
SA	FA	DJ	ME	OL	CL	IN	SA

Secondly, the multiple moving objects' trajectories are defined as follows.

Definition 2. *DM_i is the relative moving distance (0 to 100) of an object A over I_i, compared with that of an object B. That is, DM_i is 50 when the moving distance of A is the same as that of B while DM_i becomes near to 100 as the moving distance of A is getting grater than that of B and conversely.*

Definition 3. *Let the spatio-temporal relationships (STR_i) from a moving object A to a moving object B over time interval I_i be $(R_i, \alpha_i, DM_i, I_i)$. Here R_i is the spatial relation on XY-coordinates from A to B over I_i and α_i is the direction from A to B at the start frame of I_i which is expressed as an angle with 0 to 360 degree. For a given ordered list of time intervals $[I_1, I_2,..., I_n]$, the multiple moving objects' trajectories from A to B can be described by a list of spatio-temporal relationships $[STR_1, STR_2,..., STR_n]$, i.e.*

$$[(R_i, \alpha_1, DM_1, I_1), (R_2, \alpha_2, DM_2, I_2), ...,(R_n, \alpha_n, DM_n, I_n)]$$

Example 2. Fig. 4(a) depicts that a Car(C) and a Motorcycle(M) are running a race. The multiple moving objects' trajectories from C to M can be expressed by

$$[(DJ, 260^o, 30, I_1), (DJ, 290^o, 50, I_2), (DJ, 45^o, 55, I_3)]$$

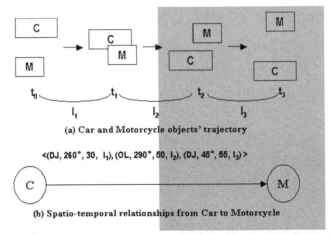

(a) Car and Motorcycle objects' trajectory

<(DJ, 260°, 30, l$_1$),(OL, 290°, 60, l$_2$), (DJ, 45°, 55, l$_3$) >

(b) Spatio-temporal relationships from Car to Motorcycle

Fig. 4. Multiple motion trajectories and their spatio-temporal relationships

4   New Spatio-temporal Representation Scheme

Most of similarity measure algorithms for spatio-temporal representation schemes mainly depend on only spatial relationships to calculate the similarity between a user query and moving objects in video databases. However, since the moving distance of an object during a time interval plays an important role in calculating the similarity between a user query and moving objects more effectively, we propose new similarity measure algorithms to consider the moving distance of objects as well as their spatial relationships. The proposed similarity measures allow us to retrieve precise video results based on the moving distance of objects as well as to provide ranking for the retrieved video results to answer a user query. For a single motion trajectory, we first propose SDST(Similarity measure based on moving Distances for Single object's Trajectories) in the following.

Definition 4. *For a single moving object's trajectory VS={ VS$_1$, VS$_2$, ..., VS$_M$} in video databases and a query trajectory QS={ QS$_1$, QS$_2$, ..., QS$_N$} (1≤N≤M) , the difference between the angle of a video motion VS$_i$ and that of a query motion QS$_i$, D$_{ang}$(VS$_i$, QS$_i$), is defined as*

$$\text{If} |\text{VS}_i - \text{QS}_i| \geq 180^o$$
$$D_{ang}(\text{VS}_i, \text{QS}_i) = (360^o - |\text{VS}_i - \text{QS}_i|)$$
$$\text{otherwise}$$
$$D_{ang}(\text{VS}_i, \text{QS}_i) = |\text{VS}_i - \text{QS}_i|$$

Example 3. For a given video trajectory V and query trajectory Q, the difference between the angle of a video motion V$_i$ and that of a query motion Q$_i$, D$_{ang}$(V$_i$, Q$_i$), is as follows :

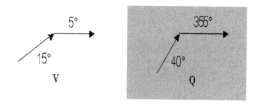

$$D_{ang}(V_1, Q_1) = |15° - 40| = 25°$$
$$D_{ang}(V_2, Q_2) = (360° - |5° - 355|) = 10°$$

Definition 5. *Given a single video moving object's trajectory VS={VS₁, VS₂, ..., VSₘ} and a query trajectory QS={QS₁, QS₂, ..., QSₙ} (1≤N≤M), the similarity between the direction of a video motion VSᵢ and that of a query motion QSᵢ, SRᵢ(VSᵢ, QSᵢ), is defined as follows. Because cos(0°) = 1 and cos(180°) = -1, SRᵢ(VSᵢ, QSᵢ) has a value between 0 to 1.*

$$SR_i(VS_i, QS_i) = \frac{cos(D_{ang}(VS_i, QS_i)) + 1}{2}$$

Definition 6. *Given a single video moving object's trajectory VS={VS₁, VS₂, ..., VSₘ} and a query trajectory QS={QS₁, QS₂, ..., QSₙ} (1≤N≤M), the similarity between the moving distance of a video motion VSᵢ and that of a query motion QSᵢ, SDᵢ(VSᵢ, QSᵢ), is defined as*

$$SD_i(VS_i, QS_i) = 1 - \frac{|D_i^{VS} - D_i^{QS}|}{Max(D_i^{VS}, D_i^{QS})}$$

Definition 7. *Given a single video moving object's trajectory VS={VS₁, VS₂, ..., VSₘ} and a query trajectory QS={QS₁, QS₂, ..., QSₙ} (1≤N≤M), the similarity between a video trajectory VS and a query trajectory QS, SDST(VS, QS), by using definition 4 and 5 is defined as follows. Here, ω₁ and ω₂ mean the weight of the direction and that of the distance, respectively.*

$$SDST(VS, QS) = MAX\{\frac{\sum_{i=1}^{N} SR_{i+j}^{(1-\omega_1)} * SD_{i+j}^{(1-\omega_2)}}{N}\} \qquad (\forall_j, 0 \le j \le M-N)$$

Secondly, we propose SDMT (Similarity measure based on moving Distance for Multiple objects' Trajectories) for multiple moving objects' trajectories. The SDMT computes the similarity based on the moving distance of objects as well as topological and directional relations in the following.

Definition 8. *Given a video trajectory of multiple moving objects VM={VM₁, VM₂, ..., VMₘ} and a query trajectory QM={QM₁, QM₂, ..., QMₙ} (1≤N≤M), the similarity of the topological relation between VMᵢ and QMᵢ, STᵢ(VMᵢ, QMᵢ),*

Table 4. Similarity distance between topological operators(Sim_Dist)

D	FA	DJ	ME	OL	CL	SA	IN
FA	0	1	2	3	4	5	4
DJ	1	0	1	2	3	4	3
ME	2	1	0	1	2	3	2
OL	3	2	1	0	1	2	2
CL	4	3	2	1	0	1	2
SA	5	4	3	2	1	0	1
IN	4	3	2	1	2	1	0

is defined as follows. Here, Fig. 5 shows the similarity distance graph between topological relaitons. Sim_Dist(VR₁, VR₂) means the similarity distance between VR_1 and VR_2 as shown in Table 4. $ST_i(VM_i, QM_i)$ is reversely in proportion to the square of Sim_Dist(VR₁, VR₂). So, λ is used to smooth the curve of $ST_i(VM_i, QM_i)$.

$$ST_i(VM_i, QM_i) = \frac{\lambda}{\lambda + Sim\_Dist(VR_i, QR_i)^2}$$

Fig. 5. Similarity distance graph

Definition 9. Given a video trajectory of multiple moving objects VM={VM₁, VM₂, ..., VM_M} and a query trajectory QM={QM₁, QM₂, ..., QM_N} (1≤N≤M), the difference between the moving distance of a video motion VM_i and that of a query motion QM_i, $SDM_i(VM_i, QM_i)$, is defined as follows. Because $|DM_i^{VM} - DM_i^{QM}|$ is range from 0 to 100, $SDM_i(VM_i, QM_i)$ has a value between 0 and 1.

$$SDM_i(VM_i, QM_i) = 1 - \frac{|DM_i^{VM} - DM_i^{QM}|}{100}$$

Definition 10. *Given a video trajectory of multiple moving objects $VM=\{VM_1,$ $VM_2, ..., VM_M\}$ and a query trajectory $QM=\{QM_1, QM_2, ..., QM_N\}$ $(1{\leq}N{\leq}M)$, the similarity between a video trajectory VM and a query trajectory QM by using definition (4), (7) and (8), SDMT(VM, QM), is defined as follows. Here, ω_1 and ω_2 and ω_3 means the weight of topological relations, that of the direction, that of the distance, respectively.*

$$SDMT(VM, QM) = MAX\{\frac{\sum_{i=1}^{N} ST_{i+j}^{(1-\omega_1)} * SR_{i+j}^{(1-\omega_2)} * SDM_{i+j}^{(1-\omega_3)}}{N}\}$$

$$(\forall_j, 0 \leq j \leq M - N)$$

5 Performance Analysis

In order to verify the usefulness of our spatio-temporal representation scheme, we do our experiment with the video data of soccer (football) games. Because users generally consider a soccer ball as a salient object in a soccer game video, we extract the trajectories of the soccer ball from the video data. Most of video data used in our experiment which are formatted as MPEG file (*. mpeg) include a shot of "*getting a goal*". We extract the trajectory of a soccer ball by manually tracing the soccer ball in soccer filed. Fig. 6 and 7 show an example to extract the single trajectory of a soccer ball from the video data and an example to extract the multiple trajectories between a soccer ball and a player, respectively.

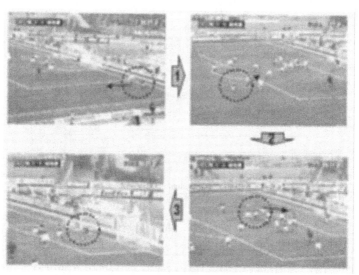

(a) Original Video Frame

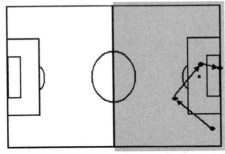

(b) Single object's trajectory extracted from (a)
Fig. 6. Example of single trajectory

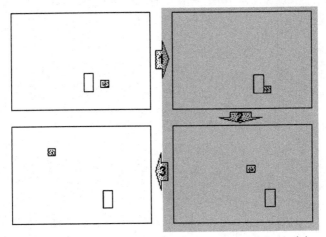

(a) Original Video Frame

(b) Multiple objects' trajectories extracted from (a)
Fig. 7. Example of multiple trajectories

Table 5. Experimental data set

	Single object's trajectory	Multiple objects' trajectories
# of video shots in the data set	350	200
# of motions in a shot	$2 - 15$	$2 - 10$
# of query types	40	10
# of motions in a query	$2 - 3$	$3 - 4$

For our experiment, we make use of the data set for single moving object's trajectory and multiple moving objects' trajectories as shown in Table 2, respectively. By considering possible "*getting a goal*" trajectories as single moving object's trajectory, we make forty query trajectories consisting of twenty in "*the right field*" and twenty in "*the left field*" from the half line of the soccer field. In addition, for multiple moving objects' trajectories, we make ten query trajectories consisting of five in "*the right field*" and five in "*the left field*" from the half line of the soccer field. For smoothing *Sim_Dist* curve, we choose $\lambda = 10$. We also do experiment by $\omega_1 = \omega_2 = 0.5$ for single moving object's trajectory and $\omega_1 = \omega_2 = \omega_3 = 0.33$ for mulitple moving objects' trajectories because their weights are assumed to be same.

For our performance analysis, we implemented our spatio-temporal representation scheme as well as Li's and Shan's schemes under Windows PC with 128 MB memory by using Microsoft-Visual C++. We compare our scheme with the Li's and Shan's schemes in terms of retrieval effectiveness, that is, precision and recall measures[GS1]. Let RVR (Relevant Video data that are Retrieved) be the number of relevant video data retrieved by a given query, RVD (Relevant Video data in Database) be the number of relevant video data to the query by manual, and RVQ (Retrieved Video data by Query) be the total number of video data retrieved by the query. To compute RVD, we make a test panel which finds relevant video data manually from the database. The test panel is composed of 10 graduate school students from our Computer Engineering department. The precision is defined as the proportion of retrieved video data being relevant and the recall is defined as the proportion of relevant video data being retrieved as follows.

$$Precision = \frac{RVR}{RVQ} \qquad\qquad Recall = \frac{RVR}{RVD}$$

For our performance comparison, we adopt the 11-point measure[SM1] which is most widely used for measuring the precision and the recall. Table 3 shows the average precision and the average recall values of our scheme, Li's scheme and Shan's scheme for single and multiple moving objects' trajectories, respectively. In the single trajectory, our scheme is outperforms the Li's scheme in terms of both precision and recall. That is, our scheme holds about 20% higher precision and about 10% higher recall. Our scheme also achieves 17% higher precision than the Shan's scheme while it holds about the same recall. In the multiple

Table 6. Comparison of retrieval effectiveness

	Single object's trajectory		Multiple objects' trajectories	
	Average Precision	Average Recall	Average Precision	Average Recall
Li's scheme	0.23	0.42	0.36	0.50
Shan's scheme	0.26	0.46	0.21	0.39
Our scheme	0.43	0.44	0.45	0.54

trajectories, our scheme holds about 10% higher precision and about 5% higher recall than Li's scheme. Our scheme also achieves about 20% higher precision and about 15% higher recall than Shan's scheme. Fig. 8 shows the recall-precision graph of our scheme, Li's one and Shan's one.

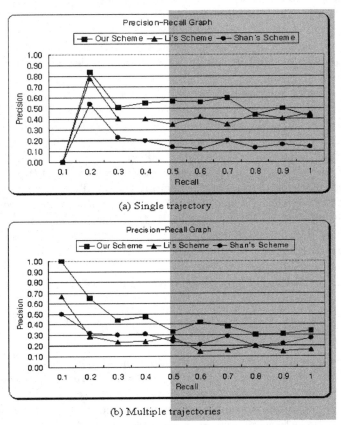

(a) Single trajectory

(b) Multiple trajectories

Fig. 8. Recall-precision graph for single and multiple trajectory

6   Conclusions

For efficient content-based retrieval on video data, we proposed a new spatio-temporal representation scheme for moving objects in video data in order to represent a spatio-temporal relationship between moving objects more precisely. In addition, we proposed two similarity measures, called SDST and SDMT, which consider the moving distance of an object during a given time interval as well as its spatial relations so that we may calculate the similarity between a user query and moving objects more effectively. They allow us to retrieve precise video results based on the moving distance of objects as well as to provide ranking for the retrieved video results to answer a user query. For our performance analysis, we implement our spatio-temporal representation scheme and compare it with Li's and Shan's schemes in terms of retrieval effectiveness. We finally show from our two experiment that for single object's trajectory, our scheme achieves about 20% higher precision while it holds about the same recall, compared with Li's and Shan's scheme. For multiple objects' trajectories, our scheme achieves about 10-20% higher precision while it holds about 5-15% higher recall. In our future work, it is necessary to prove the usefulness of our spatio-temporal representation scheme by applying it to real applications dealing with a large number of soccer game video data.

Acknowledgement

This work was supported by grant No. 97-0100-0101-3 from the Basic Research Program of the Korea Science & Engineering Foundation.

References

[WN1]   W. Niblack, et. al.: The QBIC project: Quering by Iamge Content Using Color, Texture, and Shape. In Procceedings of SPIE Storage and Retrieval for Image and Video Databases(1993) 173–187

[PH1]   P. Aigram, H.Zhang and D.Petkovi: Content-Based Representation and Retrieval of Visual Media : A state-of-the-ART Review. Multimedia Tools and Applications, Vol. 3(1996) 179–202

[JS1]   J. R. Smith, S. F. Chang: VisualSEEk: a Fully Automated Content-Based Image Query System. ACM Multimedia Systems(1996)

[TG1]   T.D.C. Little, G. Ahanger, R.J. Folz, et. al.: A Digital On-Demand Video Service Supporting Content-Based Queries. In Proceedings of the International Conference on ACM Multimedia(1993) 427–436

[VE1]   Virginia, E.Ogle and Michael Stonebraker: Chabot: Retrieval from a Relational Database of images. IEEE Computer, 28(9) (1995) 40–48

[NF1]   N. Dimitrova and F. Golshani: Rx for semantic video database retrieval. In Proceedings of the 2nd ACM International Conference on Multimedia(1994) 219–226

[SA1]   S. S. Intille and A. F. Bobick: Visual tracking using closed-worlds. In Proceedings of the International Conference on Computer Vision(1995)

[HS1]   H. S. Sawhney, S. Ayer, and M. Gorkani: Model-based 2D&3D dominant motion estimation for mosaicing and video representation. In Proceedings of International Conference on Computer Vision(1995)

[GD1]   G. Ahanger, D. Benson, and T.D.C Little: Video query formulation. In Proceedings of Storage and Retrieval for Images and Video Databases , SPIE Symposium on Electronic Imaging Science and Technology(1995) 280–291

[AM1]   A. Yoshitaka, M. Yoshimitsu, M. Hirakawa, and T. Ichikawa: V-QBE: Video database retrieval by means of example motion of objects. In Proceedings of IEEE International Conference on Multimedia Computing and Systems(1996) 453–457

[JF1]   J. F. Allen: Maintaining Knowledge about Temporal Intervals. Communication of the ACM(1993) 832–843

[SQ1]   S. K. Chang, Q. Y. Shi and C. W. Yan: Iconic Indexing by 2D Strings. IEEE Trans. Pattern Analysis, Machine Intelligence, Vol. 9(1987) 413–428

[JY1]   J. W. Chang, Y. J. Kim and K. J. Chang: A Spatial Match Reprensentation Scheme Indexing and Querying in Icnoic Image Databases. ACM International Conference on Information and Knowledge Management(1997) 169–176

[JM1]   John Z. Li, Iqbal A. Goralwalla, M. Tamer Ozsu, Duane Szafron: Video Modeling and Its Integration in a Temporal Object Model. Technical Report TR 96-02, University of Alberta(1996)

[JM2]   John Z. Li, M. Tamer Ozsu, Duane Szafron: Modeling Video Spatial Relationships in an Object Model. Technical Report TR 96-06, University of Alberta(1996)

[MS1]   Man-Kwan Shan and Suh-Yin Lee: Content-based Video Retrieval via Motion Trajectories. In Proceedings of the International Conference on SPIE, Vol. 3561(1998) 52–61

[GS1]   G. Salton: A New Comparison between Conventional Indexing (MEDLARS) and Automatic Text Processing(SMART). Journal of the American Society for Information Science, Vol. 23, No. 2(1972) 75–84

[SM1]   Salton, G., and M. McGill: An introduction to Modern Information Retrieval. McGraw-Hill(1993)

Node-to-Set Disjoint Paths Problem in Rotator Graphs

Keiichi Kaneko and Yasuto Suzuki

Tokyo University of Agriculture and Technology, Tokyo 184-8588, Japan

Abstract. In this paper, we give an algorithm for the node-to-set disjoint paths problem in rotator graphs. The algorithm is based on recursion and it is divided into cases according to the distribution of destination nodes in classes into which all the nodes in a rotator graph are categorized. The proof of correctness of our algorithm, the sum of the length of paths, and the time complexity are also given.

1 Introduction

As an unrestricted improvement in the performance of sequential computation is currently difficult to achieve, studies of parallel and distributed computation are becoming more significant. Moreover, research on so-called massively parallel machines which have very large number of processing elements has been conducted enthusiastically in recent years. Hence many complex topologies of interconnection networks have been proposed to replace the simple networks such as a hypercube and a mesh[1,4,5,8,9,10]. Unfortunately, there still remain unknowns in several metrics for these topologies, making a clear comparison of them difficult. A rotator graph by Corbett[3] is one of the new topologies that shows promise in that it has a low degree and a small diameter in comparison with the number of nodes[2,12]. However, it is not yet cleared in some metrics, amongst which is included the node-to-set disjoint paths problem: Given a source node s and a set $D = \{d_1, d_2, \cdots, d_k\}$ ($s \notin D$) of k destination nodes in a k-connected graph $G = (V, E)$, find k paths from s to d_i ($1 \le i \le k$) which are node-disjoint except for s. This is one of the most important issues in the design and implementation of parallel and distributed computing systems[6,11]. In general, node-disjoint paths can be obtained by making use of the maximum flow algorithm in polynomial order of $|V|$. In an n-rotator graph, the number of nodes is equal to $n!$, so its complexity is not considered efficient. In this paper, we give an answer to this problem which is of polynomial order of n instead of $n!$ and it is explained in detail with proof of its correctness.

2 Preliminaries

In this section, we first give a definition of a rotator graph, then give some comparisons between a rotator graph and other major network topologies for several elementary indices.

J. He and M. Sato (Eds.): ASIAN 2000, LNCS 1961, pp. 119–132, 2000.
© Springer-Verlag Berlin Heidelberg 2000

Definition 1. *An n-rotator graph, P_n, is a directed graph which has n! nodes. Each node has a unique label $(a_1, a_2, \cdots, a_n)$ comprised of a permutation of n figures: $1, 2, \cdots, n$. In addition, there exists an edge $(\boldsymbol{a}, \boldsymbol{b})$ between two nodes $\boldsymbol{a} = (a_1, a_2, \cdots, a_n)$ and $\boldsymbol{b} = (b_1, b_2, \cdots, b_n)$ if and only if there exists i $(2 \leq i \leq n)$ such that $b_1 = a_2, b_2 = a_3, \cdots, b_{i-1} = a_i, b_i = a_1, b_{i+1} = a_{i+1}, \cdots, b_n = a_n$. Here, let R_i represent the operation to obtain the node $\boldsymbol{b}$ from the node $\boldsymbol{a}$.*

An n-rotator graph P_n contains n different $(n-1)$-subrotator graphs. All of the nodes in each subrotator graph P_{n-1} share the same last figure k in their labels and the subrotator graph is specified by $P_{n-1}k$. Then any edge between two nodes which belong to different subrotator graphs $P_{n-1}h$ and $P_{n-1}k$ $(h \neq k)$ is given only by the operation R_n. Fig. 1 presents some examples of rotator graphs.

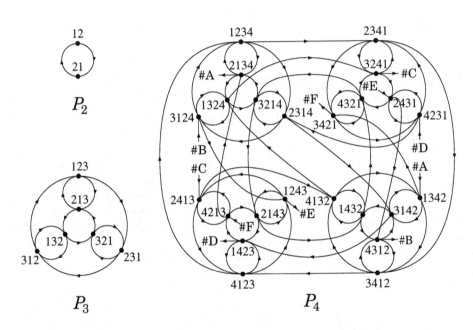

Fig. 1. Examples of rotator graphs.

Table 1 shows the comparison of an n-rotator graph with an n-star graph and an n-cube. From this table, we can see that the n-rotator graph shows better performance against other two topologies. In addition, connectivities also means the number of paths which must be constructed in the node-to-set disjoint paths problem.

Next, we define a class, which is a subset of nodes, and the node-to-set disjoint paths problem.

Table 1. Comparison of a rotator graph with other topologies.

	n-rotator graph	n-star graph	n-cube
number of nodes	$n!$	$n!$	2^n
number of edges	$(n-1) \times n!$	$(n-1) \times n!$	$n2^n$
diameter	$n-1$	$\lfloor 3(n-1)/2 \rfloor$	n
connectivity	$n-1$	$n-1$	n

Definition 2. *A class of an n-rotator graph is a set of nodes in which for any pair of nodes a and b, the node a is obtained from the node b by iterative application of the operation R_n.*

The class to which a node a belongs is specified by $C(a)$. The following are properties of classes.

1. Each class has n nodes which form a directed ring structure.
2. Every node in P_n belongs to exactly one class.
3. Every node in P_n has $n-1$ parent nodes, all of which belong to different classes.

Definition 3. *The node-to-set disjoint paths problem in an n-rotator graph is to find $n-1$ paths from a source node s to each node in the destination node set $D = \{d_1, d_2, \cdots, d_{n-1}\}$ which are disjoint except for s.*

3   Algorithm

In this section we give an algorithm for the node-to-set disjoint paths problem and it is proved by induction with respect to n. Because of the symmetry of P_n, we can fix the source node s to be $(1, 2, \cdots, n)$ without any loss of generality. For a 2-rotator graph P_2, the problem is trivial and we assume that $n > 2$ in the following. Let $D = \{d_1, d_2, \cdots, d_{n-1}\}$ represent the set of destination nodes. Our algorithm is composed of procedures corresponding to the cases given below.

Case I: There exists at least one single class with multiple destination nodes in P_n.

Case II: Each class in P_n has at most one destination node.

    Case II-1: The class $C(s)$ includes exactly one destination node.

    Case II-2: $C(s)$ has no destination node.

        Case II-2-A: All the destination nodes in P_n belong to $P_{n-1}n$.

        Case II-2-B: At least one destination node in P_n belongs to a subrotator graph other than $P_{n-1}n$.

            Case II-2-B-a: Each subrotator graph of P_n other than $P_{n-1}n$ has at most one destination node.

            Case II-2-B-b: There is a subrotator graph of P_n other than $P_{n-1}n$ which includes mutiple destination nodes.

The following subsections present procedures for the leaf cases, that is, Case I, Case II-1, Case II-2-A, Case II-2-B-a and Case II-2-B-b, as well as proofs of their correctness.

3.1   Case I

In this subsection, we will consider the case that there exist multiple destination nodes in a single class. Let $C = \{C_1, C_2, \cdots, C_k\}$ $(k < n - 1)$ be the collection of classes to which destination nodes belong. Using Procedure 1 below, we can construct $n - 1$ paths from the source node s to the $n - 1$ destination nodes in D which are disjoint except for s.

Procedure 1

1. Let D_1 be a node set constructed by choosing one destination node from each class in C such that the figure n occurs in the label of the node in the right most position compared to all the other destination nodes in the class. That is, any destination node in D_1 is nearest from the subrotator graph $P_{n-1}n$ with respect to the operation R_n amongst the other destination nodes which belong to the same class as the destination. Additionally, let D_2 be the rest of the destination nodes $D - D_1$. Then, $|D_1| = k, |D_2| = n - k - 1$. Without loss of generality, we can assume that $D_2 = \{d_1, d_2, \cdots, d_{n-k-1}\}$. See Fig. 2.

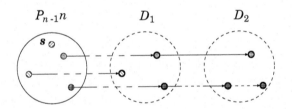

Fig. 2. The sets D_1 and D_2.

2. For each node d_i in $\{d_1, d_2, \cdots, d_{n-k-2}\}$, select a parent node c_i satisfying the following two conditions in a greedy manner. Note that the node d_{n-k-1} is not considered in this step because the probability of obtaining some gain due to its parent is very small in compared to the cost to be paid.

Condition 1 : If $i \neq j$, $C(c_i) \neq C(c_j)$.
Condition 2 : $\forall i, C(c_i) \notin C$.

3. Let $D_1 \leftarrow D_1 \cup \{c_i | 1 \leq i \leq n-k-2\}$, and $C \leftarrow C \cup \{C(c_i) | 1 \leq i \leq n-k-2\}$. Then, $|C| = n - 2$.
4. (a) In the case that $C(s) \in C$: (See Fig. 3.)

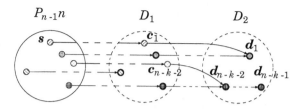

Fig. 3. Case $C(s) \in \mathcal{C}$.

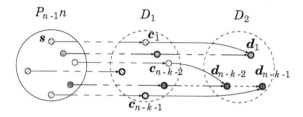

Fig. 4. Selection of a parent node c_{n-k-1}.

i. For a node d_{n-k-1}, select a parent node c_{n-k-1} of d_{n-k-1} which satisfies the following condition in a greedy manner.

$$\text{Condition}: C(c_{n-k-1}) \notin \mathcal{C}.$$

ii. Let $D_1 \leftarrow D_1 \cup \{c_{n-k-1}\}$, and $\mathcal{C} \leftarrow \mathcal{C} \cup C(c_{n-k-1}) - C(s)$. See Fig. 4.

iii. Let v_i $(1 \le i \le n-2)$ be nodes which belong to the classes in $\mathcal{C}$ and also belong to the subrotator graph $P_{n-1}n$.

iv. In $P_{n-1}n$, obtain $n-2$ paths from s to v_i $(1 \le i \le n-2)$ which are disjoint except for s by calling the algorithm recursively.

v. Establish paths from v_i $(1 \le i \le n-2)$ and s to corresponding nodes in D_1 within the classes.

vi. Select edges $c_i \to d_i$ $(1 \le i \le n-k-1)$. See Fig. 5.

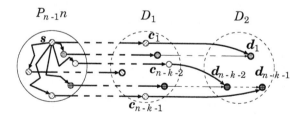

Fig. 5. Establishment of paths.

(b) In the case that $C(\boldsymbol{s}) \notin \mathcal{C}$: (See Fig. 6.)

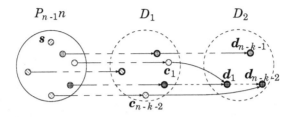

Fig. 6. Case $C(s) \notin \mathcal{C}$

i. Let $\boldsymbol{v}_i$ $(1 \leq i \leq n - 2)$ be the nodes which belong to the classes in $\mathcal{C}$ and also belong to the subrotator graph $P_{n-1}n$.
ii. In $P_{n-1}n$, obtain $n - 2$ paths from the node $\boldsymbol{s}$ to $\boldsymbol{v}_i$ $(1 \leq i \leq n - 2)$ which are disjoint except for $\boldsymbol{s}$ by calling the algorithm recursively.
iii. Establish paths from $\boldsymbol{v}_i$ $(1 \leq i \leq n - 2)$ to corresponding nodes in D_1 within the classes.
iv. Select edges $\boldsymbol{c}_i \rightarrow \boldsymbol{d}_i$ $(1 \leq i \leq n - k - 2)$. See Fig. 7.

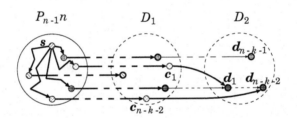

Fig. 7. Selection of edges $c_i \rightarrow d_i$.

v. Let $P_{n-1}l$ be the subrotator graph which includes $\boldsymbol{d}_{n-k-1}$.
vi. Let $\tilde{\boldsymbol{s}}$ represent a node which belongs to $C(\boldsymbol{s})$ and $P_{n-1}l$. Then we can select a path from $\boldsymbol{s}$ to the node $\tilde{\boldsymbol{s}}$ within the class $C(\boldsymbol{s})$.
vii. Let $\boldsymbol{l}_i$ $(1 \leq i \leq n - 2)$ represent the nodes which belong to the classes in $\mathcal{C}$ and also belong to the subrotator graph $P_{n-1}l$.
viii. In $P_{n-1}l$, construct $n - 2$ internally disjoint paths from $\tilde{\boldsymbol{s}}$ to $\boldsymbol{d}_{n-k-1}$[7]. Select a path $\tilde{\boldsymbol{s}} \rightarrow \boldsymbol{d}_{n-k-1}$ among them which does not include none of $n - 3$ nodes $\{\boldsymbol{l}_1, \boldsymbol{l}_2, \cdots, \boldsymbol{l}_{n-2}\} - \{\boldsymbol{d}_{n-k-1}\}$. See Fig. 8.

Lemma 4. *The $n - 1$ paths $\boldsymbol{s} \rightarrow \boldsymbol{d}_i$ $(1 \leq i \leq n - 1)$ established in Procedure 1 are disjoint except for $\boldsymbol{s}$. Additionally, the sum of the length of paths established in Procedure 1 excluding those which are constructed by the recursive call of this algorithm is of $O(n^2)$.*

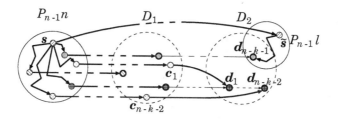

Fig. 8. Establishment of paths.

Proof. The proof is divided into two cases depending on whether $C(s)$ is included in $\mathcal{C}$ or not.

1. $C(s) \in \mathcal{C}$

   The paths selected in step 4(a)iv of Procedure 1 are disjoint except for s by the induction hypothesis. The $n-1$ paths selected in step 4(a)v are known to be disjoint because of property 2 of classes. The paths selected in step 4(a)v and the edges in step 4(a)vi are apparently disjoint except for the nodes c_i $(1 \le i \le n - k - 1)$. All the nodes which are used to construct the paths selected in step 4(a)iv have the figure n in the last position of their labels. In addition, all the nodes which are used to construct the paths selected in step 4(a)v and the edges selected in step 4(a)vi have last figures other than n in their labels except for v_i $(1 \le i \le n - 2)$ and s. Hence, the paths selected in step 4(a)iv and the paths and edges selected in steps 4(a)v and 4(a)vi are trivially disjoint. Therefore, if $C(s)$ is in the collection $\mathcal{C}$, the $n - 1$ paths constructed by Procedure 1 are disjoint except for node s.

   In addition, the sum of the length of the $n - 1$ paths established in step 4(a)v is of $O(n^2)$. The sum of the length of the $n - k - 1$ edges selected in step 4(a)vi is of $O(n)$. Summing up them, in the case of $C(s) \in \mathcal{C}$, the sum of the length of paths established in Procedure 1 excluding those which are constructed by the recursive call of the algorithm is of $O(n^2)$.

2. $C(s) \notin \mathcal{C}$

   Following similar reasoning as in the case of $C(s) \in \mathcal{C}$, the paths selected in steps 4(b)ii to 4(b)iv are disjoint except for s by using the induction hypothesis. The $n - 2$ paths selected in steps 4(b)ii to 4(b)iv and the edges selected in step 4(b)vi are known to be disjoint except for s because of property 2 of classes. The path $\tilde{s} \to d_{n-k-1}$ selected in step 4(b)viii and the paths selected in steps 4(b)ii to 4(b)vi are disjoint except for $\tilde{s}$. Therefore, if the class $C(s)$ is not in the collection $\mathcal{C}$, the $n-1$ paths selected in Procedure 1 are disjoint except for s.

   Moreover, the sum of the length of the $n - 2$ paths established in step 4(b)iii is of $O(n^2)$. The sum of the length of the $n - k - 2$ edges selected in step 4(b)iv is of $O(n)$. In addition, the length of each path selected in steps 4(b)vi and 4(b)viii is of $O(n)$. Summing up them, in the case of $C(s) \notin \mathcal{C}$, the sum of the length of paths established in Procedure 1 excluding those which are constructed by the recursive call of the algorithm is of $O(n^2)$. □

3.2   Case II-1

In this subsection, we will consider the case that there is at most one destination node in each class and there is a destination node in the class to which the source node s belongs. By Procedure 2 below, we can construct $n - 1$ paths from s to $n - 1$ nodes in D which are disjoint except for s.

Procedure 2

1. Let $\tilde{b}$ be the destination node which belongs to the class $C(s)$.
2. Select paths within the class $C(s)$ from s to $\tilde{b}$.
3. Let v_i ($1 \leq i \leq n - 2$) represent the nodes in $P_{n-1}n$ and also in the classes to which the $n - 2$ nodes in the set $D - \{\tilde{b}\}$ belong.
4. Obtain the paths from s to v_i ($1 \leq i \leq n - 2$) which are disjoint except for s by calling the algorithm recursively.
5. Select a path within the class from each node v_i ($1 \leq i \leq n - 2$) to the corresponding node in $D - \{\tilde{b}\}$.

Lemma 5. *The $n - 1$ paths, $s \rightarrow d_i$ ($1 \leq i \leq n - 1$), selected in Procedure 2 are disjoint except for s. Additionally, the sum of the length of paths established in Procedure 2 excluding those which are constructed by the recursive call of this algorithm is of $O(n^2)$.*

Proof. The paths selected in step 4 of Procedure 2 are disjoint except for s by the induction hypothesis. The paths selected in step 2 and the paths selected in step 5 are disjoint because of property 2 of classes. All the nodes on the paths selected in step 4 have the figure n in the last position of their labels. In addition, all the nodes which are used to construct paths selected in steps 2 and 5 have last figures other than n in their labels, except for s and v_i ($1 \leq i \leq n - 2$). Hence, the paths selected in step 4 and the paths selected in steps 2 and 5 are disjoint except for s and v_i ($1 \leq i \leq n - 2$). Therefore, the $n - 1$ paths constructed in Procedure 2 are disjoint except for the source node s.

Moreover, the length of the path selected in step 2 is of $O(n)$ and the sum of the length of paths selected in step 5 is of $O(n^2)$. Summing up them, the sum of the length of paths established in Procedure 2 excluding those which are constructed by the recursive call of the algorithm is of $O(n^2)$.   □

3.3   Case II-2-A

In this subsection, we will consider the case that there is at most one destination node in each class, there is no destination node in the class to which the source node s belongs and all the destination nodes belong to the subrotator graph $P_{n-1}n$ to which the source node s belongs. Procedure 3 below gives the $n - 1$ paths from s to $n - 1$ destination nodes in D which are disjoint except for s.

Procedure 3

1. Let $D_1 = \{d_i | 1 \leq i \leq n - 2\}$ and $D_2 = \{d_{n-1}\}$.
2. Obtain $n - 2$ paths from s to $n - 2$ destination nodes in D_1 which are disjoint except for the node s by calling the algorithm recursively. Here, if the destination node d_{n-1} is on one of the paths obtained, say, a path from s to a node d_k, then exchange the specifications of nodes d_{n-1} and d_k.
3. Let v represent a node in $P_{n-1}1$ which belongs to the class $C(d_{n-1})$.
4. Select an edge $s \rightarrow (2, 3, \cdots, n, 1)$.
5. In $P_{n-1}1$, establish the shortest path from $(2, 3, \cdots, n, 1)$ to v.
6. Construct a path from v to the destination node d_{n-1} within the class.

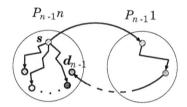

Fig. 9. Case II-2-A.

Lemma 6. *The $n - 1$ paths $s \rightarrow d_i$ $(1 \leq i \leq n - 1)$ selected in Procedure 3 are disjoint except for s. Additionally, the sum of the length of paths established in Procedure 3 excluding those which are constructed by the recursive call of this algorithm is of $O(n)$.*

Proof. The $n - 2$ paths selected in step 2 of Procedure 3 are disjoint except for s by the induction hypothesis. The nodes on the paths selected in step 2 have figure n in the last position of their labels. In addition, the nodes on the paths selected in steps 4 to 6 have figures other than n in the last position of their labels, except for s and d_{n-1}. Hence, the paths selected in step 2 and the paths selected in steps 4 to 6 are disjoint except for s and d_{n-1}. Moreover, the node d_{n-1} does not appear on the paths selected in step 2. Therefore, the $n - 1$ paths established in Procedure 3 are disjoint except for s.

Moreover, the length of the edge selected in step 4 is of $O(1)$. The length of the shortest path in step 5 is of $O(n)$. In addition, the length of the path constructed in step 6 is of $O(n)$. Summing up them, the sum of the length of paths established in Procedure 3 excluding those which are constructed by the recursive call of the algorithm is of $O(n)$. □

3.4   Case II-2-B-a

In this subsection, we will consider the case which is characterized as follows:

- there is at most one destination node in each class,
- there is no destination node in the class to which the source node s belongs,
- there are some destination nodes which do not belong to the subrotator graph $P_{n-1}n$, and
- at most one destination node exists in a subrotator graph other than $P_{n-1}n$.

By Procedure 4 below, we can construct the $n-1$ paths from s to $n-1$ destination nodes in D which are disjoint except for s.

Procedure 4

1. Let D_1 and D_2 represent the set of destination nodes in $P_{n-1}n$ and other destinations, respectively. Here, we can assume $D_2 = \{d_1, d_2, \cdots, d_k\}$ $(1 \leq k \leq n-1)$ without loss of generality.
2. Additionally, we can assume without loss of generality that the node d_k has the smallest figure in the last position in its label among the nodes in D_2.
3. Let each destination node d_i belong to the subrotator graph $P_{n-1}l_i$ $(1 \leq i \leq k-1)$.
4. Select $k-1$ nodes v_i $(1 \leq i \leq k-1)$ in $P_{n-1}n$ which satisfy following conditions in a greedy manner.

    Condition 1 : The first figure of the label of v_i is l_i.
    Condition 2 : $v_i \notin D_1$.

5. Obtain $n-2$ paths from s to $D_1 \cup \{v_i | 1 \leq i \leq k-1\}$ which are disjoint except for s by calling the algorithm recursively.
6. For each v_i $(1 \leq i \leq k-1)$, select $v_i \rightarrow R_n(v_i)$.
7. For each $R_n(v_i)$ $(1 \leq i \leq k-1)$, select a shortest path from $R_n(v_i)$ to d_i.
8. Let $P_{n-1}l$ be a subrotator graph to which d_k belongs.
9. Let $\tilde{s}$ be a node which is in the class $C(s)$ and also belongs to $P_{n-1}l$.
10. Select a path from s to $\tilde{s}$ within the class $C(s)$.
11. Establish a shortest path from $\tilde{s}$ to d_k.

Lemma 7. *The $n-1$ paths $s \rightarrow d_i$ $(1 \leq i \leq n-1)$ selected in Procedure 4 are disjoint except for s. Additionally, the sum of the length of paths established in Procedure 4 excluding those which are constructed by the recursive call of this algorithm is of $O(n^2)$.*

Proof. The paths selected in step 5 of Procedure 4 are disjoint except for s by the induction hypothesis. The paths selected in steps 6 and 7 have the figure l_i in the last positions of their labels. Hence, they are disjoint. The nodes on the paths selected in step 5 have the figure n in the last position of their labels. Additionally, the nodes on the paths selected in steps 6 and 7 have figures other than n in the last positions of their labels except for v_i $(1 \leq i \leq k-1)$. Hence, the paths selected in step 5 and the paths selected in steps 6 and 7 are disjoint except for s and v_i $(1 \leq i \leq k-1)$. Similarly, the paths selected in steps 10 and

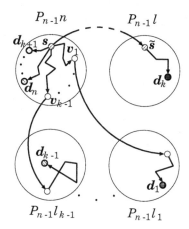

Fig. 10. Case II-2-B-a.

11 and the paths selected in steps 5 to 7 are easily proved to be disjoint except for s. Therefore, the $n - 1$ paths established in Procedure 4 are disjoint except for s.

Additionally, the sum of the length of the $k - 1$ edges selected in step 6 is of $O(n)$. the sum of the length of the $k - 1$ shortest paths selected in step 7 is of $O(n^2)$, and the sum of the length of the path selected in step 10 is of $O(n)$. Finally, the shortest path established in step 11 has of $O(n)$ length. Summing up them, the sum of the length of paths established in Procedure 4 excluding those which are constructed by the recursive call of the algorithm is of $O(n^2)$. □

3.5   Case II-2-B-b

Finally, in this subsection, we will consider the case which is characterized as follows:

- there is at most one destination node in each class,
- there is no destination node in the class to which the source node s belongs,
- there are some destination nodes which do not belong to the subrotator graph $P_{n-1}n$, and
- there exist multiple destination nodes in a subrotator graph other than $P_{n-1}n$.

Procedure 5 below constructs $n - 1$ paths from s to $n - 1$ destination nodes in D which are disjoint except for the source s.

Procedure 5

1. Select a path from s to the node of a subrotator graph which has multiple destination nodes within the class $C(s)$. Let $P_{n-1}l$ and $\tilde{s}$ represent the subrotator graph and the node, respectively. Additionally, let $D_1 = \{d_1, d_2, \cdots, d_k\}$ $(k \leq n - 1)$ be the set of destination nodes in $P_{n-1}l$.

2. For each class to which $n-2$ destination nodes in $D - \{d_1\}$ belong, let each l_i $(1 \leq i \leq n-2)$ represent a node which is in the class and belongs to $P_{n-1}l$.

3. In $P_{n-1}l$, construct $n-2$ internally disjoint paths from $\tilde{s}$ to d_1[7]. If each path includes one of l_i's, the subpath from $\tilde{s}$ to d_2 is selected, and let $D_2 \leftarrow \{d_2\}$. Otherwise, one of the paths from $\tilde{s}$ to d_1 which do not include the nodes l_i's at all is selected, and let $D_2 \leftarrow \{d_1\}$.

4. For each of $n-2$ classes to which each node in $D - D_2$ belongs, let each v_i $(1 \leq i \leq n-2)$ represent the node which is in the class and also belongs to $P_{n-1}n$.

5. Obtain the paths from s to v_i $(1 \leq i \leq n-2)$ which are disjoint except for s by calling the algorithm recursively.

6. Select paths from each v_i $(1 \leq i \leq n-2)$ to the corresponding node in $D - D_2$ within the class.

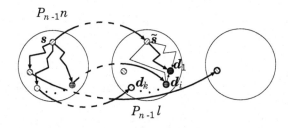

Fig. 11. Case II-2-B-b.

Lemma 8. *The $n-1$ paths $s \to d_i$ $(1 \leq i \leq n-1)$ constructed in Procedure 5 are disjoint except for s. Additionally, the sum of the length of paths established in Procedure 5 excluding those which are constructed by the recursive call of this algorithm is of $O(n^2)$.*

Proof. The paths selected in the step 5 in Procedure 5 are disjoint except for s from the hypothesis of induction. From the property 2 of classes, the paths selected in the step 6 are disjoint. The nodes on the paths selected in the step 5 have the figure n in the last positions of their labels. Additionally, the nodes on the paths selected in the step 6 have other figures than n in the last position of their labels except for v_i $(1 \leq i \leq n-2)$. Hence, the paths selected in the step 5 and the paths selected in the step 6 are disjoint except for s and v_i $(1 \leq i \leq n-2)$. Similarly, the paths selected in the steps 1 and 3 and the paths selected in the steps 5 and 6 are easily proved to be disjoint except for s. Therefore, the $n-1$ paths established in Procedure 5 are disjoint except for s.

Additionally, the lengths of the paths selected in step 1 and 3 are both of $O(n)$. The sum of the length of the $n-2$ paths selected in step 6 is of $O(n^2)$, Summing up them, the sum of the length of paths established in Procedure 5 excluding those which are constructed by the recursive call of the algorithm is of $O(n^2)$. □

Theorem 9. *The $n-1$ paths constructed by Procedures from 1 to 5 are disjoint except for s. The sum of the length of paths is of $O(n^3)$.*

Proof. From Lemmas 4 to 8, the proof is trivial. □

Theorem 10. *The complexity of the algorithm is $O(n^5)$.*

Proof. We assume that a label of a node is represented by a linear array of n elements. Let $T(n)$ represent the time complexity of our algorithm for an n-rotator graph.

The first case branching operation in our algorithm is begun with calculation of nodes each of which belongs to the same class as each destination node and also belongs to the subrotator graph $P_{n-1}n$. These nodes can be used as representatives of classes to which destination nodes belong. This calculation takes $O(n^3)$ of time complexity. The other tests for other branching can be performed less than $O(n^3)$. Now, the destination nodes are classified into classes and each class has a subset of destination nodes.

In Procedure 1, steps 2 and 4(b)viii are governing and they take $O(n^4)$ of time complexity. The algorithm for the node-to-node disjoint paths problem included in step 4(b)viii is of $O(n^3)$ of time complexity and the sum of the length of paths is of $O(n^2)$[7]. Hence, the time complexity of Procedure 1 is $T(n) = T(n-1) + O(n^4)$.

Procedure 2 is governed by step 5 which is of $O(n^2)$ of complexity. Therefore, the time complexity of Procedure 2 is $T(n) = T(n-1) + O(n^2)$.

In Procedure 3, the check after the recursive call in step 2 is governing. The sum of length of paths is of $O(n^3)$, and it take $O(n)$ of time to compare two labels, step 3 requires $O(n^4)$ of time complexity. Hence, the complexity of Procedure 3 is $T(n) = T(n-1) + O(n^4)$.

In Procedure 4, step 4 and 7 takes $O(n^4)$ of time complexity and it is governing. So, the complexity of Procedure 4 is $T(n) = T(n-1) + O(n^4)$.

Procedure 5 is governed by step 3 which is similar to step 4(b)viii of Procedure 1 and takes $O(n^4)$ of time complexity. Therefore, the time complexity of Procedure 5 is $T(n) = T(n-1) + O(n^4)$.

From above discussion, the time complexity of our algorithm is represented by $T(n) = T(n-1) + O(n^4)$ which results in $T(n) = O(n^5)$. □

4   Conclusions

In this paper, we have presented an algorithm for the node-to-set disjoint paths problem in n-rotator graphs which is of polynomial order of n. Future works include measurement of average sum of paths by computer simulation and improvement of the algorithm.

References

1. Akers, S. B. and Krishnamurthy, B.: A group theoretic model for symmetric interconnection networks. IEEE Trans. Comp. **38** (1989) 555–566
2. Bao, F., et al.: Reliable broadcasting and secure distributing in channel networks. IEICE Trans. Fundamentals **E81-A** (1998) 796–806
3. Corbett, P. F.: Rotator graphs: An efficient topology for point-to-point multiprocessor networks. IEEE Trans. Parallel and Distributed Systems **3** (1992) 622–626
4. Dandamudi, S. P. and Eager, D. L.: Hierarchical interconnection networks for multicomputer systems. IEEE Trans. Comp. **39** (1990) 786–797
5. Ghose, K. and Desai, K. R.: Hierarchical cubic networks. IEEE Trans. Parallel and Distributed Systems **6**(1995) 427–435
6. Gu, Q.-P. and Peng, S.: Node-to-set disjoint paths problem in star graphs. Information Processing Letters **62**(1997) 201–207
7. Hamada, Y., et al.: Nonadaptive fault-tolerant file transmission in rotator graphs. IEICE Trans. Fundamentals **E79-A** (1996) 477–482
8. Hwang, K. and Ghosh, J.: Hypernet — A communication-efficient architecture for constructing massively parallel computers. IEEE. Trans. Comp. **C-36** (1987) 1450–1466
9. Malluhi, Q. M. and Bayoumi, M. A.: The hierarchical hypercube — A new interconnection topology for massively parallel systems. IEEE Trans. Parallel and Distributed Systems **5** (1994) 17–30
10. Preparata, F. P. and Vuillemin, J.: The cube-connected cycles — A versatile network for parallel computation. CACM **24** (1981), 300–309
11. Rabin, M. O.: Efficient dispersal of information for security, load balancing, and fault tolerance. JACM **36** (1989), 335–348
12. Wan, P.-J.: Conflict-free channel set assignment for an optical cluster interconnection network based on rotator digraphs. Theoretical Computer Science **207** (1998) 193–201

On Simulation-Checking with Sequential Systems

Antonín Kučera*

Faculty of Informatics, Masaryk University, Czech Republic (tony@fi.muni.cz)

Abstract. We present new complexity results for simulation-checking and model-checking with infinite-state systems generated by pushdown automata and their proper subclasses of one-counter automata and one-counter nets (one-counter nets are 'weak' one-counter automata computationally equivalent to Petri nets with at most one unbounded place).

As for simulation-checking, we show the following: a) simulation equivalence between pushdown processes and finite-state processes is **EXPTIME**-complete; b) simulation equivalence between processes of one-counter automata and finite-state processes is **coNP**-hard; c) simulation equivalence between processes of one-counter nets and finite-state processes is in **P** (to the best of our knowledge, it is the first (and rather tight) polynomiality result for simulation with infinite-state processes).

As for model-checking, we prove that a) the problem of simulation-checking between processes of pushdown automata (or one-counter automata, or one-counter nets) and finite-state processes are polynomially reducible to the model-checking problem with a fixed formula $\varphi \equiv \nu X.[z]\langle z \rangle X$ of the modal μ-calculus. Consequently, model-checking with φ is **EXPTIME**-complete for pushdown processes and **coNP**-hard for processes of one-counter automata; b) model-checking with a fixed formula $\Diamond[a]\Diamond[b]\mathtt{ff}$ of the logic EF (a simple fragment of CTL) is **NP**-hard for processes of OC nets, and model-checking with another fixed formula $\Box\langle a \rangle\Box\langle b \rangle\mathtt{tt}$ of EF is **coNP**-hard. Consequently, model-checking with any temporal logic which can express these simple formulae is computationally hard even for the (very simple) sequential processes of OC-nets.

1 Introduction

Two important approaches to formal verification of concurrent systems are *equivalence-checking* and *model-checking*. In both cases, a process is formally understood to be (associated with) a state in a *transition system*, which is a triple $\mathcal{T} = (S, Act, \rightarrow)$ where S is a set of *states*, Act is a finite set of *actions*, and $\rightarrow \subseteq S \times Act \times S$ is a *transition relation*. We write $s \xrightarrow{a} t$ instead of $(s, a, t) \in \rightarrow$ and we extend this notation to elements of Act^* in the natural way. A state t is *reachable* from a state s, written $s \rightarrow^* t$, iff $s \xrightarrow{w} t$ for some $w \in Act^*$.

In the equivalence-checking approach, one describes the *specification* (the intended behavior) and the actual *implementation* of a concurrent process as states in transition systems, and then it is shown that they are *equivalent*. Here the notion of equivalence can be formalized in various ways according to specific needs of a given practical

---

* Supported by the Grant Agency of the Czech Republic, grants No. 201/98/P046 and No. 201/00/1023.

problem (see, e.g., [24] for an overview). A favorite approach is the one of *simulation* equivalence which has been found appropriate in many situations and consequently its accompanying theory has been developed very intensively. Let $\mathcal{T} = (S, Act, \rightarrow)$ be a transition system. A binary relation $R \subseteq S \times S$ is a *simulation* iff whenever $(s, t) \in R$, then for each $s \xrightarrow{a} s'$ there is some $t \xrightarrow{a} t'$ such that $(s', t') \in R$. A process s is *simulated* by t, written $s \sqsubseteq_s t$, iff there is a simulation R such that $(s, t) \in R$. Processes s, t are *simulation equivalent*, written $s =_s t$, iff they can simulate each other. Simulation can also be viewed as a *game* — imagine there are two tokens put on states s and t. Now two players, Al and Ex, start to play a *simulation game* which consists of a (possibly infinite) number of *rounds* where each round is performed as follows: Al takes the token which was put on s originally and moves it along a transition labelled by (some) a; the task of Ex is to move the other token along a transition with the same label. Al wins the game iff after a finite number of rounds Ex cannot respond to Al's final attack. We see that $s \sqsubseteq_s t$ iff Ex has a universal defending strategy, i.e., Al never wins provided Ex plays in a sufficiently 'clever' way. We use simulation game as some points to give a more intuitive justification for our claims. Finally, let us note that simulation can also be used to relate states of *different* transition systems; formally, two systems are considered to be a single one by taking their disjoint union.

In the model-checking approach, desired properties of the implementation are encoded as formulae of certain temporal logic (interpreted over transition systems) and then it is demonstrated that the implementation satisfies the formulae. There are many systems of temporal logic differing in their expressive power, decidability, complexity, and other aspects (see, e.g., [23,6]). In this paper we only work with one (fixed) formula $\varphi \equiv \nu X.[z]\langle z \rangle X$ of the *modal μ-calculus* [13] and some other (fixed) formulae of its very simple fragment which is known as the *EF logic* (the logic EF can also be seen as a natural fragment of CTL [6]). A formal definition of the syntax and semantics of the modal μ-calculus is omitted due to space constraints (we refer, e.g., to [13]). However, we do explain the meaning of φ in Section 3. Formulae of the logic EF look as follows:

$$\psi ::= \texttt{tt} \mid \psi \wedge \psi \mid \neg \psi \mid \langle a \rangle \psi \mid \Diamond \psi$$

Here a ranges over a given set of atomic actions. Dual operators to $\langle a \rangle$ and $\Diamond$ are $[a]$ and $\Box$, defined by $[a]\psi \equiv \neg \langle a \rangle \neg \psi$ and $\Box \psi \equiv \neg \Diamond \neg \psi$, respectively. Let $\mathcal{T} = (S, Act, \rightarrow)$ be a transition system. The *denotation* $\llbracket \psi \rrbracket$ of a formula ψ is the set of states where the formula *holds*; it is defined as follows:

$$\llbracket \texttt{tt} \rrbracket = S$$
$$\llbracket \psi_1 \wedge \psi_2 \rrbracket = \llbracket \psi_1 \rrbracket \cap \llbracket \psi_2 \rrbracket$$
$$\llbracket \neg \psi \rrbracket = S - \llbracket \psi \rrbracket$$
$$\llbracket \langle a \rangle \psi \rrbracket = \{ s \in S \mid \exists t \in S : s \xrightarrow{a} t \wedge t \in \llbracket \psi \rrbracket \}$$
$$\llbracket \Diamond \psi \rrbracket = \{ s \in S \mid \exists t \in S : s \rightarrow^* t \wedge t \in \llbracket \psi \rrbracket \}$$

The 'language' of transition systems is not very practical – concurrent systems often have a very large (or even infinite) state-space and hence it is not feasible to define their semantics 'directly' by means of transition systems. Therefore, 'higher' languages allowing to construct compact definitions of large systems have been proposed and studied. In this paper we mainly work with (subclasses of) pushdown automata, which are considered as a fundamental model of sequential behaviors in the framework of concurrency theory (for example, one can conveniently model programs consisting of mutually recursive procedures in the syntax of PDA, and existing verification techniques for PDA are then applicable to, e.g., some problems of data-flow analysis [7]). Formally, a *pushdown automaton* is a tuple $\Delta = (Q, \Gamma, Act, \delta)$ where Q is a finite set of *control states*, Γ is a finite *stack alphabet*, Act is a finite *input alphabet*, and $\delta : (Q \times \Gamma) \to 2^{Act \times (Q \times \Gamma^*)}$ is a *transition function* with finite image. We can assume (w.l.o.g.) that each transition increases the height (or length) of the stack at most by one (each PDA can be efficiently transformed to this kind of normal form). In the rest of this paper we adopt a more intuitive notation, writing $pA \xrightarrow{a} q\beta \in \delta$ instead of $(a, (q, \beta)) \in \delta(p, A)$. To Δ we associate the transition system $\mathcal{T}_\Delta$ where $Q \times \Gamma^*$ is the set of states (we write $p\alpha$ instead of (p, α)), Act is the set of actions, and the transition relation is determined by $pA\alpha \xrightarrow{a} q\beta\alpha \iff pA \xrightarrow{a} q\beta \in \delta$.

A natural and important subclass of pushdown automata is the class of *one-counter automata* where the stack behaves like a *counter*. Such a restriction is reasonable because in practice we often meet systems which can be abstracted to finite-state programs operating on a single unbounded variable. For example, network protocols can maintain the count on how many unacknowledged messages have been sent, printer spool should know how many processes are waiting in the input queue, etc. Formally, a *one-counter automaton* $\mathcal{A}$ is a pushdown automaton with just two stack symbols I and Z; the transition function δ of Δ is a union of functions δ_Z and δ_I where $\delta_Z : (Q \times \{Z\}) \to 2^{Act \times (Q \times (\{I\}^*\{Z\}))}$ and $\delta_I : (Q \times \{I\}) \to 2^{Act \times (Q \times \{I\}^*)}$. Hence, Z works like a bottom symbol (which cannot be removed), and the number of pushed I's represents the counter value. Processes of $\mathcal{A}$ (i.e., states of $\mathcal{T}_\Delta$) are of the form pI^iZ which is abbreviated to $p(i)$ in the rest of this paper. Again, we assume (w.l.o.g) that each transition increases the counter at most by one. A proper subclass of one-counter automata of its own interest are *one-counter nets*. Intuitively, OC-nets are 'weak' OC-automata which cannot test for zero explicitly. They are computationally equivalent to a subclass of Petri nets [22] with (at most) one unbounded place. Hence, one-counter nets can be used, e.g., to model systems consisting of producers and consumers which share an infinite buffer (a non-empty buffer enables the execution of consumers but it need not be tested for zero explicitly). Formally, a *one-counter net* $\mathcal{N}$ is a one-counter automaton such that whenever $pZ \xrightarrow{a} qI^iZ \in \delta$, then $pI \xrightarrow{a} qI^{i+1} \in \delta$. In other words, each transition which is enabled at zero-level is also enabled at (each) non-zero-level. Hence, there are no 'zero-specific' transitions which could be used to 'test for zero'.

The state of the art: Let **PDA**, **BPA**, **OC-A**, **OC-N**, and **FS** be the classes of all processes of pushdown automata, stateless pushdown automata, one-counter automata, one-counter nets, and finite-state systems, respectively. Moreover, let **PN**, **BPP**, and **PA** denote the classes of all processes of Petri nets [22], basic parallel processes [5], and process algebra [4], respectively. The problems of simulation preorder and simulation equivalence between processes of classes **A** and **B** are denoted by $\mathbf{A} \sqsubseteq_s \mathbf{B}$ and $\mathbf{A} =_s \mathbf{B}$, respectively. The problem of simulation-checking with (certain classes of) infinite-state systems has been attracting attention for almost a decade; here we only mention some of the most relevant results. First, it was shown in [8] that the problems **BPA** $\sqsubseteq_s$ **BPA**

and **BPA** $=_s$ **BPA** are undecidable. The undecidability of **BPP** $\sqsubseteq_s$ **BPP** and **BPP** $=_s$ **BPP** was proved in [9]. An interesting positive result is [1] where it is shown that **OC-N** $\sqsubseteq_s$ **OC-N** (and hence also **OC-N** $=_s$ **OC-N**) is decidable. However, **OC-A** $\sqsubseteq_s$ **OC-A** and **OC-A** $=_s$ **OC-A** are already undecidable [12]. The problem of checking simulation between infinite and finite-state systems was first examined in [11] where it is shown that **PN** $\sqsubseteq_s$ **FS**, **FS** $\sqsubseteq_s$ **PN**, and **PN** $=_s$ **FS** are decidable. A similar positive result was later demonstrated in [16] for the **PDA** $\sqsubseteq_s$ **FS**, **FS** $\sqsubseteq_s$ **PDA**, and **PDA** $=_s$ **FS** problems; some complexity estimation were also given (see below). Moreover, the problems **PA** $\sqsubseteq_s$ **FS**, **FS** $\sqsubseteq_s$ **PA**, and **PA** $=_s$ **FS** are proved to be undecidable.

The decidability and complexity of checking other behavioral equivalences (in particular, *strong* and *weak bisimilarity* [21,20]) between infinite and finite state systems also exist; we give a short comparison in the final section.

Our contribution: In our paper we present new complexity results for simulation-checking and model-checking problems with the above mentioned subclasses of pushdown processes. The most significant original contributions are summarized below together with a short discussion on previous work.

- **PDA** $=_s$ **FS** is **EXPTIME**-complete. Previously, there was a **coNP** lower bound for the problem [16] (this lower bound also works for **BPA** processes). In the same paper, the membership of **PDA** $=_s$ **FS** to **EXPTIME** has also been shown, hence here we only need to prove the **EXPTIME** lower bound.
- **OC-A** $=_s$ **FS** is **coNP**-hard. The problem whether this lower bound is tight is left open. Intuitively, the problem should be expected easier then for PDA processes, because there is a substantial simplification in the case of strong bisimilarity – the problem of strong bisimilarity with finite-state processes is in **P** for **OC-A** processes [14], but **PSPACE**-complete for **PDA** processes [19].
- **OC-N** $=_s$ **FS** is in **P**. In fact, we show that **OC-N** $\sqsubseteq_s$ **FS** and **FS** $\sqsubseteq_s$ **OC-N** are in **P**. To the best of our knowledge, this is the first (and rather tight) polynomiality result for simulation with infinite-state systems. Let us note that some equivalence-checking problems between processes of OC-nets and FS processes are still hard (for example, weak bisimilarity is **DP**-hard [14]), so the result is not immediate (see also the comments below).
- Next, we show that the problems of simulation preorder/equivalence between processes of **PDA** (or **OC-A**, or **OC-N**) and **FS** processes are reducible to the model-checking problem for the fixed formula $\varphi \equiv \nu X.[z]\langle z \rangle X$ of (the alternation-free fragment of) the modal μ-calculus. It is essentially a simple observation which was (in a similar form) used already in [2,16,18]. The point is that (due to the previous hardness results) we can conclude that the problem of model-checking with φ is **EXPTIME**-complete for **PDA** processes (the upper-bound is due to [25]) and **coNP**-hard for **OC-A** processes. An interesting thing is that the model-checking problem for stateless pushdown (i.e., **BPA**) processes and *any* fixed formula of the modal μ-calculus is already polynomial [25]. The classes of **BPA** and **OC-A** processes are rather natural but *incomparable* subclasses of **PDA** processes – we see that the absence of a finite control is a 'stronger' simplification than the replacement of the storage device (counter instead of stack) in this case.

As simulation between **OC-N** and **FS** processes is in **P**, the aforementioned technique does not yield any hardness result for model-checking with **OC-N** processes.

Therefore, we examine the problem directly – we prove that even model-checking with a simple fixed formula $\Diamond[a]\Diamond[b]\texttt{ff}$ of the logic EF is **NP**-hard for **OC-N** processes, and model-checking with another fixed formula $\Box\langle a\rangle\Box\langle b\rangle\texttt{tt}$ is **coNP**-hard. Hence, we can forget about an efficient model-checking procedure for **OC-N** processes and any modal logic which can express these simple formulae (unless **P = NP**).

2 Results about Equivalence-Checking

Theorem 1. *The problem of simulation equivalence between PDA processes and deterministic FS processes is **EXPTIME**-hard.*

Proof. We show **EXPTIME**-hardness by reduction from the acceptance problem for alternating LBA (which is known to be **EXPTIME**-complete). An *alternating LBA* is a tuple $\mathcal{M} = (Q, \Sigma, \delta, q_0, \vdash, \dashv, p)$ where $Q, \Sigma, \delta, q_0, \vdash$, and $\dashv$ are defined as for ordinary non-deterministic LBA (in particular, $\vdash$ and $\dashv$ are the left-end and right-end markers, resp.), and $p : Q \rightarrow \{\forall, \exists, acc, rej\}$ is a function which partitions the states of Q into *universal, existential, accepting*, and *rejecting*, respectively. We assume (w.l.o.g.) that δ is defined so that 'terminated' configurations (i.e., the ones from which there are no further computational steps) are exactly accepting and rejecting configurations. A *computational tree* for $\mathcal{M}$ on a word $w \in \Sigma^*$ is any (finite or infinite) tree T satisfying the following: the root of T is (labeled by) the initial configuration $q_0 \vdash w \dashv$ of $\mathcal{M}$, and if N is a node of $\mathcal{M}$ labeled by a configuration uqv where $u, v \in \Sigma^*$ and $q \in Q$, then the following holds:

- if q is accepting or rejecting, then T is a leaf;
- if q is existential, then T has one successor whose label is (some) configuration which can be reached from uqv in one computational step (according to δ);
- if q is universal, then T has m successors where m is the number of *all* configurations which can be reached from uqv in one step; those configurations are used as labels of the successors in one-to-one fashion.

$\mathcal{M}$ accepts w iff there is a finite computational tree T such that all leaves of T are accepting configurations.

Now we describe a polynomial algorithm which for a given alternating LBA $\mathcal{M} = (Q, \Sigma, \delta, q_0, \vdash, \dashv, p)$ and a word $w \in \Sigma^*$ constructs a process P of a PDA system Δ and a process F of a finite-state system $\mathcal{F}$ such that

- $P \sqsubseteq_s F$, and
- $F \sqsubseteq_s P$ iff $\mathcal{M}$ does not accept w.

Hence, $\mathcal{M}$ accepts w iff $P \neq_s F$ and we are (virtually) done.

Intuition: The underlying system $\mathcal{F}$ of F looks as follows (note the $\mathcal{F}$ is deterministic):

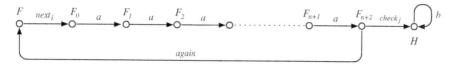

Intuitively, the goal of F is to demonstrate that there is an accepting computational tree for $\mathcal{M}$ on w, while P aims to show the converse. The game starts with the initial configuration $q_0 \vdash w \dashv$ stored in the stack of P. Now F 'chooses' the next configuration (i.e., the rule of δ which is to be applied to the current configuration stored at the top of stack) by emitting one of the $next_i$ actions. The quotes are important here because P is constructed in such a way that it has to accept the choice of F only if the control state of the current configuration is *existential*. If it is *universal*, P can 'ignore' the dictate of F and choose the next configuration according to its own will. The new configuration is then pushed to the stack of P (technically, it is done by guessing individual symbols and an auxiliary verification mechanism is added so that P cannot gain anything if it starts to cheat). As soon as P enters an accepting configuration, it 'dies' (i.e., it is not able to emit any action); and as soon as it enters a rejecting configuration, it starts to behave identically as F. Hence, if there is an accepting computational tree for $\mathcal{M}$ on w, then F can force P to enter an accepting configuration in finitely many rounds (and hence $F \not\sqsubseteq_s P$). If there is no accepting computational tree, then P can successfully defend; it either enters a rejecting configuration or the game goes forever. It means, in both cases, that $F \sqsubseteq_s P$. Moreover, a careful design of P ensures that $P \sqsubseteq_s F$ regardless whether $\mathcal{M}$ accept w or not. A full (formal) proof is omitted due to space constraints; it can be found in [15].   □

In the proof of our next theorem we use the technique for encoding assignments of Boolean variables in the structure of one-counter automata discovered in [14].

Theorem 2. *The problem of simulation equivalence between OC-A processes and FS processes is* **coNP**-*hard.*

Proof. We show **coNP**-hardness by reduction of the **coNP**-complete problem UNSAT. An instance is a Boolean formula ψ in CNF. The question is whether ψ is unsatisfiable.

Let $\psi \equiv C_1 \wedge \cdots \wedge C_m$ be a formula in CNF where C_i are clauses over propositional variables $x_1, \cdots, x_n$. We construct (in polynomial time) a process P of a OC-A system Δ and a process F of a finite-state system $\mathcal{F}$ such that $P \sqsubseteq_s F$ iff ψ is unsatisfiable. Then we simply consider the processes P' and F' which have the following outgoing transitions: $P' \xrightarrow{x} P, P' \xrightarrow{x} F$, and $F' \xrightarrow{x} F$ where x is a fresh action. Observe that P' is easily definable in the syntax of one-counter processes and F' in the syntax of finite-state processes. Clearly $F' \sqsubseteq_s P'$, and $P' \sqsubseteq_s F'$ iff $P \sqsubseteq_s F$. In other words, $P' =_s F'$ iff ψ is unsatisfiable and it proves our theorem.

It remains to show the construction of P, Δ, F, and $\mathcal{F}$. The set of actions of Δ and $\mathcal{F}$ is $Act = \{a, b, c_1, \ldots, c_m\}$. Let $A_i = Act - \{a, c_i\}$. The set of states of $\mathcal{F}$ is $\{F, F_1, \ldots, F_m\}$ and its transitions are $F \xrightarrow{a} F$, $F \xrightarrow{b} F_i$ for each $1 \le i \le m$, and $F_i \xrightarrow{y} F_i$ for each $y \in A_i$ and each $1 \le i \le m$. Hence, the system $\mathcal{F}$ looks as follows:

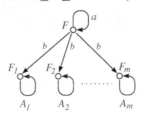

In the construction of Δ we rely on the following theorem of number theory (see, e.g., [3]): Let p_i be the ith prime number, and let $f : \mathbb{N} \to \mathbb{N}$ be a function which assigns to each n the sum $\sum_{i=1}^{n} p_i$. Then f is $\mathcal{O}(n^3)$. This fact ensures that Δ has only polynomially-many control states (see below).

The set of control states Q of Δ is $\{s, r\} \cup \{s_{\langle p_i, j \rangle} \mid 1 \leq i \leq n, 0 \leq j < p_i\}$. For each $1 \leq i \leq n$ we now define two sets of actions.

- $B_i = \{c_j \mid 1 \leq j \leq m,$ the variable x_i appears positively in the clause $C_j\}$
- $\overline{B}_i = \{c_j \mid 1 \leq j \leq m,$ the variable x_i appears negatively in the clause $C_j\}$

Transitions of Δ are defined as follows:

- $sZ \xrightarrow{a} sIZ, sI \xrightarrow{a} sII, sI \xrightarrow{b} rI$,
- $rI \xrightarrow{b} s_{\langle p_i, 0 \rangle} I$ for each $1 \leq i \leq n$,
- $s_{\langle p_i, j \rangle} I \xrightarrow{b} s_{\langle p_i, (j+1) \bmod p_i \rangle} \varepsilon$ for each $1 \leq i \leq n$ and each $0 \leq j < p_i$,
- $s_{\langle p_i, 0 \rangle} Z \xrightarrow{y} s_{\langle p_i, 0 \rangle} Z$ for each $0 \leq i \leq n$ and each $y \in B_i$.
- $s_{\langle p_i, j \rangle} Z \xrightarrow{y} s_{\langle p_i, j \rangle} Z$ for each $0 \leq i \leq n$, each $1 \leq j < p_i$, and each $y \in \overline{B}_i$.

The structure of the transition system associated to Δ is depicted in the following figure (transition systems associated to OC systems can be viewed as two-dimensional 'tables' with an infinite height where control states are used as column indexes and counter values as row indexes; as the outgoing transitions of a process $p(i)$ for $i > 0$ do not depend on the exact value of i, it suffices to depict the out-going transitions at the zero level and (some) non-zero level):

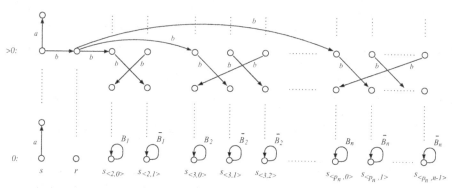

The initial state is $s(0)$. Intuitively, P first increases its counter, emitting a sequence of a's. Then it emits the first b action and changes its control state to r (preserving the value stored in the counter). To each state $r(l)$ we associate the (unique) assignment ν_l defined by $\nu_l(x_i) = \mathtt{tt}$ iff $r(l) \to^* s_{\langle p_i, 0 \rangle}(0)$ (i.e., $\nu_l(x_i) = \mathtt{ff}$ iff $r(l) \to^* s_{\langle p_i, j \rangle}(0)$ for some $1 \leq j < p_i$). Conversely, for each assignment ν there is $l \in \mathbb{N}$ such that $\nu = \nu_l$ (for example, we can put $l = \Pi_{j=0}^{n} f(j)$, where $f(j) = p_j$ if $\nu(x_j) = \mathtt{tt}$, and $f(j) = 1$ otherwise). Now it is easy to check that a clause C_k is true for an assignment ν_l iff at least one of the 'bottom' states $s_{\langle p_i, j \rangle}(0)$ where a c_k-loop is enabled (see above) is reachable from $r(l)$.

Let $s(l)$ be a state of P such that $\nu_l(\psi) = \mathtt{ff}$. It means that there is $1 \le k \le m$ such that $\nu_l(C_k) = \mathtt{ff}$. Hence, the process F can safely match the transition $s(l) \overset{b}{\to} r(l)$ by $F \overset{b}{\to} F_k$ (from that point on it can do everything except c_k). However, if there is some l such that $\nu_l(\psi) = \mathtt{tt}$, then F does not have any 'safe' matching move for the transition $s(l) \overset{b}{\to} r(l)$ because none of its F_k successors can do all of the c_i actions. Hence, ψ is unsatisfiable iff $s(0) \sqsubseteq_s F$. $\qquad\square$

Now we prove that simulation preorder and simulation equivalence between processes of one-counter *nets* and finite-state processes can be decided in polynomial time. To the best of our knowledge, these are the first polynomiality results for simulation with infinite-state systems. Intuitively, the crucial property which makes our proofs possible (and which does not hold for general one-counter automata) is the following kind of 'monotonicity' — if $p(i)$ is a process of a one-counter net, then $p(i) \sqsubseteq_s p(j)$ for every $j \ge i$.

It should be noted that in our next constructions we prefer simplicity to optimality. Therefore, it does not pay to evaluate the degrees of polynomials explicitly (though it would be of course possible) because they would considerably decrease after some straightforward optimizations. Our only aim here is to prove the membership to **P**.

Let $\mathcal{T} = (S, Act, \to)$ be a transition system. A family of $\sqsubseteq_s^i$, $i \in \mathbb{N}_0$ relations is defined inductively as follows:

- $s \sqsubseteq_s^0 t$ for all $s, t \in S$;
- $s \sqsubseteq_s^{i+1} t$ iff $s \sqsubseteq_s^i t$ and for each $s \overset{a}{\to} s'$ there is some $t \overset{a}{\to} t'$ such that $s' \sqsubseteq_s^i t'$.

Intuitively, $s \sqsubseteq_s^i t$ iff Ex has a defending strategy for the first i rounds of the simulation game. If we restrict ourselves to processes of *finitely-branching* transition systems (where each state has only finitely many a-successors for every action a), then $s \sqsubseteq_s t$ iff $s \sqsubseteq_s^i t$ for every $i \in \mathbb{N}_0$ (observe that transition systems generated by PDA are finitely-branching). This enables the following (straightforward) polynomial-time algorithm for checking simulation between finite-state processes:

Lemma 1. *Let $\mathcal{F} = (F, Act, \to)$ and $\mathcal{G} = (G, Act, \to)$ be finite-state systems with m and n states, respectively. Let $k = m \cdot n$. For all $f \in F$ and $g \in G$ we have that $f \sqsubseteq_s^k g$ iff $f \sqsubseteq_s^{k+1} g$ iff $f \sqsubseteq_s g$. Moreover, the relation $\sqsubseteq_s^k$ can be computed in time which is polynomial in the size of $\mathcal{F}$ and $\mathcal{G}$.*

Proof. If we start to construct the family of '$\sqsubseteq_s^i$' relations according to the above stated definition, we must reach the greatest fixed-point after (at most) k refinement rounds, because '$\sqsubseteq_s^0$' contains only k elements and $\sqsubseteq_s^i \subseteq \sqsubseteq_s^{i+1}$ for each $i \in \mathbb{N}_0$. It is clear that each refinement step can be computed in time which is polynomial in the size of $\mathcal{F}$ and $\mathcal{G}$. $\qquad\square$

Lemma 2. *The problem whether a OC-N process can be simulated by a finite-state process is in **P**.*

Proof. Let $\mathcal{N} = (Q, \{I, Z\}, Act, \delta)$ be a one-counter net and $\mathcal{F} = (F, Act, \to)$ a finite-state system. We show that (a description of) the simulation preorder between processes of $\mathcal{N}$ and $\mathcal{F}$ can be computed in time which is polynomial in the size of $\mathcal{N}$ and $\mathcal{F}$.

The first step of our algorithm is a construction of a *characteristic finite-state system* of $\mathcal{N}$, denoted $\mathcal{F}_\mathcal{N}$, which is defined as follows: $\mathcal{F}_\mathcal{N} = (\overline{Q}, Act, \rightarrow)$ where $\overline{Q} = \{\overline{p} \mid p \in Q\}$ and $\overline{p} \overset{a}{\rightarrow} \overline{q}$ iff $pI \overset{a}{\rightarrow} qI^i \in \delta(p, I)$ for some $i \in \mathbb{N}_0$. Hence, a process $\overline{p}$ of $\mathcal{F}_\mathcal{N}$ intuitively corresponds to a 'limit process' $p(\infty)$ of $\mathcal{N}$ (in particular, observe that $p(i) \sqsubseteq_s \overline{p}$ for all $p \in Q$ and $i \in \mathbb{N}_0$). It is obvious that the system $\mathcal{F}_\mathcal{N}$ can be constructed in linear time.

Next, for all $\overline{p} \in \overline{Q}$ and $f \in F$ we check whether $\overline{p} \sqsubseteq_s f$. It can be done in polynomial time (see Lemma 1). Now observe that if $\overline{p} \sqsubseteq_s f$ for given $\overline{p}$ and f, we can conclude that $p(i) \sqsubseteq_s f$ for *any* $i \in \mathbb{N}_0$, because $p(i) \sqsubseteq_s \overline{p}$. If $\overline{p} \not\sqsubseteq_s f$, then $\overline{p} \not\sqsubseteq_s^k f$ where $k = |Q| \cdot |F|$ (see Lemma 1). Hence, $\overline{p}$ can win the simulation game over f in (at most) k steps. It is clear that the process $p(k)$ can 'mimic' this winning strategy of $\overline{p}$, because the counter can be decreased at most by k within the first k moves (note that if we allowed to test the counter for zero, then $p(k)$ *could not* mimic the first k moves of $\overline{p}$ in general). The same applies to *any* process $p(i)$ where $i \geq k$, because then $p(k) \sqsubseteq_s p(i)$. To sum up, at this point we know if $p(i) \sqsubseteq_s f$ for all $p \in Q, f \in F$, and $i \geq k$. It remains to decide simulation between pairs of the form $(p(i), f)$ where $0 \leq i < k$. As there are only $|Q| \cdot |F| \cdot k = |Q|^2 \cdot |F|^2$ such states, we can use a simple refinement technique similar to the one of Lemma 1. Formally, we define a family of $\mathcal{R}^j$ relations inductively as follows:

- $\mathcal{R}^0 = \{(p(i), f) \mid i < k, p \in Q, f \in F\}$
- $\mathcal{R}^{j+1}$ consists of those pairs of the form $(p(i), f)$ for which we either have that
  · $\overline{p} \sqsubseteq_s g$, or $(p(i), f) \in \mathcal{R}^j$ and for each move $p(i) \overset{a}{\rightarrow} q(l)$ there is a move $f \overset{a}{\rightarrow} g$ such that $\overline{q} \sqsubseteq_s g$ or $(q(l), g) \in \mathcal{R}^j$.

Let $\mathcal{R}$ be the greatest fixed point of this refinement procedure. First, observe that $\mathcal{R}$ is computable in **P** because it is reached in (at most) $|Q|^2 \cdot |F|^2$ refinement steps and each step can be obviously computed in polynomial time. Now let us consider a pair of the form $(p(i), f)$ where $p \in Q$, $i < k$, and $f \in F$. If $(p(i), f) \notin \mathcal{R}$, then obviously $p(i) \not\sqsubseteq_s f$. On the other hand, if $(p(i), f) \in \mathcal{R}$, then $p(i) \sqsubseteq_s f$ because we can readily confirm that the relation $\mathcal{R} \cup \{(q(l), g) \mid q \in Q, l \in \mathbb{N}_0, g \in F, \overline{q} \sqsubseteq_s g\}$ is a simulation.

$\square$

Lemma 3. *The problem whether a finite-state process can be simulated by a OC-N process is in* **P**.

Proof. Let $\mathcal{N} = (Q, \{I, Z\}, Act, \delta)$ be a one-counter net and $\mathcal{F} = (F, Act, \rightarrow)$ a finite-state system. Similarly as in the previous lemma we show that (a description of) the simulation preorder between processes of $\mathcal{F}$ and $\mathcal{N}$ can be computed in time which is polynomial in the size of $\mathcal{N}$ and $\mathcal{F}$. However, the argument is slightly more complicated in this case.

We start with one auxiliary definition. For all $f \in F$ and $p \in Q$ we define the *frontier counter value*, denoted $\mathcal{V}(f, p)$, to be the least $i \in \mathbb{N}_0$ such that $f \sqsubseteq_s p(i)$; if there is no such i, we put $\mathcal{V}(f, p) = -1$. Our aim is to show that every frontier counter value is bounded by $|Q| \cdot |F|$, i.e., $\mathcal{V}(f, p) \leq |Q| \cdot |F|$ for all $f \in F$ and $p \in Q$. Let m

be the maximal frontier value. It suffices to prove that for each n such that $1 \leq n \leq m$ there are $f \in F$ and $p \in Q$ such that $\mathcal{V}(f,p) = n$. Let us suppose the converse, i.e., there is some $n \geq 1$ such that there is at least one frontier value greater then n, some frontier values are (possibly) less than n, but no frontier value equals to n. It follows directly from the definition of frontier points that the greatest simulation among the processes of $\mathcal{F}$ and $\mathcal{N}$ is the following relation $\mathcal{R}$:

$$\mathcal{R} = \{(f, p(i)) \mid f \in F, p \in Q, \mathcal{V}(f,p) \geq 0, i \geq \mathcal{V}(f,p)\}$$

Now we show that if there is some n with the above stated properties, than we can actually construct a simulation which is strictly larger than $\mathcal{R}$, which is a contradiction. Let $\mathcal{R}'$ be the following finite relation:

$$\mathcal{R}' = \{(g, q(c)) \mid g \in F, q \in Q, \mathcal{V}(g,q) > n, c = \mathcal{V}(g,q) - 1\}$$

As $n < m$, $\mathcal{R}'$ is clearly nonempty. We show that $\mathcal{R} \cup \mathcal{R}'$ is a simulation. To do that, it suffices to check the simulation condition for pairs of $\mathcal{R}'$, because $\mathcal{R}$ itself is a simulation. Let $(g, q(c)) \in \mathcal{R}'$ and $g \xrightarrow{a} h$. We need to find some move $q(c) \xrightarrow{a} \alpha$ such that the pair (h, α) is related by $\mathcal{R} \cup \mathcal{R}'$. However, as $(g, q(c)) \in \mathcal{R}'$, we have that $c = \mathcal{V}(g,q) - 1$ and hence $(g, q(c+1)) \in \mathcal{R}$. Therefore, there must be some move $q(c+1) \xrightarrow{a} r(l)$ such that $(h, r(l)) \in \mathcal{R}$ (also observe that $l \geq n$). It means that $q(c) \xrightarrow{a} r(l-1)$ (here we use the fact that $c \geq 1$). Now if $(h, r(l-1)) \in \mathcal{R}$, we are done immediately. If it is not the case, then l is the frontier counter value for h and r by definition, i.e., $l = \mathcal{V}(h,r)$. As $l \geq n$ and there is no frontier value which equals to n, we conclude that $l > n$ — but it means that $(h, r(l-1)) \in \mathcal{R}'$ by definition of $\mathcal{R}'$.

Let $k = |Q| \cdot |F|$. Now let us realize that if we could decide simulation for all pairs of the form $(f, p(k))$ in polynomial time, we would be done — observe that if $f \sqsubseteq_s p(k)$, then clearly $f \sqsubseteq_s p(i)$ for all $i \geq k$. As all frontier counter values are bounded by k (see above), we can also conclude that if $f \not\sqsubseteq_s p(k)$ then $f \not\sqsubseteq_s p(i)$ for all $i \geq k$. Simulation between the k^2 remaining pairs of the form $(f, p(i))$ where $i < k$ could be then decided in the same way as the previous lemma, i.e., by computing the greatest fixed-point of a refinement procedure defined by

- $\mathcal{R}^0 = \{(f, p(i)) \mid f \in F, p \in Q, i < k\}$
- $\mathcal{R}^{j+1}$ consists of those pairs of the form $(f, p(i))$ such that $(f, p(i)) \in \mathcal{R}^j$ and for each move $f \xrightarrow{a} g$ there is a move $p(i) \xrightarrow{a} q(l)$ such that either $(g, q(l)) \in \mathcal{R}^j$, or $l = k$ and $g \sqsubseteq_s q(k)$.

The greatest fixed-point is reached after (at most) k^2 refinement steps and each step can be computed in polynomial time.

Now we prove that simulation for the pairs of the form $(f, p(k))$ can be indeed decided in polynomial time. To do that, we show that $f \sqsubseteq_s p(k)$ iff $f \sqsubseteq_s^{2k^2} p(k)$. It clearly suffices — as $p(k)$ cannot increase the counter to more than $2k^2 + k$ in $2k^2$ moves, we can decide whether $f \sqsubseteq_s^{2k^2} p(k)$ simply by computing the '$\sqsubseteq_s^{2k^2}$' relation between the states of the system $\mathcal{F}$ and a finite-state system $(S, \Sigma, \rightarrow)$ where $S = \{(p, i) \mid p \in Q, 0 \leq i < 2k^2 + k\}$ and $\rightarrow$ is given by $(p, i) \xrightarrow{a} (q, j)$ iff $p(i) \xrightarrow{a} q(j)$;

then we just look if $f \sqsubseteq_s^{2k^2} (p, k)$. This can be of course done in polynomial time (see Lemma 1).

Let $j \in \mathbb{N}_0$ be the least number such that $f \not\sqsubseteq_s^j p(k)$. Then Al can win the simulation game in j rounds, which means that there is a sequence

$$(f_j, p_j(l_j)) \xrightarrow{a_j} (f_{j-1}, p_{j-1}(l_{j-1})) \xrightarrow{a_{j-1}} \cdots \xrightarrow{a_2} (f_1, p_1(l_1)) \xrightarrow{a_1} (f_0, -)$$

of game positions where $f = f_j$, $p(k) = p_j(l_j)$, and $f_i \not\sqsubseteq_s^i p_i(l_i)$ for each $1 \le i \le j$. The Al's attack at a position $(f_i, p_i(l_i))$ is $f_i \xrightarrow{a_i} f_{i-1}$, and Ex's defending move is $p_i(l_i) \xrightarrow{a_i} p_{i-1}(l_{i-1})$ (observe that, in particular, $f_1 \not\sqsubseteq_s^1 p_1(l_1)$ and hence $p_1(l_1)$ cannot emit the action a_1). Moreover, we assume (w.l.o.g.) that Ex defends 'optimally', i.e., $f_i \sqsubseteq_s^{i-1} p_i(l_i)$ for each $1 \le i \le j$. The first step is to show that $l_i \le 2k$ for each $1 \le i \le j$. Suppose the converse, i.e., there is some i with $l_i > 2k$. As the counter can be increased at most by one in a single transition, we can select a (strictly) increasing sequence of indexes $s_0, s_1, \ldots, s_k$ such that $l_{s_i} = k + i$ for each $0 \le i \le k$. Furthermore, as $k = |Q| \cdot |F|$, there must be two indexes s_u, s_v where $u < v$ such that $f_{s_u} = f_{s_v}$ and $p_{s_u} = p_{s_v}$. Let us denote $f_{s_u} = f_{s_v}$ by f' and $p_{s_u} = p_{s_v}$ by p'. Now we see (due to the optimality assumption) that $f' \sqsubseteq_s^{s_u-1} p'(k + u)$ and $f' \not\sqsubseteq_s^{s_v} p'(k + v)$. As $s_u - 1 \ge s_v$, we also have $f' \not\sqsubseteq_s^{s_u-1} p'(k + v)$. However, as $u < v$ we obtain $f' \sqsubseteq_s^{s_u-1} p'(k + u) \sqsubseteq_s p'(k + v)$, hence $f' \sqsubseteq_s^{s_u-1} p'(k + v)$ and we derived a contradiction. The rest is now easy — if $j > 2k^2$ (i.e., if Al cannot win in $2k^2$ rounds) then there must be some $u > v$ such that $f_u = f_v$, $p_u = p_v$, and $l_u = l_v$. It follows directly from the fact that $k = |Q| \cdot |F|$ and that each l_i is at most $2k$. Now we can derive a contradiction in the same way as above — denoting $f_u = f_v$ by f', $p_u = p_v$ by p', and $l_u = l_v$ by l', we obtain (due to the optimality assumption) that $f' \sqsubseteq_s^{u-1} p'(l')$ and $f' \not\sqsubseteq_s^v p'(l')$. As $u - 1 \ge v$, we have the desired contradiction. $\square$

An immediate consequence of Lemma 2 and Lemma 3 is the following theorem:

Theorem 3. *The problem of simulation equivalence between OC-N processes and FS processes is in* **P**.

3   Results about Model-Checking

In this section we show that there is a close relationship between simulation-checking problems and the model-checking problem for the formula $\varphi \equiv \nu X.[z]\langle z \rangle X$ of the modal μ-calculus. It is essentially a simple observation which was (in a similar form) used already in [2,16,18].

As we omitted a formal definition of syntax and semantics of this logic, we clarify the meaning of φ at this point. Let $\mathcal{T} = (S, Act, \rightarrow)$ be a transition system. Let $f_\varphi : 2^S \rightarrow 2^S$ be a function defined as follows:

$$f_\varphi(M) = \{s \in S \mid \forall (s \xrightarrow{z} s') \text{ we have that } \exists (s' \xrightarrow{z} s'') \text{ such that } s'' \in M\}$$

The denotation of φ (i.e., the set of states where φ holds), written $[\![\varphi]\!]$, is defined by

$$[\![\varphi]\!] = \bigcup \{U \subseteq S \mid U \subseteq f_\varphi(U)\}$$

Hence, $[\![\varphi]\!]$ is the greatest fixed-point of the (monotonic) function f_φ. As usual, we write $t \models \varphi$ instead of $t \in [\![\varphi]\!]$.

Theorem 4. *Let P be a process of a PDA system $\Delta = (Q, \Gamma, Act, \delta)$, and F a process of a finite-state system $\mathcal{F} = (S, Act, \rightarrow)$. Then it possible to construct (in polynomial time) processes A, B of a PDA system Δ_1 and a process C of a PDA system Δ_2 such that $P \sqsubseteq_s F$ iff $A \models \varphi$, $F \sqsubseteq_s P$ iff $B \models \varphi$, and $P =_s F$ iff $C \models \varphi$.*

Proof. Intuitively, the processes A, B and C 'alternate' the transitions of P and F in an appropriate way. We start with the definition of Δ_1. The set of control states of Δ_1 is $Q \times S \times (Act \cup \{?\}) \times \{0, 1\}$, the set of actions is Act, the stack alphabet $\overline{\Gamma}$ is $\Gamma \cup \{Z\}$ where $Z \notin \Gamma$ is a fresh symbol (bottom of stack). The set of transitions is the least set $\overline{\delta}$ satisfying the following:

- if $pX \xrightarrow{a} q\alpha$ is a rule of δ, then $(p, F, ?, 0)X \xrightarrow{z} (q, F, a, 1)\alpha$ and $(p, F, a, 0)X \xrightarrow{z} (q, F, ?, 1)\alpha$ are rules of $\overline{\delta}$ for each $F \in S$;
- if $F \xrightarrow{a} F'$, then $(p, F, ?, 1)X \xrightarrow{z} (p, F', a, 0)X$ and $(p, F, a, 1)X \xrightarrow{z} (p, F', ?, 0)X$ are rules of $\overline{\delta}$ for all $p \in Q$ and $X \in \overline{\Gamma}$;

Let $P \equiv p\alpha$. We put $A \equiv (p, F, ?, 0)\alpha Z$ and $B \equiv (p, F, ?, 1)\alpha Z$. Observe that A alternates the moves of P and F — first P performs a transition whose label is stored in the finite control and passes the token to F (by changing 0 to 1); then F emits some transition with the same (stored) label and passes the token back to P. The new bottom symbol Z is added to ensure that F cannot 'die' within A just due to the emptiness of the stack. Now it is obvious that $P \sqsubseteq_s F$ iff $A \models \varphi$; the fact that $Q \sqsubseteq_s P$ iff $B \models \varphi$ can be justified in the same way.

The way how to define C is now easy to see – it suffices to ensure that the only transitions of C are $C \xrightarrow{z} C'$ and $C \xrightarrow{z} C''$ where $C' \xrightarrow{z} A$ and $C'' \xrightarrow{z} B$. It can be achieved by a straightforward extension of Δ_1. $\square$

The proof of Theorem 4 carries over to processes of one-counter automata and one-counter nets immediately (observe there is no need to add a new bottom symbol when constructing Δ_1 and Δ_2 because the zero-marker of one-counter systems is never removed from the stack by definition.

Corollary 1. *The model-checking problem for φ is*

- ***EXPTIME**-complete for PDA processes;*
- ***coNP**-hard for OC-A processes;*

As simulation between OC-N and FS processes is in **P**, Theorem 4 does not imply any hardness result for model-checking with OC-N processes. Therefore, we examine this problem 'directly' by showing that a simple fixed formula $\Diamond[a]\Diamond[b]\mathtt{ff}$ of the logic EF is **NP**-hard for OC-N processes. In our proof we use a slightly modified version of the construction which was given in [14] to prove **DP**-hardness of weak bisimilarity between OC-N and FS processes. To make this paper self-contained, we present a full proof here.

Theorem 5. *Let $p(0)$ be a process of a one-counter net $\mathcal{N}$. The problem if $p(0) \models \Diamond[a]\Diamond[b]\mathrm{ff}$ is **NP-hard**.*

Proof. Let $\varphi \equiv C_1 \wedge \cdots \wedge C_m$ be a formula in CNF where C_i are clauses over propositional variables $x_1, \cdots, x_n$. We construct a OC-N system $\mathcal{N} = (Q, \{I, Z\}, \{a, b, \tau\}, \delta)$ and its process $p(0)$ such that φ is satisfiable iff $p(0) \models \Diamond[a]\Diamond[b]\mathrm{ff}$. The construction of $\mathcal{N}$ will be described in a stepwise manner. The sets Q and δ are initialized as follows: $Q = \{q\}$, $\delta = \{qI \xrightarrow{b} qI, qZ \xrightarrow{b} qZ\}$. Now, for each clause $C_i, 1 \le i \le m$, we do the following:

- Let π_j denote the jth prime number. We add a new control state c_i to Q. Moreover, for each variable x_j and each k such that $0 \le k < \pi_j$ we add to Q a control state $\langle C_i, x_j, k \rangle$.
- For each newly added control state s we add to δ the transitions $sI \xrightarrow{a} qI, sZ \xrightarrow{a} qZ$.
- For each $1 \le j \le n$ we add to δ the transitions $c_i I \xrightarrow{\tau} \langle C_i, X_j, 0 \rangle I$.
- For all j, k such that $1 \le j \le n$ and $0 \le k < \pi_j$ we add to δ the transition $\langle C_i, x_j, k \rangle I \xrightarrow{\tau} \langle C_i, x_j, (k+1) \bmod \pi_j \rangle \varepsilon$.
- We add to δ the 'loops' $c_i I \xrightarrow{b} c_i I, c_i Z \xrightarrow{b} c_i Z$.
- For all j, k such that $1 \le j \le n$ and $0 \le k < \pi_j$ we add to δ the loop $\langle C_i, x_j, k \rangle I \xrightarrow{b} \langle C_i, x_j, k \rangle I$.
- If a variable x_j does *not* appear positively in a clause C_i, then we add to δ the loop $\langle C_i, x_j, 0 \rangle Z \xrightarrow{b} \langle C_i, x_j, 0 \rangle Z$.
- If a variable x_j does not appear negatively in a clause C_i, then we add to δ the loops $\langle C_i, x_j, k \rangle Z \xrightarrow{b} \langle C_i, x_j, k \rangle Z$ for every $1 \le k < \pi_j$.

If we draw the transition system which is generated by the current approximation of $\mathcal{N}$, we obtain a collection of G_i graphs, $1 \le i \le m$; each G_i corresponds to the 'subgraph' of the transition system associated to $\mathcal{N}$ which is obtained by restricting Q to the set of control states which have been added for the clause C_i. The structure of G_i is shown in the following picture (the a-transitions to the states of the form $q(j)$ are omitted as the picture would become too complicated).

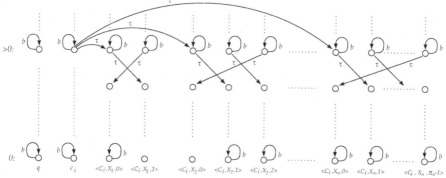

Now we can observe the following:

- For each $l > 0$, the state $c_i(l)$ 'encodes' the (unique) assignment ν_l in the same way as in the proof of Theorem 2, i.e., ν_l is defined by $\nu_l(x_j) = \mathtt{tt}$ iff $c_i(l) \to^*$ $\langle C_i, x_j, 0 \rangle(0)$; conversely, for each assignment ν there is $l \in \mathbb{N}$ such that $\nu = \nu_l$ (for example, we can put $l = \Pi_{j=0}^n f(j)$, where $f(j) = \pi_j$ if $\nu(x_j) = \mathtt{tt}$, and $f(j) = 1$ otherwise).
- For each $l > 0$ we have that $\nu_l(C_i) = \mathtt{tt}$ iff $c_i(l) \models \Diamond[b]\mathtt{ff}$. Indeed, observe that $\nu_l(C_i) = \mathtt{tt}$ iff $c_i(l)$ can reach some of the 'zero-states' where the action b is disabled.

We finish the construction of $\mathcal{N}$ by connecting the G_i components together. To do that, we add two new control states p and r to Q, and enrich δ by adding the transitions $pZ \xrightarrow{\tau} pIZ$, $pI \xrightarrow{\tau} pII$, $pI \xrightarrow{a} qI$, $pZ \xrightarrow{a} qZ$, $pI \xrightarrow{\tau} rI$, and $rI \xrightarrow{a} c_iI$ for every $1 \le i \le m$. The structure of of the transition system associated to $\mathcal{N}$ is shown below (again, the a-transitions to the states of the form $q(j)$ are omitted).

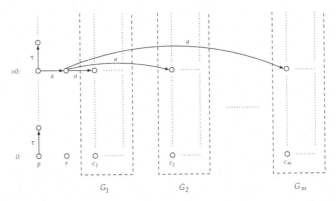

Now we can observe the following:

- The only states which can (potentially) satisfy the formula $[a]\Diamond[b]\mathtt{ff}$ are those of the form $r(l)$, because all other states have an a-transition to a state of the form $q(j)$ where is it impossible to get rid of b's.
- A state $r(l)$ satisfies the formula $[a]\Diamond[b]\mathtt{ff}$ iff $c_i(l) \models \Diamond[b]\mathtt{ff}$ for all $1 \le i \le m$ iff $\nu_l(C_i) = \mathtt{tt}$ for each $1 \le i \le m$ (due to the previous observations) iff $\nu_l(\varphi) = \mathtt{tt}$.

Hence, φ is satisfiable iff there is $l \in \mathbb{N}$ such that $r(l)$ satisfies $[a]\Diamond[b]\mathtt{ff}$ iff $p(0) \models \Diamond[a]\Diamond[b]\mathtt{ff}$. $\square$

Corollary 2. *Let $p(0)$ be a process of a one-counter net $\mathcal{N}$. The problem if $p(0) \models \Box\langle a\rangle\Box\langle b\rangle\mathtt{tt}$ is **coNP-hard**.*

4   Conclusions

This paper fills some gaps in our knowledge on complexity of simulation-checking and model-checking with (subclasses of) pushdown automata. The following table gives a summary of known results (contributions of this paper are in boldface). For comparison, related results about checking strong and weak bisimilarity (denoted by $\sim$ and $\approx$, respectively) with finite-state processes are also shown. The overview supports the claim that simulation tends to be computationally harder than bisimilarity; to the best of our knowledge, there is so far no result violating this 'rule of thumb'.

	PDA	BPA	OC-A	OC-N
$\sim$ FS	PSPACE-complete [19]	$\in$ P [17]	$\in$ P [14]	$\in$ P [14]
$\approx$ FS	PSPACE-hard [19] $\in$ EXPTIME [10]	$\in$ P [17]	DP-hard [14]	DP-hard [14]
$=_s$ FS	**EXPTIME-complete**	coNP-hard [16]	**coNP-hard**	$\in$ **P**

References

1. P.A. Abdulla and K. Čerāns. Simulation is decidable for one-counter nets. In *Proceedings of CONCUR'98*, volume 1466 of *Lecture Notes in Computer Science*, pages 253–268. Springer, 1998.
2. H.R. Andersen. *Verification of Temporal Properties of Concurrent Systems*. PhD thesis, Arhus University, 1993.
3. E. Bach and J. Shallit. *Algorithmic Number Theory. Vol. 1, Efficient Algorithms*. The MIT Press, 1996.
4. J.C.M. Baeten and W.P. Weijland. *Process Algebra*. Number 18 in Cambridge Tracts in Theoretical Computer Science. Cambridge University Press, 1990.
5. S. Christensen. *Decidability and Decomposition in Process Algebras*. PhD thesis, The University of Edinburgh, 1993.
6. E.A. Emerson. Temporal and modal logic. *Handbook of Theoretical Computer Science*, B, 1991.
7. J. Esparza and J. Knop. An automata-theoretic approach to interprocedural data-flow analysis. In *Proceedings of FoSSaCS'99*, volume 1578 of *Lecture Notes in Computer Science*, pages 14–30. Springer, 1999.
8. J.F. Groote and H. Hüttel. Undecidable equivalences for basic process algebra. *Information and Computation*, 115(2):353–371, 1994.
9. Y. Hirshfeld. Petri nets and the equivalence problem. In *Proceedings of CSL'93*, volume 832 of *Lecture Notes in Computer Science*, pages 165–174. Springer, 1994.
10. P. Jančar, A. Kučera, and R. Mayr. Deciding bisimulation-like equivalences with finite-state processes. In *Proceedings of ICALP'98*, volume 1443 of *Lecture Notes in Computer Science*, pages 200–211. Springer, 1998.
11. P. Jančar and F. Moller. Checking regular properties of Petri nets. In *Proceedings of CONCUR'95*, volume 962 of *Lecture Notes in Computer Science*, pages 348–362. Springer, 1995.
12. P. Jančar, F. Moller, and Z. Sawa. Simulation problems for one-counter machines. In *Proceedings of SOFSEM'99*, volume 1725 of *Lecture Notes in Computer Science*, pages 404–413. Springer, 1999.
13. D. Kozen. Results on the propositional μ-calculus. *Theoretical Computer Science*, 27:333–354, 1983.
14. A. Kučera. Efficient verification algorithms for one-counter processes. In *Proceedings of ICALP 2000*, volume 1853 of *Lecture Notes in Computer Science*, pages 317–328. Springer, 2000.
15. A. Kučera. On simulation-checking with sequential systems. Technical report FIMU-RS-2000-05, Faculty of Informatics, Masaryk University, 2000.

16. A. Kučera and R. Mayr. Simulation preorder on simple process algebras. In *Proceedings of ICALP'99*, volume 1644 of *Lecture Notes in Computer Science*, pages 503–512. Springer, 1999.

17. A. Kučera and R. Mayr. Weak bisimilarity with infinite-state systems can be decided in polynomial time. In *Proceedings of CONCUR'99*, volume 1664 of *Lecture Notes in Computer Science*, pages 368–382. Springer, 1999.

18. F. Laroussinie and Ph. Schnoebelen. The state explosion problem from trace to bisimulation equivalence. In *Proceedings of FoSSaCS 2000*, volume 1784 of *Lecture Notes in Computer Science*, pages 192–207. Springer, 2000.

19. R. Mayr. On the complexity of bisimulation problems for pushdown automata. In *Proceedings of IFIP TCS'2000*, volume 1872 of *Lecture Notes in Computer Science*. Springer, 2000.

20. R. Milner. *Communication and Concurrency*. Prentice-Hall, 1989.

21. D.M.R. Park. Concurrency and automata on infinite sequences. In *Proceedings 5th GI Conference*, volume 104 of *Lecture Notes in Computer Science*, pages 167–183. Springer, 1981.

22. W. Reisig. *Petri Nets—An Introduction*. Springer, 1985.

23. C. Stirling. Modal and temporal logics. *Handbook of Logic in Computer Science*, 2:477–563, 1992.

24. R.J. van Glabbeek. The linear time—branching time spectrum. In *Proceedings of CONCUR'90*, volume 458 of *Lecture Notes in Computer Science*, pages 278–297. Springer, 1990.

25. I. Walukiewicz. Pushdown processes: Games and model checking. In *Proceedings of CAV'96*, volume 1102 of *Lecture Notes in Computer Science*, pages 62–74. Springer, 1996.

Reusing Animations in Databases for Multimedia Presentations

Zhiyong Huang, Binjia Jiao, B. Prabhakaran, and Conrado R. Ruiz, Jr.

School of Computing
National University of Singapore
Singapore 117543
{huangzy,jiaobinj,prabha,conradod}@comp.nus.edu.sg
http://www.comp.nus.edu.sg

Abstract. Multimedia presentations and their applications are becoming more and more popular in most spheres of industry and everyday life. A database approach could help in querying presentations and reusing parts of existing presentations to create new ones. In this paper, we propose an object-oriented model built on a temporal interval tree structure for managing multimedia presentations as temporal databases. This model is based on a class hierarchy that reflects the temporal relationships among multimedia data comprising a presentation. Specifically, we will discuss extending this approach to reusing animations in our presentation database system. Hence, in this paper, based on the object-oriented data model and the database system, we propose storing animations in a database of 3D geometric models and motion descriptions. The reuse of 3D models is a common practice, unlike reusing motion which is rare because it is not as straightforward. Thus, we will explore more on motion reuse techniques. A set of generic and animation-oriented operations are given, which can be used to query and adapt animations for multimedia presentations based on their metadata.

1 Introduction

Currently, multimedia presentations are increasingly being used in most areas where computers are utilized. Multimedia-supported lectures, instruction manuals, animated presentations are only a small part of the examples. Therefore, the need to set up a system to manage multimedia presentations elegantly with authoring, querying, and integrated browsing features should be obvious. Databases have evolved through years and have found applications in numerous areas. A database approach to solve the multimedia presentation's querying and authoring problem will not only make it easier for users to learn, but also will make the presentation system more powerful with the mature techniques in database domains.

Simultaneously, animations are also becoming a popular medium in multimedia presentations. Despite this trend however, computer animated sequences are still difficult to produce, even with the advent of fast and powerful machines,

J. He and M. Sato (Eds.): ASIAN 2000, LNCS 1961, pp. 149–161, 2000.
© Springer-Verlag Berlin Heidelberg 2000

graphics accelerators, and high-end graphics authoring software. Thus, novice users that require animations in their multimedia presentations may find it difficult to produce good animation sequences. The difficulty primary comes from generating motion. Creating motion of good quality requires considerable effort of skilled animators, actors, and engineers, for example using motion capture technology.

Despite its high cost, motion is not commonly reusable. Motion for a particular model is very specific and is unusable for other models and scenarios. For instance, the motion of a man picking up a glass will be precisely that - the motion will be difficult to reuse for having the character pick up other objects from the ground, or even for a different character to pick up the same glass. Computer animation research has evolved 4 general strategies to the problem of producing motion. The first one is to improve the tools used for key framing. The second one uses procedural methods to generate motions based on descriptions of goals. The third one tracks motion of real world actors or objects. The fourth one attempts to adapt existing motion generated by some other methods.

The fourth approach could put animation capabilities in the hands of inexperienced animators and allow the use of motion created by others in new scenarios and with other characters. It can also enable "on-the-fly" adaptation of motions. One promising approach to motion adaptation, presented by Bruderlin and Williams [3], treats motions as signals and applies some traditional signal processing to adapt them, while preserving aspects of their character. A variant of their interesting methods, motion-displacement mapping, was simultaneously introduced as "motion warping" by Witkin and Popovic [8].

Database aspects for multimedia presentations are explored in this paper by providing a set of algebraic database operations designed for multimedia presentations based on the temporal model. These operations help in creating and querying presentation databases, together with the user interactive operations such as forward, rewind, skip, and link to other database.

This paper focuses on extending the database approach to animation by exploiting motion reuse. This approach is intended for novice or non-skilled animators requiring fast and considerably good animations for multimedia applications. We view animations in a high-level abstracted view and store them in databases. From a pool of animation resources, in VRML format, we add descriptions or meta-data to the database. The user can then search the animations and find particular objects and motion that he requires for his intended animation. He can query scenes or characters using filters or conditions such as color or using spatial properties.

The query results can then be combined and manipulated to make the scene. We provide manipulations for scaling, translation and rotation. Temporal aspects of the animation can also be altered, such as extracting only a portion of the animation. We also provide a set of motion editing operators for greater flexibility. Motion of other characters can be reused to other characters with similar structure.

2   Related Work

Most advanced animation tools focus mainly on rendering realistic models and is intended for skilled animators. However, there are several software tools that caters to novice users. Simply 3D created by Metacreations [9] provides a catalog of 3D models that could be dragged into a scene. It also provides features to animate the models. However, the results are simple translations, rotations, and trivial combinations of the two.

Creating a database of both models and motion shows great potential. However, the main obstacle is how to reuse motion. Recently, there has been a considerable effort to develop techniques for retargeting motion for new characters and scenes. Examples of such works are that of Gleicher's [4], Popovic [10] and Hodgins [6].

One related work that makes use of databases in animation is done by Kakizaki [7], who uses a scene graph and an animated agent in multimedia presentations. The animated agent performs a presentation based on a text description. In order to generate the agent's motion automatically, he categorized the motion of the agent in the presentation into three classes, namely pointing, moving, and gesturing. To determine what the target object is and to extract detailed information about the object, the system accesses a scene graph that contains all the information about the virtual environments. This information, stored in a database, is used for determining details to generate the agent's motion.

Similarly, Ayadin et al. [1] have used databases to guide the grasp movement of virtual actors. Their approach creates a database based on divisions of the reachable space of a virtual actor. Objects are classified into a set of primitives such as blocks, cylinder, and sphere. Both attempts of storing objects into databases have been fairly successful. However, the problem of motion reuse is not addressed.

3   Object-Oriented Data Model

To understand the data model we consider an example multimedia presentation with six objects, as shown in Figure 1. The start and end of an object presentation can be considered as left and right end points of a line segment. The endpoints of these line segments (corresponding to each object presentation) are sorted (with duplicates removed) to obtain the sequence $y_0, y_1, ..., y_m$ ($m < 2N$, N being the number of objects in a multimedia presentation). The primary structure of the interval tree is a complete binary tree with m+1 external (i.e., leaf) nodes such that when the tree is flattened and the non-leaf nodes are removed, external node i corresponds to y_i (the ith endpoint corresponding to the start/end of object(s) presentation) [5,11]. Each leaf node is labeled with its corresponding endpoint, i.e., y_i for the ith leaf node. Non-leaf nodes are labeled with a value that lies between maximum value in its left subtree and the minimum value in the right subtree (usually, the average of these values are used to label the node). Hence, each non-leaf node, say v, serves as a key to a pair of secondary structures LS and RS. LS and RS represent the sets of left and right end points of the temporal intervals for which v is a common ancestor. Temporal relationships in a multimedia presentation can be viewed as an interval tree. For instance, Figure 2 describes the interval tree structure for the example multimedia presentation in Figure 1. The interval tree also has two other structures, secondary and tertiary, to help in handling different temporal queries. From multimedia authoring point of view, we focus on the primary structure of the interval tree discussed here.

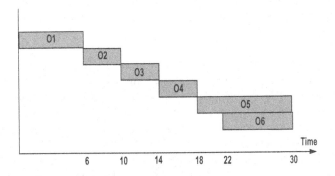

Fig. 1. An Example Multimedia Presentation

The interval tree representation of temporal relationships in a multimedia presentation can be viewed as a class hierarchy in an object-oriented environment, as described in Figure 3. Root node that corresponds to the entire presentation interval represents the *multimedia presentation* class. This class has two subclasses: *non-leaf* and *leaf*. Non-leaf class represents an internal node of the interval tree whose interval lies within its parent interval. Leaf class represents an external node of the tree whose interval index lies within its parent interval. *Multimedia data* to be presented is a subclass of the leaf nodes. This subclass represents the start or the end of the multimedia data presentation corresponding to this leaf node. This subclass may also represent the fact that the data is being presented *during* the interval index represented by the leaf class. A multimedia data class can have different choices for rendering purposes, based on the languages (of audio, text), data/compression formats, or object qualities (to take care of varying availability of system resources such as network bandwidth). These choices are represented by *multimedia data choice class* that forms a subclass of multimedia data class.

A multimedia presentation can have *links* to other presentation databases or objects within the same database. These links are represented as a link or button class, that forms a subclass of leaf class in the proposed object-oriented model. Ultimately all these classes belong to a general class that can be described as the multimedia presentation class. IS-A relationship, that is valid in an object-

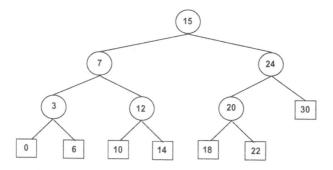

Fig. 2. Interval Tree Representation for the Example Multimedia Presentation

oriented environment is also true for this case. For example, non-leaf class IS-A multimedia presentation class and *multimedia data* class IS-A leaf class.

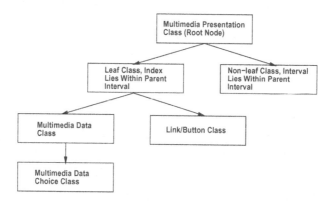

Fig. 3. Object-oriented Representation of Multimedia Presentation

4   Animation Database

Animation is a special kind of multimedia data class. It is stored in its own database because of its inherent complexity and special attributes. Consequently, a presentation of an animation is therefore a part of the leaf class of an interval tree. This section discusses how an animation at a particular time is stored in the database.

Geometric models and motion are the two indispensable components of computer animations. In virtual reality systems, information about the objects in the environment is stored in a scene graph [7]. Here we adapt the concept of the scene graph to break down an animation into atomic objects, which can be extracted, replaced, or deleted.

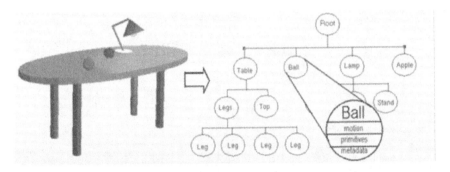

Fig. 4. An animation of a ball rolling on a table. The scene graph for this example decomposes the scene into a tree of its atomic objects. The nodes contain information about the object including motion.

The scene graph was originally designed for real-time 3D graphics system. It contains data about the objects in a scene, such as their shape, size, color, and position. Each piece of information is stored as a node in the scene graph. These nodes are arranged hierarchically in the form of a tree structure.

We have included information about the motion of the object and metadata for the motion. Motion can be represented in a number of ways. It can be stored as a set of interpolation points, an equation, or a signal. Presently, we store motion as a set of interpolation points in our database.

The queries to retrieve particular objects can be done by looking up the metadata in the scene graph database. We use Virtual Reality Modeling Language (VRML) for the purpose of demonstration. Currently, the metadata are made manually, but we are working on making it automatic. To be able to achieve this we are proposing to integrate some information into the VRML files by including them as comments. Since comments do not affect the VRML browser, it is possible to associate metadata with VRML nodes.

To provide a consistent framework, we also represent the animation in an object-oriented data model. The class diagram is shown in Figure 5. An animation is stored as a scene class which has categories and objects. Objects in turn have a motion class and may also be made up of other objects. This model can represent the scene graph of a particular animation and add categories for indexing.

An important consideration is how to store an abstract entity, such as motion in a database. To realize this goal we consider Gleicher's representation of motion. Using Gleicher's framework [4], we can denote motion as a set of signals for a particular model. Consequently, we use his representation, denoting $\mathbf{p}$ as a vector and p_i as an individual scalar parameter. We therefore have $p(t)$, a function of time, defining the model's configuration. They are represented in the system by a set of samples of keyframe points. To use the set of points, we interpolate them to create a continuous signal which will then be resampled to

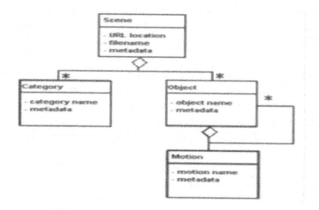

Fig. 5. Object-oriented Representation of an Animation.

produce the new animation. The motion signal is therefore defined by

$$p(t) = interp(t, keys), \tag{1}$$

where *keys* are the keyframe coordinates. They are then stored in the database as a set of points.

5   Proposed Operations

5.1   Generic Database Operations

Operations for manipulating multimedia presentation structure include insert, delete, append, and merge. These operations modify the object hierarchy of a presentation database depending on the changes to the interval tree structure.

1. **Insert:** insert a specified object or a group of objects in the presentation database for the given presentation duration and starting point. The insert operation is carried out, modifying the interval tree structure associated with the multimedia presentation.
2. **Delete:** delete a specified object from the presentation database. This operation again modifies the interval tree structure associated with the presentation and hence the object hierarchy associated with the database.
3. **Append:** append a presentation database to another. This operation integrates the objects in the two specified presentation databases sequentially in time domain.
4. **Merge:** merge two presentation databases with the same domain. This operation integrates the interval tree structure of the two presentation databases, by preserving the temporal relationships of both the databases.
5. **Browse:** browse a multimedia presentation based on the interval tree structure.

6. **Select:** select a multimedia presentation database based on the specified conditions. The conditions associated with the select operation can involve an object-search term or interval-search term or both. This operation does not modify the interval tree structure, and it returns a set of objects as response (without the interval tree structure).

7. **Project:** project desirable portions of the interval tree associated with a multimedia presentation database. Conditions associated with project operation can involve an object-search term or interval-search term or both. The response is a set of objects whose hierarchy reflects the interval tree structure of the projected portion of the multimedia presentation database.

8. **Join:** join two multimedia presentation databases. It is different from the merge operation in the sense that join operation can have conditions that need to be satisfied for an object to be part of the response. These conditions can involve interval conditions and/or object attribute conditions.

5.2   User Interactive Operations

During a multimedia presentation, the user can interact by giving different types of inputs. Inputs such as skip and reverse presentation can work on the interval tree structure to achieve the desired effect. Inputs such as scaling the speed of presentation can modify the intervals associated with interval tree to reflect the change in the presentation speed. For carrying out these user interactive operations, the proposed object-oriented model supports the following operations.

1. **Compress Interval:** the operation helps in scaling down the interval durations in a multimedia presentation database by a specified factor.

2. **Expand Interval:** the operation helps in scaling up the interval durations in a presentation database by a specified factor. This operation together with compress interval help in handling scaling the speed of data delivery during an actual multimedia presentation.

3. **Skip Interval:** the operation helps in moving to a time index in a multimedia presentation by skipping the specified interval, and hence skipping the presentation of multimedia data that lie in the skipped interval.

4. **Reverse Browse:** the operation helps in traversing the interval tree associated with a multimedia presentation database in the reverse order. This operation can be combined with compress/expand interval operations to simulate fast or slow rewind VCR type operation.

These user interactive operations can be provided as functions in the multimedia presentation class. In a similar manner, functions can be provided in the multimedia presentation class for making choices on languages, data/compression formats, or quality of media objects, based on user preferences and/or system parameters.

5.3   Animation Database Operations

We adapt some of the generic operations to cater to animation. The framework comprises of two sets of operators to create animation sequences. They are the query operators and the authoring operators. The query operators are used to search for specific characters, scenes, and motion based on some conditions. The query operators may use the 12 relationships of the objects: *before, behind, inside, contain, meet, overlap, above, under, start, finish, left, and right.* The user may alternately use the metadata of the scenes, objects, categories, and motion.

The authoring operators are then used on the queried results. These are operations that can be performed on the database for an animation represented in VRML format. There are two aspects in authoring animations. The first aspect is the spatial aspect. In animation, combining objects may require changing the position, size, and orientation of objects. The operations shown in Table 1 are used to query and manipulate the spatial attributes of the animation.

Table 1. Animation Database Operations and Syntax

Operation	Syntax	Brief Description
Insert	INSERT *object* TO *scene* [AT (x, y, z)] [WHEN start time UNTIL stop time]	Insert object to a scene under specified conditions
Delete	DELETE *object* FROM *scene*	Delete object from a scene
Extract	EXTRACT *objects* FROM *scene*	Extract the specified objects
Select	SELECT *objects* FROM *scene* WHERE [condition]	Select the objects based on specified conditions
Project	PROJECT *newscene* FROM *oldscene* WHERE [object/temporal condition]	Project a specific time interval from an animation in a scene under specified conditions
Join	JOIN *scene1 scene2* WHERE [object/temporal condition]	Join animations of two scenes based on specified conditions

The second aspect is concerned with the temporal information of animation, which is basically motion. Motion is an integral part of any animation. Here, we propose several authoring operations for retargeting motion for new characters and scenes. The operations for manipulating motion are *use, get, and disregard.* The syntax is shown in Table 2.

Table 2. Motion Operations and Syntax

Operation	Syntax	Brief Description
Use	USE *motion* TO *object*	Utilize the motion on a character
Get	GET *motion* FROM *object*	Extract motion from a character
Disregard	DISREGARD *motion* OF *object*	Delete a motion from an object

Among the three operations listed in Table 2, the *use* is most difficult. We have adapted the constraint-based approach proposed by Gleicher [4]. This approach combines constraint methods with the motion-signal processing methods. It enables us to adapt motion to a new character while retaining the desired quality of the original motion.

6   System Design and Implementation

We have used JDK1.2 on Solaris system to implement the object-oriented model, the database, the user interface, and the link operations. JMF2.0 is employed to enable the control operations on media data. Java Project X is used to process the XML representation of the object-oriented model.

As in Figure 6, visualized creation of a multimedia presentation provides convenience to author a presentation as a whole, by giving temporal interval line on timing coordinates and then defining or querying their associated objects whose spatial and system parameters are defined during creation. Animation is created by importing VRML files and specifying the temporal constraints of the files to create desired animations. Visualized creation together with proposed database operations supply a full package for authoring and manipulating purposes.

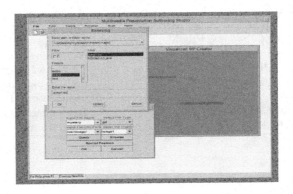

Fig. 6. Visualized Creation of a Multimedia Presentation

Presentation browser shown in Figure 7 can display the presentation spatially and temporally as predefined. Each media file player can also be interactively controlled by end users in the course of delivery. Among the players, an animation player is included, which is used to view and modify the animation as shown in Figure 7.

6.1   Example

In this section, we describe an example for creating an animation for a multimedia presentation using the operations described above. In this example, the

Fig. 7. Delivery of A Multimedia Presentation

user needs an animation of a walking woman in a room with a brown door. The user starts by querying and collecting the necessary models and motion. After the query, the user inserts them into a VRML scene with the specified temporal parameters. One snapshot of the resulting animation is shown in Figure 8. The order of the operations is as follows:

SELECT *door* FROM *allobjects* WHERE COLOR=brown
EXTRACT *woman* FROM *scene*
GET *walking* FROM *walkingman*
USE *walking* TO *woman*
SELECT *room* FROM *allobjects* WHERE TYPE=HDB5A
INSERT *door* -scale(30,30,30) TO *room* AT [50,50,50] WHEN [0,10]
INSERT *woman* TO *room* WHEN [6,12]

7   Conclusion and Future Work

Authoring, querying, and browsing are three major aspects in multimedia presentation area. It can easily be deduced that integrating these three features with popular database approaches would be a solution to the increasing needs in multimedia presentations. In this paper, we have proposed an object-oriented data model for multimedia presentation databases. Class hierarchy for this model is constructed based on the interval tree structure of temporal relationships in a multimedia presentation.

More specifically, we focus on animation database aspects in this paper, by exploring animation database operations and animation scene modeling based on the object-oriented model. Hence, it provides a consistent framework for authoring and reuse.

We plan to extend the system to be used on the Internet. It may be possible to create a web-based database of the VRML files on the net. These files can

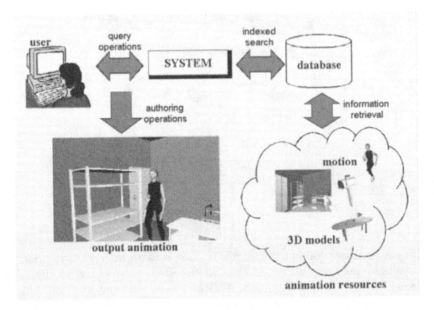

Fig. 8. Abstracted view of the proposed system. The animation is produced by using the operations to reuse existing models and motion. Woman model courtesy of Ballreich [2].

then be queried and reused to create the new animation. Since the goal of the research is to provide an easier approach to animation, we consequently plan to offer more levels of abstraction. We plan to make the framework more flexible to make it possible to be adapted for other animation formats.

References

1. Aydin, Y., Takahashi, H. and Nakajima, M.: Database Guided Animation of Grasp Movement for Virtual Actors. Proc. Multimedia Modeling '97 (1997) 213-225
2. Ballreich, C.: Nancy - 3D Model. 3Name3D, http://www.ballreich.net/vrml/h-anim/nancy_h-anim.wrl. (1997)
3. Bruderlin, A., and Williams, L.: Motion Signal Processing. Proc. ACM SIG-GRAPH '95. (1995) 97-104
4. Gleicher, M.: Retargeting Motion for New Characters. Proc. ACM SIGGRAPH '98 (1998) 33-42
5. Hamblin, C.: Instants and intervals. Proc. International Conf. of the Study of Time, J.T. Fraser, et al., Eds, New Hamsphire, (1972) 324-331
6. Hodgins, J., and Pollard, N.: Adapting Simulated Behaviors For New Characters. Proc. ACM SIGGRAPH '97, Los Angeles, CA. (1997) 153-162
7. Kakizaki, K.: Generating the Animation of a 3D Agent from Explanatory Text. Proc. ACM MM'98(1998) 139-144

8. Lasseter, J.: Principles of Traditional Animation Applied to 3D Animation. Proc. ACM SIGGRAPH '87 (1987) 35-44
9. Micrografx, Inc.: Products: Micrografx Simply 3D: Product Info. http://www.micrografx.com/mgxproducts
10. Popovic, Z., and Witkin, A.: Physically Based Motion Transformation. Proc. ACM SIGGRAPH '99(1999) 11-19
11. Samet, H.: The Design and Analysis of Spatial Data Structures. Addison-Wesley Publishing Company, INC. (1989)

Reflecting BDDs in Coq

Kumar Neeraj Verma[1], Jean Goubault-Larrecq[1], Sanjiva Prasad[2], and S. Arun-Kumar[2]

[1] GIE Dyade and INRIA Rocquencourt
[2] IIT Delhi

Abstract. We describe an implementation and a proof of correctness of binary decision diagrams (BDDs), completely formalized in Coq. This allows us to run BDD-based algorithms inside Coq and paves the way for a smooth integration of symbolic model checking in the Coq proof assistant by using reflection. It also gives us, by Coq's extraction mechanism, certified BDD algorithms implemented in Caml. We also implement and prove correct a garbage collector for our implementation of BDDs inside Coq. Our experiments show that this approach works in practice, and is able to solve both relatively hard propositional problems and actual industrial hardware verification tasks.

1 Introduction

Binary Decision Diagrams (BDDs for short) [9] are a compact and canonical representation of propositional formulae up to propositional equivalence, or equivalently of Boolean functions. BDDs and related data structures are at the heart of modern automated verification systems, based on model-checking [24] or on direct evaluation of observable equivalence between finite-state machines [10]. These techniques have enabled solving huge verification problems automatically. On the other hand, proof assistants like Coq [3], Lego [23] or HOL [15] are *expressive*, in that they can address a vast amount of rich mathematical theory (not just finite-state machines or Boolean functions). The expressiveness provided by such systems makes them eminently suitable for diverse verification tasks, such as expressing modular properties of hardware circuits [22].

Proof assistants are also *safe*, in that they rest on firm logical foundations, for which consistency proofs are known. While implementations of proof assistants might of course be faulty, some design principles help limit this to an absolute minimum. In HOL, the main design principle, inherited from LCF [16], is that every deduction, whatever its size may be, must be justified in terms of a a small number of indisputable elementary logical principles. In Coq and Lego, every proof-search phase is followed by an independent proof-checking phase, so that buggy proof-search algorithms cannot fool the system into believing logically incorrect arguments.

However, proof assistants are not automatic, even when it comes to specialized domains like Boolean functions. In particular, proof assistants today cannot perform automatic model-checking (PVS [27] is a notable exception, see below.)

J. He and M. Sato (Eds.): ASIAN 2000, LNCS 1961, pp. 162–181, 2000.

To combine the expressiveness and safety of proof assistants with model-checking capabilities, there have been proposals to integrate BDDs with proof assistants (some are discussed below), which may involve certain trade-offs. If the proof assistant is to remain safe, we cannot just force it to rely on the results provided by an external model-checker. We might instrument an external model-checker so that it returns an actual proof, which the given proof assistant will then be able to check. But model-checkers actually enumerate state spaces of astronomical sizes, and mimicking this enumeration — at least naively, see related work below — with proof rules inside the proof assistant would be foolish.

One remedy to this model-checker (automatic, fast) vs proof assistant (expressive, safe) antinomy is to use *reflection* [32,7,1,4,6], which in this context can roughly be thought of as "replacing proofs in the logic by computations" (see Section 3). Reflection is particularly applicable in Coq, since Coq is based on the calculus of inductive constructions, a logic which is essentially a typed lambda-calculus, a quintessential programming language.

In this paper we describe an implementation of BDDs in Coq using reflection. We model BDDs, implement the basic logical operations on them, and prove their correctness, all within Coq. This provides a formal proof of the BDD algorithms, and also makes available these techniques within the proof assistant. Our BDD implementation employs garbage collection. We describe how we implement a provably correct garbage collector for our BDD implementation. We provide experimental results about our BDD implementation on relatively hard propositional problems as well as industrial hardware verification benchmarks.

We must clarify that the aim of this work is not to improve on current verification technology, as far as efficiency or the size of systems verified is concerned. Our goal is to produce certified model-checkers, and also reflected model-checkers that could work as subsystems of Coq. Given that the Common Criteria (CC) certification [26] requires the use of certified formal methods at evaluation levels 5 and higher, our work may be viewed as enriching the set of tools available to people and industries engaged in the CC certification process to include proved BDD techniques, running at an acceptable speed. It has to be noted that there is also increasing interest in independent proof-checking of machine-checked proofs: here, Coq is a particularly interesting system to work with, since its core logic is so small that stand-alone, independent proof-checkers for it are not too hard to implement. In fact, such a proof-checker exists that has even been formally certified in Coq [2] (augmented with a strong normalization axiom to get around Gödel's second incompleteness theorem).

The plan of the paper is as follows. We review some related work in the rest of the introduction, then give short descriptions of BDDs in Section 2, and of Coq in Section 3. Sections 4 and 5 are the technical core of this paper: in Section 4 we describe how BDDs are not only modeled but actually programmed and proved in Coq. This involves a number of difficulties; to name a few: we have to describe memory allocation, sharing, recursion over BDDs, memoization, and to prove that they all work as expected. The organization of the correctness proofs is on classical lines: we state representational invariants, which we show are maintained by the BDD algorithms; we provide the semantics of BDDs in terms of Boolean functions, with respect to which the correctness of the algorithms is proven. For the BDD implementation to be really useful in practice, we also need to address problems related to memory management. We also describe a formally proved garbage collector for our implementation. In Section 4, we only describe the assumptions about the garbage collector and show that our BDD implementation works correctly under these assumptions. The garbage collector we implement is described and then shown to satisfy these assumptions in Section 5. The garbage collector is shown to preserve representational invariants and the semantics of all BDD nodes designated as relevant. In Section 6 we report experimental results, and discuss speed and space issues. We then conclude in Section 7.

The complete Coq code and proofs can be found at http://www.dyade.fr/fr/actions/vip/bdd.tgz.

Related work.

Closely related to our work is John Harrison's interfacing of a BDD library with the HOL prover [19]. The author's goal was to solve the validity problem for propositional logic formulae rather than to perform model-checking. Reflection cannot be employed in HOL, since its logical language does not contain a programming sub-language. To be precise, it does contain a λ-calculus with βη-equality, but this equality is not implemented as a reduction process as in Coq, but through the use of axioms defining it, which then have to be invoked explicitly. Therefore, the BDD library must log every BDD reduction step and translate each as a proper HOL inference, which HOL will then check. This logging process is difficult to implement, produces huge logs, and it is necessary to use a few tricks in the HOL implementation to keep the HOL proof-checking phase reasonably efficient.

There have also been several publications on integrating model checking with theorem proving. Indeed, this is one of the main aims of PVS [27]; but the internal model-checker of PVS is itself not checked formally, for now at least. Yu and Luo have built a model checker LegoMC [33] which returns a proof term expressing why it believes the given formula to hold on the given program. Safety is achieved through Lego checking the latter proof-term. However such methods do not seem to scale up to complex problems, since they are not symbolic checking methods like those based on BDDs.

Gordon and his colleagues have combined the HOL proof assistant with an external BDD package [13,14], allowing the HOL prover to accept results from the external BDD package, without any rechecking by HOL. While this approach is likely to work faster, its safety is dependent on the reliability of the external BDD package as well as the mechanisms for communication between HOL and the BDD package. Our approach involves more work but is completely safe.

There have also been several works on verifying garbage collectors inside proof assistants. Goguen *et al.* [11] model memory as a directed graph, define basic operations that a mutator may apply to memory, then show that adding a garbage collector (abstracted as Dijkstra *et al's* tricolor marking collector) gives a bisimilar, hence behaviorally equivalent, process. Their high-level view does not take into account any particular algorithmic detail, whereas we implement actual code that is part of a BDD implementation running in Coq and show that our implementation works as expected in the presence of this garbage collector. Moreover, they verify a garbage-collector for a fairly classical memory architecture, which does not include persistent hash-tables that should be purged of freed elements. So not only do we verify actual code, we also prove a more complex garbage collection architecture. This last aspect is also a difference between our work and others such as [12,21,25,29].

2   Binary Decision Diagrams

BDDs represent a propositional logic formula (built from variables and the connectives $\wedge, \vee, \neg, \Rightarrow, \Leftrightarrow$) as graphs. It is based on Shannon's decomposition of any formula F as $(A \Rightarrow F[A := 1]) \wedge (\neg A \Rightarrow F[A := 0])$, where $F[A := G]$ denotes substitution of G for A in F, 1 is `true` and 0 is `false`. We also use the convenient notation $F = A \longrightarrow F[A := 1]; F[A := 0]$. By choosing a variable A occurring in F, decomposing with respect to it, and recursively continuing the process for $F[A := 1]$ and $F[A := 0]$, we get a binary tree (a *Shannon tree*) whose internal nodes have variables and leaf nodes are 1 and 0.

BDDs are *shared*, *reduced* and *ordered* versions of Shannon trees. *Sharing* means that all isomorphic subtrees are stored at the same address in memory. This gives us directed acyclic graphs instead of trees. It is also the main reason why BDDs are very small in many applications. Sharing is accomplished by having a sharing map which remembers all the BDDs that have been previously constructed. *Reducing* means that a BDD node with identical children represents a redundant comparison and can be replaced by a child node. *Ordering* means that we fix some ordering on the variables and have all the variables along any path in a BDD occur in that order. These conditions ensure that BDDs are canonical forms for propositional formulae up to propositional equivalence [9].

One reason why BDDs are interesting is that they are usually compact. Furthermore, they are easy to work with, at least in principle: all the usual logical operations are easily definable by recursive descent on BDDs. Negation, for example, is defined by $\neg 1 =_{df} 0$, $\neg 0 =_{df} 1$, $\neg(A \longrightarrow F; G) =_{df} A \longrightarrow \neg F; \neg G$, and any other Boolean operation $\oplus$ (ranging over $\vee, \wedge, \Rightarrow, \Leftrightarrow$, etc.) is defined as $(A \longrightarrow F_1; G_1) \oplus (A \longrightarrow F_2; G_2) =_{df} A \longrightarrow (F_1 \oplus F_2); (G_1 \oplus G_2)$, with the usual definitions on 1 and 0. This is called *orthogonality* of operation $\oplus$.

By remembering in a cache the results of previous computations, negation can be computed in linear time, and binary operations in quadratic time w.r.t. the sizes of the input BDDs, a notion sometimes called *memoizing* or *tabulating*.

3   An Overview of Coq

Coq is a proof assistant based on the Calculus of Inductive Constructions (CIC), a type theory that is powerful enough to formalize most of mathematics. It properly includes higher-order intuitionistic logic, augmented with definitional mechanisms for inductively defined types, sets, propositions and relations. CIC is also a typed λ-calculus, and can therefore also be used as a programming language. For a gentle introduction, see [20]. We shall describe here the main features of Coq that we shall need later, and also what reflection means in our setting.

The *sorts* of CIC are Prop, the sort of all propositions; Set, the sort of all specifications, programs and data types; and $Type_i$, $i \in \mathbb{N}$, which we won't need. The typing rules for sorts include Prop : $Type_0$, Set : $Type_0$, $Type_i$: $Type_{i+1}$.

What it means for Prop to be the sort of propositions is that any object F : Prop (read: F of type Prop) denotes a proposition, i.e., a formula. If F and G are propositions, F -> G is a proposition (read: "F implies G"), and $(x : T)G$ is a proposition, for any type T (read: "for every x of type T, G"). In turn, any object $\pi : F$ is a *proof* π of F. A formula is considered proved in Coq whenever we have succeeded to find a proof of it. Proofs are written, at least internally, as λ-terms, but we shall be content to know that we can produce them with the help of *tactics*, allowing one to write proofs by reducing the goal to subgoals, and eventually to immediate, basic inferences.

Similarly, any object t : Set denotes a data type, like the data type nat of natural numbers, or the type nat -> nat of all functions from naturals to naturals. Data types can, and will usually be, defined inductively. For instance, the standard definition of the type nat of natural numbers in Coq reads:

```
Inductive nat : Set :=
   O : nat
 | S : nat -> nat.
```

which means that nat is of type Set, hence is a data type, that O (zero) is a natural number, that S is a function from naturals to naturals (successor), and that every natural number must be of the form (S (S ...(S O)...)) (induction).

Then, if t : Set, and p : t, we say that p is a *program* of type t. Programs in Coq are purely functional programs: the language of programs is based on a λ-calculus with variables, application (p q) of p to q (in general, (p q₁ ... qₙ) will denote the same as (...(p q₁)...qₙ)), abstraction [x : t]p (where x is a variable; this denotes the function mapping x of type t to p), case splits (e.g., Cases n of O => v | (S m) => (f m) end either returns v if the natural number n is zero (O) or (f m) if n is the successor of some integer m), and functions defined by structural recursion on their last argument. For the latter, consider the following definition in Coq's standard prelude:

```
Fixpoint plus [n:nat] : nat -> nat :=
  [m:nat] Cases n of
          O => m
        | (S p) => (S (plus p m))
          end
```

This is the standard definition of addition of natural numbers, by primitive recursion over the first argument. For soundness reasons, Coq refuses to accept any non-terminating function. In fact, Coq refuses to acknowledge any `Fixpoint` definition that is not primitive recursive, even though its termination might be obvious.

In general, propositions and programs can be mixed. We shall exploit this mixing of propositions and programs in a very limited form: when π and π' are programs (a.k.a., descriptions of data), then $\pi=\pi'$ is a proposition, expressing that π and π' have the same value. Reflection can then be implemented as follows: given a property P : t -> `Prop`, write a program π : t -> `bool` deciding P. (Note, by the way, that `bool` is defined by `Inductive bool : Set := true : bool | false : bool.` and should be distinguished from `Prop`). Then prove the correctness lemma:

$$(x : t) \ (\pi \ x) = \text{true} \ \text{->} \ (P \ x)$$

To show that P holds of some concrete data x_0 (without any free Coq variable), you can then compute $(\pi \ x_0)$ in Coq's *programming language*. If the result is `true`, then $(\pi \ x_0)$`=true` holds, and the correctness lemma then allows you to conclude that $(P \ x_0)$ holds in Coq's *logic*.

More concretely, assume we are interested in the validity of Boolean expressions. The type of Boolean expressions is:

```
Inductive bool_expr : Set :=
      Zero : bool_expr                              (* false *)
    | One : bool_expr                               (* true *)
    | Var : BDDvar->bool_expr                       (* propositional variables *)
    | Neg : bool_expr->bool_expr                    (* negation *)
    | Or : bool_expr->bool_expr->bool_expr          (* disjunction *)
    | And : bool_expr->bool_expr->bool_expr         (* conjunction *)
    | Impl : bool_expr->bool_expr->bool_expr        (* implication *)
    | Iff : bool_expr->bool_expr->bool_expr.        (* logical equivalence *)
```

(The type `BDDvar` of variables will be described in Section 4.1.) Given an environment ρ mapping variables to truth values (in `bool`), it is easy to define the truth-value of a given Boolean expression `be` under ρ, by standard evaluation rules: `Zero` is always false, (`Var` x) is true if and only if $\rho(x)$ is, (`And` be_1 be_2) is true provided both be_1 and be_2 are, and so on. A Boolean expression is *valid* if and only if its value is true under every environment ρ.

It is often the case that we are interested in showing that a given Boolean expression `be` is valid. The standard proof of it is to list its free variables, say $x_1, \ldots, x_n$, then do a case analysis on the truth-value of x_1; in each of the two cases (x_1 true, or x_1 false), do a case analysis on x_2, and so on. In the worst case, this requires writing a proof of size $O(2^n)$, which is tedious or even infeasible for n large enough. Furthermore, even though writing this proof may in principle be automated, by writing a computer program whose role is to output all the necessary proof steps to be fed to the Coq proof engine, the sheer size of it will make its verification consume too much time and space to be feasible at all, for $n \geq 30$ at least on current machines.

Bypassing this problem can be accomplished by devising proof rules, and showing that they are sound with respect to the semantics of Boolean expressions. We then let the user, or some computer program implementing a decision procedure for propositional logic, generate the proper sequence of applications of these proof rules to establish that be is valid (which is possible provided these proof rules are complete), and the proof assistant will then re-check that this sequence of applications is correct. This is what Boutin [6] calls *partial reflection*. This is also what Harrison [19] implemented in HOL, using BDDs as decision procedure; we have already seen in Section 1 why this solution was not completely satisfactory.

Our solution is to use *total reflection* [6]: we write a function is_tauto in Coq's λ-calculus that takes a Boolean expression be as input and returns whether the BDD for be is the distinguished 1 or not. We then prove the fundamental correctness lemma is_tauto_lemma, which states that if (is_tauto be) equals true, then be is valid. (The actual definitions are slightly more elaborate, see Section 4 for the precise formulation, implementation and proof strategies.) The task of any user wishing to show that a given Boolean expression be is valid will then be as follows: submit this claim to Coq, which will ask for a proof; then type Apply is_tauto_lemma: Coq now asks for a proof of (is_tauto be)=true. Finally, type Reflexivity to instruct Coq that both sides of the equals sign in fact have the same value. Since they are not syntactically the same, Coq will start computing, and simplify both until either they are equal (in which case the proof succeeds), or until they are not and no simplification is possible (then the proof fails).

At this point, the proof is finished. It has been completely automated, it is small (the size of the generated proof-term is only that of the goal we proved plus some constant overhead, since computation steps are not recorded), and it is as safe as the rest of Coq (we never had to trust an external BDD package blindly, in particular).

4   Implementing BDDs in Coq

In this section we describe how we model BDDs in Coq and implement and prove the basic algorithms on them. We first describe the data structures used for modeling BDDs, for implementing sharing and memoization, and for garbage collection. We define the invariants of our representation, define the semantics of BDDs in terms of Boolean functions and prove the correctness of the algorithms in terms of this semantics. In this process we also prove the uniqueness of BDDs for our representation. The garbage collector is described in Section 5. Here we describe the main BDD algorithms, with the necessary assumptions about the garbage collector. Since the Coq formalization assures technical correctness of our results, our endeavor will be to convey the underlying intuition, with only a few actual Coq definitions shown. The formal definitions and details may be found in the complete Coq code and proofs.

4.1   Representation

We use a library of maps [18] to model a *state* i.e. the memory in which all the BDDs are to be stored, and also the sharing maps that support sharing of BDDs. This library contains an implementation of finite sets and maps. The type (Map A) consists of maps denoting finite functions from addresses (of type ad, which consists of binary representations of integers) to the set A. (MapGet ? m a) returns (NONE A) if the address a is not in the domain of the map m, or (SOME A x) if m maps a to the element x (of type A). (Note the use of the question mark to abbreviate a type argument, here A, that the Coq type-checker is able to infer by itself. In the above case, (MapGet ? m a) is understood by Coq as (MapGet A m a).) (NONE A) and (SOME A x) are the elements of type (option A). (MapPut ? m a x) changes the map m by mapping the address a to x in m. Equality of addresses is defined by ad_eq. Addresses can be converted to natural numbers (of type nat) by nat_of_ad.

```
Definition BDDstate := (Map (BDDvar * ad * ad)).
Definition BDDsharing_map := (Map (Map (Map ad))).
```

A BDDstate maps addresses to triples consisting of a variable and two other addresses which represent the left and right sub-BDDs. Variables and addresses are both represented by the type ad (i.e. BDDvar = ad). The constants BDDzero and BDDone are the addresses zero and one and are used for the leaf nodes **0** and **1** respectively. Having variables as integers gives us a natural ordering on the variables. It also makes it easy to define the sharing map by giving it the type (Map (Map (Map ad))) (the domain of maps can only be addresses). A sharing map represents the inverse function of a BDD state and (in curried form) maps left hand addresses to maps from right hand addresses to maps from variables to addresses. We also have maps for memoization. The memoization map for negation (of type BDDneg_memo, defined as (Map ad)) maps addresses to other addresses representing the negated BDD. Memoization maps for disjunction have the type BDDor_memo, defined as (Map (Map ad)). They map pairs of addresses to addresses.

To implement allocation of new nodes and to do garbage collection, we also keep some other information in our configuration. We have a free list (of type BDDfree_list defined as (list ad)) which contains addresses that are freed during garbage collection. We also have a counter (of type ad), that is an address beyond which all addresses are unused. The type BDDconfig consists of tuples with the six components described above. All the algorithms also take in as input a *used list* (of type (list ad)) which contains addresses representing BDDs which are used by the user, and is used to inform the garbage collector that these BDDs should not be freed.

4.2   Invariants

Next we define the invariants of our representation to ensure that firstly, they represent well formed BDDs (i.e. directed, acyclic graphs with leaf nodes **1** and **0**, with the reducedness and ordering condition), and secondly, the various components of the data structures are consistent with each other.

Our first invariant, (BDDbounded bs node n), states that all the nodes in the BDD rooted at node have variables less than n. It also states the fact that the BDDs are reduced and ordered:

```
Inductive BDDbounded [bs:BDDstate] : ad -> BDDvar -> Prop :=
  BDDbounded_0 : (n:BDDvar) (BDDbounded bs BDDzero n)
| BDDbounded_1 : (n:BDDvar) (BDDbounded bs BDDone n)
| BDDbounded_2 : (node:ad) (n:BDDvar) (x:BDDvar) (l,r:ad)
  (MapGet ? bs node)=(SOME ? (x, (l, r)))
  -> (BDDcompare x n)=INFERIEUR -> ~l=r -> (BDDbounded bs l x) -> (BDDbounded bs r x)
  -> (BDDbounded bs node n).
```

We shall constantly require our BDD nodes node to be *bounded* by n (in a given state bs), in the sense that they satisfy (BDDbounded bs node n). Formally, the definition above states that the set B_n of BDD nodes bounded by n is the smallest containing 0 and 1 (clauses BDDbounded_0 and BDDbounded_1), and such that if node points to (x, (l, r)) in bs, then node is in B_n provided x < n and l and r are in B_x (ordering condition: this implies that all variables are less than n and in decreasing order along each path from the root), and provided l ≠ r (reducedness). The BDDbounded predicate makes no statement about canonicity of BDDs yet: that BDDs are canonical will follow not only from all BDDs being bounded, but also from other invariants involving the well-formedness of the state bs as well as of the sharing maps (see Lemma BDDunique_1 in Section 4.3).

Observe that we have chosen to have the variables in decreasing order on all paths. This is contrary to usual convention. However it allows us to use the fact that < is well-founded on ad, so the conditions defined in BDDbounded additionally imply that any bounded BDD node is the root of a *finite* graph, which is therefore in particular also *acyclic*. Without BDDbounded, enforcing acyclicity would have been much trickier.

This choice of ordering also gives a natural induction principle for doing all the proofs related to BDDs. In most paper-proofs of BDD algorithms, induction is done either on the structure of BDDs or on their sizes. But the structure of BDDs is not apparent to Coq—at least BDDs are not just inductive trees, and instead appear to Coq as a mesh of pointers—and size must itself be defined by induction over BDDs—so a more basic induction principle is needed to define size. Enforcing BDD nodes to be bounded by some number provides us with an easy way out: we just induct on a canonical number that is strictly larger than any variable in the given BDD. More precisely, the value that we use for induction in most of the proofs is bs_var' (see below), which is one more than the variable stored at the root node of the BDD. In case of leaf nodes, it is zero, thus ensuring that bs_var' strictly decreases from a node to its children, even if the children are leaf nodes:

```
Definition bs_var' := [bs:BDDstate; node:ad]
  Cases (MapGet ? bs node) of
     NONE => ad_z          (* leaf node; return ad_z (representing zero) *)
   | (SOME (x,(l,r))) => (ad_S x)    (* ad_S is the successor function *)
  end.
```

As far as the other needed invariants are concerned, let us mention the underlying ideas, rather than display the (fairly straightforward) Coq definitions. The predicate `BDDstate_OK` says that there is nothing stored in the BDD state at the addresses zero and one (since they are reserved for leaf nodes), and any node containing the variable `n` is bounded by `n + 1`. (i.e. satisfies the `BDDbounded` predicate). Sharing is ensured by the predicate `BDDsharing_OK` which says that the sharing map and the BDD state represent inverse functions. The predicate `BDDfree_list_OK` says that the free list stores exactly those nodes between `1` and counter (excluding them) which are not in the domain of the BDD state; we also require that it does not contain duplicates, as this is needed for correct behavior. The predicate `counter_OK` means that the counter is strictly greater than one and there is nothing stored in the BDD state starting from this address. The predicates `BDDneg_memo_OK` and `BDDor_memo_OK` define the invariants on the memoization maps. A memoization map is OK if all entries refer to nodes that are OK, (a *node is OK* if it is in the domain of the BDD state or is a leaf node) and the interpretation of the nodes as Boolean functions (see Section 4.3) are related as expected.

We have the predicate `BDDconfig_OK` for BDD configurations which encapsulates the six invariants described above.

Besides that, we have the predicate `used_list_OK` for the *used list* that is passed to all the functions as argument, which says that the used list should only contain nodes which are OK.

4.3   Interpretation as Boolean Functions

A *Boolean function* (of type `bool_fun`) maps environments to Booleans and an *environment* maps variables to Booleans. `bool_fun_zero` and `bool_fun_one` are the constant Boolean functions. Extensional equality is defined by `bool_fun_eq`. We also have the usual operations `bool_fun_and`, `bool_fun_or`, `bool_fun_neg`, `bool_fun_impl`, `bool_fun_iff`, `bool_fun_if` which are easy to define. A node `node` in the BDD state `bs` is interpreted as a Boolean function in the expected way by the following function, which we discuss below.

```
Fixpoint bool_fun_of_BDD_1 [bs:BDDstate; node:ad; bound:nat] : bool_fun :=
  Cases bound of O => (* Error *) bool_fun_zero
  | (S bound') => Cases (MapGet ? bs node) of
      NONE => (* leaf node *) if (ad_eq node BDDzero) then bool_fun_zero
                              else bool_fun_one
  | (SOME (x,(l,r))) => (bool_fun_if x (bool_fun_of_BDD_1 bs r bound')
                                       (bool_fun_of_BDD_1 bs l bound'))
      end end.
```

We come up against a difficulty while defining this function, namely that Coq only allows recursive functions which use structural induction on the last argument—this is a design principle of Coq ensuring that Coq is strongly normalizing and consistent. We would indeed like to define `bool_fun_of_BDD_1` as a function of just `bs` and `node`, by induction on the structure of the BDD stored at `node`. However we have no direct way of doing so since BDDs are not represented as trees (since it would have prevented us from dealing with sharing). This problem is solved by supplying an extra bound `bound` of type `nat`. This argument is decreased by one in the recursive calls to the function, which makes

Coq happy. (This is sometimes known as "Boyer's trick.") We then supply a bound which is greater than the maximum depth of recursion we expect. This bound can be very easily computed from the variable that is stored at the root node (to be precise, it is one more than the quantity `bs_var`'). The semantics function `bool_fun_of_BDD_bs` (omitted here) is defined accordingly, using the above function. We also prove a theorem stating that the value returned by this function is independent of the bound passed as argument, provided that this bound is sufficiently large. We employ a similar tack in all the other functions (negation, disjunction etc.) where we need to recurse on the structure of the BDDs.

We prove the uniqueness of BDDs for our representation in terms of the addresses where they are stored. The uniqueness lemma says that if the Boolean functions represented by two nodes in a BDD state are equal then the two nodes are equal (i.e. they are at the same address). In the statement of the lemma we have the extra argument `n` which is equal to the maximum of the `bs_var`'s of the two nodes. This then enables us to apply well founded induction on `n`.

```
Lemma BDDunique_1 : (bs:BDDstate; share:BDDsharing_map) (BDDstate_OK bs)
  -> (BDDsharing_OK bs share) -> (n:nat)(node1,node2:ad)
  n=(max (nat_of_ad (bs_var' bs node1)) (nat_of_ad (bs_var' bs node2)))
  -> (node_OK bs node1) -> (node_OK bs node2)
  -> (bool_fun_eq (bool_fun_of_BDD_bs bs node1) (bool_fun_of_BDD_bs bs node2))
  ->node1=node2.
```

The proof takes around 500 steps, and is along expected lines.

Outline of proof: The cases where both `node1` and `node2` are leaf nodes are easy. If `node1` is a leaf node, then `node2` cannot be a non-leaf node because then both its children would have the same semantics, and consequently would be equal (from induction hypothesis,) violating the fact that BDDs are reduced (from the conditions in the `BDDbounded` predicate.) In case both `node1` and `node2` are non-leaf nodes, we first show that they contain the same variable, which requires us to separately prove a lemma stating that the Boolean function represented by a node in a configuration is independent of the variables greater than the variable at the root node. We then use the induction hypothesis to derive that the left children are equal and the right children are equal. Finally we apply the conditions in the `BDDsharing_OK` predicate to show that the two nodes are equal.   □

4.4   Assumptions about the Garbage Collector

As mentioned earlier, our implementation employs garbage collection. We factor the verification into two parts – proving the BDD algorithms are correct assuming the garbage collector satisfies certain specifications, and then showing (in Section 5) that the garbage collector we implement satisfies these specifications. This factoring also gives us the flexibility to change the garbage collector (like changing the conditions when memory should be freed) at some later time independently of the BDD algorithms.

The specifications of the garbage collection function are: it takes in as input a BDD configuration and a used list and returns a new configuration. Its behavior is specified using the predicate gc_OK, which says that the new configuration returned by the garbage collector is OK, the contents of all nodes reachable from the used list are preserved and no new nodes are added into the configuration.

4.5   Memory Allocation

The main function responsible for changing the store is BDDmake. All the BDD algorithms modify the store by calling this function. It takes in as input a variable x and two BDD nodes l and r and returns a node representing the Boolean function "if x then bfr else bfl", where bfr and bfl are the Boolean functions represented by r and l respectively. It first checks whether such a node is already present in the configuration, and if not then it calls the function to allocate a new node. The allocation function, as well as all the other BDD algorithms are parameterized by a garbage collection function gc. The allocator first calls gc (which may or may not choose to free memory depending on the requirements), then allocates a node from the free list, if available, or otherwise it allocates the node at the address pointed to by the counter and the counter is incremented by one.

4.6   BDD Algorithms

We implement negation and disjunction as the basic operations on which the rest of the operations (conjunction, implication and double implication) are based. Thus we have two memoization tables in the configuration. The algorithms work by simple recursion on the structure of the BDDs. However the extra complexity is because of the fact that these algorithms are not purely functional in nature and need to modify the store. Each recursive call to the function returns a new configuration. Finally we call BDDmake which returns another configuration.

We use the following function for negation. As described in Section 4.3, recursion on the structure of BDDs is accomplished by having an extra argument of bound type nat to bind the maximum depth of recursion. gc is the garbage collection function, ul is the used list and node is the node whose negation is to be computed. The function returns a new configuration and a new node in it representing the negated BDD. The computed result is memoized by the function BDDneg_memo_put.

```
Fixpoint BDDneg_1 [gc:(BDDconfig->(list ad)->BDDconfig); cfg:BDDconfig;
                 ul:(list ad); node:ad; bound:nat] : BDDconfig*ad :=
Cases bound of O => (* Error *) (initBDDconfig,BDDzero)
  | (S bound') =>
Cases (MapGet ? (negm_of_cfg cfg) node) of        (* lookup memoization map *)
  (SOME node') => (cfg,node')                     (* return the node found *)
| NONE => Cases (MapGet ? (bs_of_cfg cfg) node) of
    NONE => (* leaf node *) (if (ad_eq node BDDzero) then
            ((BDDneg_memo_put cfg BDDzero BDDone),BDDone) else
            ((BDDneg_memo_put cfg BDDone BDDzero),BDDzero))
  | (SOME (x,(l,r))) => (* internal node: recursively compute negations of *)
Cases (BDDneg_1 cfg ul l bound') of (cfgl,nodel) =>          (* child nodes *)
Cases (BDDneg_1 cfgl (cons nodel ul) r bound') of (cfgr,noder) =>
Cases (BDDmake gc cfgr x nodel noder (cons noder (cons nodel ul))) of
(cfg',node') => ((BDDneg_memo_put cfg' node node'),node')
end end end end end.
```

Negation, as well as other algorithms, are computed by *state threading*. Recursive calls to the function, as well as calls to other functions return a new state. So the state needs to be passed around through this sequence of calls and the new state returned by each call is used in the next call.

4.7 Proofs of the Algorithms

We prove the expected semantics of BDDmake and the BDD algorithms in terms of Boolean functions. In addition, there are some other common things that need to be proved about all of them. Since all these functions change the store, we need to prove that the new configurations returned by them are OK. We also need to show that the new nodes returned are OK and the nodes in the old configuration that were reachable from the input list of nodes remain undisturbed in the new configuration (their semantics as Boolean functions remains unchanged). The assumptions are that the input configurations and nodes are OK.

The proofs are straightforward but long. This is specially so in the case of negation and disjunction, where we prove all these invariants together since all of them are required together for the induction to go through. As an example, we give the correctness lemma for negation, BDDneg_1_lemma, below. It says that for any garbage collector gc satisfying gc_OK, and for any bound bound, configuration cfg, used list ul and node node, if bound is greater than (bs_var' node cfg), cfg is OK, ul is OK with respect to cfg and node is reachable from ul, then the new configuration new_cfg returned by (BDDneg_1 gc cfg ul node bound) is OK, the new node new_node is OK in new_cfg, all nodes reachable from ul in cfg are preserved in new_cfg, the variable at new_node in new_cfg is same as that at node in cfg, and the semantics of new_node in new_cfg is negation of the semantics of node in cfg.

```
Lemma BDDneg_1_lemma : (gc:(BDDconfig->(list ad)->BDDconfig)) (gc_OK gc)
-> (bound:nat; cfg:BDDconfig; ul:(list ad))
(lt (nat_of_ad (var' cfg node)) bound) -> (BDDconfig_OK cfg)
-> (used_list_OK cfg ul) -> (used_node' cfg ul node) (* "node" is
                            reachable from a node in "ul" or is a leaf node *)
-> (BDDconfig_OK (Fst (BDDneg_1 gc cfg ul node bound)))
   /\ (config_node_OK (Fst (BDDneg_1 gc cfg ul node bound))
                      (Snd (BDDneg_1 gc cfg ul node bound)))
   /\ (used_nodes_preserved cfg (Fst (BDDneg_1 gc cfg ul node bound)) ul)
(* all used nodes from old configuration are preserved in the new one *)
   /\ (ad_eq (var' (Fst (BDDneg_1 gc cfg ul node bound))
                   (Snd (BDDneg_1 gc cfg ul node bound)))
   (var' cfg node))=true (* variables at input and output nodes are same *)
   /\ (bool_fun_eq (bool_fun_of_BDD (Fst (BDDneg_1 gc cfg ul node bound))
                                    (Snd (BDDneg_1 gc cfg ul node bound)))
   (bool_fun_neg (bool_fun_of_BDD gc cfg node))).
```

This theorem is proved in around a thousand steps. The proof of disjunction is around three times larger. We prove the above lemma using induction on bound. It differs from normal paper-proofs of the same algorithms in that we don't just have to reason about the BDDs on which the operations are applied, but about other parts of the store as well. We need to show that all the invariants are preserved in all the states and that other parts of the configuration remain unchanged. Also, we require the condition that the bound **bound**, which binds the maximum depth of recursion, is sufficiently high.

The main reason why these proofs are long is that we need to worry more about the store and less about the actual BDD on which we are computing. We require complex invariants to state that the configuration remains OK and that the store remains mostly unchanged by the operations. It might be interesting in the future to develop some general proof techniques which allow forgetting about the store and worrying only about the functional aspects of the programs.

The proofs of the BDD algorithms finally allow us to implement a tautology checker **is_tauto** for Boolean expressions, parameterized by the garbage collector. It works by building a BDD for the given Boolean expression, using the various BDD algorithms, and then checking that the resulting node is the leaf node **BDDone**. We prove the following correctness lemma **is_tauto_lemma** for the tautology checker, which says that **is_tauto** returns **true** exactly when the Boolean expression represents the constantly true Boolean function. Boolean expressions are defined using the inductive type **bool_expr** and are interpreted as Boolean functions by the function **bool_fun_of_bool_expr** in the obvious way. As usual, we have the assumption that the garbage collector passed as argument satisfies the predicate **gc_OK**.

```
Lemma is_tauto_lemma : (gc:(BDDconfig->(list ad)->BDDconfig))(gc_OK gc)
->(be:bool_expr)
(is_tauto gc be)=true<->(bool_fun_eq bool_fun_one (bool_fun_of_bool_expr be)).
```

A final note on implementing BDDs in Coq: it might seem preferable to use Typed Decision Graphs [5], a.k.a. *complement edges* [8], instead of plain BDDs. Their main value over plain BDDs is that negation operates in constant time. Here, it would allow us to dispense with the memoization table for negation, which would seem to simplify our proof work. However, disjunction is more complex to define and to reason about using complement edges. Moreover, the memoization map for disjunction, which mapped pairs of BDD nodes to BDD nodes in the plain BDD case, would map triples consisting of two BDD nodes plus a Boolean sign to pairs of BDD nodes and a Boolean sign: the latter would have to be defined under Coq as two memoization tables, one for the plus sign, one for the minus sign. This is clearly no advantage over having one memoization table for disjunction and one for negation. Still, the fact that negation is faster with complement edges means that it might be a good idea to implement and prove them, as well as any more elaborate BDD representation in the future.

5   Garbage Collection

The garbage collector implementation with which we instantiate our BDD implementation is a mark and sweep garbage collector in the style of [17]. Although reference counting is the usual choice in imperative frameworks, we believe that formalizing it in Coq is difficult, since its invariants seem more complex and a modular decomposition of its verification not entirely obvious to us. Our algorithm consists of three phases. In the mark phase, we mark all the nodes reachable from the set of nodes in the used list using depth first search. In the first sweep phase, we remove all nodes from the BDD state which are not marked and add them to the free list. In the next sweep phase, we clean the sharing and memoization maps of all invalid references (because of nodes that have now been freed).

Let us describe some Coq code from the mark phase: The following function `add_used_nodes_1` adds all the nodes reachable from a node `node` to another set of nodes `marked`. A set of nodes is implemented by the type (`Map unit`), `unit` being the trivial type with only one element `tt`. The function `mark` computes the set of all reachable nodes by iterating over each node in the input list of used nodes.

```
Fixpoint add_used_nodes_1
  [bs:BDDstate; node:ad; marked:(Map unit); bound:nat] : (Map unit) :=
  Cases bound of O => (* Error *) (MO unit)
  | (S bound') => Cases (MapGet ? marked node) of
      NONE => Cases (MapGet ? bs node) of NONE => marked
                      | (SOME (x,(l,r))) =>
(MapPut ? (add_used_nodes_1 bs r (add_used_nodes_1 bs l marked bound') bound') node tt)
              end
      | (SOME tt) => marked
    end end.

Definition add_used_nodes := [bs:BDDstate; node:ad; marked:(Map unit)]
  (add_used_nodes_1 bs node marked (S (nat_of_ad (bs_var' bs node)))).

Definition mark:=[bs:BDDstate;used:(list ad)](fold_right (add_used_nodes bs) (MO unit) used).
(* here fold right iterates the function add_used_nodes for each element in used *)
```

The new BDD state is computed by restricting the domain of the original BDD state to the set of marked nodes. This can be done using the function `MapDomRestrTo` from the map library.

```
Definition new_bs := [bs:BDDstate; used:(list ad)] (MapDomRestrTo ? ? bs (mark bs used)).
```

The new free list is computed by adding to the original free list, all the nodes from the old BDD state that are not marked. The sharing and memoization maps are cleaned by looking at each entry in them and keeping only those that refer only to marked nodes. Different functions are used for cleaning different memoization maps and sharing maps, e.g., a function `clean'1` for the memoization map for negation which is of type (`Map ad`), and a function `clean'2` (which calls the function `clean'1`) for the memoization map for disjunction (of type (`Map (Map ad)`)). We omit the definitions of these functions here as they are quite long and fairly unreadable.

We prove all the results about the garbage collector mentioned in Section 4.4. We show that after garbage collection, the resulting BDD configuration is OK, by showing that the new BDD state is OK (the reducedness, ordering conditions stated in `BDDbounded` are satisfied), and that the new free list, sharing and memoization maps are OK with respect to the new BDD state. We also show that addresses that were reachable from the input list of used nodes are left undisturbed (implying that the *semantics* of all the nodes in the list as Boolean functions remains unchanged). The proofs related to the functions `clean'1`, clean'2 mostly involve tedious arithmetical arguments related to the way addresses are stored in the maps and require proving a series of lemmas to say that the new maps contain some entry if and only if it is present in the original maps and satisfies some other conditions notably that the nodes referred to are marked. The proofs have less to do with BDDs and more to do with the details of how maps have been implemented.

6   Experimental Results

n	40	80	120	160
Coq Time	166.57	597.96	2042.38	2861.62
Caml Time	0.84	3.94	10.84	15.68
Speedup	198	152	188	182
Coq Space	33.1	68.2	39.5	48.8
Caml Space	0.4	4.1	1.0	0.9
Sp. Saving	31	12	19	30.3
#nodes	1000	10000	2000	5000

Fig. 1. Urquhart's formulae U_n

n	1	2	3	4	5	6	7	8	9	10
Coq Time	0.09	0.83	3.79	13.43	43.6	129.91	385.92	—	—	—
Caml Time	0	0.01	0.02	0.07	0.3	1.04	3.55	22.47	33.17	155.84
Speedup	—	83	190	192	145	125	109	—	—	—
Coq Space	20.7	21.6	23	27.7	34.1	49.5	84.5	—	—	—
Caml Space	36.10^{-6}	0.007	0.056	0.064	0.059	0.479	2.23	6.30	16.78	27.47
Sp. Saving	—	131	44.23	111	23	60	29	—	—	—
#nodes	8	70	270	854	2498	7006	19030	50000	129162	250000

Fig. 2. Pigeonhole formulae

We conducted several experiments to see whether this implementation is able to solve practical problems, how it scales up with problem complexity and the speed and space gained by extracting the implementation to OCaml and running the resulting, compiled programs. We give here the results for the following kinds of formulae.

- Urquhart's U-formulae [30,28]: U_n is defined as $x_1 \Leftrightarrow (x_2 \Leftrightarrow \ldots \Leftrightarrow (x_n \Leftrightarrow (x_1 \Leftrightarrow (x_2 \Leftrightarrow \ldots \Leftrightarrow (x_{n-1} \Leftrightarrow x_n) \ldots))) \ldots)$.
- Pigeonhole formulae [28]: pig_n states that you cannot put $n+1$ pigeons in n holes with no more than one pigeon per hole.
- The 1990 IMEC benchmarks [31]: these are actual hardware verification benchmarks. We give the results for the benchmarks in the ex subdirectory: 3 to 8-bit multipliers (mul03 through mul08), 2 to 8 bit ripple adders (rip02, rip04, rip06, rip08) and others (ex2, transp, ztwaalf1, ztwaalf2) and in the plasco subdirectory: werner. These involve checking equivalence between a naive and a more refined implementation of a circuit. These tests were also used by Harrison [19].

pb.	mul03	mul04	mul05	mul06	mul07	mul08	rip02	rip04	rip06	rip08
Coq Time	9.3	64.91	431.04	—	—	—	1.05	15.17	103.25	243.28
Caml Time	0.05	0.31	2.39	15.77	109.26	—	0	0.06	0.43	1.14
Speedup	186	209	180	—	—	—	—	253	240	213
#nodes	200	1854	8553	35852	100000	—	72	100	100	200

pb.	ex2	transp	ztwaalf1	ztwaalf2	werner
Coq Time	0.45	0.37	18.25	12.98	1.82
Caml Time	0	0.01	0.08	0.06	0
Speedup	—	37	228	22	—
#nodes	36	22	100	200	80

Fig. 3. IMEC benchmarks

Except for werner the other examples are tautologies. We measure the time and space requirement for building the BDD for a formula (the resulting node is 1 in case of tautologies). The policy we use is to allow more nodes to be allocated only if the garbage collector is unable to free any existing nodes. The behavior is not quite uniform with respect to the maximum number of nodes to be allocated because the garbage collector also requires space and so sometimes decreasing this number increases the total size requirements. We present here a few representative figures. Time is measured in seconds, and space in thousands of kilobytes. "Speedup" row gives the ratio of times takes by Coq and Caml for a formula. Space saving is computed as $(a-b)/c$ where a is the size of Coq process after building the BDD, b is the size beforehand, and c is the size of OCaml data (found by (stat()).livewords).

The extracted OCaml programs run around 150 times faster. Space savings are around 40-60. For pigeonhole formulae, seven pigeons is the limit for Coq and ten for the OCaml programs. Comparatively, a C version of the same algorithms is able to go up to twelve pigeons. For actual verification problems, even the Coq implementation runs in only a few seconds and difficult problems only require a few minutes (except for the multipliers, which are well known to be too hard to solve with standard BDDs). The files containing the formulas for `mul07` and `mul08` are 607 and 789 lines long respectively.

Although the Coq implementation is relatively slow and consumes a lot of memory, it is actually a pleasant surprise that such an implementation in an interpreted λ-calculus atop a simulated store runs in an acceptable amount of time and memory at all. In fact, it works on examples of quite respectable sizes, including both hard problems like pigeonhole problems and real-life problems like the IMEC benchmarks.

7   Conclusion

The import of this work is 4-fold. First, to our knowledge, this is the first complete formal proof of BDD algorithms; thanks to the Coq extraction mechanism, this yields a certified implementation in OCaml. Secondly, the BDD algorithms have not just been modeled in Coq, but completely implemented in Coq itself viewed as a programming language. This allows us and other users to replace proofs of propositional formulae in Coq's logic by mere computations in Coq's λ-calculus, and as such provides a seamless integration of BDD techniques with the Coq proof assistant. We plan to extend this to integrate a whole symbolic model checker inside Coq. Thirdly, contrary to first expectations, BDD algorithms implemented in Coq's λ-calculus atop a simulated store perform well in practice, even on hard and industrial problems. Finally, to our knowledge, this work is also the first to prove a garbage collection algorithm in full detail — what we prove is not just a model of a garbage collector, but an actual implementation that runs inside Coq itself. Furthermore, this algorithm is more complex than usual garbage collector algorithms in that it also reclaims space from memoization tables, which is not accounted for by the standard garbage collection algorithms but is needed in the context of BDDs.

Acknowledgments

We would like to thank the members of the Coq working group at INRIA Rocquencourt and at LRI, Orsay, as well as the anonymous referees for their valuable comments.

References

1. S. F. Allen, R. L. Constable, D. J. Howe, and W. E. Aitken. The semantics of reflected proof. In *LICS'90*. IEEE Computer Society Press, June 1990.
2. B. Barras. *Auto-validation d'un système de preuves avec familles inductives*. PhD thesis, University Paris VII, Nov. 1999. Code and Coq proofs available at http://www.cl.cam.ac.uk/~bb236/home/coq-in-coq.tar.gz.

3. B. Barras, S. Boutin, C. Cornes, J. Courant, Y. Coscoy, D. Delahaye, D. de Rauglaudre, J.-C. Filliâtre, E. Giménez, H. Herbelin, G. Huet, H. Laulhère, C. Muñoz, C. Murthy, C. Parent-Vigouroux, P. Loiseleur, C. Paulin-Mohring, A. Saïbi, and B. Werner. The Coq proof assistant reference manual. Version 6.2.41, available at http://coq.inria.fr/doc/main.html, Jan. 1999.

4. D. A. Basin and R. Constable. Metalogical frameworks. In G. Huet and G. Plotkin, editors, *Logical Environments*, pages 1–29. Cambridge University Press, 1993. Also available as Technical Report MPI-I-92-205.

5. J.-P. Billon. Perfect normal forms for discrete functions. Technical Report 87019, Bull S.A. Research Center, June 1987.

6. S. Boutin. Using reflection to build efficient and certified decision procedures. In M. Abadi and T. Ito, editors, *TACS'97*. Springer-Verlag LNCS 1281, 1997.

7. R. Boyer and J. S. Moore. Metafunctions: Proving them correct and using them efficiently as new proof procedures. In *The Correctness Problem in Computer Science*, London, 1981. Academic Press.

8. K. S. Brace, R. L. Rudell, and R. E. Bryant. Efficient implementation of a BDD package. In *DAC'90*. ACM/IEEE, 1990.

9. R. E. Bryant. Graph-based algorithms for Boolean function manipulation. *IEEE Transactions on Computers*, C35(8), Aug. 1986.

10. O. Coudert. *SIAM : Une Boîte à Outils Pour la Preuve Formelle de Systèmes Séquentiels*. PhD thesis, Ecole Nationale Supérieure des Télécommunications, Paris, Oct. 1991.

11. H. Goguen, R. Brooksby, and R. Burstall. Memory management: An abstract formulation of incremental tracing. In *Types'99*. Springer Verlag LNCS, 1999. Submitted.

12. G. Gonthier. Verifying the safety of a practical concurrent garbage collector. In *CAV'96*. Springer Verlag LNCS 1102, July 1996.

13. M. Gordon. Programming combinations of deduction and BDD-based symbolic calculation. Technical Report 480, University of Cambridge Computer Laboratory, Dec. 1999.

14. M. Gordon and K. F. Larsen. Combining the Hol98 proof assistant with the BuDDy BDD package. Technical Report 481, University of Cambridge Computer Laboratory, Dec. 1999.

15. M. J. C. Gordon and T. F. Melham. *Introduction to HOL: A theorem proving environment for higher order logic*. Cambridge University Press, 1993.

16. M. J. C. Gordon, R. Milner, and C. Wadsworth. Edinburgh LCF, a mechanical logic of computation. Report CSR-11-77 (in 2 parts), Dept. of Computer Science, U. Edinburgh, 1977.

17. J. Goubault. Standard ML with fast sets and maps. In *ML'94*. ACM Press, June 1994.

18. J. Goubault-Larrecq. Satisfiability of inequality constraints and detection of cycles with negative weight in graphs. Part of the Coq contribs, available at http://pauillac.inria.fr/coq/contribs/graphs.html, 1998.

19. J. Harrison. Binary decision diagrams as a HOL derived rule. *The Computer Journal*, 38, 1995.

20. G. Huet, G. Kahn, and C. Paulin-Mohring. *The Coq Proof Assistant, A Tutorial*. Coq Project, Inria, 1998. Draft, version 6.2.4. Available at http://coq.inria.fr/doc/tutorial.html.

21. P. Jackson. Verifying a garbage collection algorithm. In *TPHOL'98*. Springer Verlag LNCS 1479, 1998.

22. R. Kumar, K. Schneider, and T. Kropf. Structuring and automating hardware proofs in a higher-order theorem-proving environment. *Journal of Formal System Design*, 1993.

23. Z. Luo and R. Pollack. The LEGO proof development system: A user's manual. Technical Report ECS-LFCS-92-211, U. of Edinburgh, May 1992.

24. K. L. McMillan. *Symbolic Model Checking: An Approach to the State Explosion Problem*. Kluwer Academic Publishers, 1993.

25. G. Morrisett, M. Felleisen, and R. Harper. Abstract models of memory management. In *Functional Programming and Computer Architecture*, June 1995.

26. NIST. Common criteria for information technology security evaluation. *ISO International Standard (IS) 15408*, Jan. 2000. Version 2.1.

27. S. Owre, J. M. Rushby, and N. Shankar. PVS: A prototype verification system. In D. Kapur, editor, *CADE'92*. Springer Verlag LNAI 607, June 1992.

28. F. J. Pelletier. Seventy-five problems for testing automatic theorem provers. *Journal of Automated Reasoning*, 2, 1986. Errata: Pelletier, Francis Jeffry, JAR 4, pp. 235–236 and Pelletier, Francis Jeffry and Sutcliffe, Geoff, JAR 18(1), p. 135.

29. D. M. Russinoff. A mechanically verified garbage collector. *Formal Aspects of Computing*, 6, 1994.

30. A. Urquhart. Hard examples for resolution. *Journal of the ACM*, 34(1), 1987.

31. D. Verkest and L. Claesen. Special benchmark session on tautology checking. In L. Claesen, editor, *IMEC-IFIP Workshop on Applied Formal Methods for Correct VLSI Design*, 1990.

32. R. W. Weyhrauch. Prolegomena to a theory of mechanized formal reasoning. *Artifical Intelligence*, 13(1, 2), 1980.

33. S. Yu and Z. Luo. Implementing a model checker for LEGO. In J. Fitzgerald, C. B. Jones, and P. Lucas, editors, *FME'97*. Springer-Verlag LNCS 1313, Sept. 1997.

On Model Checking Synchronised Hardware Circuits

Martin Leucker

RWTH Aachen
Lehrstuhl für Informatik II
Ahornstr. 55, D-52074 Aachen, Germany
leucker@informatik.rwth-aachen.de

Abstract. In this paper, we present a framework for specifying and verifying an important class of hardware systems. These systems are build up from a parallel composition of circuits switching by a global clock. They can equivalently be characterised by *Petri nets* with a *maximal step semantics*. As a semantic model for these systems we introduce *Distributed Synchronous Transition Systems* (DSTS) which are distributed transition systems with a global clock synchronising the executions of actions. We show the relations to asynchronous behaviour of distributed transition systems employing Mazurkiewicz trace theory which allows a uniform treatment of synchronous as well as asynchronous executions. We introduce a process algebra like calculus for defining DSTS which we call *Synchronous Process Systems*. Furthermore, we present *Foata Lineartime Temporal Logic* (FLTL) which is a temporal logic with a flavour of LTL adapted for specifying properties of DSTS. Our important contributions are the developed decision procedures for satisfiability as well as model checking of FLTL formulas, both based on alternating Büchi automata.

1 Introduction

Many digital circuits, especially embedded controllers, can be modelled as transition systems wrt. their logical behaviour. The controller is in one of finitely many states and executes one of its commands which we will call *actions* in this paper. The action modifies the current state transforming it into a new one. Usually, the executions are synchronised by a global clock or oscillator. Every time *tick*, an action takes place.[1] Several circuits or controllers for different tasks are combined on a switching board. The global clock synchronises the execution.

However, the circuits have to coordinate their work. Therefore, they have to *communicate*. Typically, the circuits communicate among each other or to other resources like a shared memory via a common *bus*. To coordinate the access to this bus, an *arbiter* is employed. Every circuit has to ask the arbiter which grants the access to the bus. The circuits and the arbiter communicate

---

[1] Actions lasting for more than one tick can be modelled by a sequence of single–tick actions.

J. He and M. Sato (Eds.): ASIAN 2000, LNCS 1961, pp. 182–198, 2000.

via common actions. Figure 1 shows an example of four circuits. Every circuit is connected by two wires to the arbiter, one is employed for requesting the bus (ri), the second one for granting it (gi). A request of Circuit 1 recognised by the arbiter can be modelled by the common action r1. If the arbiter is not in the state for receiving the request, Circuit 1 suspends. Note, that in every *tick*, the other circuits may execute *independent* actions.[2]

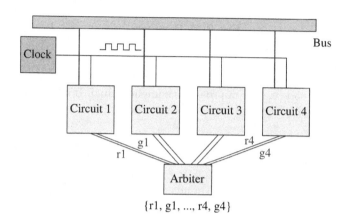

Fig. 1. Synchronised digital circuits

We introduce *Distributed Synchronous Transition Systems* (DSTS) which are distributed transition systems with a global clock synchronising the executions of actions. They can be understood as a model for the parallel composition of hardware circuits as described above.

Distributed Synchronous Transition Systems can also be interpreted as a model for the well–known *Petri nets* with a *maximal step semantics* [Rei86]. We assume that the reader is familiar with the notion of Petri nets and just give an example of a Petri net together with a maximal step run. Figure 2 shows a place–transition–net. The maximal step semantics is obtained by the rule that all transitions which are capable of firing simultaneously, fire simultaneously. A possible execution sequence for the presented Petri net would be $\{a, e\}\{b\}\{c\}\{d, f\}\{g\}\{h\}$ where each set mentions the actions occurring concurrently.

Distributed transition systems (DTS) are a well–known model for distributed systems (cf. [Zie87, TH98]). However, usually they are considered with an asynchronous model of execution. The simultaneous execution of two independent actions a and b is modelled by the interleaving of a and b, i.e., first a and then

---

[2] The shown setup of the bus, circuits and the arbiter is described as a sample layout for the Motorola PowerPC where, for example, Circuit 1 to Circuit 3 are PowerPCs and Circuit 4 is a memory controller [Mot93].

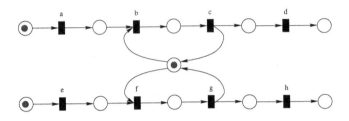

Fig. 2. A Petri net

b as well as b and then a. In this way, concurrency is reduced to sequences and non–deterministic choice. Our approach is somehow dual. If two actions a and b can occur concurrently then we require them to occur concurrently and abstract from interleaving.

Distributed transition systems can be treated formally by Mazurkiewicz trace theory [DR95]. We show that asynchronous executions of distributed transition systems are captured by the configuration graph of a trace and that the *Foata configuration graph* of a trace corresponds to one synchronous execution of the DTS.

Considering the relations between asynchronous and synchronous behaviour of distributed transition systems, it turns out that a synchronous execution can be mapped to a set of asynchronous executions differing only between the interleaving of independent actions. However, not every asynchronous execution corresponds to a synchronous one. Hence, considering asynchronous executions yields a more abstract system. For model checking linear time specifications this provides the case that one might fail to prove a property although the underlying system fulfils the requested requirement.

To simplify the task of defining DSTS, we introduce a simple calculus which we call *Synchronous Process Systems* and is inspired by Milner's CCS [Mil89]. Synchronous Process Systems consist of a set of equations, each defining a single non–deterministic sequential process. The overall behaviour of the system is obtained by taking the concurrent product of the system where the execution, synchronisation, and communication is defined in the manner described above.

Our main contribution is a logical approach for specifying properties for synchronous transition systems. We introduce *Foata Lineartime Temporal Logic* (FLTL) which is a temporal logic with a flavour of Lineartime Temporal Logic (LTL, [MP92]) adapted for specifying properties of DSTS. We give a decision procedure for FLTL as well as a model checking procedure, both based on alternating Büchi automata. It turns out that these procedures meet the known complexity bounds for LTL *viz* exponential in the length of the formula and linear in the size of the system and are essentially optimal. The model checking procedure employs an optimisation which is similar to a technique known as *partial order reduction* [Pel98]. However, instead of defining the interleaving product of the sequential processes and then trying to omit states not influencing the result of the model checking procedure, we are able to define smaller systems directly because of the underlying model.

Synchronous systems were studied by several authors. Milner defined a variant of (asynchronous) CCS for synchronous systems (SCCS, [Mil83]). Lustre [CPHP87] is a programming language for synchronous systems. Usually, these contributions concentrate on the design of the underlying systems. The problem of verification is tackled by the notion of *bisimilarity* or by *theorem proving* [BCPVD99]. Simple model–checking–based verification techniques are lacking. We present a simple model for synchronous hardware systems together with an implementation driven definition of a model checking algorithm.

In the next section, we introduce basic notions of Mazurkiewicz trace theory. Section 3 presents alternating Büchi automata which will be our tool for the decision procedure. We carry on by defining distributed transition systems and a calculus for synchronous process systems. In Sections 6, 7 and 8 we define FLTL, give a decision procedure as well as a model checking procedure, resp. We draw our conclusions in Section 9.

2   Preliminaries

A *(Mazurkiewicz) trace alphabet* is a pair (Σ, I), where Σ, the alphabet, is a finite set and $I \subseteq \Sigma \times \Sigma$ is an irreflexive and symmetric *independence relation*. (Σ, I) is sometimes also called *independence alphabet*. Usually, Σ consists of the actions performed by a distributed system while I captures a static notion of causal independence between actions. For the rest of the paper we fix a trace alphabet (Σ, I). We define $D = (\Sigma \times \Sigma) - I$ to be the *dependency relation* which is then reflexive and symmetric. For example (Σ, I) where $\Sigma = \{a, b, c, d\}$ and $I = \{(a, d), (d, a), (b, c), (c, b)\}$ is an independence alphabet.[3]

A *distributed alphabet* $\tilde{\Sigma}$ [PP95] is an n-tuple of alphabets $(\Sigma_1, \ldots, \Sigma_n)$ (not necessarily disjoint). Let $\Sigma = \Sigma_1 \cup \ldots \cup \Sigma_n$, $Proc = \{1, \ldots, n\}$. For each $a \in \Sigma$, denote by $pr(a)$ the set $\{i \in Proc \mid a \in \Sigma_i\}$. For a distributed alphabet $\tilde{\Sigma}$ we define the *independence relation* $I(\tilde{\Sigma})$ by $I(\tilde{\Sigma}) = \{(a, b) \in \Sigma \times \Sigma \mid pr(a) \cap pr(b) = \emptyset\}$.

A distributed alphabet covers the notion of a system consisting of n components or processes. Actions occurring in the intersection of several components are used for communication: They must be executed concurrently.

It is easy to see that $(\Sigma, I(\tilde{\Sigma}))$ is an independence alphabet. On the other hand, for an independence alphabet (Σ, I) we get a unique (up to the order of the alphabets) distributed alphabet $\tilde{\Sigma}$ such that $(\Sigma, I) = (\Sigma, I(\tilde{\Sigma}))$ by considering the maximal dependent subsets of Σ, i.e., the subsets $\Sigma_i \subseteq \Sigma$ such that $(a, b) \notin I$ for all $a, b \in \Sigma_i$. For example, the independence alphabet previously mentioned determines the distributed alphabet $(\{a, b\}, \{a, c\}, \{b, d\}, \{c, d\})$. Note that the maximal dependent subsets of an independence alphabet correspond to the maximal cliques when interpreting (Σ, D) as a graph. Abusing notation, we denote by $I(\Sigma)$ also the set of all pairwise independent subsets of Σ.

---

[3] We fix this alphabet for further examples.

Let $T = (E, \leq, \lambda)$ be a Σ-labelled poset. In other words, $(E, \leq)$ is a poset and $\lambda : E \to \Sigma$ is a labelling function. λ can be extended to subsets of E in the expected manner. We will refer to members of E as *events*. For $e \in E$ we define $\downarrow e = \{x \in E \mid x \leq e\}$ and $\uparrow e = \{x \in E \mid e \leq x\}$. We call $\downarrow e$ the *history* of the event e. We also let $\lessdot$ be the *covering relation* given by $x \lessdot y$ iff $x < y$ and for all $z \in E$, $x \leq z \leq y$ implies $x = z$ or $z = y$. Moreover, we let the *concurrency relation* be defined by $x \text{ co } y$ iff $x \not\leq y$ and $y \not\leq x$.

A *(Mazurkiewicz) trace* (over (Σ, I)) is a Σ-labelled poset $T = (E, \leq, \lambda)$ satisfying:

(T1) $\forall e \in E.$ $\downarrow e$ is a finite set
(T2) $\forall e, e' \in E.$ $e \lessdot e'$ implies $\lambda(e) \, D \, \lambda(e')$.
(T3) $\forall e, e' \in E.$ $\lambda(e) \, D \, \lambda(e')$ implies $e \leq e'$ or $e' \leq e$.

We shall let $TR(\Sigma, I)$ denote the class of traces over (Σ, I). As usual, a trace language L is a subset of traces, i.e. $L \subseteq TR(\Sigma, I)$. Throughout the paper we will not distinguish between isomorphic elements in $TR(\Sigma, I)$. A trace $(E, \leq, \lambda)$ is called *finite* iff E is finite.

Let $T = (E, \leq, \lambda)$ be a trace over (Σ, I). A *configuration* of T is a finite subset of events $c \subseteq E$ with $\downarrow c = c$ where $\downarrow c = \bigcup_{e \in c} \downarrow e$. The set of configurations of T will be denoted $conf(T)$. Trivially, $\emptyset \in conf(T)$ is always the case. Furthermore, we define the c-suffix of T by $T \backslash c = (E - c, \leq|_{E-c}, \lambda|_{E-c})$. It is then not hard to see that $T \backslash c \in TR(\Sigma, I)$ for any trace $T \in TR(\Sigma, I)$ and $c \in conf(T)$. For a configuration c let $top(c)$ denote its maximal elements wrt. $\leq$. Every element of $top(c)$ is called a top event or a top action (if the label of the event is considered).

Moreover, $conf(T)$ can be equipped with a natural transition relation $\longrightarrow_T \subseteq conf(T) \times \Sigma \times conf(T)$ given by $c \xrightarrow{a}_T c'$ iff there exists an $e \in E$ such that $\lambda(e) = a$, $e \notin c$ and $c' = c \cup \{e\}$.

Definition 1. *Let* $min(T) = \{e \in E \mid e \text{ is minimal in } T \text{ wrt. } \leq\}$. *The* Foata configuration graph $foata(T) = (C, \subseteq)$ *for a trace* T *is the subgraph of* $conf(T)$ *where* C *is the smallest set so that* $\emptyset \in C$ *and for every* $c \in C$ *also* $min(T \backslash c) \in C$

The idea of the Foata configuration graph is to consider the configuration sequences in which every component has made an action if possible. Figure 3 shows a trace, its configuration graph and its Foata configuration graph.[4] The formulas of the Foata temporal logic are interpreted wrt. Foata configurations of traces.

A *linearisation* of a trace $(E, \leq, \lambda)$ is a linearisation of the partial order, i.e., it is a total labelled order $(E, \leq', \lambda)$ such that $\leq \; \subseteq \; \leq'$. A trace is equal to the intersection of all its linearisations and given an independence alphabet (Σ, I) a trace T is uniquely determined by one of its linearisations T'. In this case we call T the *expansion* of T'. A linearisation of a trace $(E, \leq, \lambda)$ represents a word

---

[4] Instead of showing the events of the configurations, we present their labels. The ordering of the events is clear by the independence alphabet and by the rule that dependent events increase from left to right.

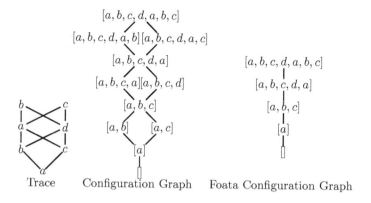

Trace   Configuration Graph   Foata Configuration Graph

Fig. 3. A trace, its configuration graph and its Foata configuration graph

by considering the sequence of labels. Furthermore, all linearisations of a trace form an equivalence class.

An ω-*linearisation* of a trace $(E, \leq, \lambda)$ is a linearisation $(E, \leq', \lambda)$ such that every event $e \in E$ has a finite history, i.e., $\forall e \in E \mid \downarrow e \mid < \infty$. An ω-linearisation of a trace corresponds to an ω-word and all ω-linearisations of a trace form an equivalence class in Σ^ω.

Definition 2. *A Foata linearisation of a trace $(E, \leq, \lambda)$ is a linearisation $(E, \leq', \lambda)$ which can be written as a product of finite traces*

$$(E, \leq', \lambda) = \prod_{i=1...\infty} (E_i, \leq'_i, \lambda_i)$$

such that for every $i \geq 1$ we have $\leq'_i = \leq' |_{E_i}$, $\lambda_i = \lambda |_{E_i}$ and E_i is a set of pairwise independent actions, i.e., $\lambda_i(E_i) \subseteq I(\Sigma)$. Furthermore, for each $i \geq 1$ and every $e \in E_{i+1}$ there is an $e' \in E_i$ such that $(\lambda(e), \lambda(e')) \in D$. Note that the product of finite traces is defined in the canonical way: $(E, \leq, \lambda)(E', \leq', \lambda') = (E \cup E', \leq \cup \leq' \cup\{(e, e') \in E \times E' \mid (\lambda(e), \lambda'(e')) \in D\}, \lambda \cup \lambda')$.

A Foata linearisation is an ω-linearisation of a trace and corresponds to an ω-word in Foata normal form which is defined similarly [DM96]: A word $w \in \Sigma^\omega$ is in Foata normal form iff

1. $w = w_1 w_2 \ldots$
2. for each $i \geq 1$ the word w_i is a product of pairwise independent actions
3. for each $i \geq 1$ and for each letter a of w_{i+1} there exist a letter b in w_i which is dependent on a $((a, b) \in D)$.

The words w_i are called *steps*. It is easy to see that for $w = w_1 w_2 \ldots$ in Foata normal form and for every i the suffix $w_i w_{i+1} \ldots$ is in Foata normal form. The steps correspond to the top actions of every configuration in the Foata configuration graph of a trace. For example, a Foata linearisation of the trace shown in Figure 3 is $(a)(bc)(ad)(bc)$ where the steps are accentuated by parenthesises.

Note that the Foata normal form as defined here is unique up to permutation of independent actions within a step. Given a total oder $\prec$ for the actions of Σ and requiring the steps to be minimal wrt. the lexicographic order derived from $\prec$ results in a unique Foata normal form for every trace. Such a word can also be considered as a word over $I(\Sigma)$. However, not every word of $I(\Sigma)$ is in Foata normal form. For example, $(b)(bc)$ can be considered as a word of $I(\Sigma)$ but its Foata normal form (as a word over Σ) would be $(bc)(b)$.

3   Alternating Büchi Automata

Nondeterminism gives an automaton the power of existential choices: A word w is accepted by an automaton iff there exists an accepting run on w. Alternation gives a machine the power of universal choices and was studied in [BL80, CKS81] (in the context of automata). In this section, we recall the notion of alternating automata along the lines of [Var96] where alternating Büchi automata are used for model checking LTL. For an introduction to Büchi automata we refer to [Tho90].

For a finite set X of variables let $\mathcal{B}^+(X)$ be the set of *positive Boolean formulas* over X, i.e., the smallest set such that

- $X \subseteq \mathcal{B}^+(X)$
- $\texttt{true}, \texttt{false} \in \mathcal{B}^+(X)$
- $\varphi, \psi \in \mathcal{B}^+(X) \Rightarrow \varphi \wedge \psi \in \mathcal{B}^+(X), \varphi \vee \psi \in \mathcal{B}^+(X)$

The dual of a formula $\varphi \in \mathcal{B}^+(X)$ denoted by $\overline{\varphi}$ is the formula where $\texttt{false}$ is replaced by $\texttt{true}$, $\texttt{true}$ by $\texttt{false}$, $\vee$ by $\wedge$ and $\wedge$ by $\vee$.

We say that a set $Y \subseteq X$ *satisfies* a formula $\varphi \in \mathcal{B}^+(X)$ $(Y \models \varphi)$ iff φ evaluates to *true* when the variables in Y are assigned to *true* and the members of $X \backslash Y$ are assigned to *false*. For example, $\{q_1, q_3\}$ as well as $\{q_1, q_4\}$ satisfy the formula $(q_1 \vee q_2) \wedge (q_3 \vee q_4)$.

Let us consider a Büchi automaton. For a state q of the automaton and an action a let $\{q_1, \ldots, q_k\} = \{q' \mid q \xrightarrow{a} q'\}$ be the set of possible next states for (q, a). The key idea for alternation is to describe the nondeterminism by the formula $q_1 \vee \cdots \vee q_k \in \mathcal{B}^+(Q)$. Hence, we write $q \xrightarrow{a} q_1 \vee \cdots \vee q_k$. If $k = 0$ we write $q \xrightarrow{a} \texttt{false}$. An alternation is introduced by allowing an arbitrary formula of $\mathcal{B}^+(Q)$. Let us be more precise:

An *Alternating Büchi Automaton* (ABA) over an alphabet Σ is a tuple $\mathcal{A} = (Q, \delta, q_0, \mathcal{F})$ such that Q is a finite nonempty set of *states*, $q_0 \in Q$ is the *initial state*, $\mathcal{F} \subseteq Q$ is a set of accepting states and $\delta : Q \times \Sigma \to \mathcal{B}^+(Q)$ is the *transition function*.

Because of universal quantification a run is no longer a sequence but a tree. A *Q-labelled tree* τ is a pair (t, T) such that t is a tree and $T : nodes(t) \to Q$. To simplify the presentation, we let $nodes(t)$ be implicitly defined and refer to its elements in the following canonical way: The root is denoted by ε and if a node s is denoted by w then a child s' labelled with q by T is denoted by wq. Since for our needs we can restrict T to be one–to–one for children of the same parent this is well–defined.

For a node s let $|s|$ denote its *height*, i.e., $|\varepsilon| = 0$, $|wq| = |w| + 1$. A branch of τ is a maximal sequence $\beta = s_0, s_1, \ldots$ of nodes of τ such that s_0 is the root of τ and s_i is the father of s_{i+1}, $i \in \mathbb{N}$. The *word induced by* β (for short β's word) is the sequence of labels of β, i.e., the sequence $T(s_0), T(s_1), \ldots$

A *run* of an alternating BA $\mathcal{A} = (Q, \delta, q_0, \mathcal{F})$ on a word $w = a_0 a_1 \ldots$ is a (possibly infinite) Q-labelled tree τ such that $T(\varepsilon) = q_0$ and the following holds:

> if x is a node with $|x| = i$, $T(x) = q$ and $\delta(q, a_i) = \varphi$ then either $\varphi \in \{\texttt{true}, \texttt{false}\}$ and x has no children or x has k children $x_1, \ldots, x_k$ for some $k \leq |Q|$ and $\{T(x_1), \ldots, T(x_k)\}$ satisfies φ.

The run τ is *accepting* if every finite branch ends on $\texttt{true}$ (i.e., $\delta(T(x), a_i) = \texttt{true}$ where x denotes the maximum element of the branch wrt. the height and i denotes its height) and every infinite branch of τ hits an element of $\mathcal{F}$ infinitively often.

It is obvious that every Büchi automaton can be turned into an equivalent (wrt. the accepted language) alternating Büchi automaton in the way described above. The converse is also true and is described for example in [Var96]. The construction involves an exponential blow up. Hence, it is easy to see that the emptiness problem for ABAs is exponential in the number of states.

4   Distributed Synchronous Transition Systems (DSTS)

We introduce a formal model for the underlying concurrent systems, *Distributed Synchronous Transition Systems*. It is based on Zielonka's asynchronous automata (without final states, [Zie87]) or the notion distributed transitions systems (described for example in [TH98]).[5] However, the definition of a run is modified to reflect the idea of a global synchronising clock. Strictly speaking, we only define *Distributed Transition Systems* (DTS) as well as their *synchronous* and *asynchronous* runs. However, to denote the context we speak of either *synchronous* or *asynchronous* DTS.

Definition 3. *A Distributed Transition System (DTS) over a distributed alphabet $\tilde{\Sigma}$ is a tuple $\mathcal{A} = (Q_1, \ldots, Q_n, \longrightarrow, \mathcal{I})$ where*

- *Each Q_i is a finite nonempty set of* local states *of the ith component.*
- *Let $\bar{Q} = \prod_{i \in Proc} Q_i$ be the set of* global states *and $\mathcal{I} \subseteq \bar{Q}$ be the set of initial states.*

---

[5] Our presentation of DTS is inspired by [PP95].

- Let $States = \prod_{i \in Proc}(Q_i \cup \{-\})$. The dummy $-$ is used as a placeholder in components which have no significance for the transition: $\longrightarrow \subseteq States \times \Sigma \times States$ is a transition relation satisfying the following condition:

$$\text{if } (\bar{q}, a, \bar{q}') \in \longrightarrow \text{ then } \bar{q}[i] = \bar{q}'[i] = - \text{ for } i \in Proc \backslash pr(a)$$

where $\bar{q}[i] \in Q_i$ denotes the ith component of $\bar{q}$.

The dummy $-$ in the definition of the transition relation $\longrightarrow$ is used for denoting components of a global state which are not affected by the transition. Given a state $\bar{q} = (q_1, \ldots, q_n) \in \bar{Q}$ we denote by $\bar{q}|_M$ the element $(q_1', \ldots, q_n') \in States$ such that $q_i = q_i'$ for $i \in M$ and $q_i' = -$ else.

Definition 4. A synchronous execution ρ of a DTS is an infinite sequence $\bar{q}_1 A_1 \bar{q}_2 \ldots$ of global states and sets of pairwise independent actions which satisfies the following conditions:

- $\bar{q}_1 \in \mathcal{I}$, i.e., $\bar{q}_1$ is an initial state.
- For $j \geq 1$ and all $a \in A_j$, $(\bar{q}_j|_{pr(a)}, a, \bar{q}_{j+1}|_{pr(a)}) \in \longrightarrow$ and $\bar{q}_j|_P = \bar{q}_{j+1}|_P$ for $P = Proc \backslash \bigcup_{a \in A_j} pr(a)$. Hence, a transition is the "parallel" execution of concurrent actions according to the local transition rules.
- Furthermore, A_j must be maximal in the following sense: For every $j \geq 1$, for all $A_j' \in I(\Sigma)$ with $A_j' \supseteq A_j$ such that there is a $\bar{q}_{j+1}'$ with $\bar{q}_j A_j' \bar{q}_{j+1}'$ we have $A_j' = A_j$. This ensures that all components being able to do a local transition participate in the global transition.

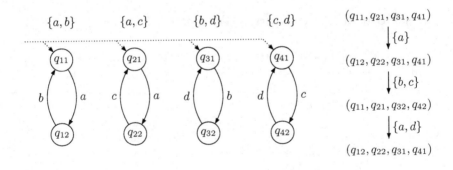

Fig. 4. A distributed transition system and a synchronous execution

Abusing notation we call a DTS also a *Distributed Synchronous Transition System* if we consider its synchronous executions. Figure 4 shows a graphical representation of a DTS and (a part of) one of its executions. The dotted line describes the initial state of the system. The crucial point of the execution is that the actions b and c must occur synchronously.

For a distributed transition system, we also define the notion of an asynchronous execution which is obtained by sequentialising and interleaving transitions.

Definition 5. *An* asynchronous execution ρ *of a DTS is an infinite sequence* $\bar{q}_1 a_1 \bar{q}_2 \ldots$ *of global states* $\bar{q}_j$ *and actions* a_j *which satisfies the following conditions:*

- $\bar{q}_1 \in \mathcal{I}$, *i.e.,* $\bar{q}_1$ *is an initial state.*
- *For every* $j \geq 1$, *we have* $(\bar{q}_j|_{pr(a_j)}, a_j, \bar{q}_{j+1}|_{pr(a_j)}) \in \longrightarrow$ *and* $\bar{q}_j|_{Proc\backslash pr(a_j)} = \bar{q}_{j+1}|_{Proc\backslash pr(a_j)}$. *The triple* $(\bar{q}_j, a_j, \bar{q}_{j+1})$ *is called the* j*th state of* ρ *and is abbreviated by* $\rho(j)$.

In the same manner we call a distributed transition system also a *distributed asynchronous transition system* when considering its asynchronous executions. For the distributed transition system presented in Figure 4

$$(q_{11}, q_{21}, q_{31}, q_{41}) \ a \ (q_{12}, q_{22}, q_{31}, q_{41}) \ b \ (q_{11}, q_{22}, q_{32}, q_{41}) \ c$$
$$(q_{11}, q_{21}, q_{32}, q_{42}) \ d \ (q_{11}, q_{21}, q_{31}, q_{41})$$

would be a (part of) an asynchronous run.

A synchronous execution can be mapped to a Foata configuration graph in the obvious way. Furthermore, given a synchronous execution an asynchronous execution can be obtained by interleaving each synchronous execution of actions A_j which we call interleaving of a synchronous run. However, it is an easy exercise to see that not every asynchronous run can be obtained by interleaving a synchronous one.

Theorem 1. *For distributed transition systems the class of (interleaved) synchronous executions is strictly contained in the class of asynchronous executions.*

Proof. Consider the system depicted in Figure 5. For every asynchronous execution corresponding to a synchronous one, there is an action d between two actions a. This does not hold for every asynchronous run.

For model checking, the previous theorem implies that considering the more abstract asynchronous behaviour of a hardware system could yield false evidence.

5   A calculus for DSTS

In this section, we introduce the process calculus *Synchronous Process System* (SPS) which may be employed to define a distributed synchronous transition system. Within the area of verification, a distributed system is preferably given in terms of such a calculus instead of directly presenting the automaton.

Let $\Gamma = \{nil^{(0)}, +^{(2)}, .^{(2)}\}$ be a ranked alphabet, Σ a finite set of nullary actions and P a variable. The set of *sequential process terms* $SPT(\Sigma, P)$ is inductively defined by

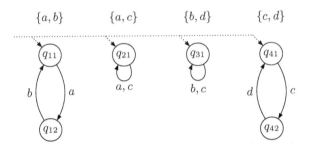

Fig. 5. Asynchronous runs and synchronous runs differ

- $P, \mathrm{nil} \in SPT(\Sigma, P)$
- $t_1, t_2 \in SPT(\Sigma, P), a \in \Sigma \Rightarrow a.t_1, t_1 + t_2 \in SPT(\Sigma, P)$

A *process definition* over (Σ, P) is an equation $P = T(P)$ where $T(P)$ is a sequential process term over (Σ, P). A *synchronous process system* over a distributed alphabet $\tilde{\Sigma} = (\Sigma_1, \ldots, \Sigma_n)$ and a finite set of process variables $\mathcal{P} = \{P, P_1, \ldots, P_n\}$ is a set of equations $(i \in \{1, \ldots, n\})$

$$\{P = P_1 \parallel \ldots \parallel P_n, P_i = t_i\}$$

where $t_i \in SPT(\Sigma_i, P_i)$ and $\parallel$ is an n-ary (parallel) operator.

The semantics of a synchronous process system is defined in two steps. The semantics of a process definition $P = t$ is a (finite) transition system $(S, \rightarrow)$ where $S = P \cup Sub(t)^6$ and $\rightarrow\ : S \times \Sigma \times S$ is a labelled transition relation defined by the following inference rules

$$\frac{}{a.t_1 \xrightarrow{a} t_1} \qquad \frac{t_1 \xrightarrow{a} t_1'}{t_1 + t_2 \xrightarrow{a} t_1'}$$

$$\frac{t \xrightarrow{a} t'}{P \xrightarrow{a} t'}\ (P{=}t) \qquad \frac{t_2 \xrightarrow{a} t_2'}{t_1 + t_2 \xrightarrow{a} t_2'}$$

The semantics of a process system $\mathcal{P} = \{P = P_1 \parallel \ldots \parallel P_n, P_i = t_i\}$ is a distributed synchronous transition system defined in the following way: For P_i let $(S_i, \rightarrow_i)$ be its semantics. Let $\longrightarrow = \{(q_1, \ldots, q_n, a, q_1', \ldots, q_n') \mid \forall i \in pr(a)\ (q_i, a, q_i') \in \rightarrow_i$ and $\forall i \in Proc\backslash pr(a)\ q_i = q_i' = -\}$. The distributed transition system for $\mathcal{P}$ is $(S_1, \ldots, S_n, \longrightarrow, (P_1, \ldots, P_n))$

A drawback of our calculus is that it is not expressive complete with respect to DSTS. It is an easy exercise to see that our calculus cannot define the trace language $\Sigma^* ac\Sigma^*$ over the alphabet $\Sigma = \{a, b, c\}$ where the only independent actions are a and c. On the contrary, this is simple when DSTS are considered.

Lemma 1. *The class of languages definable by SPS is strictly contained in the class of languages definable by DSTS.*

---

[6] $Sub(t)$ denotes the set of subterms of t defined in the usual way.

For completeness, we mention that it is easy to see that SPS define so–called regular *product languages* while DSTS define regular *trace languages* [Thi95].

6 Foata Linear Time Temporal Logic (FLTL)

In this section, we introduce *Foata Linear Time Temporal Logic* (FLTL) which is patterned after LTL and may be used to specify the behaviour of a distributed synchronous transition system. A crucial difference to LTL is that (independent) sets of actions may be employed to define atomic steps of a DSTS.

Let (Σ, I) be an independence alphabet and $I(\Sigma)$ the set of pairwise independent subsets of Σ. $\mathrm{FLTL}(\Sigma, I)$ is the least set of formulas that satisfies for all $\varphi, \psi \in \mathrm{FLTL}(\Sigma, I)$:

$$\mathrm{tt} \in \mathrm{FLTL}(\Sigma, I) \qquad\qquad \langle A \rangle \varphi \in \mathrm{FLTL}(\Sigma, I)$$
$$\neg\varphi \in \mathrm{FLTL}(\Sigma, I) \qquad\qquad O\varphi \in \mathrm{FLTL}(\Sigma, I)$$
$$\varphi \wedge \psi \in \mathrm{FLTL}(\Sigma, I) \qquad\qquad \varphi U \psi \in \mathrm{FLTL}(\Sigma, I)$$

where $A \in I(\Sigma)$.

Let T be a trace over (Σ, I) and $(foata(T), \rightarrow)$ its Foata configuration graph. The satisfaction relation for a formula $\varphi \in \mathrm{FLTL}(\Sigma, I)$ wrt. a Foata configuration c of T is inductively defined by

- $T, c \models \mathrm{tt}$,
- $T, c \models \neg\varphi \Leftrightarrow T, c \not\models \varphi$,
- $T, c \models \varphi \wedge \psi$ iff $T, c \models \varphi$ and $T, c \models \psi$,
- $T, c \models \langle A \rangle \varphi$ iff there exists an $A' \in I(\Sigma)$, $A' \supseteq A$ and $c' \in (foata(T), \rightarrow)$ such that $c \xrightarrow{A'} c'$ and $T, c' \models \varphi$ where $c \xrightarrow{A'} c'$ iff $c, c' \in foata(T)$, $\lambda(c' \setminus c) = A'$ and $c' \setminus c \in I(\Sigma)$,
- $T, c \models O\varphi$ iff there exists an $A \in I(\Sigma)$ and $c' \in (foata(T), \rightarrow)$ such that $c \xrightarrow{A} c'$ and $T, c' \models \varphi$,
- $T, c \models \varphi U \psi$ iff there exists $c' \in (foata(T), \rightarrow)$, $c' \supseteq c$ such that $T, c' \models \psi$ and for all $c'' \in (foata(T), \rightarrow)$, $c \subseteq c'' \subset c'$ $T, c'' \models \varphi$.

For formulas of the kind $\langle A \rangle \varphi$, we require a superset A' of A to exist for transforming the system from configuration c to c'. This simplifies the task of specification since the user only has to specify the actions he or she wants to see while leaving the atomic actions of the components not involved by actions of A unspecified. If we change our semantics in the way that exactly the actions specified must be employed to move from configuration $c \rightarrow c'$, we can transform every formula of our logic into this logic by taking any combination of the remaining actions. However, in general this causes an *exponential blow up* of our formula augmenting the overall complexity of deciding and model checking. It is an easy exercise to enrich our logic and algorithms by additional operators requiring A' to be a subset of A or to be equal to A without increasing its complexity.

As usual, we introduce the abbreviations of the following kind to simplify the task of specifying properties:

- $\varphi \vee \psi$ for $\neg(\neg\varphi \wedge \neg\psi)$
- $\Diamond\varphi$ for $\mathrm{tt}U\varphi$
- $\Box\varphi$ for $\neg\Diamond\neg\varphi$

Hence, it is possible to express global liveness and safety properties in a manner as known from LTL (see [MP92] for an introduction to specification via LTL).

Our logic can be understood as LTL over the alphabet $I(\Sigma)$ with the exception of the different interpretation of the next–state operator. Then one might think of employing the standard LTL algorithms for deciding FLTL. However, since not every word in $I(\Sigma)^*$ is in Foata normal form, the standard algorithms for deciding and model checking algorithm for LTL have to be modified to consider only models in Foata normal form. Furthermore, the algorithms have to be modified to respect our special form of the next–state operator(s). Concerning model checking, the models to analyse are given by distributed transition systems over the alphabet Σ. To employ a logic over $I(\Sigma)$, the transition systems have to be transformed into a single *bisimilar* one over $I(\Sigma)$. For practical reasons, this has to be carried out *on–the–fly*. Altogether, we are convinced that understanding FLTL as a logic over $I(\Sigma)$ is theoretically more elegant but is the second choice for practical algorithms. We therefore directly formulate a decision procedure and a model checking algorithm for Σ since this yields a more efficient practical implementation. However, the presentation is a little bit more technically involved.

7   Deciding FLTL

We now present a decision procedure for FLTL formulas by means of alternating Büchi automata. Given a formula $\varphi \in \mathrm{FLTL}(\Sigma, I)$, we define an automaton $\mathcal{A}_\varphi$ that for all Foata linearisations w accepts w if and only if the expansion T of w satisfies φ.

As a second step, we will define a Büchi automaton $\mathcal{A}_\mathcal{F}$ accepting a word in Σ^ω iff it is in Foata normal form. Hence, the language of the automaton accepting the intersection of the languages $\mathcal{A}_\varphi$ and $\mathcal{A}_\mathcal{F}$ is non–empty if and only if φ is satisfiable.

Definition 6. *Let* $\varphi \in \mathrm{FLTL}(\Sigma, I)$. *Then* $\mathcal{A}_\varphi = (Q, \Sigma, \delta, q_0, F)$ *is defined by* $Q = I(\Sigma) \times (Sub(\varphi) \cup \neg Sub(\varphi))$, $q_0 = (\emptyset, \varphi)$ *and* $\delta : I(\Sigma) \times Q \times \Sigma \to \mathcal{B}^+(I(\Sigma) \times Q)$ *by*

$$
\begin{aligned}
(S, \mathrm{tt}, a) &\mapsto \mathtt{true} \\
(S, \psi \wedge \eta, a) &\mapsto \delta(S, \psi, a) \wedge \delta(S, \eta, a) \\
(S, \neg\psi, a) &\mapsto \neg\delta(S, \psi, a) \\
(S, \langle A\rangle\psi, a) &\mapsto \begin{cases} \delta(\emptyset, \psi, a) & \text{if } aDS, A \subseteq S \\ \mathtt{false} & \text{if } aDS, A \not\subseteq S \\ (S \cup \{a\}, \langle A\rangle\psi) & \text{if } aIS \end{cases} \\
(S, O\psi, a) &\mapsto \begin{cases} \delta(\emptyset, \psi, a) & \text{if } aDS \\ (S \cup \{a\}, O\psi) & \text{if } aIS \end{cases} \\
(\emptyset, \psi U\eta, a) &\mapsto \delta(\emptyset, \eta \vee (\psi \wedge O(\psi U\eta)), a)
\end{aligned}
$$

The set of final states is, as usual, given by the states with negative formulas,
$F = I(\Sigma) \times \{\neg\varphi : \varphi \in Sub(\varphi)\}.$

Given a linearisation of a trace in Foata normal form, the different steps are characterised by actions dependent on the preceeding step. Hence, the transition function of the automaton $\mathcal{A}_\varphi$ for a formula $\varphi \in$ FLTL collects the independent actions of the current step and checks the formula as soon as a dependent action occurs. *until* formulas are directly unwound according to the equivalence $\varphi U \psi \equiv \psi \lor (\varphi \land O(\varphi U \psi))$. Hence, the transition function δ just treats the situation for an empty step.

Every finite branch of a run of $\mathcal{A}_\varphi$ ending in **true** gives a proof for our formula. Infinite branches only occur by infinitely often unwinding *until* formulas. Hence, they must be accepted iff the *until* formula is negated. This shows the correctness of our construction.

Now, we define an automaton $\mathcal{A}_\mathcal{F}$ accepting Foata linearisations of traces. It can be understood as a kind of filter, rejecting ω-words which cannot be a Foata linearisation of a trace. The intersection of $\mathcal{A}_\mathcal{F}$ and $\mathcal{A}_\varphi$ is the automaton to be checked for (non–)emptiness to decide the satisfiability of φ.

Definition 7. $\mathcal{A}_\mathcal{F} = (Q, \Sigma, \delta, q_0, F)$ *is defined by* $Q = 2^\Sigma \times I(\Sigma)$, $q_0 = (\Sigma, \emptyset)$, $F = Q$ *and* $\delta : Q \times \Sigma \to 2^Q$ *by* $(G, S, a) \mapsto \emptyset$ *if* $a \notin G$ *else, if* $a \in G$ *then* $(G, S, a) \mapsto \{(G', S')\}$ *where* G' *and* S' *are defined in the following way: if* aIS *then* $S' = S \cup \{a\}$, $G' = G$ *and if* aDS *then* $S' = \{a\}$, $G' = D(S) = \{b \in \Sigma : \exists c \in S \ bDc\}$.

According to the definition of the Foata normal form (see Section 2) a word is in Foata normal form if it can be written as product of steps. A step is a word of pairwise independent letters. Furthermore, for every step (excluding the first one) there is a dependent action in the previous one. $\mathcal{A}_\mathcal{F}$ reads a word step by step. A part of a step is stored in S. An action independent on actions of the current step must belong to the current step. Hence it is added to S. As soon as an action is read which is dependent on one of the actions of the current step it must be part of the next step which is initialised by this action. Furthermore, to reflect the second requirement for the steps, we store in G the actions dependent on S. These are the *good* actions which we allow to be read from now on. This ensures that all actions read from now on are dependent on the previous step (because of $(G, S, a) \mapsto \emptyset$ if $a \notin G$).

Complexity It is easy to see that for $\varphi \in$ FLTL the size of $\mathcal{A}_\varphi$ is linear in the size of φ. Hence, the size of the resulting Büchi automaton is exponential in the size of φ. $\mathcal{A}_\mathcal{F}$ is independent of φ, so is its size. Hence, deciding whether there is a model for φ is exponential in its length. This is optimal since for the empty independence relation, we are in the situation of LTL.

8   Model Checking for DSTS and FLTL

In this section, we present a model checking algorithm for FLTL wrt. the executions of a distributed synchronous transition system. Given a DSTS $\mathcal{A}$ and a formula φ, we construct a Büchi automaton $\mathcal{B}_{\mathcal{A}}$ accepting for every synchronous execution of $\mathcal{A}$ a *single* asynchronous one. In contrast to accepting every asynchronous execution, this reduces the number of possible transitions and, more important, the number of reachable states. For the negation of φ, we construct an ABA and transform it into a Büchi automaton $\mathcal{B}_{\neg\varphi}$ as described in the previous section. Testing the intersection of $\mathcal{B}_{\mathcal{A}}$ and $\mathcal{B}_{\neg\varphi}$ for emptiness answers whether there is an execution of $\mathcal{A}$ violating φ.

Definition 8. *Let* $\mathcal{A} = (Q_1, \ldots, Q_n, \longrightarrow, \mathcal{I})$ *be a* DSTS. *Then let* $\mathcal{B}_{\mathcal{A}} = (Q, \delta, \mathcal{I} \times \{\emptyset\}, F)$ *be the BA defined by* $Q = Q_1 \times \cdots \times Q_n \times I(\Sigma)$ *and* $F = Q \times I(\Sigma)$, *i.e., every state is also a final state. Fix a linear order* $\prec$ *on the alphabet* Σ.[7] *We call an action* a *enabled in* $\bar{q}$ *iff there is a* $\bar{q}' \in \bar{Q}$ *such that* $(\bar{q}|_{pr(a)}, a, \bar{q}'|_{pr(a)}) \in \longrightarrow$. *Let* $((\bar{q}, S), a, (\bar{q}', S')) \in \delta$ *iff*

1. $(\bar{q}|_{pr(a)}, a, \bar{q}'|_{pr(a)}) \in \longrightarrow$, *i.e., it is a valid transition according to the underlying* DTS, *and*
2. *if* aDS *then*
   (a) $\{b \in \Sigma \mid bIS \text{ and } b \text{ enabled in } \bar{q}\} = \emptyset$, *i.e., there is no action independent to the current step left for execution, and*
   (b) a *is strictly smaller than each element of the set* $\{b \in \Sigma \mid bIa \text{ and } b \text{ enabled in } \bar{q}\}$ *wrt.* $\prec$, $S' = \{a\}$
   else
3. *if* aIS *then* a *is strictly smaller than each element of* $\{b \in \Sigma \mid bIa, bIS \text{ and } b \text{ enabled in } \bar{q}\}$ *wrt.* $\prec$, $S' = S \cup \{a\}$.

Item 2.(a) guarantees that the next step is considered only if the current one is "full". Items 2.(b) and 3 handle the selection of "equivalent" transitions. The rule is: Just let the smallest action wrt. $\prec$ make a transition. The new current step S' is treated as in the definition of $\mathcal{A}_{\mathcal{F}}$ (see Section 7). Note that we do not have to concentrate on *good* actions since our selection strategy ensures to fill a step before considering the next one. This shows that $\mathcal{B}_{\mathcal{A}}$ accepts for every synchronous execution of $\mathcal{A}$ exactly one linearisation. For example, $\mathcal{B}_{\mathcal{A}}$ for $\mathcal{A}$ as in Figure 4 is shown in Figure 6

Complexity Model Checking is exponential in the size of the formula and linear in the size of $\mathcal{B}_{\mathcal{A}}$. The size of $\mathcal{B}_{\mathcal{A}}$ is exponential in the size number of components of $\mathcal{A}$. The experiences gained by partial order reduction [Pel98] allow the conclusion that the number of reachable states is in the average case much smaller.

9   Conclusion

In this paper we presented a framework for verifying synchronous hardware systems. We introduced a suitable semantic model, *Distributed Synchronous Transition Systems* (DSTS), which are distributed transition systems with a global

---

[7] Note that it suffices to define $\prec$ of pairs of independent actions only. Hence, $\Sigma_1, \ldots, \Sigma_n$ induces an appropriate $\prec$.

$$(q_{11}, q_{21}, q_{31}, q_{41}, \emptyset)$$
$$\downarrow a$$
$$(q_{12}, q_{22}, q_{31}, q_{41}, \{a\})$$
$$\downarrow b$$
$$(q_{11}, q_{22}, q_{32}, q_{41}, \{b\})\longleftarrow$$
$$\downarrow c$$
$$(q_{11}, q_{21}, q_{32}, q_{42}, \{b, c\})$$
$$\downarrow d \qquad\qquad b$$
$$(q_{12}, q_{22}, q_{32}, q_{42}, \{a\})$$
$$\downarrow a$$
$$(q_{12}, q_{22}, q_{31}, q_{41}, \{a, d\})$$

Fig. 6. A Büchi automaton for the DSTS shown in Figure 4

clock synchronising the executions of actions. Considering a sample layout for PowerPC systems, we proved that our approach is adequate for hardware systems. We also presented a characterisation by the *maximal step semantics* for *Petri nets*. We pointed out that, considering asynchronous executions of the underlying system instead of its synchronous behaviour, one might fail to prove some of its properties. We explained that executions of distributed transition systems can be described within Mazurkiewicz trace theory, especially by *Foata configuration graphs of traces*. To enrich our approach, we introduced the calculus *Synchronous Process Systems* simplifying the task of defining DSTS.

The main advantage of our approach is the support by temporal logic specifications and automatic decision procedures for satisfiability and model checking. We defined *Foata Lineartime Temporal Logic* (FLTL) which is a temporal logic with a flavour of LTL adapted for specifying properties of DSTS. We developed a decision procedure for satisfiability as well as a model checking FLTL specifications, both based on alternating Büchi automata. As future work, we plan to integrate this model together with FLTL in the verification platform TRUTH [LLNT99].

References

[BCPVD99] S. Bensalem, P. Caspi, C. Parent-Vigouroux, and C. Dumas. A methodology for proving control systems with Lustre and PVS. In Charles B. Weinstock and John Rushby, editors, *Dependable Computing for Critical Applications—7*, volume 12 of *Dependable Computing and Fault Tolerant Systems*, pages 89–107, San Jose, CA, January 1999. IEEE Computer Society.

[BL80] J.A. Brzozowski and E. Leiss. On equations for regular languages, finite automata, and sequential networks. *Theoretical Computer Science*, 10:19–35, 1980.

[CKS81] Ashok K. Chandra, Dexter C. Kozen, and Larry J. Stockmeyer. Alternation. *Journal of the ACM*, 28(1):114–133, January 1981.

[CPHP87] P. Caspi, D. Pilaud, N. Halbwachs, and J. A. Plaice. LUSTRE: A declarative language for programming synchronous systems. In *Conference Record of the Fourteenth Annual ACM Symposium on Principles of Programming Languages*, pages 178–188, Munich, West Germany, January 21–23, 1987. ACM SIGACT-SIGPLAN, ACM Press.

[DM96]   Volker Diekert and Yves Métivier. Partial commutation and traces. Technical Report TR-1996-02, Universität Stuttgart, Fakultät Informatik, Germany, March 1996.

[DR95]   Volker Diekert and Grzegorz Rozenberg, editors. *The Book of Traces*. World Scientific, Singapore, 1995.

[LLNT99] M. Lange, M. Leucker, T. Noll, and S. Tobies. Truth – a verification platform for concurrent systems. In *Tool Support for System Specification, Development, and Verification*, Advances in Computing Science. Springer-Verlag Wien New York, 1999.

[Mil83]   R. Milner. Calculi for synchrony and asynchrony. *Theoretical Computer Science*, 25(3):267–310, July 1983.

[Mil89]   R. Milner. *Communication and Concurrency*. International Series in Computer Science. Prentice Hall, 1989.

[Mot93]   Motorola, editor. *The PowerPC (TM) 601 User's Manual*. Motorola, 1993.

[MP92]   Zohar Manna and Amir Pnueli. *The Temporal Logic of Reactive and Concurrent Systems*. Springer, New York, 1992.

[Pel98]   Doron Peled. Ten years of partial order reduction. In *CAV, Computer Aided Verification*, number 1427 in LNCS, pages 17–28, Vancouver, BC, Canada, 1998. Springer.

[PP95]   Doron Peled and Wojciech Penczek. Using asynchronous buchi automata for efficient model-checking of concurrent systems. In *Protocol Specification Testing and Verification*, pages 90–100, Warsaw, Poland, 1995. Chapman & Hall.

[Rei86]   Wolfgang Reisig. *Petrinetze*. Springer-Verlag, Berlin Heidelberg New York Tokyo, 2 edition, 1986.

[TH98]   P. S. Thiagarajan and J. G. Henriksen. Distributed versions of linear time temporal logic: A trace perspective. *Lecture Notes in Computer Science*, 1492:643–681, 1998.

[Thi95]   P. S. Thiagarajan. A trace consistent subset of PTL. In Insup Lee and Scott A. Smolka, editors, *CONCUR '95: Concurrency Theory, 6th International Conference*, volume 962 of *Lecture Notes in Computer Science*, pages 438–452, Philadelphia, Pennsylvania, 21–24 August 1995. Springer-Verlag.

[Tho90]   Wolfgang Thomas. Automata on infinite objects. In J. van Leeuwen, editor, *Handbook of Theoretical Computer Science*, chapter 4, pages 133–191. Elsevier Science Publishers B. V., 1990.

[Var96]   Moshe Y. Vardi. *An Automata-Theoretic Approach to Linear Temporal Logic*, volume 1043 of *Lecture Notes in Computer Science*, pages 238–266. Springer-Verlag Inc., New York, NY, USA, 1996.

[Zie87]   Wiesław Zielonka. Notes on finite asynchronous automata. *R.A.I.R.O. — Informatique Théorique et Applications*, 21:99–135, 1987.

Safe Ambients:
Control Flow Analysis and Security

Pierpaolo Degano, Francesca Levi, and Chiara Bodei

Dipartimento di Informatica, Università di Pisa
Corso Italia 40, I-56100 Pisa, Italy
{degano,levifran,chiara}@di.unipi.it

Abstract. We present a Control Flow Analysis (CFA) for the Safe Ambients, a variant of the calculus of Mobile Ambients. The analysis refines [12] and computes an approximation of the run-time topology of processes. We use the result of the analysis to establish a secrecy property.

1 Introduction

Mobile Ambients (MA [6]) has recently emerged as a core programming language for the Web and, at the same time, as a model for reasoning about properties of mobile processes. Differently from other process algebras based on name communication like the π-calculus [11], MA is based on the notion of *ambient*. An ambient is a bounded place, where multi-threaded computation happens; in a sense, it generalizes both the idea of agent and the idea of location. Each ambient has a *name*, a collection of *local processes* and a collection of *subambients*. Ambients are organized in a hierarchy that can be dynamically modified, according to three basic capabilities, associated with ambient names and used for access control. They are the following: $\mathbf{in}\,n$ allows an ambient to enter into ambient (named) n: $(m[\,\mathbf{in}\,n.\,P_1 \mid P_2\,] \mid n[\,Q\,] \longrightarrow n[\,m[\,P_1 \mid P_2\,] \mid Q\,])$; $\mathbf{out}\,n$ allows an ambient to exit from ambient n: $(n[\,m[\,\mathbf{out}\,n.\,P_1 \mid P_2\,] \mid Q\,] \longrightarrow m[\,P_1 \mid P_2\,] \mid n[\,Q\,])$; $\mathbf{open}\,n$ allows to destroy the boundary of ambient n: $(\mathbf{open}\,n.\,P \mid n[\,Q\,] \longrightarrow P \mid Q)$. As shown by the rules, an ambient m moves as a whole with all its subambients. The movements of m only depend on the capabilities exercised by the local processes contained at its top level (for instance $\mathbf{in}\,n.\,P_1$ in the first rule); instead the local processes of subambients of m cannot directly influence the movements of their parent m. Also, the ambient n, that is affected by the rules, has no control on whether or not the action takes place.

Safe Ambients (SA [10]) is a modification of MA, where a movement or an ambient dissolution can take place only when the affected ambient agrees, offering the corresponding *coaction*: $\overline{\mathbf{in}}\,n, \overline{\mathbf{out}}\,n, \overline{\mathbf{open}}\,n$. This variation does not change the expressiveness of MA, yet makes it easier both to write programs and to formally prove their correctness, especially by using behavioural equivalences.

Several techniques, both dynamic and static, have been devised to study and establish various security properties of mobile calculi, based on notions of classifications and information flow. Encouraging results have been obtained by the use of static approaches, such as Type Systems [10,4,3,5] and Control Flow Analysis (CFA) [12,13,14]. These techniques predict safe and computable approximations to the set of values or behaviours arising dynamically. For example, in calculi for concurrency, the approximations concern the values that variables may assume at run-time or the values that may flow on channels. In the ambient calculi, particularly relevant for security issues is information about the dynamic evolution of the ambient hierarchy and about which and where capabilities may be exercised.

The CFA given in [12] computes an approximation of the (run-time) topological structure of MA processes and follows the lines of previous work on the π-calculus [1]. More in detail, the analysis predicts for each ambient n, which ambients and capabilities (say α) may be contained at top level inside n. The analysis has been applied to prove a security property of the firewall protocol from [6,7].

In this paper, we refine the analysis of [12], adapted to SA, by introducing a sort of contextual information, extending the proposal made in [9]. The analysis predicts for each ambient n:

1. which ambient surrounds ambient n whenever α (capability or ambient) is contained inside at top level;
2. which ambient surrounds n whenever α (capability or ambient), besides being contained inside (at top level), is also ready to interact.

Such a contextual information allows to considerably restrict the space of possible movements. In this way we gain in precision, and thus we may consider more properties and prove statically more programs safe.

As a simple example, we apply the result of the analysis for proving a *secrecy* property. We classify ambients into *trustworthy* and *untrustworthy*. Secrecy of data is preserved if an untrustworthy ambient can never open a trustworthy one. We show that if a program passes a simple static test, then its secret information is dynamically protected.

In proving a security property it is essential to be able to guarantee that properties are preserved when programs work in unknown, possibly hostile contexts. In general, not all contexts preserve our property, but we can say which of them do. As expected, the needed restrictions concern the usage of names. Actually, some of them cannot occur as ambient names in the context, but can occur inside its capabilities (cf. the assumption made in [12]). We define a tester process E that represents the most hostile context matching these requirements. If a process P in parallel with E passes the static test, then the secrecy property holds dynamically in any context represented by E.

Due to lack of space, we omit all the proofs.

2   Mobile Safe Ambients

In this section we briefly recall the *Mobile Safe Ambients* ([10]) calculus, without communication primitives. The only difference with the syntax of MA is given by coactions $\overline{\text{in}}\, n, \overline{\text{out}}\, n, \overline{\text{open}}\, n$.

Because of a peculiar treatment of bound names (see below), we partition names as follows. Given $\widehat{\mathcal{N}} = \{n, h, k, \ldots\}$ the infinite set of *names*, let $\mathcal{N}' = \biguplus_{n \in \widehat{\mathcal{N}}} \mathcal{N}_n$, where $\mathcal{N}_n = \{n_0, n_1, \ldots\}$. The name n stands for a generic element of $\mathcal{N}_n$.

Definition 2.1 (syntax). Processes *(denoted by $P, Q, R, \ldots \in \mathcal{P}$) and capabilities (denoted by $M, N, \ldots \in \mathcal{C}$) Processes are built according to the following syntax*

$P ::=$	*processes*	$M ::=$	*capabilities*
$\mathbf{0}$	*nil*	$\text{in}\, n$	*enter n*
$M.P$	*prefix*	$\overline{\text{in}}\, n$	*allow enter n*
$n[P]$	*ambient*	$\text{out}\, n$	*exit n*
$P \mid P$	*parallel composition*	$\overline{\text{out}}\, n$	*allow exit n*
$(\nu n)P$	*restriction*	$\text{open}\, n$	*open n*
$!P$	*replication*	$\overline{\text{open}}\, n$	*allow open n*

In the following capabilities are ranged over by $M, N \ldots$, actions by μ and *coactions* by $\bar{\mu}$. Furthermore, capabilities and names are ranged over by α. Standard syntactical conventions are used: the trailing $\mathbf{0}$ in processes $M.\mathbf{0}$ is omitted, and parallel composition has the least syntactic precedence.

We refer to the usual notions of names, free names, and bound names of a process P, denoted by $\text{n}(P)$, $\text{fn}(P)$, $\text{bn}(P)$, respectively. Hereafter, it will be convenient to assume an external ambient, $\top \notin \mathcal{N}'$, so we let $\mathcal{N} = \mathcal{N}' \cup \{\top\}$.

The *structural congruence* $\equiv$ on processes is defined as the least congruence satisfying the following clauses:

- $(\nu n_i)P \equiv (\nu n_j)P\{n_j/n_i\}$, if $n_j \notin \text{fn}(P)$;
- $(\mathcal{P}/_\equiv, \mid, \mathbf{0})$ is a commutative monoid;
- $M.P \equiv M.Q$ if $P \equiv Q$;
- $n[P] \equiv n[Q]$ if $P \equiv Q$;
- $(\nu n)P \equiv (\nu n)Q$ if $P \equiv Q$;
- $(\nu n)\mathbf{0} \equiv \mathbf{0}$, $(\nu n)(\nu n')P \equiv (\nu n')(\nu n)P$, $(\nu n)P \equiv P$ if $n \notin \text{fn}(P)$,
  $(\nu n)(P \mid Q) \equiv (\nu n)P \mid Q$ if $n \notin \text{fn}(Q)$,
  $m[(\nu n)P] \equiv (\nu n)m[P]$ if $n \neq m$;
- $!P \equiv P \mid !P$.

The structural congruence is the standard one, apart from the treatment of α-conversion. A name $n_i \in \mathcal{N}_n$ the name n_i can only be replaced by a name $n_j \in \mathcal{N}_n$ (not occurring free in the process). Moreover, we assume that the names occurring bound inside restrictions are all distinct from each other and from free variables. These assumptions are only used to keep the definition of our analysis more compact, and can be easily removed (see, e.g. [1]).

The reduction relation $\longrightarrow$ of SA in Table 1 is defined in the usual way. The only differences with the reduction semantics of MA are the basic movement rules. We write $\Longrightarrow$ for the reflexive and transitive closure of $\longrightarrow$.

We introduce some notions which are necessary to formalize the soundness of the analysis and also the security property.

$$\text{In}: \; n[\,\text{in}\, m.\, P_1 \mid P_2\,] \mid m[\,\overline{\text{in}}\; m.\, Q_1 \mid Q_2\,] \longrightarrow m[\,n[\,P_1 \mid P_2\,] \mid Q_1 \mid Q_2\,]$$

$$\text{Out}: \; m[\,n[\,\text{out}\, m.\, P_1 \mid P_2\,] \mid \overline{\text{out}}\; m.\, Q_1 \mid Q_2\,] \longrightarrow n[\,P_1 \mid P_2\,] \mid m[\,Q_1 \mid Q_2\,]$$

$$\text{Open}: \; m[\,\overline{\text{open}}\, m.\, P_1 \mid P_2\,] \mid \text{open}\, m.\, Q_1 \mid Q_2 \longrightarrow P_1 \mid P_2 \mid Q_1 \mid Q_2$$

$$\text{Res}: \; \frac{P \longrightarrow P'}{(\nu n)P \longrightarrow (\nu n)P'} \qquad \text{Par}: \; \frac{P \longrightarrow P'}{P \mid Q \longrightarrow P' \mid Q}$$

$$\text{Amb}: \; \frac{P \longrightarrow P'}{n[\,P\,] \longrightarrow n[\,P'\,]} \qquad \text{Struct}: \; \frac{P \equiv P' \;\; P' \longrightarrow P'' \;\; P'' \equiv P'''}{P \longrightarrow P'''}$$

Table 1. Reduction Rules for SA.

Definition 2.2. *Let P be a process and $\alpha \in \mathcal{N} \cup \mathcal{C}$ a name or a capability. We say that α is*

1. top level *in P iff α does not occur inside any ambient of P;*
2. enabled *in P iff α is top level in P and it does not occur underneath a prefix.*

For instance, in $P = \text{in}\, k.\, \overline{\text{out}}\, n \mid m[\,\text{out}\, n.\, \overline{\text{open}}\, m.\, \text{in}\, a\,]$, both capabilities $\text{in}\, k$ and $\overline{\text{out}}\, n$ and ambient m are top level. Capability $\text{in}\, k$ and ambient m are also enabled, while $\overline{\text{out}}\, n$ is only top level. Intuitively, if α is enabled, then it can be exercised (if it is a capability) and can interact with other processes at the same level (if it is an ambient). Hence, whenever P is placed inside an ambient with name n, capability $\text{in}\, k$ may be exercised and cause a movement of n and ambient m may interact inside n. By contrast, capability $\overline{\text{out}}\, n$ is not ready to be exercised, because it is guarded by $\text{in}\, k$: it is top level but not enabled.

We say that a *context* $C[-]$ (a process with a hole) is *flat* iff the hole is enabled in $C[-]$. Also, we call Q *configuration* of P if $P \equiv C[Q]$, and we write $\top[P]$ when C is empty.

3   Control Flow Analysis for *SA*

Our analysis predicts for each ambient n which capabilities and ambients *may* be contained inside n at run-time, when it occurs within a selected ambient. The solution to the analysis of a process P is a function ϕ, such that a typical element of $\phi(n)$ is $\alpha^{(\ell_1, \ell_2)}$, where α is either a name or a capability and ℓ_1, ℓ_2 are sets of names. Intuitively, when $\alpha^{(\ell_1, \ell_2)} \in \phi(n)$, the analysis says that the derivatives of P may include the following configurations:

1. for each $k \in \ell_1$, $k[\,\nu \tilde{p}\, (R \mid n[\,Q\,])\,]$ where α is *top level* in Q;

2. for each $k \in \ell_2$, $k[\boldsymbol{\nu}\tilde{p}\,(R \mid n[\,P\,])\,]$ where α is *enabled* in P.

Before introducing the formal definitions we illustrate the above through a simple example. We omit brackets in singletons.

Example 3.1. Consider the process

$$P = n[\,\text{in}\,k.\,\overline{\text{out}}\,n \mid m[\,\text{out}\,n.\,\overline{\text{open}}\,m.\,\text{in}\,a\,]\,] \mid k[\,\overline{\text{in}}\,k.\,\text{open}\,m\,].$$

The process P evolves (only) as follows. The ambient n can go inside k

$$P \longrightarrow k[\,\text{open}\,m \mid n[\,\overline{\text{out}}\,n \mid m[\,\text{out}\,n.\,\overline{\text{open}}\,m.\,\text{in}\,a\,]\,]\,] = Q$$

When n is inside k, the ambient m can exit from n

$$Q \longrightarrow k[\,\text{open}\,m \mid n[\,\mathbf{0}\,] \mid m[\,\overline{\text{open}}\,m.\,\text{in}\,a\,]\,] = R$$

When m is inside k, it can be opened and it liberates the capability $\text{in}\,a$ inside k

$$R \longrightarrow k[\,n[\,\mathbf{0}\,] \mid \text{in}\,a\,] = S.$$

A solution for the analysis of P is as follows

$\phi(\top)$	$\{n^{(\emptyset,\emptyset)},\,k^{(\emptyset,\emptyset)}\}$
$\phi(n)$	$\{m^{(\{\top,k\},\{\top,k\})},\,\text{in}\,k^{(\top,\top)},\,\overline{\text{out}}\,n^{(\{\top,k\},k)}\}$
$\phi(m)$	$\{\text{out}\,n^{(n,n)},\,\overline{\text{open}}\,m^{(\{n,k\},k)},\,\text{in}\,a^{(\{n,k\},k)}\}$
$\phi(k)$	$\{\overline{\text{in}}\,k^{(\top,\top)},\,\text{open}\,m^{(\top,\top)},\,\text{in}\,a^{(\{n,k,\top\},\{k,\top\})},\,n^{(\top,\top)},\,m^{(\top,\top)}\}$

- $\phi(\top)$ contains ambients n and k with label $(\emptyset,\emptyset)$, to indicate that they occur at the outermost level.
- $\phi(n)$ contains: $m^{(\{\top,k\},\{\top,k\})}$, to predict that m is enabled when n is inside $\top$ or k (see processes P and Q); $\text{in}\,k^{(\top,\top)}$, to show that $\text{in}\,k$ is enabled, when n is inside $\top$ (see P) and will be consumed when n moves elsewhere (see Q and R); $\overline{\text{out}}\,n^{(\{\top,k\},k)}$ recording that $\overline{\text{out}}\,n$ is top level when n is inside $\top$ or k (see P and Q), while it is only enabled when $\text{in}\,k$ has been consumed, and thus n has moved inside k (see Q).

- $\phi(m)$ contains: $\mathsf{out}\, n^{(n,n)}$ predicting that $\mathsf{out}\, n$ is enabled when m is inside n (see P and Q); $\overline{\mathsf{open}}\, m^{(\{n,k\},k)}$ showing that $\overline{\mathsf{open}}\, m$ is top level when m is inside n or k (see P and Q), while it is only enabled after the execution of $\mathsf{out}\, n$, that is in k (see R). Similarly for $\mathsf{in}\, a^{(\{n,k\},k)}$.
- $\phi(k)$ contains: n and m with label $(\top, \top)$ to indicate that both ambients may enter in k (n by exercing $\mathsf{in}\, k$ and m by exercing $\mathsf{out}\, n$); $\overline{\mathsf{in}}\, k$ and $\mathsf{open}\, m$ with label $(\top, \top)$, showing that m does not move from $\top$. Moreover, it contains also $\mathsf{in}\, a^{(\{n,k,\top\},\{k,\top\})}$, to predict that $\mathsf{in}\, a$ is top level and enabled when k is inside $\top$ (see S).

Although, when $\alpha^L \in \phi(n)$, $\ell_2 \subseteq \ell_1$ (α enabled is also top level), both sets are useful for an accurate prediction of process behaviour:

1. ℓ_1 approximates the set of ambients that surround n when α is top level and that therefore may acquire α by opening n. For instance, in Example 3.1 the ambient k acquires capability $\mathsf{in}\, a$ from $\phi(m)$ through $\mathsf{open}\, m$, because k belongs to (the first component of) its label. Capabilities $\mathsf{out}\, n$ and $\overline{\mathsf{open}}\, m$ are not acquired, because they are not top level when m is inside k.
2. ℓ_2 approximates the set of ambients that surround n when α is enabled, namely when α is ready to interact. Hence, ℓ_2 can be used to say if a capability is executable and to predict its effect. For instance, in Example 3.1 the (second component of the) labels of $\overline{\mathsf{out}}\, n$ in $\phi(n)$ and of $\mathsf{out}\, n$ in $\phi(m)$ are used to predict the effect of $\mathsf{out}\, n$ on the ambient m. Since $\mathsf{out}\, n$ is enabled when m is inside n and $\overline{\mathsf{out}}\, n$ is enabled when n is inside k, m may go out of n and may end up inside k, the current parent ambient of n.

NOTATION. In the following we shall make use of some notation and abbreviations. The set of *labels* is $\mathcal{L} = \{(\ell_1, \ell_2) \mid \ell_1, \ell_2 \in \wp(\mathcal{N}) \wedge \ell_2 \subseteq \ell_1\}$. Hereafter, L will stand for (ℓ_1, ℓ_2) and L_i will stand for $(\ell_{1,i}, \ell_{2,i})$. Inclusion and union of labels are defined componentwise. Moreover, with an abuse of notation, for $N \in \wp(\mathcal{N})$ we write $L \subseteq N$ in place of $L \subseteq (N, N)$ and $L \cup N$ in place of $L \cup (N, N)$.

The set of *located capabilities* and *names* is denoted $\mathcal{LCA}$, ranged over by α^L, where α is either a capability or an ambient name and L is a label. An *element* I is a subset of $\mathcal{LCA}$. Over elements we define

1. $\alpha^{L_1} \in I$ if $\alpha^{L_2} \in I$ and $L_1 \subseteq L_2$;
2. $I_1 \sqsubseteq I_2$ iff $\alpha^L \in I_1$ implies $\alpha^L \in I_2$.

For example $\{\mathsf{in}\, n^{(k,k)}\} \sqsubseteq \{\mathsf{in}\, n^{(\{h,k\},k)}\}$.

THE ANALYSIS. We now formalize the intuition given above. Our CFA does not distinguish among different elements of the same equivalence class $\mathcal{N}_n$. This amounts to saying that $\phi(n)$ stands for the analysis of every n_i and, similarly, each n occurring in a located capability stands for every n_i, as well. In this way, we statically maintain the identity of names that may be lost by applying the standard α-conversion: for a different approach see the naming environment and the stable names in [12].

Definition 3.2 (Solutions). *Given a process P, let $\mathrm{n}(P) \cup \{\top\} \subseteq N_P$. A solution for P is a total function $\phi : N_P \to \wp(\mathcal{LCA})$.*
Furthermore, we order solutions by letting $\phi_1 \sqsubseteq \phi_2$ iff $\forall n \in N_P.\ \phi_1(n) \sqsubseteq \phi_2(n)$.

A solution ϕ for a process Q is *validated* if and only if $\phi \models^{\top,(\emptyset,\emptyset)}_{\phi(\top)} Q$ (shortly $\phi \models Q$) according to the set of clauses in Table 2. Clauses operate on judgments of the form

$$\phi \models^{k,L}_I P,$$

where k is a name of an ambient or $\top$, L is a label, and I is an element. The rules in Table 2 use some auxiliary notions that follow.

AUXILIARY NOTIONS. Let ϕ be a solution for P and $n, k \in N_P$. Some of the functions defined below depend on ϕ, that we shall often omit when clear from the context.

We introduce a function $\mathbf{f}$ that collects for each ambient n a superset of its possible fathers or parent ambients, i.e. the ambients that may surround n. In the same definition, we introduce the function ENAB which, given an ambient n and a capability M, collects those fathers of n in which M may be enabled. Moreover, we define a sort of transitive closure w.r.t. the open operation.

Definition 3.3 (Fathers, ENAB, $k^\uparrow$).

- $\mathbf{f}^\phi(n) = \{k \mid n^L \in \phi(k)\}$;
- $\text{ENAB}^\phi(M, n) = \{\ell_2 \mid M^{(\ell_1, \ell_2)} \in \phi(n)\}$;
- $k^\uparrow_\phi$ *is the least set of names such that $k \in k^\uparrow_\phi$ and $\forall h \in k^\uparrow_\phi$,*
  if $n \in \text{ENAB}^\phi(\overline{\text{open}}\, h, h)$ and $\text{open}\, h^L \in \phi(n)$ then $n \in k^\uparrow_\phi$.

For instance in Example 3.1 $\text{ENAB}(\overline{\text{out}}\, n, n) = k$ and $\text{ENAB}(\text{in}\, k, n) = \top$ which show that $\overline{\text{out}}\, n$ may be exercised when n is inside k only, and that $\text{in}\, k$ may be exercised when n is inside $\top$ only.

Based on the above, the function $\mathbf{t}$ predicts the target ambients in which an ambient ends up after a movement action (in or out).

Definition 3.4 (Target). *The target of α in k, $\mathbf{t}^\phi(\alpha, k) \subseteq N_P$, is given by*

1. $\mathbf{t}^\phi(\text{in}\, n, k) = \begin{cases} n & \text{if } \bigcup_{h \in k^\uparrow_\phi} \text{ENAB}^\phi(\text{in}\, n, h) \cap \text{ENAB}^\phi(\overline{\text{in}}\, n, n) \neq \emptyset \\ \emptyset & \text{otherwise} \end{cases}$

2. $\mathbf{t}^\phi(\text{out}\, n, k) = \begin{cases} \text{ENAB}^\phi(\overline{\text{out}}\, n, n) & \text{if } n \in \bigcup_{h \in k^\uparrow_\phi} \text{ENAB}^\phi(\text{out}\, n, h) \\ \emptyset & \text{otherwise} \end{cases}$

3. $\mathbf{t}^\phi(\alpha, k) = \emptyset$ *if $\alpha \in \{\text{open}\, n, \overline{\text{in}}\, n, \overline{\text{out}}\, n, \overline{\text{open}}\, n\}$.*

The target of a movement capability is empty whenever the capability is deadlocked. In details: $\text{in}\, n$ may be executed only if there exists an ambient h, such that $\text{in}\, n$ is enabled when k in inside h and $\overline{\text{in}}\, n$ is enabled when n is also inside h; $\text{out}\, n$ is executable only if it is enabled when k is also inside n. When a capability $\text{in } n$ is executable, its effect is that of moving the ambient k inside n; when a capability $\text{out } n$ is executable, its effect is that of moving the ambient k inside some of the fathers of n, the ones where $\overline{\text{out}}\, n$ is enabled.

For instance in Example 3.1, $\mathbf{t}(\text{in } k, n) = k$, since $\text{in } k$ is enabled when n is inside $\top$, while $\overline{\text{in}}\, n$ is enabled when n is inside $\top$. Moreover, $\mathbf{t}(\text{out } n, m) = k$ since $\text{out } n$ is enabled when m is inside n and $\overline{\text{out}}\, n$ is enabled when n is inside k.

We introduce also some operators acting on elements, i.e. on subsets of $\mathcal{LCA}$. They are used in the clauses (**open**) and (**par**): we shall give some intuition later on.

Definition 3.5. *We define*

- $I \triangleleft k = \{\alpha^L \mid \alpha^L \in I \ \wedge \ k \in \ell_1\}$;
- $\gamma^\phi(k, I, n) = \begin{cases} I \triangleleft k \ \text{if } k \in \mathit{ENAB}^\phi(\overline{\text{open}}\, n, n) \\ \emptyset \qquad\quad otherwise \end{cases}$;
- $I \oplus L = \{\alpha^{L' \cup L} \mid \alpha^{L'} \in I\}$;
- $I_1 \otimes_n^\phi I_2 = \left(I_1 \oplus \{\mathbf{t}^\phi(M, n) \mid M^L \in I_2\}\right) \cup \left(I_2 \oplus \{\mathbf{t}^\phi(M, n) \mid M^L \in I_1\}\right)$.

By abuse of notation, we write $I_1 \oplus I_2$ for $I_1 \oplus (I_2, I_2)$.

Intuition on the CFA clauses The intuitive meaning of the elements of judgement $\phi \models_I^{k,L} P$, with $L = (\ell_1, \ell_2)$, is the following: the process P to be examined is (statically) contained in the current ambient k; the element I, subset of $\phi(k)$, contains enough information to validate process P assuming the following configurations are reachable:

1. for any $m \in \ell_1$, $m[\boldsymbol{\nu}\tilde{p}\,(R \mid k[Q])]$, where P is a subprocess of Q (possibly equal to Q itself), and
2. for any $m \in \ell_2$, $m[\boldsymbol{\nu}\tilde{p}\,(R \mid k[P])]$.

Using subsets of $\phi(k)$ increases the accuracy of the analysis, especially in the case of parallel processes (see the explanation of clause (**par**) below). The clauses operate on the structure of process P, updating k, L and I. The current ambient k is updated, whenever we pass inside a new ambient. The current label L is updated in the same situation and whenever we pass a movement capability (input and output). Each time an ambient or a capability is under consideration, the analysis checks that the current element I contains the corresponding located component. The check skips to another element I' to analyse the continuation of the process in almost every clause, except for **pref** and $\overline{\textbf{pref}}$. The new element I' or a suitable modification of it must be part of the old subset I (and finally part of the analysis of the current ambient). We now illustrate the more relevant clauses.

(**amb**) Ambient n is (statically) contained inside the ambient k. Label L says that n may be enabled, when k is inside an ambient of ℓ_2, while it may be top level but not necessarily enabled, when k is inside an ambient of ℓ_1.

Hence, the located ambient n^L has to occur in I, i.e. in the solution for k. The process P has to be validated in the ambient n with label (k, k), because

nil: $\phi \models_I^{k,L} \mathbf{0}$ iff true

amb: $\phi \models_I^{k,L} n[\,P\,]$ iff $n^L \in I \ \wedge \exists I' : \phi \models_{I'}^{n,(k,k)} P \ \wedge \ I' \sqsubseteq \phi(n)$

pref: $\phi \models_I^{k,L} \mu.\,P \ \wedge \ \mu \neq \mathsf{open}\,n$ iff $\begin{cases} \mu^L \in I \ \wedge \ \phi \models_I^{k,(\ell_1 \cup \mathsf{t}(\mu,k),\mathsf{t}(\mu,k))} P \ \wedge \\[2mm] \forall h \in \mathsf{t}(\mu,k) : k^{(\mathsf{f}(h),\mathsf{f}(h))} \in \phi(h) \end{cases}$

$\overline{\mathbf{pref}}\ \phi \models_I^{k,L} \overline{\mu}.\,P$ iff $\overline{\mu}^L \in I \wedge \ \phi \models_I^{k,L} P$

open: $\phi \models_I^{k,L} \mathsf{open}\,n.\,P$ iff $\begin{cases} (\mathsf{open}\,n^L \in I) \ \wedge \ \exists I_1 : \ \phi \models_{I_1}^{k,L} P \ \wedge \\[2mm] I_1 \otimes_k (\gamma(k,\phi(n),n) \oplus L) \sqsubseteq I \ \wedge \\[2mm] \forall k \in \mathrm{ENAB}(\overline{\mathsf{open}}\,n, n), \ h \in \mathcal{N}, \\ \alpha^L \in \phi(h) : \ n \in \ell_i \Rightarrow k \in \ell_i, \ \forall i = 1,2 \end{cases}$

par: $\phi \models_I^{k,L} P \mid Q$ iff $\begin{cases} \exists I_1, I_2 : \phi \models_{I_1}^{k,L} P \ \wedge \ x\phi \models_{I_2}^{k,L} Q \ \wedge \\[2mm] I_1 \otimes_k I_2 \sqsubseteq I \end{cases}$

repl: $\phi \models_I^{k,L} !P$ iff $\exists I' : \phi \models_{I'}^{k,L} P \ \wedge \ I' \otimes_k I' \sqsubseteq I$

Table 2. Control Flow Analysis for SA

the configuration $k[\, \boldsymbol{\nu}\tilde{p}\,(R \mid n[\, P\,])\,]$ may be reachable. To analyse P it suffices then to find out an element I' such that $I' \sqsubseteq \phi(n)$.

(**pref**) As in the previous rule the located capability μ^L must belong to the element I. The residual process P has to be validated still inside the ambient k considering that ambient k, as effect of μ, may have moved. Indeed, function $\mathsf{t}(\mu, k)$ gives the set of ambients in which k may enter because of the execution of μ. Hence, the following configurations may be reachable: $m[\, \boldsymbol{\nu}\tilde{p}\,(R \mid k[\, P\,])\,]$, for $m \in \mathsf{t}(\mu, k)$, and $m[\, \boldsymbol{\nu}\tilde{p}\,(R \mid k[\, Q\,])\,]$, where P is a subprocess of Q, for $m \in \ell_1 \cup \mathsf{t}(\mu, k)$. Label $(\ell_1 \cup \mathsf{t}(\mu, k), \mathsf{t}(\mu, k))$ is thus used to validate P.

For instance in Example 3.1 we have $\overline{\mathsf{out}}\, n^{(\top, k\}, k)} \in \phi(n)$, because $\mathsf{t}(\mathsf{in}\, k, n) = k$ and

$$\phi \models_I^{n,(\top,\top)} \mathsf{in}\, k.\, \overline{\mathsf{out}}\, n \text{ requires } \phi \models_I^{n,(\{\top,k\},k)} \overline{\mathsf{out}}\, n$$

while

$$\phi \models_I^{n,(\{k,\top\},k)} \overline{\mathsf{out}}\, n \text{ requires } \overline{\mathsf{out}}\, n^{(\{k,\top\},k)} \in I \sqsubseteq \phi(n).$$

The remaining condition guarantees that $\mathsf{t}(\mu, k)$ have been recorded as possible fathers of k.

(**par**) The main idea is that of validating separately the process P and the process Q and to combine the results through the operator $\otimes$. Consider the process $R = \mathsf{in}\, n \mid \mathsf{out}\, m$. We obtain for instance

$$\phi \models_{I_1}^{k,L} \mathsf{in}\, n \text{ and } \phi \models_{I_2}^{k,L} \mathsf{out}\, m$$

for $I_1 = \{\mathsf{in}\, n^L\}$, $I_2 = \{\mathsf{out}\, m^L\}$. Neither I_1 nor I_2 contains enough information to validate R, because capabilities $\mathsf{in}\, n$ and $\mathsf{out}\, m$ may be executed in every order. Hence, the solution is sound only if it predicts that $\mathsf{out}\, m$ may be exercised in ℓ_2 and *also* after $\mathsf{in}\, n$, i.e. when k is inside n. Symmetrically it predicts that $\mathsf{in}\, n$ may be exercised in ℓ_2 and *also* after $\mathsf{out}\, m$, namely when k has moved out of m. Since label L does not contain this information, the labels of capabilities and ambients of the solutions I_1 and I_2 have to be updated according to the movements of the parallel processes. The operation $\otimes$ derives from elements I_1 and I_2 a correct element for R. Assuming that $\mathsf{t}(\mathsf{in}\, n, k) = n$ and $\mathsf{t}(\mathsf{out}\, m, k) = \mathsf{f}(m)$, we have

$$I_1 \otimes_k I_2 = \{\mathsf{in}\, n^{(\ell_1 \cup \{\mathsf{f}(m)\}, \ell_2 \cup \{\mathsf{f}(m)\})}, \mathsf{out}\, m^{(\ell_1 \cup \{n\}, \ell_2 \cup \{n\})}\}.$$

(**open**) The effect of an $\mathsf{open}\, n$ exercised inside k is that of liberating the process (say Q), which is currently contained in n, and to place it in parallel with the continuation of $\mathsf{open}\, n$ (say P). Considering a simplified case where $P = \mathbf{0}$ we have that $k[\, \mathsf{open}\, n \mid n[\, \overline{\mathsf{open}}\, n.\, Q\,]\,]$ reduces to $k[\, Q\,]$.

The idea is that the element I is valid iff also $\phi \models_I^{k,L} Q$, i.e. if I contains the ambients and capabilities which may be liberated inside k by opening n. If $\alpha^L \in \phi(n)$ and $k \in \ell_1$, then the the following configurations may be reachable $k[\, \boldsymbol{\nu}\tilde{p}\,(R \mid n[\, S\,])\,]$, where α is top level of S and may be acquired by k by opening n. Hence, the subset of $\phi(n)$, $\phi(n) \lhd k$ (that is the set of α^L such that $k \in \ell_1$), gives an approximation of the ambients and capabilities that k may acquire.

To be more precise we require that $\phi(n) \lhd k$ is a subset of the element I only when $\mathtt{open}\, n$ is executable, i.e. when $\overline{\mathtt{open}}\, n$ is enabled when n is inside k (see Definition 3.5 of γ).

For instance in Example 3.1 we have

$$\phi(m) = \{\mathtt{out}\, n^{(n,n)}, \overline{\mathtt{open}}\, m^{(\{n,k\},k)}, \mathtt{in}\, a^{(\{n,k\},k)}\}.$$

Therefore, $\gamma(k, \phi(m), m) = \{\mathtt{in}\, a^{(\{n,k\},k)}\}$: only capability $\mathtt{in}\, a$ is acquired by k through $\mathtt{open}\, m$.

If $\mathtt{open}\, n$ has a continuation P then $k[\,\mathtt{open}\, n.\, P \mid n[\,\overline{\mathtt{open}}\, n.\, Q\,]\,]$ reduces to $k[\, P \mid Q\,]$. Hence, the element $\gamma(k, \phi(n), n)$ has to be combined in parallel with the element that validates P. The remaining condition in the clause ensures that the effect of $\mathtt{open}\, n$ is properly recorded in all the labels. Since n may be dissolved inside k, every capability or ambient which was enabled (or top level) in n is also enabled (or top level) in k.

Remark 3.6. Now, we can better comment the role of labels ℓ_1 and ℓ_2: label ℓ_1 is used to handle more accurately the effect of $\mathtt{open}\, n$ (see rule (**open**)); label ℓ_2 restricts the cases where capabilities are executable and also allows one to predict more precisely where an ambient may end up after its execution (see Definition 3.4 of $\mathtt{t}$).

If capabilities and ambients were not labelled in our manner the prediction of the analysis would be less precise. For instance in Example 3.1, the analysis in [12] would imprecisely predict that k may acquire by opening m also $\mathtt{out}\, n$ and $\overline{\mathtt{open}}\, m$, i.e. the whole set $\phi(m)$. Moreover, the same analysis would imprecisely predict that the ambient m may end up, by executing $\mathtt{out}\, n$, in any father of n, thus in k and also in $\top$.

4   Properties of the analysis

We state some standard results of our analysis. First there always exists a least solution which is valid according to the clauses of Table 2. It is enough to show that the set of valid solutions is a complete lattice w.r.t. $\sqsubseteq$ (here defined componentwise), and that it forms a Moore Family [1] [8,15].

Theorem 4.1. *The set $\mathcal{J} = \{\phi \mid \phi \models_I^{k,L} P\}$ is a Moore family.*

The analysis satisfies a standard Subject Reduction theorem: validity of solutions is preserved under reduction.

Theorem 4.2. *Let $\phi \models_I^{k,L} P$, $I \sqsubseteq \phi(k)$ and $L \subseteq \mathtt{f}(k)$. If $P \Longrightarrow Q$ then there exists I' such that $\phi \models_{I'}^{k,L} Q$ and $I \sqsubseteq I' \sqsubseteq \phi(k)$.*

Corollary 4.3. *Let $\phi \models_{\phi(\top)}^{\top,(\emptyset,\emptyset)} P$. If $P \Longrightarrow Q$ then $\phi \models_{\phi(\top)}^{\top,(\emptyset,\emptyset)} Q$.*

---

[1] $(\mathcal{I}, \sqsubseteq)$ is a Moore family whenever any of its subsets admits a g.l.b. in $\mathcal{I}$

The following theorem states the relation between the dynamic and static behaviour. It says that a valid solution for a process P contains all the configurations of any derivative of P. In details, for every configuration $k[\,\boldsymbol{\nu}\tilde{p}(R_2 \mid n[\,R_1\,])\,]$ of any derivative of P, and for every α (capability or name) top level (resp. enabled) in R_1, the solution for n contains α^L where $k \in \ell_2$ (resp. $k \in \ell_1$).

Theorem 4.4 (Correctness). *Let $\alpha \in \mathcal{N} \cup \mathcal{C}$ and $n, k \in \mathcal{N}$. Whenever $\phi \models P$, $P \Longrightarrow Q$, and $k[\boldsymbol{\nu}\tilde{p}\,(n[\,R_1\,] \mid R_2)]$ is a configuration of Q:*

1. *if α is enabled in R_1, then $\alpha^{(\ell_1, \ell_2 \cup \{k\})} \in \phi(n)$;*
2. *if α is top level in R_1, then $\alpha^{(\ell_1 \cup \{k\}, \ell_2)} \in \phi(n)$.*

5 A Security Property

An ambient m may acquire the information contained in another ambient by opening it. We wish to maintain some information confidential to a group of ambients, considered trustworthy. To do so, names $\mathcal{N}$ (including $\top$) are partitioned into *trustworthy* $\mathcal{T}$ and *untrustworthy* $\mathcal{U}$. Secrecy of data is preserved if an untrustworthy ambient can never open a trustworthy one. Based on this partition, we first formalise our dynamic notion of secrecy: *protection*; then we give a static notion that implies the dynamic one.

We say that n is *opened* by k in P iff $k[\,\boldsymbol{\nu}\tilde{p}\,(n[\,R_1\,] \mid R_2)\,]$ is a configuration of P and $\overline{\mathbf{open}}\,n$ and $\mathbf{open}\,n$ are enabled in R_1 and in R_2, respectively.

Definition 5.1 (Dynamic Property). *A process P is protected iff $\forall k \in \mathcal{N}$, $n \in \mathcal{T}$, whenever $P \Longrightarrow Q$ and n is opened by k in Q then $k \in \mathcal{T}$.*

Definition 5.2 (Static Property). *A process P is defended if there exists a solution ϕ such that $\phi \models P$ and, $\forall k \in \mathcal{N}$, $n \in \mathcal{T}$, whenever $\mathbf{open}\,n^{L_1} \in \phi(k)$, $\overline{\mathbf{open}}\,n^{L_2} \in \phi(n)$ and $k \in \ell_{2,2}$, then $k \in \mathcal{T}$.*

Our static property is a correct approximation of the dynamic one. In fact, Theorem 4.4 suffices to prove the following.

Lemma 5.3. *If P is defended then it is protected.*

The property above is not enough, because it does not guarantee that a *defended* process P will still be such when plugged in a hostile context $C[-]$, unless the whole $C[P]$ is analysed again and proved to be *defended*. However, we can characterize those contexts that do not break the secrecy of P and for which there is no need to analyse $C[P]$. Technically, we first define a tester process, called enemy, which represents the most hostile context in which P can be put. The enemy satisfies some mild conditions on the names of its ambients: they should not clash with a subset N of those occurring in P. Note that the enemy may know the names of P, even if trustworthy: they need not to be kept secret (e.g. by restricting them). Also, the check on the names of the enemy can be done at run-time by P: entering, leaving or opening an ambient n of the enemy should be forbidden if $n \in N$. This can be easily done by a dynamic check.

Then, we show that if the system where P and its enemy run in parallel is *defended*, then P is *protected* in any context represented by the enemy.

Definition 5.4 (Enemy). *The* enemy *of a process P w.r.t. $N \subseteq \mathrm{fn}(P)$ is*

$$E(P, N) = (|_{m \in \mathrm{fn}(P) \backslash N} \; m[Q]) \mid Q$$

where $Q =|_{n \in \mathrm{fn}(P)} (!\mathbf{in}\, n \mid !\mathbf{out}\, n \mid !\mathbf{open}\, n \mid !\overline{\mathbf{in}}\, n \mid !\overline{\mathbf{out}}\, n \mid !\overline{\mathbf{open}}\, n).$

Theorem 5.5. *If $P \mid E(P, N)$ is* defended *for $N \subseteq \mathrm{fn}(P)$ then $C[P]$ is* protected *for every flat context $C[-]$ with no configuration $n[Q]$, $n \in N$.*

Note that it is not necessary to actually analyse $E(P, N)$: its solutions have all the same shape and can be easily built. Furthermore, given the standard solution for $E(P, N)$ and a solution for P, it is possible to build a valid solution for $P \mid E(P, N)$.

6 An Example

Consider an ambient a willing to send a message to an ambient b. Since the ambient calculus has no primitives for remote communication, a message is delivered by enclosing it in an ambient that moves inside the receiver. This acquires the message by opening it. When the message is secret, it is essential to guarantee that no ambient can open the ambient carrying the message, except for the designated receiver b. In other words, we would like our system to be *protected* (but we do not consider whether b receives the message or not).

Assuming that the path from a to b is known, an abstract specification could be the following, where *mail* carries the message D [2]:

$$SYS \; = a[\,\overline{\mathbf{out}}\, a.\, \overline{\mathbf{in}}\, a \mid \mathbf{open}\, mail \mid MAIL\,] \mid b[\,\overline{\mathbf{in}}\, b.\, \mathbf{open}\, msg\,]$$

$$MAIL = mail[\,\mathbf{out}\, a.\, \mathbf{in}\, b.\, \overline{\mathbf{out}}\, mail.\, \mathbf{out}\, b.\, \mathbf{in}\, a.\, \overline{\mathbf{open}}\, mail \mid$$
$$msg[\,\mathbf{out}\, mail.\, \overline{\mathbf{open}}\, msg.\, D\,]\,]$$

The ambient *mail* goes out of a and carries within b the message, included in *msg*. When there, *msg* exits from *mail* and b reads D through $\mathbf{open}\, msg$. Then, *mail* goes back to a, willing to deliver the ack of b through $\overline{\mathbf{open}}\, mail$.

When the message is secret, it is essential to guarantee that no ambient can open *msg* and therefore read the message, except for the receiver b. Assume that $\mathcal{T} = \{b, msg\}$ is the set of trustworthy ambients and that all the other ambients

---

[2] For the sake of simplicity, we assume here that D is a passive datum, that may only occur in the same position of **0** in processes, and that requires no analysis.

(including) $\top$, are trustworthy and form the complementary set $\mathcal{U}$. We wish to prove that SYS is protected (even when placed into a context which knows names msg, $mail$ and b.)

Actually, we show that $P = SYS \mid E(SYS, \{b, msg, mail\})$ is defended. Then, Theorem 5.5 suffices to prove that $C[SYS]$ is protected in any context where there are no ambients with name b, msg and $mail$.

The solution in Table 3 is valid for P and shows it protected. Indeed ϕ satisfies the requirements of Definition 5.2:

1. msg can be opened in b only because $\overline{\text{open}}\, msg^{(\mathcal{U}\cup\{b\},b)} \in \phi(msg)$;
2. ambient b is locked (it is not openable), because $\overline{\text{open}}\, b$ does not occur in $\phi(b)$.

$\phi(mail)$	$\{\text{out } a^{(\mathcal{U},\mathcal{U})}, \text{in } b^{(\mathcal{U},\mathcal{U})}, \overline{\text{out}}\, mail^{(\mathcal{U}\cup\{b\},b)}, \text{out } b^{(\mathcal{U}\cup\{b\},\mathcal{U}\cup\{b\})},$ $\text{in } a^{(\mathcal{U}\cup\{b\},\mathcal{U})}, \overline{\text{open}}\, msg^{(\mathcal{U}\cup\{b\},a)}\} \cup \{msg^{(\mathcal{U}\cup\{b\},\mathcal{U}\cup\{b\})}\}$
$\phi(b)$	$\{\bigcup_{n\in\mathcal{U}} n^{\mathcal{U},\mathcal{U}}, msg^{(\mathcal{U},\mathcal{U})}\} \cup$ $\{\overline{\text{in}}\, b^{(\mathcal{U},\mathcal{U})}, D^{(\mathcal{U}\cup\{b\},\mathcal{U}\cup b\})}, \text{open } msg^{(\mathcal{U},\mathcal{U})}\}$
$\phi(msg)$	$\{\text{out } mail^{(\mathcal{U},\mathcal{U})}, \overline{\text{open}}\, msg^{(\mathcal{U}\cup\{b\},b)}, D^{(\mathcal{U}\cup\{b\},b)}\}$
$\phi(n)$	$\{\bigcup_{m\in\mathcal{U}\cup\mathcal{T}} m^{(\mathcal{U},\mathcal{U})}\} \cup \{\bigcup_{m\in\mathcal{U}\cup\mathcal{T}} \mu^{(\mathcal{U},\mathcal{U})}, \bar{\mu}^{(\mathcal{U},\mathcal{U})}\},\ n \in \{a, \top\}$

Table 3. A Solution for SYS

Now we can better explain why the restrictions on the use of names in the context are necessary. The constraint on the use of trustworthy names b and msg are necessary for both the dynamic and the static property to hold. Dynamically, a context may contain a trustworthy ambient, say msg, that accept to be opened inside any other ambients. From a static point of view, ϕ is a function and so ambients with the same name are mapped to the same element. So, there is no way to distinguish the located capabilities and ambients of the "good" and trustworthy ambient $mail$ and the ones of the "bad " and trustworthy ambient $mail$ occurring in the context.

Note that labels are essential to prove (statically) that SYS satisfies the security property (see the discussion on the precision of the analysis contained in Remark 3.6).

7 Conclusions

The idea of using static techniques, such as those based on CFA [12,13,14] and type systems [10,4,3,5], to prove properties of mobile ambients is not new. The analysis of [12] is similar to ours but less accurate (if adapted to SA), since it does not use any contextual information (see Remark 3.6). The analyses contained in [13,14] show how to perform a rational reconstruction of the analysis [12] in the framework of Abstract Interpretation as well as how to specify stronger analyses using powerful counting analyses. Moreover, in [2] it is proposed an approach similar to our, even though based on type systems.

Many research lines are still open, besides the use of shape analysis [14] for improving the precision of our analysis in the case of recursive processes. Among them, there is the problem of constructing solutions efficiently and of considering also communication. Furthermore, the generality of the analysis (which is not ad hoc for a specific property) suggests to define other static tests on the solutions for establishing other security properties, like for instance mobility and locking of [3,5] or integrity.

It is worth mentioning that, even though SA was not introduced for security reasons, it seems to be more adequate than MA for better writing secure programs. Coaction $\overline{open}\, n$ for instance offers a control on the access to the private resources of the ambient n. In the example of Section 6 a proper use of coactions guarantees that trustworthy ambients may be contained inside untrustworthy ambients without being opened. The protocol should be substantially complicated to achieve the same security property if MA is used.

Acknowledgments. We wish to thank Flemming and Hanne Riis Nielson for many useful discussions. This work has been partially supported by MURST Project TOSCA.

References

1. C. Bodei, P. Degano, F. Nielson and H. Riis Nielson. *Static Analysis for the π-calculus with their application to security.* To appear in *Information and Computation.* Also available at http://www.di.unipi.it/~chiara/publ-40/BDNNi00.ps.
2. M. Bugliesi and G. Castagna *Secure Safe Ambients and JVM Security.* Proceedings of the Workshop on Issues in the Theory of Security 2000 (co-located with ICALP'00), pages 18-23, 2000.
3. L. Cardelli, G. Ghelli and A. Gordon *Mobility types for mobile ambients.* Proceedings of ICALP' 99, LNCS 1644, pages 230-239. Springer-Verlag, 1999.
4. L. Cardelli and A. Gordon *Types for mobile ambients.* Proceedings of 26th ACM Principles of Programming Languages (POPL' 99), pages 79-92. ACM Press, 1999.

5. L. Cardelli and G. Ghelli *Ambient Groups and Mobility Types.* Proceedings of IFIP TCS 2000. To appear.
6. L. Cardelli and A. Gordon. *Mobile Ambients* Proceedings of FoSSaCS' 98, LNCS 1378, pages 140-155. Springer-Verlag, 1998.
7. L. Cardelli and A. Gordon. *Equational Properties of Mobile Ambients* Proceedings of FoSSaCS' 99, LNCS 1578, pages 212-226. Springer-Verlag, 1999.
8. P. Cousot and R. Cousot, *Systematic Design of Program Analysis Frameworks,* Proceedings of POPL '79, pages 269–282, ACM Press, 1979.
9. F. Levi and C. Bodei *Security Analysis of Mobile Ambients.* Proceedings of the Workshop on Issues in the Theory of Security 2000 (co-located with ICALP'00), pages 18-23, 2000.
10. F. Levi and D. Sangiorgi *Controlling Interference in Ambients.* Proceedings of the 27th ACM Principles of Programming Languages (POPL' 00), pages 352-364. ACM Press, 2000.
11. R. Milner and J. Parrow and D. Walker. *A calculus of mobile processes, (Part I and II)* Information and Computation, number 100, pages 1-77, 1992.
12. F. Nielson, H.R. Nielson, R.R. Hansen and J.G. Jensen *Validating firewalls in mobile ambients.* Proceedings of CONCUR' 99, LNCS 1664, pages 463-477. Springer-Verlag, 1999.
13. R. R. Hansen and J. G. Jensen and F. Nielson and H. R.Nielson *Abstract Interpretation of Mobile Ambients* Proceedings of SAS'99, LNCS 1694, pages 135-148, Springer-Verlag, 1999.
14. H. R. Nielson and F. Nielson *Shape Analysis for Mobile Ambients* Proceedings of POPL' 00, pages 135-148, ACM Press, 2000.
15. F. Nielson and H. R. Nielson and C. Hankin, *Principles of Program Analysis,* Springer,1999.

Security Types for Mobile Safe Ambients*

M. Dezani-Ciancaglini and I. Salvo

Dipartimento di Informatica, Università di Torino
Corso Svizzera 185, 10149 Torino, Italy
{dezani,salvo}@di.unito.it

Abstract. The *Ambient Calculus* and the *Safe Ambient Calculus* have been recently successfully proposed as models for the Web. They are based on the notions of ambient *movement* and ambient *opening*. Different type disciplines have been devised for them in order to avoid unwanted behaviours of processes.
In the present paper we propose a type discipline for safe mobile ambients which is essentially motivated by ensuring *security* properties. We associate security levels to ambients and we require that an ambient at security level s can only be traversed or opened by ambients at security level at least s. Since the movement and opening rights can be unrelated, we consider two partial orders between security levels.
We also discuss some meaningful examples of use of our type discipline.

1 Introduction

The *Ambient Calculus* [4] has been recently successfully proposed as a model for the Web. An ambient is a named location: it may contain processes and sub-ambients. A process may:

- communicate in an asynchronous way with a process in the same ambient;
- cause the enclosing ambient to move inside or outside other ambients;
- destroy the boundary of a sub-ambient, causing the contents of the sub-ambient to spill into the parent ambient.

In order to have a richer algebraic theory, in the *Safe Ambient Calculus* [9] the activity of processes is better controlled since:

- an ambient may traverse an ambient n only if at least one process inside n agrees;
- a process may destroy the boundary of an ambient n only if at least one process inside n agrees.

A standard way of forbidding unwanted behaviours is to impose a *type discipline*.

Different type disciplines have been proposed for the Ambient Calculus, taking advantage of several papers on typing for mobile processes, with or without localities, see for example [11], [6] and [10]. In [5] the types assure the correctness of communications. The type system of [2] guarantees also that only ambients

---

* Partially supported by MURST Cofin '99 TOSCA Project.

which are declared as mobile will move and only ambients which are declared as openable will be opened. Adding subtyping allows us to obtain a more flexible type discipline [12]. Lastly, by means of *group* names [3], the type of an ambient n controls the set of ambients n may cross and the set of ambients n may open. Moreover the possibility of creating fresh group names gives a flexible way of statically preventing unwanted propagation of names.

A powerful type discipline for the Safe Ambient Calculus has been devised in [9]. The main features are the control of ambient mobility and the removing of all *grave interferences*, i.e. of all non-deterministic choices between logically incompatible interactions. This is achieved by means of types which can be derived only for *single-threaded* ambients, i.e. ambients which at every step offer at most one interaction with external or internal ambients.

The secure safe ambient calculus of [1] is a typed variant of Safe Ambients in which ambient types are protection domains expressing behavioural invariants.

Security plays a crucial role in the theory and practice of distributed systems. In the present paper we propose a type discipline for safe mobile ambients which is essentially motivated by ensuring *security* properties. The type of an ambient name specifies a security level s. We require that an ambient at security level s can only be traversed or opened by ambients at security level at least s. For example the movement of an ambient n inside an ambient m:

$$n[\textbf{in } m.P_1 \mid P_2] \mid m[\overline{\textbf{in}} \ m.Q_1 \mid Q_2]$$

can correctly be typed only if the security level of n is greater than or equal to that of m. Moreover, we consider also *passive* security levels, which forbid an ambient to influence the behaviour of a surrounding ambient belonging to a higher security level.

Since the movement and opening rights can be unrelated, we consider two partial orders between security levels.

As in the above-mentioned type discipline with group names, each ambient name belongs to a security level. However, we do not consider the possibility of creating fresh, private security levels, since we consider two global partial orders defined on security levels and it is not clear how to include the new level. Moreover, thanks to the order relations, in the type of an ambient name we do not need to list explicitly all security levels of ambients it may traverse or open.

In the simple case in which the movement rights are all equal and there are only two opening rights we classify the ambients as trustworthy and untrustworthy. Then the types can assure the secrecy property considered in [8] that an untrustworthy ambient can never open a trustworthy one.

The paper is organized as follows. Section 2 recalls the definitions of Mobile Safe Ambients. For the sake of readability, we present our type system in two steps. Section 3 discusses a simpler version, which introduces the notion of security level in ambient types. The full system is motivated by the requirement of obtaining more refined typings, in particular to type as immobile an ambient which opens a mobile ambient that, when opened, does not unleash mobility capabilities. To do this we need to distinguish the behaviours of processes before and after an ambient is opened (Section 4). Section 5 gives some examples of use of our type discipline. A first protocol models a mailserver with different mailboxes and users: each user is allowed to enter only his own mailbox and this is achieved via type constraints imposed on the security level order. A second example shows that we can encode the security policy for reading and writing discussed in [7] for the π-calculus. Lastly, we present the renaming, firewall and channel protocols which are already typed in [2] and in [9] for comparisons and for showing how some behavioural conditions can be expressed in our system as type constraints. Some final remarks are done in Section 6.

2   Untyped Mobile Safe Ambients

The calculus of Mobile Safe Ambients [9] is a refinement of the calculus of Mobile Ambients [4] which allows a better control of the actions and therefore a richer algebraic theory of processes. We will use here the calculus of Mobile Safe Ambients, the only difference being that we describe infinite behaviours by $!P$ instead of $\mathbf{rec}X.P$, since this slightly simplifies the typing rules. The syntax is given in Figure 1 starting from an infinite countable set of names.

Figure 2 contains the reduction relation which uses the structural congruence $\equiv$. As customary, the structural congruence $\equiv$ is defined as the minimal reflexive, transitive and symmetric relation which is a congruence and moreover:

- satisfies $!P \equiv !P \mid P$;
- makes the operator $\mid$ commutative, associative, with $\mathbf{0}$ as zero element;
- allows to stretch the scopes of restrictions, to permute restrictions and to cancel a restriction followed only by $\mathbf{0}$;
- satisfies $\epsilon.P \equiv P$ and $(M.M').P \equiv M.M'.P$.

$M, N ::=$	**expression**		$P, Q ::=$	**process**
n	name		$(\nu\, n : W)P$	restriction
$\mathbf{in}\ M$	can inter into M		$\mathbf{0}$	inactivity
$\overline{\mathbf{in}}\ M$	M allow enter		$P \mid Q$	parallel
$\mathbf{out}\ M$	can exit out of M		$!P$	replication
$\overline{\mathbf{out}}\ M$	M allow exit		$M.P$	action
$\mathbf{open}\ M$	can open M		$M[P]$	ambient
$\overline{\mathbf{open}}\ M$	M allow open		$\langle M_1 \ldots M_k \rangle$	output action
ϵ	empty path		$(x_1 : W_1, \ldots, x_k : W_k).P$	input action
$M.M'$	path			

Fig. 1. Expressions and Processes

3   Security Types

The basic idea of our type system is to control at type level access and opening rights of ambients. Each ambient name has a type that represents its *security*

(R-in) $n[\textbf{in } m.P_1 \mid P_2] \mid m[\overline{\textbf{in}} \ m.Q_1 \mid Q_2]$ $\longrightarrow m[n[P_1 \mid P_2] \mid Q_1 \mid Q_2]$

(R-out) $m[n[\textbf{out } m.P_1 \mid P_2] \mid \overline{\textbf{out}} \ m.Q_1 \mid Q_2]$ $\longrightarrow n[P_1 \mid P_2] \mid m[Q_1 \mid Q_2]$

(R-open) $\textbf{open } n.P \mid n[\overline{\textbf{open}} \ n.Q_1 \mid Q_2]$ $\longrightarrow P \mid Q_1 \mid Q_2$

(R-I/O) $\langle M_1, \ldots, M_k \rangle \mid (n_1 : W_1, \ldots, n_k : W_k).P \longrightarrow P\{n_1 := M_1, \ldots, n_k := M_k\}$

(R-par) $P \longrightarrow Q$ $\Rightarrow P \mid R \longrightarrow Q \mid R$

(R-res) $P \longrightarrow Q$ $\Rightarrow (\nu n : W)P \longrightarrow (\nu n : W)Q$

(R-amb) $P \longrightarrow Q$ $\Rightarrow n[P] \longrightarrow n[Q]$

(R-$\equiv$) $P' \equiv P \quad P \longrightarrow Q \quad Q \equiv Q'$ $\Rightarrow P' \longrightarrow Q'$

Fig. 2. Reduction

level: a process inside an ambient can perform actions according to the ambient security level. A security level defines mobility and opening rights of ambients which belong to. As in previous type systems for Mobile Ambients [5,2], the type of an ambient keeps information about the type of messages exchanged inside it, if the ambient can move and if it can be opened. Moreover, in the type of an ambient name, we consider also type annotations that say if the ambient can be traversed and if it can open other ambients. In Section 5, we successfully exploit security levels to model a mailserver where unauthorized accesses are forbidden as non-well typed processes (Subsection 5.1) and to model an information flow policy in an ambient encoding of π-calculus channels.

Types. Types are defined starting from an universe $\mathcal{U}$ of *active security levels* and an universe $\overline{\mathcal{U}}$ of *passive* security levels: each element s in $\mathcal{U}$ has a corresponding element $\overline{\mathsf{s}}$ in $\overline{\mathcal{U}}$. The universe $\mathcal{U}$ comes equipped with two partial order relations, $\leq^{\frown}$ for mobility rights and $\leq^{\circ}$ for opening rights. These orders are mirrored in $\overline{\mathcal{U}}$.

We denote by $\mathsf{s}, \mathsf{s}', \mathsf{s}_1, \ldots$ elements of $\mathcal{U}$, by $\overline{\mathsf{s}}, \overline{\mathsf{s}}', \overline{\mathsf{s}}_1, \ldots$ elements of $\overline{\mathcal{U}}$, and by $\mathsf{S}, \mathsf{S}', \mathsf{S}_1, \ldots$ subsets of $\mathcal{U} \cup \overline{\mathcal{U}}$.

As usual [5] the exchange types are Shh when no exchange is allowed and tuples whose elements are either ambient types or capability types.

An ambient type has the shape $\mathsf{s}_V^Y[T_U^Z]$ where:

- s is the security level to which the ambient belongs (similar to the group of [3]);
- T is the type of exchanges the ambient allows within (as in [5]);
- Y says if the ambient is locked ($\bullet$) or unlocked ($\circ$) and only unlocked ambients can be opened (as in [2]);
- V says if the ambient can ($\overline{\circ}$) or cannot ($\overline{\bullet}$) open another ambient which belongs to a security level lower or equal in the order $\leq^{\circ}$;
- Z says if the ambient can move ($\frown$) or if it is immobile ($\vee$) (as in [2]);
- U says if the ambient can ($\leftrightarrow$) or cannot ($\oplus$) be traversed by another ambient which belongs to a security level greater or equal in the order $\leq^{\frown}$.

A capability type has the shape $Cap[F]$ where F is an effect.

An effect has the shape $\mathsf{S}_1, \mathsf{S}_2, T$, where T is the type of exchanges which can be unleashed by an **open** action (as in [3]). The set S_1 contains the security levels of the ambients which can be traversed. The set S_2 contains the security levels of the ambients which can be opened. In S_1 and S_2 the levels are active or passive according to the ambient is in an action or in a co-action.

The sets of type annotations and of types are respectively given in Figures 3 and 4.

$$
\begin{array}{ll}
Z := & \textbf{mobility annotation} \\
& \curvearrowright \text{ mobile} \\
& \vee \text{ immobile} \\
U := & \textbf{traversing annotation} \\
& \leftrightarrow \text{ can be traversed} \\
& \oplus \text{ cannot be traversed}
\end{array}
\qquad
\begin{array}{ll}
V := & \textbf{opening annotation} \\
& \bar{\mathsf{o}} \text{ can open} \\
& \bar{\bullet} \text{ cannot open} \\
Y := & \textbf{locking annotation} \\
& \circ \text{ unlocked} \\
& \bullet \text{ locked}
\end{array}
$$

Fig. 3. Type annotations

$$
\begin{array}{lll}
F & ::= & \textbf{effect} \\
& \mathsf{S}_1, \mathsf{S}_2, T & \text{moves and is traversed according to } \mathsf{S}_1, \text{ open and} \\
& & \text{can be opened according to } \mathsf{S}_2, \text{ exchange } T \\
W & ::= & \textbf{message type} \\
& \mathsf{s}_V^Y[T_U^Z] & \text{ambient name in security level } \mathsf{s} \\
& & \text{(contains processes whose effects agree with } \{Y, V, Z, U\}) \\
& Cap[F] & \text{capability (unleashes F effects)} \\
T & ::= & \textbf{exchange type} \\
& Shh & \text{no exchange} \\
& W_1 \times \ldots \times W_k & \text{tuple exchange}
\end{array}
$$

Fig. 4. Types

Typing Rules. As usual an environment E associates names with ambient and capability types:
$$E ::= \varnothing \mid E, n : W.$$
The domain of E (notation $dom(E)$) is defined by:
$$
dom(E) = \begin{cases} \varnothing & \text{if } E = \varnothing \\ dom(E') \cup \{n\} & \text{if } E = E', n : W \end{cases}
$$

The typing judgments are relative to a given universe $\mathcal{U}$ of security levels and to a given environment E. There are six kinds of judgments:

$$
\begin{array}{ll}
\mathcal{U}, E \vdash \diamond & \text{good environment} \\
\mathcal{U}, E \vdash T & \text{good exchange type } T \\
\mathcal{U}, E \vdash F & \text{good effect } F \\
\mathcal{U}, E \vdash W & \text{good message type } W \\
\mathcal{U}, E \vdash M : W & \text{good expression } M \text{ of message type } W \\
\mathcal{U}, E \vdash P : F & \text{good process } P \text{ with effect } F.
\end{array}
$$

Figure 5 contains the rules for deriving judgments of the four first kinds. These rules follow in a standard way the syntax of types given in Figure 4.

$$\frac{}{\mathcal{U} \vdash \diamond} \text{ (Empty Env)} \qquad \frac{\mathcal{U}, E \vdash W \quad n \notin dom(E)}{\mathcal{U}, E, n : W \vdash \diamond} \text{ (Env Formation)}$$

$$\frac{\mathcal{U}, E \vdash \diamond}{\mathcal{U}, E \vdash Shh} \text{ (Shh)} \qquad \frac{\mathcal{U}, E \vdash W_1 \quad \ldots \quad \mathcal{U}, E \vdash W_k}{\mathcal{U}, E \vdash W_1 \times \ldots \times W_k} \text{ (Prod)}$$

$$\frac{\mathcal{U}, E \vdash T \quad s \in \mathcal{U}}{\mathcal{U}, E \vdash s_V^Y[T_U^Z]} \text{ (Amb)} \qquad \frac{\mathcal{U}, E \vdash F}{\mathcal{U}, E \vdash Cap[F]} \text{ (Cap)}$$

$$\frac{\mathcal{U}, E \vdash T \quad \bigcup_{1 \leq i \leq 2} S_i \subseteq \mathcal{U} \cup \overline{\mathcal{U}}}{\mathcal{U}, E \vdash S_1, S_2, T} \text{ (Effect)}$$

Fig. 5. Good Environments and Types

The capabilities unleashed by opening an ambient n are the maximal capabilities consistent with respect to the type annotations and the security level in the type of n, therefore to give the typing rules for the **open** expression we need to define when *two sets* S, S' *of security levels* agree ($\bowtie$) *with the type annotation* $\{V, Z, U\}$. This means that:

-- if S contains an active security level then Z says that the ambient is mobile;
-- if S contains a passive security level then U says that the ambient can be traversed;
-- if S' contains an active security level then V says that the ambient can open.

This allows us to build the pair of maximal sets $\Im(\{V, Z, U\}, s)$ which agree with a given type annotation $\{V, Z, U\}$ and contain only a given security level (active) s and (passive) $\overline{s}$. See Figure 6.

$$S, S' \bowtie \{V, Z, U\} \iff \begin{array}{l} \exists s \in S \Rightarrow Z = \curvearrowright \quad \& \\ \exists \overline{s} \in S \Rightarrow U = \leftrightarrow \quad \& \\ \exists s \in S' \Rightarrow V = \overline{o} \end{array}$$

$$\Im(\{V, Z, U\}, s) = max \, S, S'.S \cup S' \subseteq \{s, \overline{s}\} \, \& \, S, S' \bowtie \{V, Z, U\}$$

Fig. 6. Agreement between sets of security levels and type annotations

To determine the effect of a path of expressions, we combine two effects for obtaining a new effect. As usual, we can combine two effects only if they share the same exchange type. The *combination of effects* is just componentwise set union, more precisely (overloading the symbol $\cup$):

$$(\mathsf{S}_1, \mathsf{S}_2, T) \cup (\mathsf{S}_3, \mathsf{S}_4, T) = \mathsf{S}_1 \cup \mathsf{S}_3, \mathsf{S}_2 \cup \mathsf{S}_4, T.$$

The typing of a mobility action, **in** M or **out** M, checks if the ambient M can be traversed and builds a simple capability by putting the active security level of M in the first set. The typing of a mobility co-action, $\overline{\textbf{in}}$ M or $\overline{\textbf{out}}$ M, is similar, except that the passive security level is put in the first set.

The typing of an open action, **open** M, checks if the ambient M can be opened, using the information given by the type of M, that has the shape $\mathsf{s}_V^Y[T_U^Z]$. If Y is $\circ$, the ambient can be opened and in the type of **open** M we must take into account the effects unleashed by the ambient M after being opened. This effect must contain a pair of sets S, S' which agree with $\{V, Z, U\}$. Since we have to take into account the maximal possible effect, we build S, S' as $\Im(\{V, Z, U\}, \mathsf{s})$. The final effect will be $\mathsf{S}, \{\mathsf{s}\} \cup \mathsf{S}', T$, where we add s to take into account the open action.

An open co-action, $\overline{\textbf{open}}$ M, can be typed only if the annotation Y in the type of M is $\circ$ and the effect is simply $\{\ \}, \{\overline{\mathsf{s}}\}, T$. Figure 7 gives the typing rules for expressions.

Typing an ambient requires to check if the ambient type agrees with the effect of the process running inside it. An *effect* $\mathsf{S}, \mathsf{S}', T$ agrees *with an ambient type* $\mathsf{s}_V^Y[T_U'^Z]$ iff:

- $T = T'$;
- the sets S, S' agree with the type annotations $\{V, Z, U\}$;
- if S' contains a passive security level then Y says that the ambient can be opened;
- all active security levels in S are $\leq^\frown \mathsf{s}$ and all passive security levels in S are $\leq^\frown \overline{\mathsf{s}}$;
- all active security levels in S' are $\leq^\circ \mathsf{s}$ and all passive security levels in S' are $\leq^\circ \overline{\mathsf{s}}$.

Conditions on passive security levels ensure that opening an ambient does not influence, unleashing co-capabilities, the behaviour of a surrounding ambient which belongs to a higher security level.

In Figure 8 we formally define when an effect $\mathsf{S}, \mathsf{S}', T$ agrees with $\mathsf{s}_V^Y[T_U'^Z]$ using the definitions of Figure 6.

Figure 9 gives the typing rules for processes. Rule (Proc Amb) checks that the effect of P agrees with the ambient type of n before building the process $n[P]$. Now $n[P]$ has no action, and therefore its effect is $\{\ \}, \{\ \}, T$ for an arbitrary T. The remaining typing rules are almost standard.

Properties of Well-Typed Processes. The effects we derive for processes are rather informative of their behaviours. More precisely if $\mathcal{U}, E \vdash P : \mathsf{S}, \mathsf{S}', T$ we can show that:

- if P may perform a move action then $\mathsf{S} \cap \mathcal{U} \neq \varnothing$,
- if P may perform a move co-action then $\mathsf{S} \cap \overline{\mathcal{U}} \neq \varnothing$,
- if P may perform an open action then $\mathsf{S}' \cap \mathcal{U} \neq \varnothing$,
- if P may perform an open co-action then $\mathsf{S}' \cap \overline{\mathcal{U}} \neq \varnothing$.

It turns out that a process P has no thread [9], i.e. P cannot do actions, whenever we can derive the judgement $\mathcal{U}, E \vdash P : \mathsf{S}, \mathsf{S}', T$ with $(\mathsf{S} \cup \mathsf{S}') \cap \mathcal{U} = \varnothing$.

$$\frac{\mathcal{U}, E, n : W, E' \vdash \diamond}{\mathcal{U}, E, n : W, E' \vdash n : W} \text{ (Exp } n) \qquad \frac{\mathcal{U}, E \vdash \diamond}{\mathcal{U}, E \vdash \epsilon : \{\}, \{\}, T} \text{ (Exp } \epsilon)$$

$$\frac{\mathcal{U}, E \vdash M : Cap[F] \quad \mathcal{U}, E \vdash M' : Cap[F']}{\mathcal{U}, E \vdash M.M' : Cap[F \cup F']} \text{ (Exp .)}$$

$$\frac{\mathcal{U}, E \vdash M : \mathsf{s}_V^Y[T_\hookrightarrow^Z] \quad \mathcal{U}, E \vdash T'}{\mathcal{U}, E \vdash \mathbf{in} \ M : Cap[\{\mathsf{s}\}, \{\ \}, T']} \text{ (Exp } \mathbf{in})$$

$$\frac{\mathcal{U}, E \vdash M : \mathsf{s}_V^Y[T_\hookrightarrow^Z] \quad \mathcal{U}, E \vdash T'}{\mathcal{U}, E \vdash \overline{\mathbf{in}} \ M : Cap[\{\bar{\mathsf{s}}\}, \{\ \}, T']} \text{ (Exp } \overline{\mathbf{in}})$$

$$\frac{\mathcal{U}, E \vdash M : \mathsf{s}_V^Y[T_\hookrightarrow^Z] \quad \mathcal{U}, E \vdash T'}{\mathcal{U}, E \vdash \mathbf{out} \ M : Cap[\{\mathsf{s}\}, \{\ \}, T']} \text{ (Exp } \mathbf{out})$$

$$\frac{\mathcal{U}, E \vdash M : \mathsf{s}_V^Y[T_\hookrightarrow^Z] \quad \mathcal{U}, E \vdash T'}{\mathcal{U}, E \vdash \overline{\mathbf{out}} \ M : Cap[\{\bar{\mathsf{s}}\}, \{\ \}, T']} \text{ (Exp } \overline{\mathbf{out}})$$

$$\frac{\mathcal{U}, E \vdash M : \mathsf{s}_V^\circ[T_U^Z] \quad \Im(\{V, Z, U\}, \mathsf{s}) = \mathsf{S}, \mathsf{S}'}{\mathcal{U}, E \vdash \mathbf{open} \ M : Cap[\mathsf{S}, \{\mathsf{s}\} \cup \mathsf{S}', T]} \text{ (Exp } \mathbf{open})$$

$$\frac{\mathcal{U}, E \vdash M : \mathsf{s}_V^\circ[T_U^Z]}{\mathcal{U}, E \vdash \overline{\mathbf{open}} \ M : Cap[\{\ \}, \{\bar{\mathsf{s}}\}, T]} \text{ (Exp } \overline{\mathbf{open}})$$

Fig. 7. Good Expressions

$$\mathsf{S}, \mathsf{S}', T \bowtie \mathsf{s}_V^Y[T_U'^Z] \iff \begin{array}{l} T = T' \ \& \\ \mathsf{S}, \mathsf{S}' \bowtie \{V, Z, U\} \ \& \\ \exists \bar{\mathsf{s}} \in \mathsf{S}' \Rightarrow Y = \circ \ \& \\ \forall \mathsf{s}', \bar{\mathsf{s}}' \in \mathsf{S}.\mathsf{s}' \leq^\frown \mathsf{s} \ \& \ \bar{\mathsf{s}}' \leq^\frown \bar{\mathsf{s}} \ \& \\ \forall \mathsf{s}', \bar{\mathsf{s}}' \in \mathsf{S}'.\mathsf{s}' \leq^\circ \mathsf{s} \ \& \ \bar{\mathsf{s}}' \leq^\circ \bar{\mathsf{s}} \end{array}$$

Fig. 8. Agreement between effects and ambient types

$$\frac{\mathcal{U}, E \vdash M : Cap[F] \quad \mathcal{U}, E \vdash P : F'}{\mathcal{U}, E \vdash M.P : F \cup F'} \text{ (Proc Action)}$$

$$\frac{\mathcal{U}, E \vdash M : s_V^Y[T_U^Z] \quad \mathcal{U}, E \vdash P : F \quad F \bowtie s_V^Y[T_U^Z] \quad \mathcal{U}, E \vdash T}{\mathcal{U}, E \vdash M[P] : \{\,\}, \{\,\}, T} \text{ (Proc Amb)}$$

$$\frac{\mathcal{U}, E, n : s_V^Y[T_U^Z] \vdash P : F}{\mathcal{U}, E \vdash (\nu\, n : s_V^Y[T_U^Z])P : F} \text{ (Proc Res)} \qquad \frac{\mathcal{U}, E \vdash T}{\mathcal{U}, E \vdash \mathbf{0} : \{\,\}, \{\,\}, T} \text{ (Proc 0)}$$

$$\frac{\mathcal{U}, E \vdash P : F \quad \mathcal{U}, E \vdash Q : F'}{\mathcal{U}, E \vdash P \mid Q : F \cup F'} \text{ (Proc Par)} \qquad \frac{\mathcal{U}, E \vdash P : F}{\mathcal{U}, E \vdash\, !P : F} \text{ (Proc Repl)}$$

$$\frac{\mathcal{U}, E, n_1 : W_1, \ldots, n_k : W_k \vdash P : S, S', W_1 \times \ldots \times W_k}{\mathcal{U}, E \vdash (n_1 : W_1, \ldots, n_k : W_k).P : S, S', W_1 \times \ldots \times W_k} \text{ (Proc Input)}$$

$$\frac{\mathcal{U}, E \vdash M_1 : W_1 \quad \ldots \quad \mathcal{U}, E \vdash M_k : W_k}{\mathcal{U}, E \vdash \langle M_1, \ldots, M_k \rangle : \{\,\}, \{\,\}, W_1 \times \ldots \times W_k} \text{ (Proc Output)}$$

Fig. 9. Good Processes

This implies that we can type only single threaded processes if we restrict rule (Proc Par) as follows:

$$\frac{\mathcal{U}, E \vdash P : F \quad \mathcal{U}, E \vdash Q : F' \quad st(F) \text{ or } st(F')}{\mathcal{U}, E \vdash P \mid Q : F \cup F'}$$

where $st(S, S', T)$ is short for $(S \cup S') \cap \mathcal{U} = \varnothing$. A more refined typing for single threaded processes is given in [9].

As usual, the soundness of the typing rules is assured by a Subject Reduction Theorem. Since the effects precisely describe the actions which can be performed by a process, and the reduction consumes actions, in general we can derive a "better" effect for the reduced process. To formally state this, we introduce an order $\sqsubseteq$ on effects: $F' \sqsubseteq F$ means that sets in F "cover" with respect to the appropriate order the corresponding sets in F'. We say that a set S' *covers* a set S with respect to the order $\leq^*$ ($S \sqsubseteq^* S'$) iff for all $s \in S$ we can find $s' \in S'$ such that $s \leq^* s'$ and similarly for passive security levels. Figure 10 defines this order.

$$S \sqsubseteq^* S' \qquad \Longleftrightarrow \quad \forall s \in S. \exists s' \in S'.s \leq^* s' \,\&\, \forall \bar{s} \in S. \exists \bar{s}' \in S'.\bar{s} \leq^* \bar{s}' \quad (* \in \{\curvearrowright, \circ\})$$
$$S_1, S_2, T \sqsubseteq S_1', S_2', T \Longleftrightarrow S_1 \sqsubseteq^\curvearrowright S_1' \,\&\, S_2 \sqsubseteq^\circ S_2'$$

Fig. 10. Partial order of effects

Theorem 1. *If* $\mathcal{U}, E \vdash P : F$ *and* $P \longrightarrow Q$ *then* $\mathcal{U}, E \vdash Q : F'$ *for some* F' *such that* $F' \sqsubseteq F$.

We will prove the soundness of the full system (Theorem 2) which implies that of the present one.

The subject reduction property means that:

- every communication is well-typed;
- no locked ambient will ever be opened, and an unlocked ambient will only be opened inside an ambient which can open and which has a higher or equal security level in the order $\leq^\circ$;
- no immobile ambient will ever move, and a mobile ambient will only traverse ambients which can be traversed and which have lower or equal security levels in the order $\leq^\frown$.

4 Security Types with Opening Control

As pointed out in [9], better control over the ambient behaviours helps in deriving a richer algebraic theory and hence easier proofs of correctness.

One important lack of the type system introduced in previous section, with respect of the type system of [9], is that it is not possible to type as immobile an ambient that opens mobile ambients. This is not satisfactory. As an example think to a message sent to a server: the message is a mobile entity, whereas the server is not. Reasonably, in an Ambient Calculus encoding, the ambient representing the server has to open the ambient representing the message. A message is represented by a mobile ambient, but opening it does not unleash movement capabilities. We will further discuss this problem in the example concerning a firewall protocol, in Subsection 5.3.

In this section we extend our type system in order to derive such kind of judgements. In the typical cases in which only one $\overline{\text{open}}$ appears in processes inside an ambient, exploiting the presence of co-actions, we can distinguish between effects before and after the unique $\overline{\text{open}}$ co-action and hence determine the capabilities unleashed opening such an ambient. As expected, such control over ambient behaviour rather complicates the type system.

Expanded Types. We extend the set of types as follows. The locking annotations can also have the shape:

$$Y = \circ\{V, Z, U\}$$

which means that the ambient can be opened and that processes spilled out after the opening behave according to the annotation $\{V, Z, U\}$.

Also effects can keep information about opening and mobility rights required by processes before and after the opening of their surrounding ambient. Therefore effects can be *simple effects* that, as before, have the shape $\mathsf{S}_1, \mathsf{S}_2, T$ or *expanded effects*, that have the shape $\mathsf{S}_1, \mathsf{S}_2, \{\mathsf{S}_3, \mathsf{S}_4\}, T$ which says that there is only one $\overline{\text{open}}$ and that before the execution of it we have the effect $\mathsf{S}_1, \mathsf{S}_2, T$, while after the execution of it we have the effect $\mathsf{S}_3, \mathsf{S}_4, T$. In Fig. 11 we extend the syntax of effects.

$$H ::= \qquad\qquad \textbf{opening effect}$$

S	open and can be opened according to S
$S_1, \{S_2, S_3\}$	open and can be opened according to S_1 after the open, moves and is traversed according to S_2, open and can be opened according to S_3
$F ::=$	**effect**
S, H, T	moves and is traversed according to S, open and can be opened according to H, exchange T

Fig. 11. Expanded Effects

Expanded Typing Rules. The rules for type formation must be extended by adding a rule for the formation of expanded effects:

$$\frac{\mathcal{U}, E \vdash T \quad \bigcup_{1 \le i \le 4} S_i \subseteq \mathcal{U} \cup \overline{\mathcal{U}} \quad S_2 \cap \overline{\mathcal{U}} \ne \varnothing}{\mathcal{U}, E \vdash S_1, S_2, \{S_3, S_4\}, T} \quad \text{(Effect expanded)}$$

where we require that at least one ambient can be opened with the condition $S_2 \cap \overline{\mathcal{U}} \ne \varnothing$.

The combination of two effects is still componentwise set union when the first one is simple, but now the resulting effect is either simple or expanded according to how the second effect is. If the effects are both expanded their combination is a simple effect obtained by loosing the information on what is the difference between the effects before and after the two $\overline{\text{open}}$ actions: in such case we can not foresee, typing an **open** action, which $\overline{\text{open}}$ will be involved in the reduction, and hence the extra information given by expanded effects is not useful to obtain more refined typings. If the first effect is expanded and the second is simple, the combination is an expanded effect obtained by taking into account the second effect only after the unique $\overline{\text{open}}$ action. The formal definition of combination of effects is given in Figure 12.

$$S, H, T \uplus S', H', T' = \begin{cases} S \cup S', H \cup H', T & \text{if } H \subseteq \mathcal{U} \cup \overline{\mathcal{U}} \\ S, S_1, \{S_2 \cup S', S_3 \cup H'\}, T & \text{if } H = S_1, \{S_2, S_3\} \,\& \\ & H' \subseteq \mathcal{U} \cup \overline{\mathcal{U}} \\ S \cup S' \cup S_2 \cup S_2', S_1 \cup S_1' \cup S_3 \cup S_3', T & \text{if } H = S_1, \{S_2, S_3\} \,\& \\ & H' = S_1', \{S_2', S_3'\} \end{cases}$$

Fig. 12. Combination of simple and expanded effects for expressions

In typing rules for expression we have to modify the rule for expression path (Exp .), replacing the operator $\uplus$ to set union for combination of effects. The other rules remain the same, also if Y can be $\circ\{V, Z, U\}$, and we add rules for all actions to take into account expanded effects. The new rules for typing the mobility actions allow the movement after the ambient has been opened.

Similarly to the case of simple effects, the typing of an open action, **open** M, checks if the ambient M can be opened, using the information given by the type of M, that has the shape $s_V^Y[T_U^Z]$. If Y is $\circ\{V', Z', U'\}$, the ambient can be opened and in the type of **open** M we must take into account the effects unleashed by the ambient M after being opened. This effect must contain a pair of sets S, S' which agree with $\{V', Z', U'\}$, so as for simple effects we take $\Im(\{V', Z', U'\}, s)$. The final effect will be $S, \{s\} \cup S', T$, where we add s to take into account the open action.

An open co-action, $\overline{\text{open}}\ M$, can be typed if the annotation Y in the type of M is $\circ\{V', Z', U'\}$. In this case the effect is expanded to $\{\ \}, \{\bar{s}\}, \{\{\ \}, \{\ \}\}, T$. This allows us to distinguish between the effects before and after the opening of M. Figure 13 gives the typing rules for expressions.

$$\frac{\mathcal{U}, E \vdash M : Cap[F] \quad \mathcal{U}, E \vdash M' : Cap[F']}{\mathcal{U}, E \vdash M.M' : Cap[F \uplus F']} \ (\text{Exp} \ . \ \star)$$

$$\frac{\mathcal{U}, E \vdash M : s_V^{\circ\{V', Z', \hookleftarrow\}}[T_U^Z] \quad \mathcal{U}, E \vdash T'}{\mathcal{U}, E \vdash \mathbf{in}\ M : Cap[\{s\}, \{\ \}, T']} \ (\text{Exp}\ \mathbf{in}\ \star)$$

$$\frac{\mathcal{U}, E \vdash M : s_V^{\circ\{V', Z', \hookleftarrow\}}[T_U^Z] \quad \mathcal{U}, E \vdash T'}{\mathcal{U}, E \vdash \overline{\mathbf{in}}\ M : Cap[\{\bar{s}\}, \{\ \}, T']} \ (\text{Exp}\ \overline{\mathbf{in}}\ \star)$$

$$\frac{\mathcal{U}, E \vdash M : s_V^{\circ\{V', Z', \hookleftarrow\}}[T_U^Z] \quad \mathcal{U}, E \vdash T'}{\mathcal{U}, E \vdash \mathbf{out}\ M : Cap[\{s\}, \{\ \}, T']} \ (\text{Exp}\ \mathbf{out}\ \star)$$

$$\frac{\mathcal{U}, E \vdash M : s_V^{\circ\{V', Z', \hookleftarrow\}}[T_U^Z] \quad \mathcal{U}, E \vdash T'}{\mathcal{U}, E \vdash \overline{\mathbf{out}}\ M : Cap[\{\bar{s}\}, \{\ \}, T']} \ (\text{Exp}\ \overline{\mathbf{out}}\ \star)$$

$$\frac{\mathcal{U}, E \vdash M : s_V^{\circ\{V', Z', U'\}}[T_U^Z] \quad \Im(\{V', Z', U'\}, s) = S, S'}{\mathcal{U}, E \vdash \mathbf{open}\ M : Cap[S, \{s\} \cup S', T]} \ (\text{Exp}\ \mathbf{open}\ \star)$$

$$\frac{\mathcal{U}, E \vdash M : s_V^{\circ\{V', Z', U'\}}[T_U^Z]}{\mathcal{U}, E \vdash \overline{\mathbf{open}}\ M : Cap[\{\ \}, \{\bar{s}\}, \{\{\ \}, \{\ \}\}, T]} \ (\text{Exp}\ \overline{\mathbf{open}}\ \star)$$

Fig. 13. Good expressions with expanded effects

We have also to define when an expanded effect agrees with an ambient type. An expanded effect $S_1, S_2, \{S_3, S_4\}, T$ agrees with an ambient type $s_V^Y[T_U'^Z]$ iff:

- $T = T'$;
- S_1, S_2 agree with $\{V, Z, U\}$;
- $Y = \circ\{V', Z', U'\}$ and S_3, S_4 agree with $\{V', Z', U'\}$;

- all active security levels in $S_1 \cup S_3$ are $\leq^\frown$ s and all passive security levels in $S_1 \cup S_3$ are $\leq^\frown \bar{s}$;
- all active security levels in $S_2 \cup S_4$ are $\leq^\circ$ s and all passive security levels in $S_2 \cup S_4$ are $\leq^\circ \bar{s}$.

See Figure 14 for the formal definition.

Lastly, we need to combine the effects of two processes when they are put in parallel. If both effects are simple or expanded, we can use the $\uplus$ as defined in Figure 12 obtaining in both cases a simple effect. Otherwise we have that only one process contains an $\overline{\mathsf{open}}$ co-action, so we can obtain an expanded effect in which the sets of the simple effect are considered both before and after the opening action. This definition is given in Figure 15.

In the typing rule for processes we cannot combine expanded effects by means of set union as in rules (Proc Action) and (Proc Par). The rule (Proc Action $\star$) uses the operator $\uplus$ of Figure 12, since the action M will be done before the actions in P. Instead the typing rule (Proc Par $\star$) uses the operator $\overline{\uplus}$ of Figure 15, since the actions in P and in Q will be done in parallel. Lastly rule (Proc Input $\star$) takes into account that the effects of P can be either simple or expanded. The new rules are given in Figure 16. The remaining rules do not change, but we convene that all effects can be either simple or expanded.

$$S_1, S_2, \{S_3, S_4\}, T \bowtie s_V^Y[T_U'^Z] \iff
\begin{array}{l}
T = T' \ \& \\
S_1, S_2 \bowtie \{V, U, Z\} \ \& \\
Y = \circ\{V', U', Z'\} \ \& \\
S_3, S_4 \bowtie \{V', U', Z'\} \ \& \\
\forall s', \bar{s}' \in S_1 \cup S_3. s' \leq^\frown s \ \& \ \bar{s}' \leq^\frown \bar{s} \ \& \\
\forall s', \bar{s}' \in S_2 \cup S_4. s' \leq^\circ s \ \& \ \bar{s}' \leq^\circ \bar{s}
\end{array}$$

Fig. 14. Agreement between expanded effects and ambient types

$$S, H, T \overline{\uplus} S', H', T =
\begin{cases}
S \cup S', S_1 \cup H', \{S_2 \cup S', S_3 \cup H'\}, T & \text{if } H = S_1, \{S_2, S_3\} \ \& \\
& H' \subseteq \mathcal{U} \cup \overline{\mathcal{U}} \\
S \cup S', S_1 \cup H, \{S_2 \cup S, S_3 \cup H\}, T & \text{if } H \subseteq \mathcal{U} \cup \overline{\mathcal{U}} \ \& \\
& H' = S_1, \{S_2, S_3\} \\
S, H, T \uplus S', H', T' & \text{otherwise}
\end{cases}$$

Fig. 15. Combination of simple and expanded effects for processes

Properties of Well Typed Processes. All the observations done for the system of Section 3 remain valid proviso that:

- if $\mathcal{U}, E \vdash P : S_1, S_2, \{S_3 \cup S_4\}, T$ we replace $S_1 \cup S_3$ to S and $S_2 \cup S_4$ to S';

$$\frac{\mathcal{U}, E, n_1 : W_1, \ldots, n_k : W_k \vdash P : \mathsf{S}, \mathsf{H}, W_1 \times \ldots \times W_k}{\mathcal{U}, E \vdash (n_1 : W_1, \ldots, n_k : W_k).P : \mathsf{S}, \mathsf{H}, W_1 \times \ldots \times W_k} \; (\text{Proc Input } \star)$$

$$\frac{\mathcal{U}, E \vdash M : Cap[F] \quad \mathcal{U}, E \vdash P : F'}{\mathcal{U}, E \vdash M.P : F \uplus F'} \; (\text{Proc Action } \star)$$

$$\frac{\mathcal{U}, E \vdash P : F \quad \mathcal{U}, E \vdash Q : F'}{\mathcal{U}, E \vdash P \mid Q : F \overline{\uplus} F'} \; (\text{Proc Par } \star)$$

Fig. 16. Good Processes with Expanded Effects

- we consider rule (Par Proc $\star$) instead of rule (Par Proc) in the discussion about single-threaded ambients.

Finally, to obtain a Soundness Result for the new type system we generalize the order relations to expanded effects as shown in Figure 17.

$$\begin{array}{lll}
\mathsf{S}_3, \mathsf{S}_4, T \sqsubseteq \mathsf{S}'_1, \mathsf{S}'_2, \{\mathsf{S}'_3, \mathsf{S}'_4\}, T & \Longleftrightarrow & \mathsf{S}_3 \sqsubseteq^\frown \mathsf{S}'_3 \;\&\; \mathsf{S}_4 \sqsubseteq^\circ \mathsf{S}'_4 \\
\mathsf{S}_1, \mathsf{S}_2, \{\mathsf{S}_3, \mathsf{S}_4\}, T \sqsubseteq \mathsf{S}'_1, \mathsf{S}'_2, \{\mathsf{S}'_3, \mathsf{S}'_4\}, T & \Longleftrightarrow & \mathsf{S}_i \sqsubseteq^\frown \mathsf{S}'_i \text{ for } i = 1, 3 \\
& & \&\; \mathsf{S}_i \sqsubseteq^\circ \mathsf{S}'_i \text{ for } i = 2, 4
\end{array}$$

Fig. 17. Partial order of simple and expanded effects

Theorem 2. *If* $\mathcal{U}, E \vdash P : F$ *and* $P \longrightarrow Q$ *then* $\mathcal{U}, E \vdash Q : F'$ *for some* F' *such that* $F' \sqsubseteq F$.

Proof. The proof is by induction on the definition of $\longrightarrow$.

We consider only rules (R-in) and (R-open). The case of (R-out) is similar to that of (R-in) and the other rules follow easily by induction.

For rule (R-in) the key observation is that

$$\text{if } F \bowtie \mathsf{s}_V^Y[T_U^Z] \text{ and } F' \sqsubseteq F \text{ then } F' \bowtie \mathsf{s}_V^Y[T_U^Z].$$

This follows easily from the definitions of $\bowtie$ (Figure 8) and $\sqsubseteq$ (Figure 10). The typing of the left-hand side contains the sub-derivations shown in Figure 18. The two applications of rule (Proc Amb) require respectively $((\{\mathsf{s}\}, \{ \}, T') \uplus F_1) \uplus F_2 \bowtie \mathsf{s}_{V'}^{Y'}[T_{U'}^{Z'}]$ and $((\{\bar{\mathsf{s}}\}, \{ \}, T) \uplus F'_1) \uplus F'_2 \bowtie \mathsf{s}_V^Y[T_U^Z]$. Therefore we can deduce the same type for the right-hand side as shown in Figure 19, where the two applications of rule (Proc Amb) require respectively $F_1 \uplus F_2 \bowtie \mathsf{s}_{V'}^{Y'}[T_{U'}^{Z'}]$ and $F'_1 \uplus F'_2 \bowtie \mathsf{s}_V^Y[T_U^Z]$.

For rule (R-open) notice that:

$$\text{if } \mathsf{S}_1, \mathsf{S}_2, T \bowtie \mathsf{s}_V^\circ[T_U^Z] \text{ then } \mathsf{S}_1, \mathsf{S}_2, T \sqsubseteq \Im(\{V, Z, U\}, \mathsf{s}), T;$$
$$\text{if } \mathsf{S}_1, \mathsf{S}_2, \{\mathsf{S}_3, \mathsf{S}_4\}, T \bowtie \mathsf{s}_V^{\circ\{V', Z', U'\}}[T_U^Z] \text{ then } \mathsf{S}_3, \mathsf{S}_4, T \sqsubseteq \Im(\{V', Z', U'\}, \mathsf{s}), T.$$

$$\cfrac{\cfrac{\cfrac{\cfrac{\cfrac{\mathcal{U}, E \vdash m : \mathsf{s}_V^Y[T_U^Z] \quad \mathcal{U}, E \vdash T'}{\mathcal{U}, E \vdash \mathbf{in}\ m : Cap[\{\mathsf{s}\}, \{\ \}, T'] \quad \mathcal{U}, E \vdash P_1 : F_1}}{\mathcal{U}, E \vdash \mathbf{in}\ m.P_1 : (\{\mathsf{s}\}, \{\ \}, T') \boxplus F_1 \quad \mathcal{U}, E \vdash P_2 : F_2}}{\mathcal{U}, E \vdash \mathbf{in}\ m.P_1 \mid P_2 : ((\{\mathsf{s}\}, \{\ \}, T') \boxplus F_1) \boxplus F_2} \quad}{\mathcal{U}, E \vdash n : \mathsf{s}_{V'}^{'Y'}[T_{U'}^{'Z'}] \quad \mathcal{U}, E \vdash \mathbf{in}\ m.P_1 \mid P_2 : ((\{\mathsf{s}\}, \{\ \}, T') \boxplus F_1) \boxplus F_2 \quad \mathcal{U}, E \vdash T''}}{\mathcal{U}, E \vdash n[\mathbf{in}\ m.P_1 \mid P_2] : \{\ \}, \{\ \}, T''}$$

$$\cfrac{\cfrac{\cfrac{\cfrac{\cfrac{\mathcal{U}, E \vdash m : \mathsf{s}_V^Y[T_U^Z] \quad \mathcal{U}, E \vdash T}{\mathcal{U}, E \vdash \overline{\mathbf{in}}\ m : Cap[\{\overline{\mathsf{s}}\}, \{\ \}, T] \quad \mathcal{U}, E \vdash Q_1 : F_1'}}{\mathcal{U}, E \vdash \overline{\mathbf{in}}\ m.Q_1 : (\{\overline{\mathsf{s}}\}, \{\ \}, T) \boxplus F_1' \quad \mathcal{U}, E \vdash Q_2 : F_2'}}{\mathcal{U}, E \vdash \overline{\mathbf{in}}\ m.Q_1 \mid Q_2 : ((\{\overline{\mathsf{s}}\}, \{\ \}, T) \boxplus F_1') \overline{\boxplus} F_2'} \quad}{\mathcal{U}, E \vdash m : \mathsf{s}_V^Y[T_U^Z] \quad \mathcal{U}, E \vdash \overline{\mathbf{in}}\ m.Q_1 \mid Q_2 : ((\{\overline{\mathsf{s}}\}, \{\ \}, T) \boxplus F_1') \overline{\boxplus} F_2' \quad \mathcal{U}, E \vdash T''}}{\mathcal{U}, E \vdash m[\overline{\mathbf{in}}\ m.Q_1 \mid Q_2] : \{\ \}, \{\ \}, T''}$$

Fig. 18. Typing of the left-hand side of rule (R-in)

$$\cfrac{\cfrac{\cfrac{\mathcal{U}, E \vdash n : \mathsf{s}_{V'}^{'Y'}[T_{U'}^{'Z'}] \quad \cfrac{\mathcal{U}, E \vdash P_1 : F_1 \quad \mathcal{U}, E \vdash P_2 : F_2}{\mathcal{U}, E \vdash P_1 \mid P_2 : F_1 \boxplus F_2} \quad \mathcal{U}, E \vdash T}{\mathcal{U}, E \vdash n[P_1 \mid P_2] : \{\ \}, \{\ \}, T}}{}{}$$

$$\cfrac{\cfrac{\mathcal{U}, E \vdash n[P_1 \mid P_2] : \{\ \}, \{\ \}, T \quad \cfrac{\mathcal{U}, E \vdash Q_1 : F_1' \quad \mathcal{U}, E \vdash Q_2 : F_2'}{\mathcal{U}, E \vdash Q_1 \mid Q_2 : F_1' \boxplus F_2'}}{\mathcal{U}, E \vdash n[P_1 \mid P_2] \mid Q_1 \mid Q_2 : F_1' \boxplus F_2'}}{\cfrac{\mathcal{U}, E \vdash m : \mathsf{s}_V^Y[T_U^Z] \quad \mathcal{U}, E \vdash n[P_1 \mid P_2] \mid Q_1 \mid Q_2 : F_1' \overline{\boxplus} F_2' \quad \mathcal{U}, E \vdash T''}{\mathcal{U}, E \vdash m[n[P_1 \mid P_2] \mid Q_1 \mid Q_2] : \{\ \}, \{\ \}, T''}}$$

Fig. 19. Typing of the right-hand side of rule (R-in)

This is a consequence of the definitions of $\bowtie$ (Figure 8), $\sqsubseteq$ (Figure 10), and $\Im(\ ,\ )$ (Figure 6). Figure 20 shows the typing of the left-hand side, under the assumption that $Y = \circ\{V', Z', U'\}$ and $\Im(\{V', Z', U'\}, \mathsf{s}) = \mathsf{S}, \mathsf{S}'$ (the case $Y = \circ$ and $\Im(\{V, Z, U\}, \mathsf{s}) = \mathsf{S}, \mathsf{S}'$ is similar and simpler). The application of rule (Proc Amb) requires $((\{\ \}, \{\bar{\mathsf{s}}\}, \{\{\ \}, \{\ \}\}, T) \uplus F_1) \overline{\uplus} F_2 \bowtie \mathsf{s}_V^Y[T_U^Z]$, therefore $((\{\ \}, \{\bar{\mathsf{s}}\}, \{\{\ \}, \{\ \}\}, T) \uplus F_1) \overline{\uplus} F_2$ must be an expanded effect. Let

$$((\{\ \}, \{\bar{\mathsf{s}}\}, \{\{\ \}, \{\ \}\}, T) \uplus F_1) \overline{\uplus} F_2 = \mathsf{S}_1, \mathsf{S}_2, \{\mathsf{S}_3, \mathsf{S}_4\}, T.$$

Then by the definitions of $\uplus$ (Figure 12), of $\overline{\uplus}$ (Figure 15), and of $\sqsubseteq$ we get $F_1 \overline{\uplus} F_2 \sqsubseteq \mathsf{S}_3, \mathsf{S}_4, T$. From the above remark $\mathsf{S}_1, \mathsf{S}_2, \{\mathsf{S}_3, \mathsf{S}_4\}, T \bowtie \mathsf{s}_V^Y[T_U^Z]$ implies $\mathsf{S}_3, \mathsf{S}_4, T \sqsubseteq \mathsf{S}, \mathsf{S}', T$. We obtain $F_1 \overline{\uplus} F_2 \sqsubseteq \mathsf{S}, \mathsf{S}', T$ and also $F \overline{\uplus} (F_1 \overline{\uplus} F_2) \sqsubseteq (\mathsf{S}, \{\mathsf{s}\} \cup \mathsf{S}', T) \overline{\uplus} F$ being $\overline{\uplus}$ commutative. We are done, since we can derive $F \overline{\uplus} (F_1 \overline{\uplus} F_2)$ for the right-hand side as shown in Figure 21.

$$\dfrac{\dfrac{\mathcal{U}, E \vdash n : \mathsf{s}_V^Y[T_U^Z] \quad \mathcal{U}, E \vdash T}{\mathcal{U}, E \vdash \mathbf{open}\ n : Cap[\mathsf{S}, \{\mathsf{s}\} \cup \mathsf{S}', T] \quad \mathcal{U}, E \vdash P : F}}{\mathcal{U}, E \vdash \mathbf{open}\ n.P : (\mathsf{S}, \{\mathsf{s}\} \cup \mathsf{S}', T) \overline{\uplus} F}$$

$$\dfrac{\dfrac{\dfrac{\mathcal{U}, E \vdash n : \mathsf{s}_V^Y[T_U^Z] \quad \mathcal{U}, E \vdash T}{\mathcal{U}, E \vdash \overline{\mathbf{open}}\ n : Cap[\{\ \}, \{\bar{\mathsf{s}}\}, \{\{\ \}, \{\ \}\}, T] \quad \mathcal{U}, E \vdash Q_1 : F_1}}{\dfrac{\mathcal{U}, E \vdash \overline{\mathbf{open}}\ n.Q_1 : (\{\ \}, \{\bar{\mathsf{s}}\}, \{\{\ \}, \{\ \}\}, T) \overline{\uplus} F_1 \quad \mathcal{U}, E \vdash Q_2 : F_2}{\mathcal{U}, E \vdash \overline{\mathbf{open}}\ n.Q_1 \mid Q_2 : ((\{\ \}, \{\bar{\mathsf{s}}\}, \{\{\ \}, \{\ \}\}, T) \overline{\uplus} F_1) \overline{\uplus} F_2}} \quad \mathcal{U}, E \vdash n : \mathsf{s}_V^Y[T_U^Z] \quad \mathcal{U}, E \vdash \overline{\mathbf{open}}\ n.Q_1 \mid Q_2 : ((\{\ \}, \{\bar{\mathsf{s}}\}, \{\{\ \}, \{\ \}\}, T) \overline{\uplus} F_1) \overline{\uplus} F_2 \quad \mathcal{U}, E \vdash T}{\mathcal{U}, E \vdash n[\overline{\mathbf{open}}\ n.Q_1 \mid Q_2] : \{\ \}, \{\ \}, T}$$

$$\dfrac{\mathcal{U}, E \vdash \mathbf{open}\ n.P : (\mathsf{S}, \{\mathsf{s}\} \cup \mathsf{S}', T) \overline{\uplus} F \quad \mathcal{U}, E \vdash n[\overline{\mathbf{open}}\ n.Q_1 \mid Q_2] : \{\ \}, \{\ \}, T}{\mathcal{U}, E \vdash \mathbf{open}\ n.P \mid n[\overline{\mathbf{open}}\ n.Q_1 \mid Q_2] : (\mathsf{S}, \{\mathsf{s}\} \cup \mathsf{S}', T) \overline{\uplus} F}$$

Fig. 20. Typing of the left-hand side of rule (R-open)

5   Examples

In this section we present some examples, where we assume a different security level for each ambient. Examples in Subsection 5.2, 5.3 and 5.4 are discussed both in [9] and [2]: we present them in order to show which kinds of typing

$$\frac{\mathcal{U}, E \vdash P : F \quad \dfrac{\mathcal{U}, E \vdash Q_1 : F_1 \quad \mathcal{U}, E \vdash Q_2 : F_2}{\mathcal{U}, E \vdash Q_1 \mid Q_2 : F_1 \boxed{+} F_2}}{\mathcal{U}, E \vdash P \mid Q_1 \mid Q_2 : F \boxed{+} (F_1 \boxed{+} F_2)}$$

Fig. 21. Typing of the right-hand side of rule (R-open)

are derivable in our type system and which kinds of constraints on the security levels order are required to type them. The other two examples, instead, show possible applications of our type system, in particular how to use it to ensure some security properties. Examples 5.2, 5.4 and 5.5 can be typed in the simpler system of Section 3 while the others examples require the extension discussed in Section 4.

5.1 Mailserver

In this example we model a mailserver. In our model, a mailserver MS is an ambient which contains a set of mailboxes, $MBOX_i$, for $1 \le i \le k$. A message MSG is a mobile ambient that enters first in the mailserver and then in a mailbox. Messages have high level mobility rights, whereas each user must have the same mobility rights of its mailbox. The idea is that users do not have rights to enter mailboxes of other users. A user U_i that tries to use a capability **in** mb_j, for $i \ne j$ is not a well-typed process.

$$MSG = m[\textbf{in } ms.\textbf{in } mb_i.\overline{\textbf{open}} \ m.\langle M \rangle]$$
$$MS = ms[!\overline{\textbf{in}} \ ms \ |!\overline{\textbf{out}} \ ms \mid MBOX_1 \mid \ldots \mid MBOX_k]$$
$$MBOX_i = mb_i[!\overline{\textbf{in}} \ mb_i \ |!\overline{\textbf{out}} \ mb_i]$$
$$U_i = u_i[\textbf{in } ms.\textbf{in } mbox_i.\textbf{open } m.(x : T).\textbf{out } mb_i.\textbf{out } ms.P]$$

where T is the exchange type of P.

Considering an environment E such that:

$$\mathcal{U}, E \vdash m : \mathsf{msg}_{\overline{\bullet}}^{\circ\{\overline{\bullet}, \vee, \oplus\}}[T_\oplus^\frown]$$
$$\mathcal{U}, E \vdash ms : \mathsf{mserv}_\bullet^\bullet[T_\leftrightharpoons^\vee]$$
$$\mathcal{U}, E \vdash mb_i : \mathsf{mbox}_{i\overline{\bullet}}^\bullet[T_\leftrightharpoons^\vee]$$
$$\mathcal{U}, E \vdash u_i : \mathsf{ut}_{i\overline{\circ}}^\bullet[T_\oplus^\frown]$$
$$\mathcal{U}, E \vdash M : T$$

we can type processes inside ambients as follows:

$\mathcal{U}, E \vdash \textbf{in } ms.\textbf{in } mb_i.\overline{\textbf{open}} \ m.\langle M \rangle : \{\mathsf{mserv}, \mathsf{mbox}_i\}, \{\overline{\mathsf{msg}}\}, \{\varnothing, \varnothing\}, T$

$\mathcal{U}, E \vdash !\overline{\textbf{in}} \ ms \ |!\overline{\textbf{out}} \ ms \mid MBOX_1 \mid \ldots \mid MBOX_k : \{\overline{\mathsf{mserv}}\}, \{\}, T$

$\mathcal{U}, E \vdash !\overline{\textbf{in}} \ mb_i \ |!\overline{\textbf{out}} \ mb_i : \{\overline{\mathsf{mbox}_i}\}, \{\}, T$

$\mathcal{U}, E \vdash \textbf{in } ms.\textbf{in } mb_i.\textbf{open } m.(x : T).\textbf{out } mb_i.\textbf{out } ms.P : \{\mathsf{mserv}, \mathsf{mbox}_i\}, \{\mathsf{msg}\}, T$

It easy to check that process types agree with corresponding ambient types. In order to avoid unauthorized access to mailboxes, we consider the following order defined on $\mathcal{U}$:

$$\mathsf{msg} \ge^\frown \mathsf{ut}_i =^\frown \mathsf{mbox}_i \qquad \text{for all } i$$

$$\mathsf{ut}_i \not\geq^\frown \mathsf{ut}_j \ \& \ \mathsf{ut}_j \not\geq^\frown \mathsf{ut}_i \qquad \text{for all } i \neq j$$

and

$$\mathsf{ut}_i \geq^\circ \mathsf{msg} \qquad \text{for all } i.$$

5.2 Renaming

We recall the construct given in [9] to change the name of an ambient:

$$n \ \textbf{be} \ m.P = m[\textbf{out} \ n.\overline{\textbf{in}} \ m.\textbf{open} \ n.P] \mid \overline{\textbf{out}} \ n.\textbf{in} \ m.\overline{\textbf{open}} \ n$$

Let E be an environment such that:

$$\mathcal{U}, E \vdash m : \mathsf{sm}_\circ^Y[T_U^\frown]$$
$$\mathcal{U}, E \vdash n : \mathsf{sn}_\circ^\circ[T_\leftrightarrow^\frown]$$

where Y, U and T depend on the type of P. We assume that in the environment E we can derive the following typing judgments for P and Q:

$$\mathcal{U}, E \vdash P : \mathsf{S}_1^P, \mathsf{S}_2^P, T$$
$$\mathcal{U}, E \vdash Q : \mathsf{S}_1^Q, \mathsf{S}_2^Q, T$$

The desired property is that[1]:

$$n[n \ \textbf{be} \ m.P \mid Q] \simeq m[P \mid Q]$$

for all Q such that no ambient in Q can perform an **out** n action. In our type system, this last condition can be assumed by requiring that $\mathsf{sn} \notin \mathsf{S}_1^Q$.

In such an environment we can derive the following typing for processes:

$$\mathcal{U}, E \vdash \textbf{out} \ n.\overline{\textbf{in}} \ m.\textbf{open} \ n.P :$$
$$(\{\mathsf{sn}, \overline{\mathsf{sm}}, \overline{\mathsf{sn}}\}, \{\mathsf{sn}, \overline{\mathsf{sn}}\}, T) \uplus (\mathsf{S}_1^P, \mathsf{S}_2^P, T)$$
$$\mathcal{U}, E \vdash \overline{\textbf{out}} \ n.\textbf{in} \ m.\overline{\textbf{open}} \ n : \{\overline{\mathsf{sn}}, \mathsf{sm}\}, \{\overline{\mathsf{sn}}\}, T$$

Finally we observe that we can type the renaming protocol under the following conditions on the security levels order:

$$\mathsf{sm} \geq^\circ \mathsf{sn}$$
$$\mathsf{sm} =^\frown \mathsf{sn}$$

In particular, it seems meaningful that security levels sm and sn are the same.

5.3 Firewall

The untyped protocol given in [9] for controlling access through a firewall is:

$$AG = m[\overline{\textbf{in}} \ m.\textbf{open} \ k.$$
$$(x)x.\overline{\textbf{open}} \ m.Q]$$
$$FW = (\nu w)(w[\overline{\textbf{out}} \ w.\textbf{in} \ w.\textbf{open} \ m.P$$
$$\mid k[\textbf{out} \ w.\textbf{in} \ m.\overline{\textbf{open}} \ k.\langle \mathbf{in} \ w \rangle] \ ])$$

FW represents the firewall and AG a trusted agent which crosses the firewall thanks to the pilot ambient k. The name k plays the role of a key which allows only authorized agents to cross the firewall.

---

[1] As in [9] two processes are $\simeq$-equivalent iff no closing contexts can tell them apart.

Let P and Q be such that:

$$\mathcal{U}, E \vdash Q : \{\ \}, S_2^Q, T$$
$$\mathcal{U}, E \vdash P : \{\ \}, S_2^Q, T$$

where $T = Cap[\{fw\}, \{\ \}, T']$ for some T' and we assume that processes P and Q do not perform move actions to show that in this case we can type w as immobile. Let E be an environment such that:

$$\mathcal{U}, E \vdash m : \mathsf{ag}_{\overline{\circ}}^{\circ\{\vee,\oplus,\overline{\bullet}\}}[T_{\leftrightarrow}^{\frown}]$$
$$\mathcal{U}, E \vdash w : \mathsf{fw}_{\overline{\circ}}^{\bullet}[T_{\leftrightarrow}^{\vee}]$$
$$\mathcal{U}, E \vdash k : \mathsf{aut}_{\overline{\circ}}^{\circ\{\frown,\oplus,\overline{\bullet}\}}[T_{\oplus}^{\frown}]$$

Let P_m (resp. P_w and P_k) be the process inside the ambient m (resp. w and k). In the environment E, we can derive the following judgments:

$$\mathcal{U}, E \vdash P_m : \{\mathsf{fw}, \overline{\mathsf{ag}}\}, \{\mathsf{aut}, \overline{\mathsf{ag}}, \{\{\ \}, S_2^Q\}\}, T$$
$$\mathcal{U}, E \vdash P_w : \{\overline{\mathsf{fw}}\}, \{\mathsf{ag}\}, T$$
$$\mathcal{U}, E \vdash P_k : \{\mathsf{fw}, \mathsf{ag}\}, \{\overline{\mathsf{aut}}\}, T$$

and we obtain the following typed versions of the protocols:

$$AG = m[\overline{\mathbf{in}}\ m.\mathbf{open}\ k.$$
$$(x : Cap[\{\mathsf{fw}\}, \{\ \}, T'])x.\overline{\mathbf{open}}\ m.Q]$$
$$FW = (\nu w : \mathsf{fw}_{\overline{\circ}}^{\bullet}[T_{\leftrightarrow}^{\vee}])(w[\overline{\mathbf{out}}\ w.\mathbf{in}\ w.\mathbf{open}\ m.P$$
$$|\ k[\mathbf{out}\ w.\mathbf{in}\ m.\overline{\mathbf{open}}\ k.\langle \mathbf{in}\ w\rangle]\ ])$$

We can type the ambient w as immobile, since opening the mobile ambient m does not unleash mobility capabilities. We obtain this information from the type of m and the possibility to type P_m with an expanded effect. The presence of the co-action $\overline{\mathbf{open}}\ m$ is crucial for having such control over the behaviour of an ambient.

The demanded property is that:

$$(\nu m)(AG\ |\ FW) \simeq (\nu m, w)(w[P\ |\ Q])$$

under the conditions $w \notin fn(Q)$ and $m \notin fn(P)$. These conditions are assured by $\mathsf{fw} \notin S_2^Q$ and $\mathsf{ag} \notin S_2^P$. We do not see how to express this requirement using only types in the system of [9].

Finally, we observe that the following constraints on the order relation among security levels are needed to correctly type the whole protocol:

$$\mathsf{fw} \leq^{\frown} \mathsf{ag} \leq^{\frown} \mathsf{aut}$$

and

$$\mathsf{fw} \geq^{\circ} \mathsf{ag} \geq^{\circ} \mathsf{aut}$$

5.4   Channels

The encoding of asynchronous typed π-calculus is an important test of expressiveness for the ambient calculus. Several encodings have been proposed for both typed and untyped mobile ambients and for safe ambients. Here we consider the typed version in our system of the simpler untyped protocol presented in [9]:

$$[\![p(q_1,\ldots,q_n)]\!] = p[\overline{\textbf{in}}\ p.\textbf{open}\ p.(q_1,\ldots,q_n).\overline{\textbf{open}}\ p.[\![P]\!]\ |\ \textbf{open}\ p$$
$$[\![\overline{p}\langle q_1,\ldots,q_n\rangle]\!] = p[\overline{\textbf{in}}\ p.\overline{\textbf{open}}\ p.\langle q_1,\ldots,q_n\rangle]$$
$$[\![(\nu p : T)P]\!] = (\nu p : [\![T]\!])[\![P]\!]$$
$$[\![P\ |\ Q]\!] = [\![P]\!]\ |\ [\![Q]\!]$$
$$[\![!P]\!] = ![\![P]\!]$$
$$[\![\textbf{0}]\!] = \textbf{0}$$
$$[\![Ch(T_1,\ldots,T_n)]\!] = \mathsf{Proc}_{\circ}^{\circ}[[\![T_1]\!] \times \ldots \times [\![T_n]\!]_{\leftrightarrows}^{\frown}]$$
$$[\![p : T]\!] = p : [\![T]\!]$$
$$[\![\Gamma, p : T]\!] = [\![\Gamma]\!], [\![p : T]\!]$$

where the type grammar is $T := Ch(T_1,\ldots,T_n)$, $n \geq 0$.

If $\Gamma \vdash P$ can be derived using the standard rules for the asynchronous typed π-calculus [9] then we get either $[\![\Gamma]\!] \vdash [\![P]\!] : \{\ \}, \{\mathsf{Proc}\}, Shh$ or $[\![\Gamma]\!] \vdash [\![P]\!] : \{\ \}, \{\}, Shh$.

5.5   Secure Channels

This example is inspired by the information flow analysis carried out in [7]. We want to model a π-calculus, in which to each channel p is associated a write and a read access right. Moreover, a π-calculus process can be defined as running at a given security level[2]. According with the principle that information can move only upward, the security policy imposes that a channel can communicate information only to π-calculus processes with a security level greater than its write access right and can receive information only from π-calculus processes with a security level less than its read access right. In the π-calculus process:

$$\sigma\{p\langle q\rangle\}\ |\ \rho\{p(q)P\}$$

we have that the process $\sigma\{p\langle q\rangle\}$ runs at the security level σ and the process $\rho\{p(q)P\}$ runs at the security level ρ. Communication can take place if the write access rights of p, W_p, are less or equal to ρ and if the read access rights of p, R_p, are greater or equal to σ.

We show an encoding of π-calculus channels with read and write access rights into Safe Ambients. The basic idea is to modify the above encoding of channels in Subsection 5.4 in such a way:

- the order $\leq^{\circ}$ among security levels in ambient types represents the order among π-calculus security levels;
- each channel p is represented as a pair of ambients p^w and p^r; such ambients belong to security levels w_p and r_p respectively;
- the security levels w_p and r_p play in the ambient encoding of secure channels the role of access rights W_p and R_p;
- in the encoding of a π-calculus process $\rho\{P\}$, an ambient ρ, belonging to a security level s_ρ, represents the security level of a process;

---

[2] "security level" is overloaded in this subsection, since we consider both security levels of π-calculus processes and security level of ambient types. No ambiguity arises thanks to the context.

- in the encoding of the π-calculus process $\sigma\{p\langle q\rangle\} \mid \rho\{p(q)P\}$, the communication protocol imposes that the ambient ρ must be able to open p^w, and p^r must be able to open σ, so that the protocol is well-typed only if:

$$s_\rho \geq^\circ w_p$$
$$s_\sigma \leq^\circ r_p$$

The encoding is rather complicated, because a process does not know the security level of the process with which communication will happen and hence we need two auxiliary ambients p^m and p^n. This implies that also the channel q will be represented by four ambients, q^r, q^w, q^m, q^n.

$$[\![\, \sigma\{p\langle q\rangle\}\,]\!] = \sigma[\mathbf{in}\ p^r.\overline{\mathbf{out}}\ \sigma.\overline{\mathbf{open}}\ \sigma$$
$$\mid p^m[\overline{\mathbf{out}}\ \sigma.\overline{\mathbf{open}}\ p^m.\mathbf{open}\ \sigma]$$
$$\mid p^w[\overline{\mathbf{in}}\ p^w.\mathbf{open}\ p^n.\overline{\mathbf{open}}\ p^w.\langle q^r, q^w, q^m, q^n\rangle]$$
$$]$$

$$[\![\, \rho\{p(x)P\}\,]\!] = p^r[\overline{\mathbf{in}}\ p^r.\mathbf{open}\ p^m.\overline{\mathbf{out}}\ p^r.\mathbf{in}\ \rho.\overline{\mathbf{open}}\ p^r.(x^r, x^w, x^m, x^n).[\![\,P\,]\!]$$
$$\mid p^n[\mathbf{in}\ p^w.\overline{\mathbf{open}}\ p^n.\mathbf{in}\ \rho]$$
$$\mid \rho[\overline{\mathbf{in}}\ \rho.\mathbf{open}\ p^w.\mathbf{out}\ p^r.\overline{\mathbf{in}}\ \rho.\overline{\mathbf{open}}\ \rho]$$
$$]$$
$$\mid \mathbf{open}\ p^r \mid \mathbf{open}\ \rho$$

We have that:

$$[\![\, \rho\{p(x)P\}\,]\!] \mid [\![\, \sigma\{p\langle q\rangle\}\,]\!] \longrightarrow [\![\,P\,]\!]\{x^r := q^r, x^w := q^w, x^m := q^m, x^n := q^n\}$$

Let $[\![\, Ch(T)\,]\!] = \mathsf{w}^\circ_\circ[\![\,T\,]\!]^\frown_\leftrightarrow \times \mathsf{r}^\circ_\circ[\![\,T\,]\!]^\frown_\leftrightarrow \times \mathsf{w}^\circ_\circ[\![\,T\,]\!]^\frown_\leftrightarrow \times \mathsf{r}^\circ_\circ[\![\,T\,]\!]^\frown_\leftrightarrow]$, where w (resp. r) is the write (resp. read) access right of a channel of type T and suppose the channel q has type T in the typed π-calculus. We can type the above protocol in an environment E such that:

$$\mathcal{U}, E \vdash \sigma : \mathsf{s}^\circ_{\sigma \bullet}[\![\, Ch(T)\,]\!]^\frown_\leftrightarrow]$$
$$\mathcal{U}, E \vdash \rho : \mathsf{s}^\circ_{\rho \circ}[\![\, Ch(T)\,]\!]^\frown_\leftrightarrow]$$
$$\mathcal{U}, E \vdash p^w, p^n : \mathsf{w}^\circ_{p \circ}[\![\, Ch(T)\,]\!]^\frown_\leftrightarrow]$$
$$\mathcal{U}, E \vdash p^r, p^m : \mathsf{r}^\circ_{p \circ}[\![\, Ch(T)\,]\!]^\frown_\leftrightarrow]$$
$$\mathcal{U}, E \vdash q^w, q^n : \mathsf{w}^\circ_{q \circ}[\![\, Ch(T)\,]\!]^\frown_\leftrightarrow]$$
$$\mathcal{U}, E \vdash q^r, q^m : \mathsf{r}^\circ_{q \circ}[\![\, Ch(T)\,]\!]^\frown_\leftrightarrow]$$

6   Conclusion

We presented two type systems for safe ambients that guarantee security properties. While the first one could be adapted without problems to mobile ambients, the second one requires co-actions in order to distinguish the effects before and after a (unique!) $\overline{\mathbf{open}}$ action.

Both type systems describe in a rather precise way the behaviours of ambients and could be used to establish a typed equivalence theory of ambients, similarly to what was done for the π-calculus in [11].

The typing rules are syntax directed and therefore there is a type checking algorithm quite similar to that of [12]. It is not clear to us what means type inference for systems which look for security properties, since these are just expressed by the environments and by the types of bound names.

Acknowledgment. The authors are grateful to the referees for their helpful comments.

References

1. Michele Bugliesi and Giuseppe Castagna. Secure safe ambients. In *Proceedings of the 28th ACM Symposium on Principles of Programming Languages*, 2001. To appear.
2. Luca Cardelli, Giorgio Ghelli, and Andrew D. Gordon. Mobility types for mobile ambients. In Jiří Wiederman, Peter van Emde Boas, and Mogens Nielsen, editors, *ICALP 1999*, volume 1644 of *Lecture Notes in Computer Science*, pages 230–239. Springer-Verlag, 1999.
3. Luca Cardelli, Giorgio Ghelli, and Andrew D. Gordon. Ambient groups and mobility types. In Jan van Leeuwen et al., editor, *Theoretical Computer Science: Exploring New Frontiers in Theoretical Informatics*, volume 1872 of *Lecture Notes in Computer Science*, pages 333–347. Springer-Verlag, 2000.
4. Luca Cardelli and Andrew D. Gordon. Mobile ambients. In Maurice Nivat, editor, *FoSSaCS 1998*, volume 1378 of *Lecture Notes in Computer Science*, pages 140–155. Springer-Verlag, 1998.
5. Luca Cardelli and Andrew D. Gordon. Types for mobile ambients. In *POPL'99*, pages 79–92, New York, NY, USA, 1999. ACM Press.
6. Matthew Hennessy and James Riely. Resource access control in systems of mobile agents (extended abstract). In *Proc. of 3rd International Workshop on High-Level Concurrent Languages (HLCL'98)*, 1998. Vol. 16(3) of *Electronic Notes in Theoretical Computer Science*. Full version to appear in *Information and Computation*.
7. Matthew Hennessy and James Riely. Information flow vs. resource access in the asynchronous π-calculus. In Ugo Montanari, José Rolim, and Emo Welzl, editors, *ICALP 2000*, volume 1853 of *Lecture Notes in Computer Science*, pages 415–427. Springer-Verlag, 2000.
8. Francesca Levi and Chiara Bodei. Security analysis for mobile ambients. In *Proceedings of the Workshop on Issues in the Theory of Security,* (co-located with ICALP 2000), pages 18–23, 2000.
9. Francesca Levi and Davide Sangiorgi. Controlling interference in ambients. In *POPL'00*, pages 352–364, New York, NY, USA, 2000. ACM Press.
10. Rocco De Nicola, Gianluigi Ferrari, Rosario Pugliese, and Betty Venneri. Types for access control. *Theoretical Computer Science*, 2000. Special issue on Coordination. To appear, available at http://rap.dsi.unifi.it/papers.htm.
11. Benjamin Pierce and Davide Sangiorgi. Typing and subtyping for mobile processes. In *Logic in Computer Science*, 1993. Full version in *Mathematical Structures in Computer Science*, Vol. 6, No. 5, pages 409-454, 1996.
12. Pascal Zimmer. Subtyping and typing algorithms for mobile ambients. In Jerzy Tiuryn, editor, *FoSSaCS 2000*, volume 1784 of *Lecture Notes in Computer Science*, pages 375–390. Springer-Verlag, 2000.

Improving Functional Logic Programs by Difference-Lists*

Elvira Albert[1], César Ferri[1], Frank Steiner[2], and Germán Vidal[1]

[1] DSIC, UPV, Camino de Vera s/n, E-46022 Valencia, Spain
{ealbert,cferri,gvidal}@dsic.upv.es
[2] Institut für Informatik, CAU Kiel, Olshausenstr. 40, D-24098 Kiel, Germany
fst@informatik.uni-kiel.de

Abstract. Modern multi-paradigm declarative languages integrate features from functional, logic, and concurrent programming. Since programs in these languages make extensive use of list-processing functions, we consider of much interest the development of list-processing optimization techniques. In this work, we consider the adaptation of the well-known difference-lists transformation from the logic programming paradigm to our integrated setting. Unfortunately, the use of difference-lists is impractical due to the absence of non-strict equality in lazy (call-by-name) languages. Despite all, we have developed a novel, stepwise transformation which achieves a similar effect over functional logic programs. We also show a simple and practical approach to incorporate the optimization into a real compiler. Finally, we have conducted a number of experiments which show the practicality of our proposal.

Keywords: functional logic programming, program transformation, compiler optimization

1 Introduction

In recent years, several proposals have been made to amalgamate functional and logic programming languages. These multi-paradigm languages combine features from functional programming (nested expressions, lazy evaluation), logic programming (logical variables, partial data structures), and concurrent programming (concurrent evaluation of constraints with synchronization on logical variables). The operational semantics of modern multi-paradigm languages is based on *needed narrowing*, which is currently the best narrowing strategy for lazy functional logic programs due to its optimality properties [4]. Needed narrowing provides completeness in the sense of logic programming (computation of all solutions) as well as functional programming (computation of values), and it can be efficiently implemented by pattern matching and unification.

* This work has been partially supported by CICYT TIC 98-0445-C03-01, by Acción Integrada hispano-alemana HA1997-0073, by the German Research Council (DFG) under grant Ha 2457/1-1., and by the Generalitat Valenciana under grant ESTBEC00-14-32

J. He and M. Sato (Eds.): ASIAN 2000, LNCS 1961, pp. 237–254, 2000.

Example 1. Consider the function isShorter which is defined by the equations:

$$
\begin{aligned}
\text{isShorter}([\,],\text{ys}) &= \text{True} \\
\text{isShorter}(x:\text{xs},[\,]) &= \text{False} \\
\text{isShorter}(x:\text{xs},y:\text{ys}) &= \text{isShorter}(\text{xs},\text{ys})
\end{aligned}
$$

where "$[\,]$" and "$:$" are the constructors of lists. The expression isShorter$(x : \text{xs},z)$ can be evaluated, for instance, by instantiating z to $(y{:}\text{ys})$ to apply the third equation, followed by the instantiation of xs to $[\,]$ to apply the first equation:

$$
\text{isShorter}(x:\text{xs},z) \rightsquigarrow_{\{z \mapsto y:\text{ys}\}} \text{isShorter}(\text{xs},\text{ys}) \rightsquigarrow_{\{\text{xs} \mapsto [\,]\}} \text{True}
$$

In general, given a term like isShorter(l_1, l_2), it is always necessary to evaluate l_1 (to some *head normal form*) since all three equations in Example 1 have a non-variable first argument. On the other hand, the evaluation of l_2 is only needed if l_1 is of the form $(\_:\_)$. Thus, if l_1 is a free variable, needed narrowing instantiates it to a constructor term, here $[\,]$ or $(\_:\_)$. Depending on this instantiation, either the first equation is applied or the second argument l_2 is evaluated.

Since functional (logic) programmers make extensive use of list-processing functions, we consider of much interest the development of list-processing optimization techniques. In this work, we consider a well-known list-processing optimization from the logic programming community. Most Prolog programmers know how to use *difference-lists* to improve the efficiency of list-processing programs significantly. Informally, a difference-list is a pair of lists whose second component is a suffix of the first. For example, the list 1:2:$[\,]$ is encoded as a pair $\langle 1{:}2{:}\text{xs},\text{xs}\rangle$, where xs is a logical variable. The key to succeed in optimizing programs by difference-lists is the use of a constant-time concatenation: append$(\langle x,y\rangle, \langle y,z\rangle, \langle x,z\rangle)$. Unfortunately, if we try to adapt this technique to a functional logic context, we find several problems. In particular, a common restriction in lazy functional logic languages is to require *left-linear* rules, i.e., the left-hand sides of the rules cannot contain several occurrences of the same variable. In principle, this restriction does not permit the encoding of concatenation of difference-lists as a rule of the form: append$*(\langle x,y\rangle, \langle y,z\rangle) = \langle x,z\rangle$ and, consequently, prevents us from having difference-lists in lazy functional languages (at least, at runtime). Therefore, we are interested in a transformation process in which the final program does not contain occurrences of difference-lists. To achieve this goal we considered that, in some cases, programs using difference-lists are structurally similar to programs written using "accumulating parameters" [13]. Compare, for instance, an optimized version of quicksort by difference-lists (see Sect. 4):

$$
\begin{aligned}
&\text{qs}*([\,],\langle\text{ys},\text{ys}\rangle). \\
&\text{qs}*(x{:}\text{xs},\langle\text{ys},\text{ys}'\rangle) :- \text{split}(x,\text{xs},l,r), \text{qs}*(l,\langle\text{ys},x{:}\text{w}\rangle), \text{qs}*(r,\langle\text{w},\text{ys}'\rangle).
\end{aligned}
$$

and by accumulating parameters:

$$
\begin{aligned}
&\text{qs}_{\text{acc}}([\,],\text{ys},\text{ys}). \\
&\text{qs}_{\text{acc}}(x{:}\text{xs},\text{ys}',\text{ys}) :- \text{split}(x,\text{xs},l,r), \text{qs}_{\text{acc}}(r,\text{ys}',\text{w}), \text{qs}_{\text{acc}}(l,x{:}\text{w},\text{ys}).
\end{aligned}
$$

We will show that this idea can be generalized, giving rise to an optimization technique which achieves a similar effect over functional logic programs and which always returns a program without difference-lists.

The structure of the paper is as follows. After some preliminary definitions in the next section, Sect. 3 describes the language syntax and the operational semantics referenced in our approach. Section 4 introduces a transformation technique (based on the use of difference-lists) which improves a certain class of list-processing programs and shows its correctness and effectiveness. An experimental evaluation of our optimization is shown in Sect. 5. Finally, Sect. 6 presents some related work and Sect. 7 concludes. An extended version of this paper can be found in [1].

2 Preliminaries

In this section we recall some basic notions from term rewriting [5] and functional logic programming [7]. We consider a (many-sorted) signature Σ partitioned into a set $\mathcal{C}$ of constructors and a set $\mathcal{F}$ of (defined) functions or operations. There is at least one sort $Bool$ containing the constructors $\texttt{True}$ and $\texttt{False}$. The set of constructor terms with variables (e.g., x, y, z) is obtained by using symbols from $\mathcal{C}$ and $\mathcal{X}$. The set of variables occurring in a term t is denoted by $Var(t)$. A term t is ground if $Var(t) = \emptyset$. A term is linear if it does not contain multiple occurrences of one variable. We write $\overline{o_n}$ for the list of objects $o_1, \ldots, o_n$.

A pattern is a term of the form $f(\overline{d_n})$ where $f/n \in \mathcal{F}$ and $d_1, \ldots, d_n$ are constructor terms. A term is operation-rooted if it has an operation symbol at the root. A position p in a term t is represented by a sequence of natural numbers (Λ denotes the empty sequence, i.e., the root position). $t|_p$ denotes the subterm of t at position p, and $t[s]_p$ denotes the result of replacing the subterm $t|_p$ by the term s (see [5] for details).

We denote by $\{x_1 \mapsto t_1, \ldots, x_n \mapsto t_n\}$ the substitution σ with $\sigma(x_i) = t_i$ for $i = 1, \ldots, n$ (with $x_i \neq x_j$ if $i \neq j$), and $\sigma(x) = x$ for all other variables x. The set $Dom(\sigma) = \{x \in \mathcal{X} \mid \sigma(x) \neq x\}$ is called the domain of σ. A substitution σ is (ground) constructor, if $\sigma(x)$ is (ground) constructor for all $x \in Dom(\sigma)$. The identity substitution is denoted by id. Given a substitution θ and a set of variables $V \subseteq \mathcal{X}$, we denote by $\theta_{\restriction V}$ the substitution obtained from θ by restricting its domain to V. We write $\theta = \sigma\ [V]$ if $\theta_{\restriction V} = \sigma_{\restriction V}$, and $\theta \leq \sigma\ [V]$ denotes the existence of a substitution γ such that $\gamma \circ \theta = \sigma\ [V]$.

A set of rewrite rules $l = r$ such that $l \notin \mathcal{X}$, and $Var(r) \subseteq Var(l)$ is called a term rewriting system (TRS). The terms l and r are called the left-hand side and the right-hand side of the rule, respectively. A TRS $\mathcal{R}$ is left-linear if l is linear for all $l = r \in \mathcal{R}$. A TRS is constructor-based (CB) if each left-hand side is a pattern. A rewrite step is an application of a rewrite rule to a term, i.e., $t \rightarrow_{p,R} s$ if there is a position p in t, a rewrite rule $R = (l = r)$ and a substitution σ with $t|_p = \sigma(l)$ and $s = t[\sigma(r)]_p$. In the following, a functional logic program is a left-linear CB-TRS.

To evaluate terms containing variables, narrowing non-deterministically instantiates the variables so that a rewrite step is possible. Formally, $t \leadsto_{p,R,\sigma} t'$ is a *narrowing step* if p is a non-variable position in t and $\sigma(t) \rightarrow_{p,R} t'$. We denote by $t_0 \leadsto_\sigma^* t_n$ a sequence of narrowing steps $t_0 \leadsto_{\sigma_1} \cdots \leadsto_{\sigma_n} t_n$ with $\sigma = \sigma_n \circ \cdots \circ \sigma_1$ (if $n = 0$ then $\sigma = id$). Due to the presence of free variables, an expression may be reduced to different values after instantiating free variables to different terms. In functional programming, one is interested in the computed *value* whereas logic programming emphasizes the different bindings (*answer*). In our integrated setting, given a narrowing derivation $t \leadsto_\sigma^* d$ to a constructor term d (possibly with variables), we say that d is the computed value and σ is the computed answer for t.

3   The Language

Modern functional logic languages are based on needed narrowing and inductively sequential programs. *Needed narrowing* [4] is currently the best known narrowing strategy due to its optimality properties w.r.t. the length of successful derivations and the number of computed solutions. It extends the Huet and Lévy's notion of a needed reduction [10]. The definition of inductively sequential programs and the needed narrowing strategy is based on the notion of a *definitional tree* [3]. Roughly speaking, a definitional tree for a function symbol f is a tree whose leaves contain all (and only) the rules used to define f and the inner nodes contain information to guide the pattern matching during the evaluation of expressions. Each inner node has a *pattern* and a variable position in this pattern (the *inductive position*) which is further refined in the patterns of its immediate children by using different constructor symbols. The pattern of the root node is simply $f(\overline{x_n})$, where $\overline{x_n}$ are different variables. Formally, given a program $\mathcal{R}$, a definitional tree $\mathcal{P}$ with pattern π is an expression of the form:

$\mathcal{P} = rule(\pi = r')$ where $\pi = r'$ is a variant of a program rule $l = r \in \mathcal{R}$.

$\mathcal{P} = branch(\pi, p, \mathcal{P}_1, \ldots, \mathcal{P}_n)$ where p is a variable position of π (called the inductive position), $c_1, \ldots, c_n$ are different constructors for $n > 0$, and each $\mathcal{P}_i$ is a definitional tree with pattern $\pi[c_i(x_1, \ldots, x_k)]_p$ where k is the arity of c_i and $x_1, \ldots, x_k$ are new variables.

A graphic representation of definitional trees, where each inner node is marked with a pattern, the inductive position in branches is surrounded by a box, and the leaves contain the corresponding rules is often used to illustrate this notion (see, e.g., the definitional tree for the function isShorter of Example 1 in Fig. 1, here abbreviated as sh).

A defined function is called *inductively sequential* if it has a definitional tree. A rewrite system $\mathcal{R}$ is called *inductively sequential* if all its defined functions are inductively sequential. Note that inductively sequential programs are a particular case of left-linear CB-TRSs.

In order to compute needed narrowing steps for an operation-rooted term t, we take a definitional tree $\mathcal{P}$ for the root of t and compute $\lambda(t, \mathcal{P})$. Here, λ

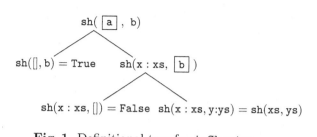

Fig. 1. Definitional tree for `isShorter`

is a *narrowing strategy* which returns triples (p, R, σ) containing a position, a rule, and a substitution. Formally, if t is an operation-rooted term and $\mathcal{P}$ is a definitional tree with pattern π, $\pi \leq t$, then $\lambda(t, \mathcal{P})$ is defined as follows [4]:

$$
\lambda(t, \mathcal{P}) \ni \begin{cases}
(\Lambda, l = r, id) & \text{if } \mathcal{P} = rule(l = r); \\
(q, l = r, \sigma \circ \tau) & \text{if } \mathcal{P} = branch(\pi, p, \mathcal{P}_1, \ldots, \mathcal{P}_k),\ t|_p = x \in \mathcal{X}, \\
& \quad \tau = \{x \mapsto c_i(\overline{x_n})\},\ pattern(\mathcal{P}_i) = \pi[c_i(\overline{x_n})]_p \\
& \quad \text{and } (q, l = r, \sigma) \in \lambda(\tau(t), \mathcal{P}_i); \\
(q, l = r, \sigma) & \text{if } \mathcal{P} = branch(\pi, p, \mathcal{P}_1, \ldots, \mathcal{P}_k),\ t|_p = c_i(\overline{t_n}), \\
& \quad pattern(\mathcal{P}_i) = \pi[c_i(\overline{x_n})]_p,\ \text{and} \\
& \quad (q, l = r, \sigma) \in \lambda(t, \mathcal{P}_i); \\
(p.q, l = r, \sigma) & \text{if } \mathcal{P} = branch(\pi, p, \mathcal{P}_1, \ldots, \mathcal{P}_k),\ t|_p = f(\overline{t_n}),\ f \in \mathcal{F}, \\
& \quad \mathcal{P}' \text{ is a definitional tree for } f,\ \text{and} \\
& \quad (q, l = r, \sigma) \in \lambda(t|_p, \mathcal{P}')
\end{cases}
$$

Then, for all $(p, R, \sigma) \in \lambda(t, \mathcal{P})$, $t \leadsto_{p, R, \sigma} t'$ is a *needed narrowing step*. Informally, needed narrowing applies a rule, if possible; otherwise, it checks the subterm corresponding to the inductive position of the branch: if it is a variable, we instantiate it to the constructor of a child; if it is already a constructor, we proceed with the corresponding child; finally, if it is a function, we evaluate it by recursively applying needed narrowing. For inductively sequential programs, needed narrowing is sound and complete w.r.t. *strict* equations (i.e., both sides must reduce to the same ground constructor term) and constructor substitutions as solutions [4].

4   Optimization by Accumulating Parameters

In this section, we introduce a new transformation for optimizing *functions that independently build different sections of a list to be later combined together* [13]. The development of this section is inspired by the well-known difference-list transformation from the logic programming community [12,13].

The idea behind the difference-list transformation of [12] is to replace certain lists by terms called *difference-lists* in order to expose opportunities for a faster concatenation. A difference-list is represented as a pair of lists whose second component is a suffix of the first. For example, the list `1:2:[]` is encoded as the pair $\langle 1{:}2{:}xs, xs \rangle$, where xs is a logical variable. Therefore, a difference-list represents the list which results from removing the suffix from the first component. Informally, a difference-list can be seen as a "list plus a pointer to its tail". By virtue of the new representation, such a pointer may avoid traversing some lists represented by difference-lists, since the concatenation of difference-lists is a constant-time operation: $\mathtt{append\_dl}(\langle x, y \rangle, \langle y, z \rangle, \langle x, z \rangle)$. Therefore, predicates using $\mathtt{append\_dl}$ take advantage from its improved runtime, as we now illustrate by considering the quicksort algorithm:

$$\mathtt{qs}([], []).$$
$$\mathtt{qs}(x{:}xs, ys) \ :- \ \mathtt{split}(x, xs, l, r),\ \mathtt{qs}(l, z),\ \mathtt{qs}(r, w),\ \mathtt{append}(z, x{:}w, ys).$$

The definition of the predicate $\mathtt{split}$ is not relevant here; it is sufficient to know that, given a call $\mathtt{split}(x, xs, l, r)$, it returns all the elements of the list xs which are lesser than x in l, and those which are greater than x in r. Following [12], the second argument of $\mathtt{qs}$ and all the arguments of $\mathtt{append}$ need to be changed to difference-lists by using the equivalences:

$$[] \quad\quad\quad \rightarrow \langle y, y \rangle$$
$$t_1{:}\dots{:}t_n{:}[] \rightarrow \langle t_1{:}\dots{:}t_n{:}y, y \rangle$$
$$x \quad\quad\quad \rightarrow \langle x, y \rangle$$

where y is a fresh variable. Thus, we obtain the program:

$$\mathtt{qs}(xs, ys) \ :- \ \mathtt{qs}{*}(xs, \langle ys, [] \rangle).$$
$$\mathtt{qs}{*}([], \langle ys, ys \rangle).$$
$$\mathtt{qs}{*}(x{:}xs, \langle ys, ys' \rangle) \ :- \ \mathtt{split}(x, xs, l, r),\ \mathtt{qs}{*}(l, \langle z, zs \rangle),\ \mathtt{qs}{*}(r, \langle w, ws \rangle),$$
$$\mathtt{append\_dl}(\langle z, zs \rangle, \langle x{:}w, ws \rangle, \langle ys, ys' \rangle).$$

Note that the first rule is introduced to relate the new predicate $\mathtt{qs}{*}$ and the original $\mathtt{qs}$ (since the difference-list $\langle ys, [] \rangle$ is equivalent to the standard list ys). By unfolding the call to $\mathtt{append\_dl}$, we get an improved definition of $\mathtt{qs}$:

$$\mathtt{qs}(xs, ys) \ :- \ \mathtt{qs}{*}(xs, \langle ys, [] \rangle).$$
$$\mathtt{qs}{*}([], \langle ys, ys \rangle).$$
$$\mathtt{qs}{*}(x{:}xs, \langle ys, ys' \rangle) :- \ \mathtt{split}(x, xs, l, r),$$
$$\mathtt{qs}{*}(l, \langle ys, x{:}w \rangle),\ \mathtt{qs}{*}(r, \langle w, ys' \rangle).$$

In an attempt to adapt this technique to a functional logic context, we find several problems. In particular, a common restriction in lazy functional logic languages is to require *left-linear* rules, i.e., the left-hand sides of the rules cannot contain several occurrences of the same variable. In principle, this restriction prevents us from encoding the concatenation of difference-lists as a rule of the form: $\mathtt{append}{*}(\langle x, y \rangle, \langle y, z \rangle) = \langle x, z \rangle$. Of course, we can transform it into:

$$\mathtt{append\_dl}(\langle x, y \rangle, \langle w, z \rangle) \ = \ \langle x, z \rangle \ \Leftarrow \ y == w$$

by using a guarded expression (i.e., a conditional expression). However, in order to keep the effectiveness of the transformation, the equality symbol "$==$" should be interpreted as syntactic unification, which is not allowed in lazy functional logic programs where only strict equality is permitted. In general, the manipulation of difference-lists requires the use of non-strict equality in order to *assign* terms to the pointers of difference-lists. Therefore, we are interested in a transformation process in which the final program does not contain occurrences of difference-lists (nor calls to append$*$).

To achieve this goal, we considered that, in some cases, programs using difference-lists are structurally similar to programs written using accumulators. For instance, quicksort can be defined using accumulators as follows:

$$qs(xs, ys) \qquad : - \; qs_{acc}(xs, [], ys).$$
$$qs_{acc}([], ys, ys).$$
$$qs_{acc}(x{:}xs, ys', ys) : - \; split(x, xs, l, r), \; qs_{acc}(r, ys', w), \; qs_{acc}(l, x{:}w, ys).$$

There are only two differences between this program and the difference-list version. The first difference is syntactic: the difference-list is represented as two independent arguments, but in reverse order, the tail preceding the head. The second difference is the goal order in the body of the recursive clause of qs_{acc}. The net effect is that the sorted list is built *bottom-up* from its tail, rather than *top-down* from its head [13].

Now we show, by means of an example, an adaptation of the difference-list transformation to a functional logic language.

4.1 An Example of the Difference-lists Transformation

Consider again the quicksort algorithm, but now with a functional (logic) syntax:

$$qs([]) \quad = []$$
$$qs(x{:}xs) = append(qs(l), x : qs(r))$$
$$\qquad \qquad \text{where } (l, r) = split(x, xs)$$

Here, both qs and split are the functional counterpart of the predicates used in the previous section.

As dictated by the method of [12], the three arguments of the predicate append as well as the second argument of the predicate qs should be changed by difference-lists. Similarly, in our functional syntax, we will replace the arguments of the function append and the *result* of both functions by difference-lists. From the previous section, we know how to transform different kinds of standard lists into difference-lists; now, however, we are faced with a new situation which arises the question: how can we transform an operation-rooted term into a difference-list? To solve this problem, we allow the *flattening* of some calls by using a sort of conditional expressions. The main difference with standard guarded expressions is that, in order to preserve the semantics, we use a syntactic (non-strict) equality "$\approx$" for the equations in the condition. In this way, we get the following transformed program:

$$qs(x) \qquad = y \; \Leftarrow \; \langle y, [] \rangle \approx qs*(x)$$
$$qs*([]) \quad = \langle x, x \rangle$$
$$qs*(x{:}xs) = append*(\langle z, zs \rangle, \langle x{:}w, ws \rangle) \; \Leftarrow \; \langle z, zs \rangle \approx qs*(l),$$
$$\qquad \qquad \qquad \qquad \qquad \qquad \qquad \qquad \langle w, ws \rangle \approx qs*(r)$$
$$\qquad \qquad \text{where } (l, r) = split(x, xs)$$

By defining the constant-time append* by the rule:

$$\text{append}*(\langle x, y\rangle, \langle y, z\rangle) = \langle x, z\rangle$$

we can unfold the calls to append* as follows:

$$
\begin{aligned}
\text{qs}(x) \quad &= y \;\Leftarrow\; \langle y, []\rangle \approx \text{qs}*(x)\\
\text{qs}*([]) \quad &= \langle x, x\rangle\\
\text{qs}*(x{:}xs) &= \langle z, ws\rangle \;\Leftarrow\; \langle z, x{:}w\rangle \approx \text{qs}*(1), \langle w, ws\rangle \approx \text{qs}*(r)\\
&\qquad\text{where } (1, r) = \text{split}(x, xs)
\end{aligned}
$$

In contrast to [12], now we want to remove difference-lists from the program. Intuitively, the idea is to detect that, since we only allow difference-lists in the result of functions, the second argument of the difference-list is somehow used to construct the final result progressively and, ᵗthus, we can change it by an "accumulating parameter".

Also, since the calls to qs* are flattened using a conditional expression, we need to move the second argument of the difference-list to the corresponding call to qs*. Thus, we obtain the program:

$$
\begin{aligned}
\text{qs}(x) \quad &= y \;\Leftarrow\; y \approx \text{qs}_{\text{acc}}(x, [])\\
\text{qs}_{\text{acc}}([], x) \quad &= x\\
\text{qs}_{\text{acc}}(x{:}xs, ws) &= z \;\Leftarrow\; z \approx \text{qs}_{\text{acc}}(1, x{:}w), \; w \approx \text{qs}_{\text{acc}}(r, ws)\\
&\qquad\text{where } (1, r) = \text{split}(x, xs)
\end{aligned}
$$

where qs* is renamed as qs_{acc}. Finally, by simplifying the equations in the conditions (i.e., by unifying them), we achieve the desired optimization:

$$
\begin{aligned}
\text{qs}(x) \quad &= \text{qs}_{\text{acc}}(x, [])\\
\text{qs}_{\text{acc}}([], x) \quad &= x\\
\text{qs}_{\text{acc}}(x{:}xs, ws) &= \text{qs}_{\text{acc}}(1, x : \text{qs}_{\text{acc}}(r, ws))\\
&\qquad\text{where } (1, r) = \text{split}(x, xs)
\end{aligned}
$$

which gives a similar improvement as the optimized predicate qs* above. Indeed, thanks to the use of accumulating parameters, we avoid the traversal of the list computed by qs(1) on each recursive call. In general, this optimization is able to produce superlinear speedups [12,13].

4.2   The Stepwise Transformation

For the purposes of formal definition and correctness results, our method is viewed in a stepwise manner:

(a) Marking Algorithm:
Given a function to be optimized, a marking algorithm is applied in order to determine which expressions should be replaced by difference-lists.

1. Input: a program $\mathcal{R}$ and a function f whose result type is a list
2. Initialization: $\mathcal{M}_0 = \{f\}$, $i = 0$

3. Repeat
   - for each function in $\mathcal{M}_i$, mark the right-hand sides of the rules defining f
   - propagate marks among expressions by applying the following rules:
   $$\underline{\texttt{append}(t_1, t_2)} \rightarrow \texttt{append}(\underline{t_1}, \underline{t_2})$$
   $$\underline{t_1 : t_2} \rightarrow \underline{t_1} : \underline{t_2}$$
   $$\underline{\texttt{g}(t_1, \ldots, t_n)} \rightarrow \texttt{g}(\underline{t_1}, \ldots, \underline{t_n})$$
   where $\texttt{g} \in \mathcal{F}$ is a defined function symbol different from append.[1]
   - if there is a marked expression $\underline{t}$ such that t is a variable, then return FAIL;
   else $\mathcal{M}_{i+1} = \{\texttt{h} \mid \underline{\texttt{h}}(t_1, \ldots, t_k)$ appears in $\mathcal{R}\}$
   until $\mathcal{M}_i = \mathcal{M}_{i+1}$

(b) <u>Introduction of Difference-lists:</u>
If the marking algorithm does not return FAIL, then we use the function τ to transform expressions rooted by a marked symbol into difference-lists:

$$\tau(\underline{[\,]}) = \langle y, y \rangle$$
$$\tau(\underline{t_1 : t_2}) = \langle t_1 : s, s' \rangle \quad \text{where } \langle s, s' \rangle := \tau(t_2)$$
$$\tau(\underline{\texttt{f}(\overline{t_n})}) = \langle y, y' \rangle \Leftarrow \langle y, y' \rangle \approx \texttt{f}(\overline{t_n})$$

where y, y' are fresh variables not appearing in the program and those occurrences of append whose arguments have been replaced by difference-lists are renamed as append*. Furthermore, we consider that all marked function symbols f in the resulting program are replaced by f*. For instance, a rule of the form $\texttt{f}(\overline{c_n}) = t_1 : t_2 : \underline{\texttt{f}(\overline{s_n})}$ is transformed into:

$$\texttt{f*}(\overline{c_n}) = \langle t_1 : t_2 : y, y' \rangle \Leftarrow \langle y, y' \rangle \approx \texttt{f*}(\overline{s_n})$$

As illustrated in the example of Sect. 4.1, when the transformation of several terms gives rise to conditional expressions, all the equations are joined into a single condition. The following equation replaces the original definition of f:

$$\texttt{f}(\overline{x_n}) = y \Leftarrow \langle y, [\,] \rangle \approx \texttt{f*}(\overline{x_n})$$

Let us remark that the introduction of non-strict equalities does not destroy the correctness of the transformation, since they can be seen as a technical artifice in this stage but will be removed from the program in stage (e).

(c) <u>Unfolding of append*:</u>
The next step consists in unfolding[2] the calls to append* using the following rule:

$$\texttt{append*}(\langle x, y \rangle, \langle y, z \rangle) = \langle x, z \rangle$$

---

[1] Note that, if the original program is well-typed, a constructor-rooted term $\texttt{c}(\overline{t_n})$ with c different from ":" is never marked, thus we do not consider this case.

[2] In particular, we use an unfolding similar to [14], but using (needed) narrowing instead of SLD-resolution (as defined in [2]).

Note that this rule is not legal in a functional logic language. It is used during the transformation but no calls to append∗ will appear in the final program.

(d) Use of Accumulating Parameters:
Then, we move the second argument of difference-lists to the corresponding function call as indicated by these rules:

$$[\mathtt{f}*(\overline{t_n}) = \langle y, y' \rangle \Leftarrow C] \rightarrow [\mathtt{f_{acc}}(\overline{t_n}, y') = y \Leftarrow C]$$
$$[t \Leftarrow \langle s, s' \rangle \approx \mathtt{f}*(\overline{t_n})] \rightarrow [t \Leftarrow s \approx \mathtt{f_{acc}}(\overline{t_n}, s')]$$

This corresponds to the idea of converting the second argument of the difference-lists into an accumulating parameter of the function in which the result will be computed.

(e) Simplification:
The final step of the transformation simplifies further the program by unfolding the (non-strict) equations in the conditional expressions (i.e., by unifying them). In this way, we guarantee that all conditional expressions are removed from the program, since the first argument of difference-lists is always a free variable.

Let us illustrate how our strategy proceeds with two examples. As an example of complete transformation, consider the following contrived example, which we use to illustrate the actions taken by each stage:

$$\mathtt{f}([], y) = y{:}[]$$
$$\mathtt{f}(x{:}xs, y) = \mathtt{append}(\mathtt{f}(xs, y), x : \mathtt{g}(xs))$$
$$\mathtt{g}([]) = []$$
$$\mathtt{g}(x{:}xs) = x : \mathtt{g}(xs)$$

If we start the marking algorithm with function $\mathtt{f}$, we get the marked program:

$$\mathtt{f}([], y) = y \underline{:} []$$
$$\mathtt{f}(x{:}xs, y) = \mathtt{append}(\underline{\mathtt{f}}(xs, y), x \underline{:} \underline{\mathtt{g}}(xs))$$
$$\mathtt{g}([]) = \underline{[]}$$
$$\mathtt{g}(x{:}xs) = x \underline{:} \underline{\mathtt{g}}(xs)$$

After replacing the marked expressions by difference-lists:

$$\mathtt{f}(x, y) = z \Leftarrow \langle z, [] \rangle \approx \mathtt{f}*(x, y)$$
$$\mathtt{f}*([], y) = \langle y{:}z, z \rangle$$
$$\mathtt{f}*(x{:}xs, y) = \mathtt{append}*(\langle z, z' \rangle, \langle x{:}w, w' \rangle) \Leftarrow \langle z, z' \rangle \approx \mathtt{f}*(xs, y),$$
$$\langle w, w' \rangle \approx \mathtt{g}*(xs)$$
$$\mathtt{g}(x) = y \Leftarrow \langle y, [] \rangle \approx \mathtt{g}*(x)$$
$$\mathtt{g}*([]) = \langle y, y \rangle$$
$$\mathtt{g}*(x{:}xs) = \langle x{:}y, y' \rangle \Leftarrow \langle y, y' \rangle \approx \mathtt{g}*(xs)$$

By unfolding the call to append∗:

$$\vdots$$

$$\mathtt{f}*(x{:}xs, y) = \langle z, w' \rangle \Leftarrow \langle z, x{:}w \rangle \approx \mathtt{f}*(xs, y), \ \langle w, w' \rangle \approx \mathtt{g}*(xs)$$

$$\vdots$$

By introducing accumulating parameters:

$$f(x, y) = z \Leftarrow z \approx f_{acc}(x, y, [])$$
$$f_{acc}([], y, z) = y{:}z$$
$$f_{acc}(x{:}xs, y, w') = z \Leftarrow z \approx f_{acc}(xs, y, x{:}w), w \approx g_{acc}(xs, w')$$
$$g(x) = y \Leftarrow y \approx g_{acc}(x, [])$$
$$g_{acc}([], y) = y$$
$$g_{acc}(x{:}xs, y') = x{:}y \Leftarrow y \approx g_{acc}(xs, y')$$

Finally, by unfolding the conditions, we get:

$$f(x, y) = f_{acc}(x, y, [])$$
$$f_{acc}([], y, z) = y{:}z$$
$$f_{acc}(x{:}xs, y, w') = f_{acc}(xs, y, x{:}g_{acc}(xs, w'))$$
$$g(x) = g_{acc}(x, [])$$
$$g_{acc}([], y) = y$$
$$g_{acc}(x{:}xs, y') = x{:}g_{acc}(xs, y')$$

Intuitively, the effect of the transformation is that, in the resulting program, the operations over the input list to f are mixed up, while in the original program they were built independently (and then combined by the function append).

As an example of program to which the transformation cannot be applied, consider the double append program:

$$dapp(x, y, z) = append(append(x, y), z)$$
$$app([], y) = y$$
$$app(x : xs, y) = x : app(xs, y)$$

If we start the marking algorithm with the function dapp, in the first iteration we get the following marked rule:

$$dapp(x, y, z) = append(append(\underline{x}, \underline{y}), \underline{z})$$

Therefore, stage (a) incurs into FAIL since the variables x, y, and z have been marked. Note that by allowing stage (b) (as it actually happens in the original difference-list transformation), we would obtain the following definition of dapp:

$$dapp(\langle x, xs \rangle, \langle xs, ys \rangle, \langle ys, z \rangle) = \langle x, z \rangle$$

However, stage (c) could not remove the difference-lists of the arguments of dapp and, thus, we would produce a non-legal program.

Notice that, even if the marking algorithm does not return FAIL, improvement is not guaranteed (although there is no significant loss of efficiency in these cases, see the function g in the example above). In order to always guarantee runtime improvement, stage (a) is only started with functions whose definitions are of the form $append(t_1, t_2)$; this way we ensure that, if the method is actually applied, at least one call to append will be removed and, consequently, some gain will be achieved. Let us note that functional (logic) programmers routinely use append to concatenate intermediate results. Therefore, the optimization pays off in practice.

4.3 Correctness

The correctness of the transformation can be derived from the correctness of stages (b) and (d), since the remaining stages do not modify the program (stage a) or are instances of the fold/unfold framework of [2] (stages c and e). In the following, we develop a proof sketch for stages (b) and (d) under certain conditions on the form of difference-lists (i.e., only *lazily* regular lists are allowed in the first argument of append∗, see below).

To prove the correctness of stage (b), we first need to define an adequate semantics for conditional expressions in transformed programs. Basically, it can be provided as follows. Let us consider an initial (marked) program $\mathcal{R}_a$ and the program $\mathcal{R}_b$ obtained from applying stage (b) to $\mathcal{R}_a$. Now, we introduce the following function τ':

$$\begin{aligned}
\tau'([]) &= [] \\
\tau'(t_1 : t_2) &= t_1 : \tau'(t_2) \\
\tau'(f(\overline{t_n})) &= y \;\Leftarrow\; y \approx f(\overline{t_n})
\end{aligned}$$

This function is used to transform the initial program $\mathcal{R}_a$ into a modified version $\mathcal{R}'_a$ with the same structure than $\mathcal{R}_b$, but without difference-lists. It should be clear that each needed narrowing derivation in $\mathcal{R}_a$ can be mimicked in $\mathcal{R}'_a$, since the only difference is that some expressions containing nested function symbols have been flattened into (non-strict) equalities. This way, we can define the semantics of conditional expressions in $\mathcal{R}_b$ in terms of the associated needed narrowing steps in the original program $\mathcal{R}_a$ (via the equivalence with $\mathcal{R}'_a$). Furthermore, when evaluating terms in $\mathcal{R}_b$, we allow the flattening of expressions, as well as the unfolding of equations, in order to preserve the equivalence with the computations in $\mathcal{R}_a$.

Once the interpretation of conditional expressions is fixed, we can establish the following equivalence between derivations in $\mathcal{R}_a$ and $\mathcal{R}_b$ where no call to append occurs. Given an operation-rooted term $e = \mathtt{f}(t_1, \ldots, t_n)$ such that $\mathtt{f}$ is marked by the algorithm in stage (a), then

$$e \leadsto^*_\sigma d:[] \;\text{ in } \mathcal{R}_a \quad \text{iff} \quad e' \leadsto^*_{\sigma'} \langle d{:}y, y \rangle \;\text{ in } \mathcal{R}_b \quad (*)$$

where $e' = \mathtt{f∗}(t_1, \ldots, t_n)$, $\sigma = \sigma'\,[Var(e)]$, and d represents a (possibly empty) sequence of elements of the form $d_1{:}\ldots{:}d_k$, $k \geq 0$. Note that, by the definition of the marking algorithm, the terms $t_1, \ldots, t_n$ cannot contain marked function symbols. This equivalence can be easily stated by induction on the length of the derivations, by considering the following three facts: i) no calls to append (resp. append∗) are produced in the first (resp. the second) derivation; ii) the left-hand sides of the applied rules are the same in both derivations since they are not changed by stage (b); and iii) the modifications in the right-hand sides can be easily proven from the equivalence between lists and difference-lists and the interpretation of conditional expressions. Therefore, we center the discussion on the correctness of the function append∗.

In [12], the notion of *regular* difference-list is introduced to ensure the correctness of append∗; namely, only calls to append∗ with a regular difference-list in the first argument are allowed. Essentially, a difference-list is regular if it is of the form $\langle t_1{:}\ldots{:}t_n{:}y, y\rangle$ and y does not appear in $t_1,\ldots,t_n$, i.e., if it denotes a finite list (here $t_1{:}\ldots{:}t_n{:}[\,]$). This notion of regularity is not appropriate in our context due to lazy evaluation, since we can have calls to append* with a non-regular difference-list in the first argument, and still preserve correctness if this argument is evaluated to a regular difference-list afterwards. To overcome this restriction (which would reduce drastically the number of programs amenable to be transformed), we introduce a lazy version of regular list as follows. Given an expression $e[d_1]_p$ containing a difference-list d_1 at some position p, we say that d_1 is *lazily* regular in a derivation $e[d_1]_p \leadsto^*_\sigma e'$ iff $\sigma(d_1)$ is regular (i.e., of the form $\langle t_1{:}\ldots{:}t_n{:}y, y\rangle$). Now, by using the notion of lazily regular lists, we can state the correctness of append* as follows.[3] Let e_1, e_2 be expressions with no calls to append and let e'_1, e'_2 be the corresponding expressions which result from replacing each call to a marked function f by the corresponding call f*. Then,

$$\text{append}(e_1, e_2) \leadsto^*_\sigma d{:}\sigma(e_2) \text{ in } \mathcal{R}_a$$
$$\text{iff}$$
$$\text{append*}(\langle x, xs\rangle, \langle y, ys\rangle) \ \Leftarrow\ \langle x, xs\rangle \approx e'_1, \langle y, ys\rangle \approx e'_2$$
$$\leadsto^*_{\sigma'} \langle d{:}y, ys\rangle \ \Leftarrow\ \langle y, ys\rangle \approx \sigma'(e'_2) \text{ in } \mathcal{R}_b$$

where e_1 is lazily regular in the second derivation, $\sigma = \sigma'\ [Var(\{e_1, e_2\})]$, and d represents a (possibly empty) sequence of elements of the form $d_1{:}\ldots{:}d_k$, $k \geq 0$.

Let us prove the claim by considering both implications:

($\Rightarrow$) Consider the derivation $\text{append}(e_1, e_2) \leadsto^*_\sigma d{:}\sigma(e_2)$ in $\mathcal{R}_a$. By definition of needed narrowing, it is immediate that $e_1 \leadsto^*_\sigma d{:}[\,]$. By equivalence (*), we have $e'_1 \leadsto^*_{\sigma'} \langle d{:}z, z\rangle$ in $\mathcal{R}_b$, where $\sigma = \sigma'\ [Var(e_1)]$. Therefore,

$$\begin{aligned}
&\text{append*}(\langle x, xs\rangle, \langle y, ys\rangle) \ \Leftarrow\ &&\langle x, xs\rangle \approx e'_1, \langle y, ys\rangle \approx e'_2\\
&\leadsto_{\{xs\mapsto y\}} &&\langle x, ys\rangle \ \Leftarrow\ \langle x, y\rangle \approx e'_1, \langle y, ys\rangle \approx e'_2\\
&\leadsto^*_{\sigma'} &&\langle x, ys\rangle \ \Leftarrow\ \langle x, y\rangle \approx \langle d{:}z, z\rangle, \langle y, ys\rangle \approx \sigma'(e'_2)\\
&\leadsto_{\{x\mapsto d{:}y, z\mapsto y\}} &&\langle d{:}y, ys\rangle \ \Leftarrow\ \langle y, ys\rangle \approx \sigma'(e'_2)
\end{aligned}$$

and the claim follows.

($\Leftarrow$) Consider the derivation

$$\begin{aligned}
&\text{append*}(\langle x, xs\rangle, \langle y, ys\rangle) \ \Leftarrow\ &&\langle x, xs\rangle \approx e'_1, \langle y, ys\rangle \approx e'_2\\
&\leadsto^*_{\sigma'} &&\langle d{:}y, ys\rangle \ \Leftarrow\ \langle y, ys\rangle \approx \sigma'(e'_2)
\end{aligned}$$

Since e'_1 is lazily regular, we have $e'_1 \leadsto_{\sigma'} \langle d{:}z, z\rangle$ in $\mathcal{R}_b$. Hence, by equivalence (*), $e_1 \leadsto_\sigma d{:}[\,]$ in $\mathcal{R}_a$, where $\sigma = \sigma'\ [Var(e_1)]$. Although the evaluation of e_1 and the calls to append are interleaved due to the laziness of append, we know that $\text{append}(e_1, e_2) \leadsto^*_\sigma d{:}\sigma(e_2)$ by definition of needed narrowing, which completes the proof.

Note that requiring e'_1 to be lazily regular is not a real restriction in our context, since terminating functions fulfill this condition by the manner in which

---

[3] Here we do not consider nested occurrences of append, although the proof scheme can be extended to cover this case by using an appropriate induction.

we introduce difference-lists in the base cases of recursive functions. On the other hand, if we were only interested in proving an equivalence w.r.t. head normal forms, we conjecture that this restriction could be safely dropped.

Now we concentrate on stages (d) and (e). Let $\mathcal{R}_c$ be the program obtained from stage (c) and $\mathcal{R}_e$ be the output of stage (e). In order to prove the correctness of this step, we prove that for each function symbol f in $\mathcal{R}_c$ (defined in terms of some $f*$) we have a semantically equivalent function f in $\mathcal{R}_e$ (defined in terms of f_{acc}). For the sake of simplicity, let us consider a recursive function of the form:

$$f(\overline{x_n}) = y \Leftarrow \langle y, [] \rangle \approx f*(\overline{x_n})$$
$$f*(\overline{a_n}) = \langle d{:}y, y \rangle$$
$$f*(\overline{b_n}) = \langle d'{:}z, y \rangle \Leftarrow \langle z, e{:}y \rangle \approx f*(\overline{s_n})$$

in $\mathcal{R}_c$, where d, d', e represent a (possibly empty) sequence of elements of the form $d_1{:}\ldots{:}d_k$, $k \geq 0$. According to the transformation rules in stages (d) and (e), we produce the following definition:

$$f(\overline{x_n}) = f_{acc}(\overline{x_n}, [])$$
$$f_{acc}(\overline{a_n}, y) = d{:}y$$
$$f_{acc}(\overline{b_n}, y) = d'{:}f_{acc}(\overline{s_n}, e{:}y)$$

in $\mathcal{R}_e$. Given a (finite) list $c_1{:}\ldots{:}c_k{:}[]$, in order to prove that $f(\overline{c_n}) \leadsto_\sigma^* c_1{:}\ldots{:}c_k{:}[]$ in $\mathcal{R}_c$ iff $f(\overline{c_n}) \leadsto_\sigma^* c_1{:}\ldots{:}c_k{:}[]$ in $\mathcal{R}_e$, it suffices to prove that $f*(\overline{c_n}) \leadsto_\sigma^* \langle c_1{:}\ldots{:}c_k{:}y, y \rangle$ in $\mathcal{R}_c$ iff $f_{acc}(\overline{c_n}, []) \leadsto_\sigma^* c_1{:}\ldots{:}c_k{:}[]$ in $\mathcal{R}_e$. To prove this claim by induction, we first generalize it as follows:

$$\langle t{:}z, y \rangle \Leftarrow \langle z, r{:}y \rangle \approx f*(\overline{c_n}) \leadsto_\sigma^* \langle t'{:}l{:}r'{:}y, y \rangle \text{ in } \mathcal{R}_c$$
$$\text{iff } t{:}f_{acc}(\overline{c_n}, r{:}[]) \leadsto_{\sigma'}^* t'{:}l{:}r'{:}[] \text{ in } \mathcal{R}_e$$

where $\sigma = \sigma' [Var(\{f*(\overline{c_n}), t, r\})]$, the expressions t, r, l represent (possibly empty) sequences of elements of the form $t_1{:}\ldots{:}t_k$, $k \geq 0$, and t', r' are constructor instances of t, r (in particular, $t' = \sigma(t), r' = \sigma(r)$). Now we proceed by induction on the length of the former derivation. The base case is immediate by applying the first rules of $f*$ and f_{acc}, respectively. Let us consider the inductive case. By applying the second rule of $f*$, we have:

$$\langle t{:}z, y \rangle \Leftarrow \langle z, r{:}y \rangle \approx f*(\overline{c_n}) \leadsto_\theta \langle t'{:}z, y \rangle \Leftarrow \langle z, r'{:}y \rangle \approx \langle d'{:}z', y' \rangle,$$
$$\langle z', e{:}y' \rangle \approx f*(\overline{s_n})$$

and, by unfolding the first equation in the condition:

$$\langle t'{:}d'{:}z', y \rangle \Leftarrow \langle z', e{:}r'{:}y \rangle \approx f*(\overline{s_n})$$

On the other hand, by applying the second rule of f_{acc} to $t{:}f_{acc}(\overline{c_n}, r{:}[])$, we have:

$$t{:}f_{acc}(\overline{c_n}, r{:}[]) \leadsto_{\theta'} t'{:}d'{:}f_{acc}(\overline{s_n}, e{:}r'{:}[])$$

where $\theta = \theta' [Var(\{f*(\overline{c_n}), t, r\})]$. The claim follows by the inductive hypothesis.

$$
\begin{aligned}
&\begin{aligned}
&f(\overline{s_n}) = [] \\
&f(\overline{t_n}) = m_1 : append(f(\overline{t_n'}), m_2 : [])
\end{aligned}
\quad\Longrightarrow\quad
\begin{aligned}
&f(\overline{x_n}) \quad= f_{acc}(\overline{x_n}, []) \\
&f_{acc}(\overline{s_n}, y) = y \\
&f_{acc}(\overline{t_n}, y) = m_1 : f_{acc}(\overline{t_n'}, m_2 : y))
\end{aligned}
\\[2ex]
&\begin{aligned}
&f(\overline{s_n}) = [] \\
&f(\overline{t_n}) = m_1 : append(f(\overline{t_n'}), m_2 : f(\overline{t_n''}))
\end{aligned}
\quad\Longrightarrow\quad
\begin{aligned}
&f(\overline{x_n}) \quad= f_{acc}(\overline{x_n}, []) \\
&f_{acc}(\overline{s_n}, y) = y \\
&f_{acc}(\overline{t_n}, y) = m_1 : f_{acc}(\overline{t_n'}, m_2 : f_{acc}(\overline{t_n''}, y))
\end{aligned}
\\[2ex]
&\begin{aligned}
&f(\overline{s_n}) = [] \\
&f(\overline{t_n}) = m_1 : append(append(f(\overline{t_n'}), m_2 : f(\overline{t_n''})), m_3 : [])
\end{aligned} \\
&\qquad\qquad\Longrightarrow\qquad
\begin{aligned}
&f(\overline{x_n}) \quad= f_{acc}(\overline{x_n}, []) \\
&f_{acc}(\overline{s_n}, y) = y \\
&f_{acc}(\overline{t_n}, y) = m_1 : f_{acc}(\overline{t_n'}, m_2 : f_{acc}(\overline{t_n''}, m_3 : y))
\end{aligned}
\end{aligned}
$$

where m_1, m_2, m_3 are (possibly empty) sequences of the form $d_1 : d_2 : \ldots : d_k$, with $k \geq 0$.

Fig. 2. Matching scheme

4.4 Effectiveness of the Transformation

Throughout this section, our aim has been to define an automatic method for achieving the effect of the difference-list transformation over functional logic programs. We have not been concerned with the efficiency of its implementation. It turns out that some of the stages that we have introduced appear to be expensive to implement. Thus, for a first attempt of integrating the method into a real compiler, we have defined a matching scheme which is both simple and effective. For our transformation, we discovered that, in practice, many doubly recursive functions ensure a gain in efficiency from the transformation (also some single recursive functions, provided they use append to concatenate some elements to the result of the recursive call). These functions are matched by three simple transformation rules (depicted in Fig. 2) and, thus, replaced by equivalent functions without calls to append.

As an example, we consider the towers of Hanoi:

$$
\begin{aligned}
&hanoi(0, a, b, c) \quad= [] \\
&hanoi(S(n), a, b, c) = append(hanoi(n, a, c, b), (a, b) : hanoi(n, c, b, a))
\end{aligned}
$$

The first argument is a natural number (constructed from 0 and S), a, b and c represent the three towers, and (a, b) a movement of a plate from a to b. By considering that m_1 is an empty sequence and $m_2 = (a, b)$, the second rule of the scheme matches and transforms the program into the following optimized version without concatenations:

$$
\begin{aligned}
&hanoi(n, a, b, c) \quad= han(n, a, b, c, []) \\
&han(0, a, b, c, y) \quad= y \\
&han(S(n), a, b, c, y) = han(n, a, c, b, (a, b) : han(n, c, b, a, y))
\end{aligned}
$$

Note that all the concatenations have actually disappeared.

5   Experimental Evaluation

In order to evaluate experimentally our transformation, we have incorporated the optimization based on the matching scheme of Fig. 2 into the PAKCS compiler for Curry [8] as an automatic source-to-source transformation which is transparent to the user. The language Curry is an international initiative to provide a common platform for the research, teaching and application of integrated functional logic languages [9]. To implement the optimization, we have used the standard intermediate representation of Curry programs: FlatCurry [8].[4]

To perform the experiments, we considered programs which are used in the literature to illustrate the benefits of difference-lists in Prolog (adapted to a functional logic syntax). The complete code of the benchmarks and a detailed description of the implementation can be found in [1]. The following table shows the performances of the original programs (Original) w.r.t. the improved versions (Optimized) by the introduction of accumulating parameters:

Benchmarks	Original	Optimized	Speedup
rev_{2000}	3470	65	53.38
$qsort_{2000}$	1010	850	1.18
$pre-order_{2000}$	104	17	6.11
$in-order_{2000}$	105	16	6.56
$post-order_{2000}$	132	16	8.25
$hanoi_{17}$	4100	2160	1.89

Times are expressed in milliseconds and are the average of 10 executions. Runtime input goals were chosen to give a reasonably long overall time. In particular, goal subindices show the number of elements in the input lists or trees. Column Speedup shows the relative improvements achieved by the transformation, obtained as the ratio Original ÷ Optimized. Results are encouraging, achieving significant speedups for some of the examples.

6   Related Work

The development of list-processing optimizations has been an active research topic both in functional and logic programming for the last decades. A related approach to difference-lists appeared early in [11], where Hughes introduced an optimized representation of lists, the so-called *abstract lists*, which are specially defined for a fast concatenation in functional programming. The idea behind their use is similar to that of logic difference-lists, although they are formulated in a different way. As opposite to our approach, the goal of [11] is not to provide an automatic algorithm to replace standard lists by abstract lists, but to introduce an efficient data structure to be used by the programmer. The idea of optimizing concatenations was taken one step forward by Wadler in [15], where he described

---

[4]   A prototype implementation, together with some examples and documentation of the system is publicly available at: http://www.dsic.upv.es/users/elp/soft.html.

local transformations for removing some concatenations from a program. The formalization of our stepwise process to introduce accumulating parameters is, apparently, not related with Wadler's transformation. Nevertheless, we strongly believe that over many examples both approaches produce a similar effect. A formal comparison between them could be useful. For instance, we think that our marking algorithm could be used within Wadler's technique to identify those functions from which concatenations will be successfully removed. On the other hand, we could benefit from the simplicity of Wadler's rules in some steps of our transformation.

The above techniques optimize functions that independently build different sections of a list to be combined later together. Apart from that kind of optimizations, there are a number of program transformations for optimizing list-processing functions which use some intermediate list to compute the result. The most popular such transformations are: Wadler's deforestation [16] and the short cut to deforestation of [6]. Also, [1] adapts the short cut deforestation technique to a functional logic setting. Although the techniques are different, their aim is essentially the same: to transform a function into another one which does not create intermediate lists. Such optimization techniques are complementary with the difference-list transformation in the sense that, generally, if a program can be improved by one of them, then, the other is not effective and vice versa (see [1] for details).

7   Conclusions and Future Work

In this paper, we have presented a novel transformation for improving list-processing functions in the context of a multi-paradigm functional logic language: an automatic transformation based on the introduction of accumulating parameters. Furthermore, it has been shown practical and effective by testing it within a real functional logic compiler, the PAKCS compiler for Curry [8].

The concept underlying difference-lists is the use of the difference operation between (incomplete) data structures to represent (partial) results of a computation. This could also be applied to other recursive data types apart from lists (see, e.g., [12,13]). A promising direction for future work is the generalization of our stepwise transformation to arbitrary (algebraic) data types. Another interesting topic is the definition of abstract measures to quantify the performance of functional logic programs, i.e., measures independent of concrete implementations. We expect that these measures also shed some light to find new optimizations and to determine their power.

References

1. E. Albert, C. Ferri, F. Steiner, and G. Vidal. List-Processing Optimizations in a Multi-Paradigm Declarative Language. Technical Report DSIC, UPV, 2000. Available from URL: http://www.dsic.upv.es/users/elp/papers.html.

2. M. Alpuente, M. Falaschi, G. Moreno, and G. Vidal. A Transformation System for Lazy Functional Logic Programs. In A. Middeldorp and T. Sato, editors, *Proc. of FLOPS'99*, pages 147–162. Springer LNCS 1722, 1999.

3. S. Antoy. Definitional trees. In *Proc. of the 3rd Int'l Conference on Algebraic and Logic Programming, ALP'92*, pages 143–157. Springer LNCS 632, 1992.

4. S. Antoy, R. Echahed, and M. Hanus. A Needed Narrowing Strategy. *Journal of the ACM*, 47(4):776–822, 2000.

5. N. Dershowitz and J.-P. Jouannaud. Rewrite Systems. In J. van Leeuwen, editor, *Handbook of Theoretical Computer Science*, volume B: Formal Models and Semantics, pages 243–320. Elsevier, Amsterdam, 1990.

6. A.J. Gill, J. Launchbury, and S.L. Peyton Jones. A Short Cut to Deforestation. In *Proc. of FPLCA'93*, pages 223–232, New York, NY (USA), 1993. ACM Press.

7. M. Hanus. The Integration of Functions into Logic Programming: From Theory to Practice. *Journal of Logic Programming*, 19&20:583–628, 1994.

8. M. Hanus, S. Antoy, J. Koj, P. Niederau, R. Sadre, and F. Steiner. PAKCS 1.2: User Manual. Technical report, CAU Kiel, 2000. Available at http://www.informatik.uni-kiel.de/~pakcs.

9. M. Hanus (ed.). Curry: An Integrated Functional Logic Language. Available at http://www.informatik.uni-kiel.de/~curry, 2000.

10. G. Huet and J.J. Lévy. Computations in orthogonal rewriting systems, Part I + II. In J.L. Lassez and G.D. Plotkin, editors, *Computational Logic – Essays in Honor of Alan Robinson*, pages 395–443, 1992.

11. J. Hughes. A Novel representation of Lists and its Application to the Function reverse. Tech. Report PMG-38, Chalmers Institute of Technology, Sweden, 1984.

12. K. Marriott and H. Søndergaard. Difference-list Transformation for Prolog. *New Generation Computing*, 11(2):125–157, October 1993.

13. L. Sterling and E. Shapiro. *The Art of Prolog: Advanced Programming Techniques*. MIT Press, 1986.

14. H. Tamaki and T. Sato. Unfold/Fold Transformations of Logic Programs. In *Proc. of Second Int'l Conf. on Logic Programming*, pages 127–139, 1984.

15. P.L. Wadler. The Concatenate Vanishes. Technical report, Department of Computing Science, University of Glasgow, UK, 1987.

16. P.L. Wadler. Deforestation: Transforming programs to eliminate trees. *Theoretical Computer Science*, 73:231–248, 1990.

A New Multihop Logical Topology for Reliable Broadband Communication

U. Bhattacharya[1], R. Chaki[2]

[1]Department of Computer Sc. & Technology, B E College (DU), Calcutta 711 103.
e-mail : ub@becs.ac.in

[2]Joint Plant Committee, 52/1A Ballygunge Circular Road, Calcutta 700 019
e-mail : rchaki@hotmail.com

Abstract : This paper presents a new logical topology GIADM-net, a generalised IADM network for enhancing the reliability of optical networks using wavelength division multiplexing. The presence of multiple number of paths of same distance between any two nodes in exchange of reasonable number of hops in the network, ensures a higher degree of reliability compared to other existing topologies in case of link failure, as well as in balancing link loading in the network so as to maximise the network throughput. This GIADM-net, connects any arbitrary no. of nodes in a regular graph as opposed to the cases in De Bruijn graph and shufflenet. The average hopping distance between two nodes, using this topology is smaller, compared to that in GEM net, shufflenet and De Bruijn Graph, at the cost of marginal increase in diameter.

1. Introduction

Optical networks[4] use interconnection of high speed wide-band fibers for transmitting information between any source-destination pair of nodes. The huge bandwidth of the optical fibers has been exploited by the wavelength division multiplexing (WDM)[6] approach, where several communication channels operate at different carrier wavelengths on a single fibre. End-users in a fibre-based WDM backbone network may communicate with one-another via all-optical channels, which are referred to as lightpaths[1]. A lightpath between end-nodes is a path between them through router(s) or star coupler(s) using a particular wavelength (often called a channel) for each segment of the fibre traversed. In an N-node network, if each node is equipped with N-1 transceivers and if there are enough wavelengths on all fiber links, then every node-pair could be connected by an all optical lightpath. But the cost of the transceivers dictate us to equip each node with only a few of them resulting to limit the number of WDM channels in a fiber to a small value d . Thus, only a limited number of lightpaths may be set up on the network. Typically, the physical topology of a network consists of nodes and fibre-links in a broadcast star or ring or bus. On any underlying physical topology, one can impose a carefully selected connectivity pattern that provides dedicated connections between certain pair of nodes. Traffic destined to a node that is not directly receiving from the transmitting

J. He and M. Sato (Eds.): ASIAN 2000, LNCS 1961, pp. 255-262, 2000.

node, must be routed through the intermediate nodes. The overlaid topology is referred to as multihop logical topology. Gem-net[2], de-Bruijn graph[1], Shuffle-net[2] etc. are examples of such existing multihop[10] logical topologies. The lightpath definition between the nodes in an optical network or the logical topology is usually represented by a directed graph (or, digraph) G = (V,E) (where V is the set of nodes and E is the set of edges) with each node of G representing a node of the network and each edge (denoted by u->v) representing a lightpath from node u to node v.

This paper considers the problem of enhancing the reliability of an optical network [4], [6], [7], [3], by overlaying a new logical topology over a wavelength routed all optical network physical topology and also compares the features of the existing logical topologies with this new topology GIADM-net.

A GIADM-net is a generalised IADM network [5], used as a multihop logical topology. The characteristic feature of having multiple numbers of paths of same distance between any two nodes in exchange of a reasonable number of hops in the network, is the major criteria for selecting such logical topology. The major problems in the optical network such as link failure or imbalance in link loading in the network can be handled properly by using this multipath property of the network, ensuring a higher degree of reliability compared to other existing logical topologies. Any arbitrary number of nodes can be connected in a regular fashion as in GEM-net but as opposed to the cases of De Bruijn Graph and Shufflenet. The property of IADM-network has been extended here to connect any number of nodes in the optical network. The average hopping distance between two nodes in GIADM logical topology is smaller compared to that the GEM-net, shufflenet and De Bruijn Graph at the expense of marginal increase in diameter of the regular graph.

After describing the GIADM net architecture, we study its construction, diameter, average hopping distance, number of paths between any source and destination and routing[8],[9]. A comparative table has been formed to discuss about the different properties of these topologies, e.g., De Bruijn Graph, GEM net and GIADM-net.

2. GIADM-Net Architecture and the Interconnection Pattern

GIADM-net is a regular multihop network architecture, which is a generalization of IADM-network. The network is a generalized one from the sense that any number of nodes may be connected with this topology Fig. 1 shows a logical GIADM-net topology connecting 6 nodes overlaid on the physical star topology network.   A   GIADM-net connecting N number of nodes are arranged in K number of columns, using the relationship : $(k-1) * (2^{k-1} - 1) < N \le k * (2^k - 1)$.

Each of (k - N mod k) number of columns has M = N div k number of nodes, whereas each of the remaining number of columns has (N div k + 1) number of nodes. Nodes in adjacent columns are arranged according to a generalization of the IADM connectivity pattern using directed links. The generalization allows any number of nodes in a column as opposed to the constraint in IADM network. The number of links from each node is 3. Node (c, r) where c is the column number and r is the node number is connected to node (c', $(r \pm 2^i)$ mod M) and node (c',r) and c' = (c+1) mod k where i = 0, 1, 2, ..., k-1.

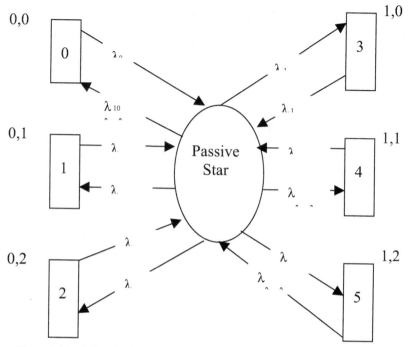

Figure 1 (a) : A 6-node GIADM –net : Physical Topology and a transceiver tuning pattern

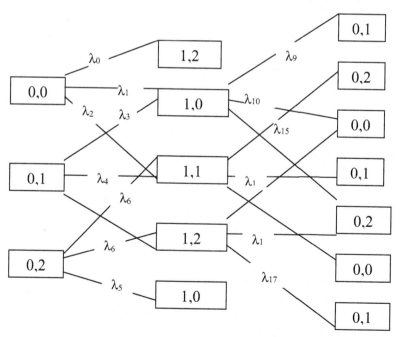

Figure 1 (b): A 6-node GIADM –net : Logical structure (virtual Topology)

2.1   Diameter

The diameter of a GIADM-net is obtained as follows :

Let $CN_{i,j}$ be the total number of nodes in stage j connected to a single node at stage i by the interconnection. $CN_{i,j+1}$ mod k is related to $CN_{i,j}$ by the following recurrence relation

$$
\begin{aligned}
CN_{i,(j+1) \bmod k} &= 2\,CN_{i,j} + 1, \text{ and}\\
CN_{i,i} &= 1 \text{ (trivial case)}\\
CN_{i,i+k-1} &= 2\,CN_{i,i+k-2} + 1\\
&= 2\,(2\,CN_{i,i+k-3} + 1) + 1\\
&\quad \cdots\cdots\cdots\cdots\cdots\cdots\\
&= 2\,(2\,(2\,(2\cdots (2\,CN_{i,i} + 1) + 1) + 1) + \cdots + 1) + 1\\
&= 2^{k-1} + 1 + 2 + 2^2 + \cdots + 2^{k-1}\\
&= 2^{k} - 1
\end{aligned}
$$

So, starting at any node, each and every node among 2^{k} -1 nodes in a particular column can be reached for the first time on (k-1)th hop. So, all these nodes which are not covered in the previously visited column will be finally covered in an additional (k-1) hops. Thus, maximum number of hops to be taken by the packets of information to communicate a source to a destination through shortest path in the network is $D = k - 1 + k-1 = 2k-2$.

2.2 Average Hopping Distance in a GIADM-Net Can Be Obtained as Follows :

$$
\left(\sum_{k=1}^{i}\ \left(\sum_{j=i+1}^{(i+k-1)\bmod k} j\,CN_{i,j} + (2^{k} - 1 - CN_{i,j})(j+k)\ \right)\bmod k\right)2/N(N-1)
$$

[2] shows the superiority of GEM-net over De Bruijn graph, regarding average hopping distance.

Some comparative results containing diameter and average hopping distance for different values of N of a GIADM-net and GEM-net are shown below :

Number of Nodes	Number of Columns k		Average Hopping distance		Diameter	
	GEM-net	GIADM	GEM-net	GIADM	GEM	GIADM
8	1-4	3	2.000-2.286	1.714	3-4	4
24	1-4	4	3.261-3.478	3.086	5-6	6
64	1-8	5	4.448-5.714	4.206	6-10	8
256	1-8	6	6.336-7.561	6.223	8-12	10
1024	1-8	8	8.297-9.517	8.22	10-14	14

2.3 Multiple Number of Node-Disjoint Paths between a Source and a Destination

Majority of the nodes are connected to a source node by shortest distance through multiple number of node-disjoint paths. The remaining nodes, connected to the source node by single shortest path through h number of hops, are connected to the same by multiple number of node-disjoint paths through h+k number of hops. It can be shown easily, that any node can be connected to any other node in the network through multiple number of node-disjoint paths requiring at most $D+1 = 2k-1$ number of hops.

2.3.1 Special Case : Computation of Number of Paths of GIADM Connecting k * (2^k-1) Number of Nodes Arranged in k Number of Columns :

Let the source node (i,p) is the node in pth position of ith stage. Let $np_{(i,p)-(j,q)}$ be the number of paths connecting the source node (i,p) to the destination node (j,q).

Following relationship holds good till $j+1 \bmod k = i+k-1$

i) $np_{(i,p)-(j+1,r)} = np_{(i,p)-(j,q)}$
   when $q = (p \pm 2^i.m) \bmod (N \text{ div } k)$
   and $r = (p \pm 2^i * CN_{i,j} \text{ div}2 + m + 1) \bmod (N \text{ div } k)$
   for $o \le m \le CN_{i,j} \text{ div } 2$

ii) $np_{(i,p)-(j+1,p)} = np_{(i,p)-(j,r)}$

iii) $np_{(i,p)-(j+1,r)} = np_{(i,p)-(j,r)} + np_{(i,p)-(j,t)}$
   where $r = (p \pm m.2^i) \bmod (N \text{ div } k)$
   and $t = (p \_ (CN_{i,j} \text{ div } 2). 2^i + (m-1).2^i) \bmod (N \text{ div } k)$
   for $1 \le m \le CN_{i,j} \text{ div } 2$
   and also,
   $np_{(i,p)-(i+1,q)} = 1$ whereas $q = p + 2^i.m$ and $m = 0,1$

After computing the number of paths from the source node (i,p) to all the nodes which are accessible in (k-1) hops, the number of paths to all other nodes which are accessible in greater than k-1 hops, can be calculated by using the following recurrence relation :

$$np_{(j+1 \bmod k, q)} = np_{(j,q)} + np_{(j,(q+2j) \bmod (N \text{ div } k))} + np_{(j,(q-2j) \bmod (N \text{ div } k))}.$$

The above relation is used till $(j+1) \bmod k = 2k-2$

2.4 Routing

A very simple routing scheme has been adapted here, using the scheme for IADM.
Let S (i,p) and D (j,q) be the source node and the destination node respectively. Where $0 \le i, j \le k - 1$ and $0 \le p, q \le 2^k - 2$

2.4.1 Case 1 : j > i

a) Destination nodes which are reachable from the source node in less than or equal to (k-1) hops :

To be able to specify any arbitrary path in the GIADM net, at least 2*(j-i) numbers of bits are required. The (j-i) low order bits represent the magnitudes of the route and the (j-i) high order bits represent the signs corresponding to the magnitudes.

Given a source input S and a routing tag F of length 2(j-i), the destination D can be calculated as :

$$D = \left[S + \sum_{s=i}^{j-1} (-1)^{f_{s+j-2i}} * f_{s-i} * 2^s \right] \bmod (N \text{ div } k)$$

b) Destination nodes which are reachable in > (k-1) hops :

Routing Tag F is of length 2 * (j-i+k). The destination D can be calculated as follows

$$D = \left[s + \sum_{s=i}^{k-1} (-1)^{f_{s+j+k-2i}} * f_{s-i} * 2^s + \sum_{s=0}^{j-1} (-1)^{f_{2k+j-2i+s}} * f_{k-i+s} * 2^s \right] \bmod (N \text{ div } K)$$

2.4.2   Case 2 : j < i

a) Destination nodes which are reachable from the source node in less than or equal to (k-1) hops :

Routing tag F is length : 2 * (k-i+j)

$$D = [s + \sum_{s=i}^{k-1} (-1)^{f_{k-2i+j+s}} * f_{s-i} * 2^s + \sum_{s=0}^{j-1} (-1)^{f_{2k-2i+j+s}} * f_{2k-2i+j+s} * 2^s] \bmod (N \text{ div } k)$$

b) Destination nodes which are reachable in greater than (k-1) hops :

Routing tag F is of length : 2 * (2k - i + j)

$$D = [s + \sum_{s=i}^{k-1} (-1)^{f_{2k-2i+j+s}} * f_{s-i} * 2^s + \sum_{s=0}^{k-1} (-1)^{f_{3k-2i+j+s}} * f_{k-i+s} * 2^s$$

$$+ \sum_{s=0}^{j-1} (-1)^{f_{4k-2i+j+s}} * f_{2k-i+s} * 2^s] \bmod (N \text{ } d \text{ } v \text{ } K)$$

3. Comparative Table Showing the Salient Features of Different Topologies with That of GIADM-Net

Different Parameters	De Bruijn Graph (λ,D)	*GEM net	GIADM-net
Nodal degree (λ)	2,3,4	2,3,4	3
Number of links	2N, 3N, 4N	2N, 3N, 4N	3N
Number of shortest paths between a source destination pair	1	1 for the best configuration	≥1
Maximum number of node-disjoint paths between a source destination pair	(λ-1) for nodal degree λ	Not discussed	3 (more than one combination may exist)
Scalability	No	Yes	Yes
Average hopping distance	d₁ (say)	D₂ (say) d₂<d₁ for the best configuration	d₃ (say) d₃ < d₂

- Data collected from [2]
- The table shown above clearly mentions the following facts:

i)   Number of shortest paths in GIADM-net between a source-destination pair is higher than that in de-Bruijn graph, and also that in GEM-net for its best configuration.

ii) Maximum number of node-disjoint paths between a source-destination pair in de-Bruijn graph is almost equal to its degree, whereas in GIADM-net, there exists more than one combination of 3 node-disjoint paths at a time.

iii) Average hopping distance is smallest in GIADM-net in comparison with other two as obtained from the statistics.

iv) GIADM-net may be scalable one as like GEM-net.

v) Nodal degree of each node is 3 in GIADM-net, whatever be the size of the network, unlike in other existing topologies. Total number of links in GIADM is 3N which is less than those in other topologies.

4. Conclusion

The proposed new topology GIADM-net, a generalised IADM work, introduces a higher degree of reliability in multihop WDM optical network, compared to the existing topologies such as De Bruijn Graph and shufflenet, by having multiple number of node disjoint paths of same distance between any two nodes in exchange of reasonable number of hops in the network. This GIADM-net was designed to be scalable like GEMnet and as opposed to the cases in De Bruijn Graph and shufflenet. The paper also summarises the information about how to compute the number of paths between any source destination pair, of a GIADM-net in a special case and also the respective routing scheme. The comparative table at the end of the paper shows that average hopping distance in GIADM-net is smallest among the existing topologies, and more than one combination of three node-disjoint paths may exist at best for a source destination pair in GIADM-net, whereas only one combination of the node disjoint paths exist in De Bruijn Graph in exchange of higher complexity of the network, compared with GIADM-net.

References

1. Kumar N. Sivarajan, Rajib Ramaswami; Lightwave Networks based on de Bruiju Graphs in IEEE/ACM TRANSACTIONS ON NETWORKING, vol. 2 no. 1, February, 1994.

2. J. Iness, S. Banerjee, B. Mukherjee; GEMNET : A Generalised, Shuffle exchange based, Regular, Scalable, Modular, Multihop, WDM Lightwave Network in IEEE/ACM TRANSACTIONS ON NETWORKING vol. 3., no. 4, August, 1995.

3. M. A. Marsan, A. Bianco, E. Leonardi, F. Neri; "A comparison of regular topologies for all optical networks" in Proc. INFOCOM '93, San Francisco, CA, March, 1993.

4. P. E. Green; "The Future of Fiber-optic Computer Networks", IEEE Computer, vol. 24, pp. 78-87, September, 1991.

5. H. J. Siegel; "Interconnection Networks for Large-Scale Parallel Processing, Theory and case studies", Mc-Graw Hill Publishing Company, 2nd edition.

6. B. Mukherjee : "Optical Communication Networks", Mc-Graw Hill Publishing Compnay, 1st edition.

7. B. Mukherjee, S. Ramamurthy, D. Banerjee and A. Mukherjee : "Some principles for designing a wide-area optical network", Proceedings IEEE INFOCOM '94, 1994.

8. A. Mokhtar and M. Azizoglu : "Adaptive wavelength routing in all optical networks", IEEE/ACM Transactions on Networking,vol. 6, No.2, April 1998.
9. H. Shen, F. Chin and Y. Pan : "Efficient fault-tolerant routing in multihop optical WDM Networks", IEEE Transactions on parallel and distributed systems, vol. 10, No. 10, October 1999.
10. B. Mukherjee : "WDM-based local lightwave networks - Part II : multihop systems", IEEE network magazine, vol 6, no 4, pp 20-32, July 1992.

A New Scalable Topology for Multihop Optical Networks

U. Bhattacharya[1], R. Chaki[2]

[1]Department of Computer Sc. & Technology, B E College (DU), Calcutta 711 103.
e-mail : ub@becs.ac.in

[2]Joint Plant Committee, 52/1A Ballygung Circular Road, Calcutta 700 019
e-mail : rchaki@hotmail.com

Abstract : A new scalable logical topology for multihop optical networks has been presented in this paper based on de-Bruijn graph. The de-Bruijn graph having simple routing property is a regular non-scalable logical topology having diameter to be of logarithmic value of number of nodes. The proposed topology adds the advantage of scalability over those in de-Bruijn graph, keeping perturbation in the network to a very low level during insertion of nodes, at the cost of marginal variance in degree of the network.

1. Introduction

High speed wide-band fibers [10] in optical networks[8],[9] are used for transmitting information between any source-destination pair of nodes. In this regard, wavelength-division-multiplexing(WDM)[1] is the approach where several communication channels operate at different carrier wavelengths on a single fibre, exploiting the huge bandwidth of the optical fibres. End-users in a fibre-based WDM backbone network may communicate with one-another via all-optical [6], [7] channels, which are referred to as lightpaths. A lightpath between end-nodes is a path between them through router(s) or star coupler(s) using a particular wavelength (often called a channel) for each segment of the fibre traversed. In an N-node network, if each node is equipped with N-1 transceivers and if there are enough wavelengths on all fiber links, then every node-pair could be connected by an all-optical lightpath. But the cost of the transceivers dictate us to equip each node with only a few of them resulting to limit the number of WDM channels in a fiber to a small value d. Thus, only a limited number of lightpaths may be set up on the network.

Typically, the physical topology of a network consists of nodes and fibre-links in a broadcast star or ring or bus. On any underlying physical topology, one can impose a carefully selected connectivity pattern that provides dedicated connections between certain pair of nodes. Traffic destined to a node that is not directly receiving from the transmitting node, must be routed through the intermediate nodes. The overlaid topology is referred to as multi-hop logical topology. GEM-net [2], de Bruijn graph [3], shuffle-net [2] etc. are examples of such existing multi-hop logical topologies. The lightpath definition between the nodes in an optical network or the logical topology is usually represented by a directed graph (or digraph) G= (V,E) (where V is the set of nodes and E is the set of edges) with each node of G representing a node of

J. He and M. Sato (Eds.): ASIAN 2000, LNCS 1961, pp. 263-272, 2000.

the network and each edge (denoted by u->v) representing a lightpath from node u to node v. The desirable criterion of this graph is (I) small nodal degree for low cost (ii) simple routing scheme for avoiding the need of complex routing tables (iii) small diameter for faster communication (iv) growth capability with least possible perturbation in the network . The de Bruijn graph being a regular topology and having a structured node-connectivity have simpler routing [4] schemes and can support a large number of nodes with a small diameter and small nodal degree . However, scalability [5] remains a problem with such regular structures where number of nodes in such a network is defined by some mathematical formulae. Irregular multi-hop structures generally address the optimality criterion directly, but the routing becomes complex due to the lack of structural connectivity pattern.

Our topology, based on topology of de-Bruijn graph seeks to address a solution to this problem. For any integer d and k, the topology becomes a de-Bruijn graph when number of nodes in the network equals d^k and $(2d)^k$, where d and 2d are the degree of the graphs respectively and k is the diameter. In the situation where d^k < number of nodes < $(2d)^k$, the irregular graph structure while keeping its diameter to the value k, still maintains a simple routing scheme. Again, during insertion of nodes one after another, perturbation as well as variance of degree in the network is kept at a low level.

Our topology, based on topology of de-Bruijn graph seeks to address a solution to this problem. For any integer d and k, the topology becomes a de-Bruijn graph when number of nodes in the network equals d^k and $(2d)^k$, where d and 2d are the degree of the graphs respectively and k is the diameter. In the situation where d^k < number of nodes < $(2d)^k$, the irregular graph structure while keeping its diameter to the value k, still maintains a simple routing scheme. Again, during insertion of nodes one after another, perturbation as well as variance of degree in the network is kept at a low level.

2. Proposed Interconnection Topology

The proposed interconnection topology gets the structure of a de-Bruijn graph when the number of nodes (N) in the network equals d^k. This directed graph has the set of nodes $\{0,1,2,.......,d-1\}^k$ with an edge from node $a_1a_2.......a_k$ to node $b_1b_2....b_k$ if and only if the condition $b_i = a_{i+1}$ is satisfied where a_i, b_i belongs to set A and A=$\{0,1,2,...,d-1\}$, $1<= i <=k-1$. Each node has indegree and outdegree d and the diameter of the graph is k. Fig. 1 shows a 2^3 de-Bruijn graph with degree 2 and diameter 3.

The proposed topology also assumes the structure of a de Bruijn graph when the number of nodes(N) in the network equals $(2d)^k$, where 2d is the indegree or outdegree of each node and k is the diameter with the set of nodes $\{0,1,2,.....,2d-1\}^k$, with an edge from node $a_1a_2.......a_k$ to node $b_1b_2....b_k$ iff the condition $b_i= a_{i+1}$ is satisfied where a_i,b_i belongs to Z , Z=$\{0,1,2,...2d-1\}$, $1<=I<=k-1$.We now consider a set X= Z-A = $\{d, d+1,........,2d-1\}$.

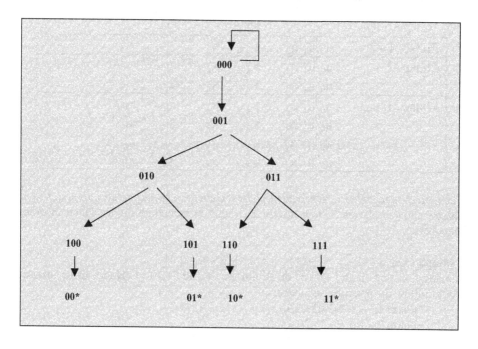

Figure 1: A de Bruijn graph with 2^3 nodes, $d = 2$ and $k = 3$

The proposed interconnection topology , when $d^k < N < (2d)^k$, assumes an insertion strategy of the nodes to be connected in the network in k number of phases as shown in table 1 (where subscript denotes the value and superscript denotes the position in its representation) :

Table 1

Phase	Node pattern	Number of nodes
1	$a_0{}^0 a_1{}^1 a_2{}^2 \ldots . a_{k-2}{}^{k-2} x_{k-1}{}^{k-1}$	d^k
2	$a_0{}^0 a_1{}^1 a_2{}^2 \ldots . a_{k-3}{}^{k-3} x_{k-2}{}^{k-2} z_{k-1}{}^{k-1}$	$2*d^k$
3	$a_0{}^0 a_1{}^1 a_2{}^2 \ldots a_{k-4}{}^{k-4} x_{k-3}{}^{k-3} z_{k-2}{}^{k-2} z_{k-1}{}^{k-1}$	2^2*d^k
.		
I	$a_0{}^0 a_1{}^1 a_2{}^2 \ldots a_{k-I-1}{}^{k-i-1} \quad\quad x_{k-i}{}^{k-i} z_{k-i+1}{}^{k-i+1}$ $\ldots\ldots . z_{k-1}{}^{k-1}$	$2^{i-1}*d^k$
.		
K	$x_0{}^0 z_1{}^1 z_2{}^2 \ldots\ldots\ldots z_{k-1}{}^{k-1}$	$2^{k-1}*d^k$

Each phase i is divided into 2^{i-1} no. of subphases. Node patterns in each phase follow the sequence as mentioned below:

Table 2

Phase 1	$a_0{}^0 a_1{}^1 a_2{}^2 .... a_{k-2}{}^{k-2} x_{k-1}{}^{k-1}$
Phase 2	$a_0{}^0 a_1{}^1 a_2{}^2 .... a_{k-3}{}^{k-3} x_{k-2}{}^{k-2} a_{k-1}{}^{k-1}$
	$a_0{}^0 a_1{}^1 a_2{}^2 .... a_{k-3}{}^{k-3} x_{k-2}{}^{k-2} x_{k-1}{}^{k-1}$
Phase 3:	$a_0{}^0 a_1{}^1 a_2{}^2 .... a_{k-4}{}^{k-4} x_{k-3}{}^{k-3} a_{k-2}{}^{k-2} a_{k-1}{}^{k-1}$
	$a_0{}^0 a_1{}^1 a_2{}^2 .... a_{k-4}{}^{k-4} x_{k-3}{}^{k-3} a_{k-2}{}^{k-2} x_{k-1}{}^{k-1}$
	$a_0{}^0 a_1{}^1 a_2{}^2 .... a_{k-4}{}^{k-4} x_{k-3}{}^{k-3} x_{k-2}{}^{k-2} a_{k-1}{}^{k-1}$
	$a_0{}^0 a_1{}^1 a_2{}^2 .... a_{k-4}{}^{k-4} x_{k-3}{}^{k-3} x_{k-2}{}^{k-2} x_{k-1}{}^{k-1}$

The pattern is repeated in subsequent phases. Generally speaking, all the nodes in all phases and sub-phases follow strictly the values in ascending order of their insertion sequence.

Example: Let $d=2, k=2$; $A=\{0,1\}$; $X=\{2,3\}$; $Z=\{0,1,2,3\}$
Already existing nodes in d^k de-Bruijn graph : 00,01,10,11. Nodes to be inserted would follow the insertion sequence:

> Phase 1:   02,03,12,13
> Phase 2: (a) 20,21,30,31
>   (b) 22,23,32,33

Insertion of all those nodes in the network would lead to form a $(2d)^k$ de Bruijn graph.

2.1. Lemma 1: At least d number of real parents of a node (to be inserted next) always exist.

Proof: The real parents of a node to be inserted in i^{th} phase $(1<=i<=k)$ having the pattern as $a_0{}^0 a_1{}^1 a_2{}^2 ... a_{k-i-1}{}^{k-i-1} x_{k-i}{}^{k-i} z_{k-i+1}{}^{k-i+1} .... z_{k-1}{}^{k-1}$ can be evaluated following the convention in de-Bruijn graph as : $*a_0{}^0 a_1{}^1 ... a_{k-i-1}{}^{k-I} x_{k-i}{}^{k-i+1} z_{k-i+1}{}^{k-i+2} .... z_{k-2}{}^{k-1}$, where * in 0th position of the pattern can take any value from Z.

The above representation of parents show that they have been inserted in i-1th phase, when * belongs to A. For i=1, the real parents are available from d^k de-Bruijn graph. So, at least d numbers of parents are always available for a node during insertion.

2.2. Lemma-2: The real children of a node following de-Bruijn graph convention during insertion may not exist.

Proof: Real Children of a node to be inserted in i^{th} phase having representation $a_0{}^0 a_1{}^1 a_2{}^2 ... a_{k-i-1}{}^{k-i-1} x_{k-i}{}^{k-i} z_{k-i+1}{}^{k-i+1} .... z_{k-1}{}^{k-1}$ may be obtained following de Bruijn graph convention by left shifting the representation one digit and inserting any digit from right. Table 1 shows the presence of all such nodes in $(i+1)^{th}$ phase whose insertion is not yet achieved.

2.3. Definitions:

Real Parent: The node to be inserted in the ith phase is of the form $a_0{}^0 a_1{}^1 a_2{}^2 \ldots \ldots a_{k-i-1}{}^{k-i-1} \, x_{k-i}{}^{k-i} z_{k-i+1}{}^{k-2} \ldots \ldots z_{k-1}{}^{k-1}$ The real parent of the node consists of the set of nodes RP{x}, where x is obtained by shifting the node bit patterns by one bit to the right and inserting a z(ε Z) bit to the leftmost position left blank by the shift process. Each x has got a bit pattern $z a_1{}^1 a_2{}^2 \ldots a_{k-i-1}{}^{k-i-1} x_{k-i}{}^{k-i} z_{k-i+1}{}^{k-i+1} \ldots \ldots z_{k-1}{}^{k-1}$.

Real Children: The node to be inserted in the ith phase is of the form $a_0{}^0 a_1{}^1 a_2{}^2 \ldots a_{k-i-1}{}^{k-i-1} \, x_{k-i}{}^{k-i} z_{k-i+1}{}^{k-2} \ldots \ldots z_{k-1}{}^{k-1}$. The real children of the node consists of the set of nodes   RC{x}, where x is obtained by shifting the node bit patterns by one bit to the left and inserting a z (ε Z) bit to rightmost position, which has been left blank by the shift process. Each x has got a bit pattern $a_1{}^0 a_2{}^1 \ldots a_{k-i-1}{}^{k-i-2} x_{k-i}{}^{k-i-1} z_{k-i+1}{}^{k-i} \ldots \ldots z_{k-1}{}^{k-2} z$.

Temporary children: The node to be inserted in ith phase is of the form : $a_0{}^0 a_1{}^1 a_2{}^2 \ldots a_{k-i-1}{}^{k-i-1} \, x_{k-i}{}^{k-i} z_{k-i+1}{}^{k-2} \ldots \ldots z_{k-1}{}^{k-1}$. Temporary children of a node consists of the set TC{x}, where x is obtained by a two-step process:

(i) d is subtracted from the leftmost x-digit of the node bit pattern.

(ii) The resultant bit pattern of the above step is shifted to the left by one bit, and a z (ε Z) bit is inserted to the rightmost position left blank by the shift operation.

Each x thus has a bit pattern as follows: $a_1{}^0 a_2{}^1 \ldots a_{k-i-1}{}^{k-i-2} (x_{k-i}{}^{k-i-1} - d) \, z_{k-i+1}{}^{k-i} \ldots \ldots z_{k-1}{}^{k-2} z$ where z in $(k-1)^{th}$ position of the pattern may take any value from Z.

2.4 Lemma 3: At least d and at most 2d number of temporary children of a node to be inserted always exist.

Proof: As referred in the definition of temporary children in 2.3, $(x_{k-i}{}^{k-i-1} - d)$ belongs to A. So, representation of the temporary children of the node to be inserted in i[th] phase takes the form : $a_1{}^0 a_2{}^1 \ldots a_{k-i}{}^{k-i-1} z_{k-i+1}{}^{k-i} \ldots \ldots z_{k-1}{}^{k-2}*$, where * in k-1th position of the pattern belongs to Z. Table 1 & table 2 shows that at least d and at most 2d number of such nodes are already present in the network. Hence, the theorem is proved.

2.5 Insertion Strategy

1. Nodes are selected in sequence as described by Table 1 and Table 2.
2. Each node is connected with at least d number of real parents (ref. 2.1).
3. Each node is connected also with it's temporary children whose numbers may vary from d to 2d (ref. 2.3 and 2.4). If the number of available temporary children is less than 2d, unavailable children are marked.
4. It is to be checked that whether the node to be inserted is the unavailable temporary child of some other nodes present in the network already. If it is so, then they would be connected by a temporary link.
5.   As obvious from table 1, nodes inserted in phase i $(1<=i<=k-1)$ and connected to their temporary children, gets their real children as soon as the nodes in phase i+1 are inserted in the network. So, insertion of a node in phase i+1 is followed by the additional step (other than steps 2, 3 and 4) of releasing the links between nodes inserted in phase i to their respective temporary children while connecting to their

real children. More precisely, insertion of a node $a_0{}^0a_1{}^1...\ a_{k-i-2}{}^{k-i-2}\ x_{k-i-1}{}^{k-i-1}z_{k-i}{}^{k-i}$ $....z_{k-1}{}^{k-1}$ in stage i+1 (1<=i<=k-1) results to establish links with its real parents $*a_0{}^1a_1{}^2...\ a_{k-i-2}{}^{k-i-1}x_{k-i-1}{}^{k-i}z_{k-i}{}^{k-i+1}\ ....z_{k-2}{}^{k-1}$, (* in 0th position belongs to A) while each of their real parents loses its link to the respective temporary child $a_0{}^0a_1{}^1...\ a_{k-i-2}{}^{k-i-2}$ $(x_{k-i-1}{}^{k-i-1}-d)z_{k-i}{}^{k-i}\ ....z_{k-1}{}^{k-1}$ to which each of them was connected in the ith phase of insertion.

Case study:
Insertion:

Let's try to insert the nodes $N_1 = 002$ and $N_2 = 003$ into the de bruijn network of Figure 1.

Parent of N_1 = *00=(000,100,200,300), two nodes from the parent set are present in the original network. Children of N_1 = 02*=(020,021,022,023), none of which is present. Hence temporary children of N_1 are found out as follows.

TC(N_1) =C(000)=00*=(001,002,000,003), two of the temporary children are present.

Similarly P(N_2) = P(003) =* 00==(000,100,200,300), and C(N_2) = 03* = (030,031,032,033), none of which is present. Hence TC(N_2) = C(001)= 01*= (010,011,012,013), hence the network becomes:

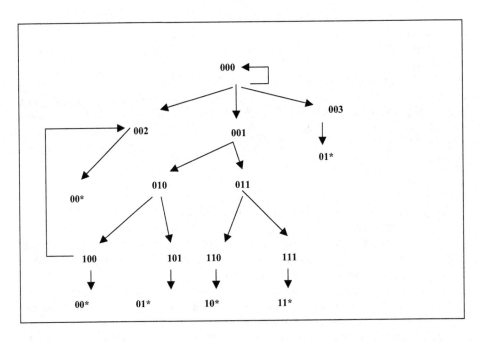

Figure 2 : The network after the insertion of nodes 002 & 003

2.6. Some Important Properties of the Topology

Some important properties of the topology has been mentioned below which can easily be concluded by using table 1, table 2, insertion strategy, lemma 1, lemma2 and lemma 3.

Property 1: At the end of insertion of all nodes in phase 1 all nodes in d^k de-Bruijn graph get all of their real children as is present in $(2d)^k$ de-Bruijn graph and the nodes inserted in that phase will get their all 2d number of temporary children whose rightmost digits constitute the set Z.

Property 2: Insertion of all the nodes in a phase i, $1<=i<k$ causes to have 2d number of temporary children for each of the nodes inserted in that phase.

Property 3: Insertion of all nodes in ith phase $(1<i<=k)$ results to replace all 2d number of temporary children with the same number of real children for the nodes inserted in i-1th phase.

Property 4: During insertion of nodes in phase i, each of the nodes in phase i-1, $1<i<=k$ remain connected with total 2d number of real and temporary children whose rightmost digits constitute the set Z.

Property 5: 2d number of temporary children is available for each node of sub-phase s, $1<=s< 2^{i-1}$ in phase $1<i<k-1$ at the time of its insertion. During insertion, at least d number of temporary children is available for the nodes in sub-phase 2^{i-1} of the phase $1<i<k$.

Property 6: 2d number of real children is available for each node of sub-phases s, $1<=s< 2^{k-1}$ in phase k at the time of its insertion. During insertion, at least d number of real children is available for the nodes in sub-phase 2^{k-1} in phase k. At the end of insertion of all nodes in phase k , all the nodes in phase k get connected with their 2d number of real children.

Property 7: During insertion of nodes in phase i, $1<i<k$ each of the nodes inserted in phase less than i-1 have 2d number of real children, each of the nodes inserted in phase i-1 gets connected to a total of 2d number of temporary and real children whose rightmost digits constitute the set Z, whereas the nodes inserted in all sub-phases s, $1<=s< 2^{i-1}$ of the phase I have 2d number of temporary children whose rightmost digits also constitute the set Z.

Property 8 :During insertion of nodes in phase k, each of the nodes in phase less than k-1 remains connected to their 2d number of real children whose rightmost digits constitute the set Z, each of the nodes in phase k-1 will get connected to a total of 2d number temporary and real children whose rightmost digit constitutes the set Z, whereas the nodes inserted in sub-phase s, $1<=s<2^{k-1}$ of phase k will get connected to 2d number of real children.

Property 9: At the end of insertion of all nodes in phase k, the nodes inserted in (k-1)[th] and k[th] phase gets connected to 2d number of real children, resulting to (2d)k de-Bruijn graph where all the nodes have their 2d number of real children.

2.7 Lemma 4: The number of links perturbed during the process of insertion of a node is at most 2d.

Proof: At each insertion of a node at most 2d number of temporary links will be released from its real parents to their respective temporary children. Hence, the theorem is proved.

2.8 Lemma- 5: The diameter of the proposed interconnection remains k.

Proof:
Case 1: Insertion of nodes in phase 1
During insertion of nodes in phase 1 the node pattern for both the source and destination is $a_0{}^0 a_1{}^1 a_2{}^2 \ldots a_{k-2}{}^{k-2} z_{k-1}{}^{k-1}$. For a source where $z_{k-1k-1}=a_{k-1}k-1$, the destination can be reached easily through at most k hops via real child at each hop. For a source where $z_{k-1}{}^{k-1} = x_{k-1}{}^{k-1}$, first hop will lead to a temporary child because of absence of any real child. Another at most k-1 hops will get real child at each hop because of their node pattern and will thus lead to the destination.

Case 2: Insertion of nodes in phase (1<i<k)
(a) Insertion of nodes in any sub-phase s $(1<=s<2^i-1)$:
In the situation as mentioned , there must exist a route connecting any source to any destination by at most k hops, where each hop will lead to either a real or a temporary child with its rightmost digit matched with the leftmost digit (not scanned yet) of the destination .
(b) Insertion of nodes in sub-phase 2i-1 of any phase 1<i<k.
We already observed that the nodes inserted in sub-phase s, $1<=s<2I-1$ of the phase i ,1<i<k , and in phases 1,2,…i-1 are already connected with 2d number of real or temporary or a combination of real and temporary children whose last digits constitutes the set Z. The insertion of nodes in sub-phase 2i-1 of this one makes these nodes to be connected with at least d number of temporary children whose last digits constitute the set A and those are present in the sub-phase 2i-1 -1 of the same phase i. The remaining d number of temporary children whose rightmost digits constitute the set X belongs to sub-phase 2i-1 itself and may still be unavailable during the insertion.
So, considering (a) a source not belonging to the sub-phase 2i-1 and destination belonging to sub-phase, (b) a source belonging to this sub-phase and destination remaining outside this sub-phase and (c) source and destination both belonging to this sub-phase, it can easily be concluded from table 2, insertion strategy and parent-child relationship that there must exist a route between them consisting of not more than k hops.

Case 3: Insertion of nodes in phase k:
As in case 2 it can easily proved that any source and any destination in such a situation are always connected through a route no longer than k hops.

2.9 Lemma 6: Degree of a node during insertion of a node varies from d to 3d.
Proof: As obvious from table 1, table 2 , properties of the topology and lemmas mentioned above.

3. Routing of the Proposed Interconnection Topology

A very simple routing strategy exists for the proposed topology to connect any source to any destination. At any moment of insertion when $dk < N < (2d)k$, all of the nodes present in the network is connected either to all available temporary children or to 2d number of real children or to a combination of real and temporary children whose rightmost digits constitute the set Z. So, the routing process starts from the source with the identification of its proper successor to reach its destination. It will select the child amongst all the children whose rightmost sub string matches most with the leftmost sub string of the destination pattern. In this way, the selected child becomes the first intermediate node in its routing to destination. The same process will continue again starting from the selected child and comparing the rightmost sub string of its children to the leftmost unused sub string of the destination pattern and ultimately the process will end when the destination has been reached.

Case Study

Let's consider the routing from S(012) to D(001). Now, C(012)=12*=(120,121, 122,123)

As seen from the figure, none of the real children of S exist. Hence the temporary children of S are found out as follows: TC(S)=TC(012)=C(010)=10*=(100,101, 102,102)

Two temporary children (100,101) are present; hence they are compared with the destination D (001). As the node (100) has the maximum sub string matching with D, it is chosen for the nest hop.

C(100)=00*=(000,001,002,003). Thus, it is seen that 001 is a child of 100, hence the routing comprises of: 012 –> 100 –> 001.

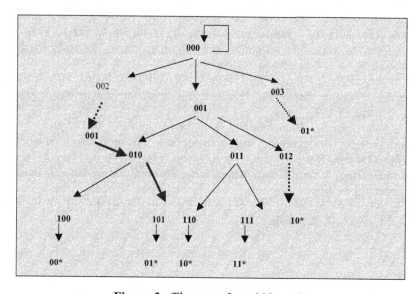

Figure 3 : The route from 002 to 101

4. Conclusion

Amongst all regular topologies in multihop optical networks, de-Bruijn graph is being considered to be a significant one due to its simple structure associated with simple routing scheme supporting a large number of nodes with small nodal degree and small diameter. The regular structures like de-Bruijn graph where total number of nodes is defined by some mathematical formulae is again associated with the problem of non-scalability. On the contrary, irregular multihop structures overcome this problem of non-scalability at the cost of complex routing schemes. This paper aims at designing an irregular scalable multihop structure based on de-Bruijn graph having simple routing scheme and maintaining same diameter as in de-Bruijn graph while perturbation in the network during insertion of nodes is maintained at a very small level.

References

1. B Mukherje, "WDM-based local lightwave networks part II " Multihop systems, IEEE Network, vol. 6, pp. 20-32, July 1992.
2. J.Ines, S. Bannerjee and B. Mukerjee, "Gemnet : a generalized shuffle exchange based regular scalable and modular network based on WDM lightwave networks ", IEEE/ACM Trans, Networking, Vol 3, No 4, Aug 1995.
3. K. Sivarajan and R. Ramaswami, "Lightwave Networks based on de bruijn graphs", IEEE INFOCOM'91, pp 1001-1011, Apr. 1991.
4. R. Ramaswami, K.N. Sivarajan, "Routing and Wavelength assignment in all-optical networks",IEEE/ACM Transactions on networking, vol. 3, Nov. 5, October 1995.
5. C.A. Brackett, A.S. Acampora, J. Sweitzer, etc."A scalable multiwavelength multihop optical network: A proposal for research on All-optical networks",Journal of lightwave technology, vol 11, no.5/6, May/June 1993.
6. T. Gipser, M. Kao, "An all-optical network architecture", Journal of lightwave technology, vol. 14, No. 5 , May 1996
7. M.A. Marsan, A. Bianco, E. Lionardi, F. Neri,"Topologies for wavelength-routing All-optical networks.",IEEE/ACM Transactions on networking, vol. 1, No. 5, October 1993.
8. B. Mukherjee, S. Ramamurthy, D. Banerjee and A. Mukherjee : " Some principles for designing a wide-area optical network", Proceedings IEEE INFOCOM '94,1994.
9. B. Mukherjee :" Optical communication Networks", Mc-graw-Hill publishing Company, 1st edition.
10. P. E. Green," The future of Fiber-optic Computer networks", IEEE Computer, vol. 24, pp 78-87, September 1991.

On Computable Tree Functions

Masahiro Kimoto* and Masako Takahashi**

Department of Mathematical and Computing Sciences
Tokyo Institute of Technology

Abstract. In order to investigate the structure of computable functions over (binary) trees, we define two classes of recursive tree functions by extending the notion of recursive functions over natural numbers in two different ways, and also define the class of functions computable by while-programs over trees. Then we show that those classes coincide with the class of conjugates of recursive functions over natural numbers via a standard coding function (between trees and natural numbers). We also study what happens when we change the coding function, and present a necessary and sufficient condition for a coding function to satisfy the property above mentioned.

0 Introduction

We consider in this paper a naive question: What are computable functions over trees. A simple answer for the question might be the following: a tree function is computable if and only if it is obtained from a computable function f over natural numbers as the conjugate $\varphi^{-1} \circ f \circ \varphi$ where φ is an appropriate coding function from trees to natural numbers and φ^{-1} is the decoding function.

Then a natural question arises: What coding functions are appropriate? Should not they be 'computable' in some sense? But then in what sense? Do we have to know the notion of computability of coding functions (from trees to natural numbers), before we study the notion of computability of tree functions?

Another question related to the tentative answer is: Does the notion of computability of tree functions depend on the choice of the coding function or not?

We try to answer the first question in a number of different ways, and also partially answer the other questions mentioned above.

Our motivation comes from the observation that a number of tree manipulating operations are found to be useful in well-known algorithms for sorting, searching, etc., and also in various application areas such as natural language processing. These are concrete examples of interesting 'computable' tree operations (or partial functions over trees), and certainly there should be many more. We would like to develop a structural theory of computable tree operations,

* Present address: Compaq Computer K.K., Tokyo 167-8533 Japan. E-mail: Masahiro.Kimoto@jp.compaq.com
** Present address: Department of Information Science, International Christian University, Tokyo 181-8585 Japan. E-mail: mth@icu.ac.jp

J. He and M. Sato (Eds.): ASIAN 2000, LNCS 1961, pp. 273–289, 2000.
© Springer-Verlag Berlin Heidelberg 2000

which hopefully will fill the gap between conventional theory of computation and algorithmic aspects of trees.

In this paper, among various tree structures with or without labels, we concentrate on binary trees without labels. This is because binary trees have the important property that any tree structure (and moreover any finite sequence of tree structures) can be nicely represented by binary trees without any coding function involved. (See, e.g., [4].) Moreover, we believe that studying unlabelled binary trees, a degenerate case of labelled binary trees, would be essential for studying the general case.

This paper is organized as follows. In the rest of this section, we summarize some notations and known facts about computable functions over $\mathbf{N} = \{0, 1, 2, ...\}$, the set of natural numbers. In Section 1, we present basic definitions about binary trees and their functions, and some of their basic properties. Then in Section 2 the notion of primitive recursive functions over binary trees is introduced, and we show that the class is equal to that of conjugates of conventional primitive recursive functions (over $\mathbf{N}$) via the standard coding function (of binary trees with natural numbers). In Section 3, two classes of recursive tree functions are introduced, one of which depends on the coding function and the other is coding-free. Then we prove that the two classes are equal to the class of conjugates of conventional recursive functions (over $\mathbf{N}$), and also equal to the class of functions computable by while-programs over binary trees. In the last section, we study how the choice of coding function affects the results; indeed we give a necessary and sufficient condition for coding functions to yield the above results.

In this paper, a function from a subset of $\mathbf{N}^n$ to $\mathbf{N}$ is called a *function over* $\mathbf{N}$ or a *numeric function*, and for such a function f we write $f : \mathbf{N}^n \rightharpoonup \mathbf{N}$ (using a special symbol $\rightharpoonup$ rather than the usual $\rightarrow$). Note that in the literature these functions are called 'partial' functions and we may occasionally use that word to stress the point. As usual, the notation $f : X^n \rightarrow Y$ means f is a (total) function from X to Y.

Recall that the class $\mathbf{PR}(\mathbf{N})$ of primitive recursive functions over $\mathbf{N}$ is defined as the least class that contains the successor function $\mathsf{suc} : \mathbf{N} \rightarrow \mathbf{N}$, the zero functions $\mathsf{zero}_n : \mathbf{N}^n \rightarrow \mathbf{N}$ and projection functions $p_{n,i} : \mathbf{N}^n \rightarrow \mathbf{N}$, and is closed under composition and primitive recursion.

Also recall that the class $\mathbf{R}(\mathbf{N})$ of recursive (partial) functions over $\mathbf{N}$ is defined as the least class that contains primitive recursive functions over $\mathbf{N}$ and their minimization functions, and is closed under composition. The minimization function $\mu f : \mathbf{N}^n \rightharpoonup \mathbf{N}$ of $f : \mathbf{N}^{n+1} \rightharpoonup \mathbf{N}$ is defined by

$$(\mu f)(\boldsymbol{x}) = x \iff \forall y \leq x [f(\boldsymbol{x}, y) = 0 \iff y = x].$$

The class $\mathbf{R}(\mathbf{N})$ is known to be equal to the class of functions computed by a (high-level) while-*program* of the form;

$$\mathsf{input}(\boldsymbol{x}); S_1; S_2; ...; S_k; \mathsf{output}(y)$$

where each S_i is a *statement*, which is either an assignment statement or a while-statement. An *assignment statement* is of the form

$$x := f(\boldsymbol{y})$$

and a while-*statement* is of the form

$$\text{while } f(\boldsymbol{y}) \neq 0 \text{ do } [S'_1; S'_2; ...; S'_l]$$

where f is an arbitrary primitive recursive function (in $\mathbf{PR(N)}$), x, y are variables (to store elements of $\mathbf{N}$), $\boldsymbol{x}$ is a sequence of distinct (input) variables, and $\boldsymbol{y}$ is any sequence of variables. S'_j's in the while-statement are statements. Then the (partial) function $f_P : \mathbf{N}^n \rightharpoonup \mathbf{N}$ *computed by* a while-program P with n input variables is defined as usual, assuming that the initial values of all variables other than input variables are set to be 0. For more about the theory of computation and related subjects, see, e.g., [6].

In the literature, the notions of $\mathbf{PR(N)}$ and $\mathbf{R(N)}$ have been extended to functions over algebraic structures other than $\mathbf{N}$ (see, e.g., [1], [2], [7], [8]). The present work may be considered as an extention of studies of word functions in [2] and [7] to the case of functions over binary trees.

1 Basic Definitions

1.1 Definition   The set $\mathbf{T}$ of *binary trees* (or simply *trees*) is defined recursively, as follows.

1. nil $\in \mathbf{T}$.
2. If $t_1, t_2 \in \mathbf{T}$, then $\mathsf{cons}(t_1, t_2) \in \mathbf{T}$.

When $t = \mathsf{cons}(t_1, t_2)$, we write $\mathsf{left}(t) = t_1$ and $\mathsf{right}(t) = t_2$. For each $t \in \mathbf{T}$, we define the size $|t| (\in \mathbf{N})$ of t recursively as

$$|\mathsf{nil}| = 0, \qquad |\mathsf{cons}(t_1, t_2)| = |t_1| + |t_2| + 1.$$

It is well-known (see e.g. [4]) that for each $n \in \mathbf{N}$ the number of binary trees of the size n is equal to the Catalan number $B(n) = \frac{1}{n+1}\binom{2n}{n}$.

1.2 Definition   For $s, t \in \mathbf{T}$, we write $s \prec t$ if one of the following conditions holds;

1. $|s| < |t|$.
2. $|s| = |t|$ and $\mathsf{left}(s) \prec \mathsf{left}(t)$.
3. $|s| = |t|$, $\mathsf{left}(s) = \mathsf{left}(t)$ and $\mathsf{right}(s) \prec \mathsf{right}(t)$.

For example,

nil $\prec$ cons(nil, nil) $\prec$ cons(nil, cons(nil, nil)) $\prec$ cons(cons(nil, nil), nil) $\prec$
cons(nil, cons(nil, cons(nil, nil))) $\prec$ cons(nil, cons(cons(nil, nil), nil)) $\prec$
cons(cons(nil, nil), cons(nil, nil)) $\prec$ cons(cons(nil, cons(nil, nil)), nil) $\prec$
cons(cons(cons(nil, nil), nil), nil) $\prec$ cons(nil, cons(nil, cons(nil, cons(nil, nil)))) $\prec$
· · ·

It is not difficult to see that the reflexive closure $\preceq$ of $\prec$ is a total order on $\mathbf{T}$.
(See [3].) Moreover the ordered set $(\mathbf{T}, \preceq)$ is shown to have the same order type
as $(\mathbf{N}, \leq)$ through bijection $\nu(t) = \mathrm{card}\{s \in \mathbf{T} | s \prec t\}$. (Note that for each $t \in \mathbf{T}$
the set $\{s \in \mathbf{T} | s \prec t\}$, being a subset of $\{s \in \mathbf{T} | \, |s| \leq |t|\}$, has a finite cardinality
not exceeding $\sum_{n \leq |t|} B(n)$.)

1.3 Definition   Let us write next(t) for min$\{s \in \mathbf{T} | t \prec s\}$, where min refers
to the order $\preceq$. Note that the inverse $\tau : \mathbf{N} \to \mathbf{T}$ of the bijection $\nu : \mathbf{T} \to \mathbf{N}$ can
be described by using next $: \mathbf{T} \to \mathbf{T}$ as

$$\tau(n) = \nu^{-1}(n) = \mathsf{next}^n(\mathsf{nil}).$$

1.4 Definition   For each $n \in \mathbf{N}$, let us write $\underline{n}$ ($\overline{n}$, respectively) for the
minimum (maximum) binary tree of the size n; that is,

$$\underline{0} = \mathsf{nil}, \qquad \underline{n+1} = \mathsf{cons}(\mathsf{nil}, \underline{n}),$$
$$\overline{0} = \mathsf{nil}, \qquad \overline{n+1} = \mathsf{cons}(\overline{n}, \mathsf{nil}).$$

We also write $\underline{\mathbf{N}} = \{\underline{n} | n \in \mathbf{N}\}$ and $\overline{\mathbf{N}} = \{\overline{n} | n \in \mathbf{N}\}$.

Using these notations, we can give recursive descriptions of functions next $:$
$\mathbf{T} \to \mathbf{T}$ and $\nu : \mathbf{T} \to \mathbf{N}$. For the proofs, see [3].

1.5 Lemma

- If $t \in \overline{\mathbf{N}}$, then next($t$) = $\underline{|t| + 1}$.
- If $t = \mathsf{cons}(t', t'') \notin \overline{\mathbf{N}}$ and
    - if $t'' \notin \overline{\mathbf{N}}$, then next($t$) = cons($t'$, next($t''$)),
    - if $t'' \in \overline{\mathbf{N}}$ and $t' \notin \overline{\mathbf{N}}$, then next($t$) = cons(next($t'$), $\underline{|t''|}$),
    - If $t'' \in \overline{\mathbf{N}}$ and $t' \in \overline{\mathbf{N}}$, then next($t$) = cons($\overline{|t'| + 1}$, $\underline{|t''| - 1}$).

Note that in the last subcase we have $|t''| > 0$ since $t' \in \overline{\mathbf{N}}$ and $t \notin \overline{\mathbf{N}}$.

1.6 Lemma

- If $t = \mathsf{nil}$, then $\nu(t) = 0$.
- If $t = \mathsf{cons}(t', t'')$, then

$$\nu(t) = \sum_{n<|t|} B(n)$$
$$+ \sum_{n<|t'|} (B(n) \times B(|t| - n - 1))$$
$$+ (\nu(t') - \nu(|t'|)) \times B(|t''|)$$
$$+ (\nu(t'') - \nu(|t''|)).$$

The notion of conjugates, which plays an essential role in this paper, can be defined, as follows.

1.7 Definition   Given a bijection $\varphi : X \to Y$ and a function $f : Y^n \to Y$ where X and Y are arbitrary sets, we define the *conjugate* $f_\varphi : X^n \to X$ of f via φ by

$$f_\varphi(x_1, x_2, ..., x_n) = \varphi^{-1}(f(\varphi(x_1), \varphi(x_2), ..., \varphi(x_n))).$$

For simplicity, one may write $\varphi(\boldsymbol{x})$ for the sequence $(\varphi(x_1), \varphi(x_2), ..., \varphi(x_n)) \in Y^n$, thus abbreviate f_φ as $\varphi^{-1} \circ f \circ \varphi$. Note that the conjugate of f_φ via φ^{-1} is f.

For example, $\mathsf{next} : \mathbf{T} \to \mathbf{T}$ is the conjugate suc_ν of $\mathsf{suc} : \mathbf{N} \to \mathbf{N}$ via $\nu : \mathbf{T} \to \mathbf{N}$, since $\mathsf{next}(\nu^{-1}(n)) = \mathsf{next}^{n+1}(\mathsf{nil}) = \nu^{-1}(n+1) = \nu^{-1}(\mathsf{suc}(n))$, thus $\mathsf{next} = \nu^{-1} \circ \mathsf{suc} \circ \nu = \mathsf{suc}_\nu$. Also, $\mathsf{suc} = \mathsf{next}_\tau$, the conjugate of next via $\tau = \nu^{-1}$.

2 Primitive Recursive Functions over T

In this section, we define the notion of primitive recursive functions over $\mathbf{T}$, and compare the functions with conjugates of primitive recursive functions over $\mathbf{N}$.

2.1 Definition   The class $\mathbf{PR}(\mathbf{T})$ of *primitive recursive functions over* $\mathbf{T}$ is defined recursively, as follows.

1. (constructors)   The binary function $\mathsf{cons} : \mathbf{T}^2 \to \mathbf{T}$ and n-ary constant functions $\mathsf{nil}_n : \mathbf{T}^n \to \mathbf{T}$ such that $\mathsf{nil}_n(t) = \mathsf{nil}$ $(n \geq 0)$ belong to $\mathbf{PR}(\mathbf{T})$.
2. (projections) $p_{n,i} : \mathbf{T}^n \to \mathbf{T}$ such that $p_{n,i}(t_1, t_2, ..., t_n) = t_i$ belong to $\mathbf{PR}(\mathbf{T})$ $(1 \leq i \leq n)$.
3. (composition) $\mathbf{PR}(\mathbf{T})$ is closed under composition. That is, if $g : \mathbf{T}^l \to \mathbf{T}$ and $g_1, g_2, ..., g_l : \mathbf{T}^n \to \mathbf{T}$ belong to $\mathbf{PR}(\mathbf{T})$, then so does the function $f : \mathbf{T}^n \to \mathbf{T}$ defined by $f(\boldsymbol{t}) = g(g_1(\boldsymbol{t}), ..., g_l(\boldsymbol{t}))$.
4. (primitive recursion)   If $g : \mathbf{T}^n \to \mathbf{T}$ and $h : \mathbf{T}^{n+4} \to \mathbf{T}$ belong to $\mathbf{PR}(\mathbf{T})$, then so does the function $f : \mathbf{T}^{n+1} \to \mathbf{T}$ defined by

$$\begin{cases} f(\boldsymbol{t}, \mathsf{nil}) = g(\boldsymbol{t}), \\ f(\boldsymbol{t}, \mathsf{cons}(t', t'')) = h(\boldsymbol{t}, t', t'', f(\boldsymbol{t}, t'), f(\boldsymbol{t}, t'')). \end{cases}$$

We will denote the function f in 3 by $g \circ (g_1, ..., g_l)$, and the one in 4 by $h * g$.

2.2 Examples   The following functions belong to $\mathbf{PR}(\mathbf{T})$.

1. The unary functions left $: \mathbf{T} \to \mathbf{T}$ and right $: \mathbf{T} \to \mathbf{T}$ defined by

$$\begin{cases} \mathsf{left}(\mathsf{nil}) = \mathsf{nil}, \\ \mathsf{left}(\mathsf{cons}(t', t'')) = t', \end{cases}$$

$$\begin{cases} \mathsf{right}(\mathsf{nil}) = \mathsf{nil}, \\ \mathsf{right}(\mathsf{cons}(t', t'')) = t''. \end{cases}$$

2. The minimum tree function mnt $: \mathbf{T} \to \mathbf{T}$ to assign the minimum tree of the same size as the argument (i.e., $\mathsf{mnt}(t) = \underline{|t|}$) can be defined by primitive recursion:

$$\begin{cases} \mathsf{mnt}(\mathsf{nil}) = \mathsf{nil}, \\ \mathsf{mnt}(\mathsf{cons}(t', t'')) = \mathsf{cons}(\mathsf{nil}, \mathsf{gr}(\mathsf{mnt}(t'), \mathsf{mnt}(t''))) \end{cases}$$

where $\mathsf{gr} : \mathbf{T}^2 \to \mathbf{T}$ is the function to graft the first argument at the rightmost leaf of the second argument;
   $\mathsf{gr}(t, \mathsf{nil}) = t, \qquad \mathsf{gr}(t, \mathsf{cons}(t', t'')) = \mathsf{cons}(t', \mathsf{gr}(t, t''))$.
Likewise, we can define the maximum tree function mxt $: \mathbf{T} \to \mathbf{T}$ such that $\mathsf{mxt}(t) = \overline{|t|}$ by

$$\begin{cases} \mathsf{mxt}(\mathsf{nil}) = \mathsf{nil}, \\ \mathsf{mxt}(\mathsf{cons}(t', t'')) = \mathsf{cons}(\mathsf{gl}(\mathsf{mxt}(t'), \mathsf{mxt}(t'')), \mathsf{nil}) \end{cases}$$

where
   $\mathsf{gl}(t, \mathsf{nil}) = t, \qquad \mathsf{gl}(t, \mathsf{cons}(t', t'')) = \mathsf{cons}(\mathsf{gl}(t, t'), t'')$.

3. The function nil? $: \mathbf{T} \to \mathbf{T}$ to tell whether the given tree is nil or not can be defined by

$$\begin{cases} \mathsf{nil?}(\mathsf{nil}) = \mathsf{true}, \\ \mathsf{nil?}(\mathsf{cons}(t', t'')) = \mathsf{false}. \end{cases}$$

Here we define true and false by nil and $\mathsf{cons}(\mathsf{nil}, \mathsf{nil})$, respectively. The characteristic functions $\underline{\mathbf{N}}? : \mathbf{T} \to \mathbf{T}$ ($\overline{\mathbf{N}}? : \mathbf{T} \to \mathbf{T}$, respectively) of the sets $\underline{\mathbf{N}} = \{\underline{n} | n \in \mathbf{N}\}$ ($\overline{\mathbf{N}} = \{\overline{n} | n \in \mathbf{N}\}$) are defined by

$$\begin{cases} \underline{\mathbf{N}}?(\mathsf{nil}) = \mathsf{true}, \\ \underline{\mathbf{N}}?(\mathsf{cons}(t', t'')) = \mathsf{if}(\mathsf{nil?}(t'), \underline{\mathbf{N}}?(t''), \mathsf{false}), \end{cases}$$

$$\begin{cases} \overline{\mathbf{N}}?(\mathsf{nil}) = \mathsf{true}, \\ \overline{\mathbf{N}}?(\mathsf{cons}(t', t'')) = \mathsf{if}(\mathsf{nil?}(t''), \overline{\mathbf{N}}?(t'), \mathsf{false}), \end{cases}$$

where

$$\begin{cases} \mathsf{if}(\mathsf{nil}, t, s) = t, \\ \mathsf{if}(\mathsf{cons}(t', t''), t, s) = s. \end{cases}$$

4. The function $\mathsf{next} : \mathbf{T} \to \mathbf{T}$ is primitive recursive, because

$$\begin{cases} \mathsf{next}(\mathsf{nil}) = \mathsf{cons}(\mathsf{nil}, \mathsf{nil}), \\ \mathsf{next}(\mathsf{cons}(t', t'')) = \mathsf{if}(\overline{\mathbf{N}}?(\mathsf{cons}(t', t'')), u, v) \end{cases}$$

where

$$u = \mathsf{cons}(\mathsf{nil}, \mathsf{mnt}(\mathsf{cons}(t', t''))) \quad (= |\mathsf{cons}(t', t'')| + 1),$$
$$v = \mathsf{if}(\overline{\mathbf{N}}?(t''), \mathsf{if}(\overline{\mathbf{N}}?(t'), w_1, w_2), \mathsf{cons}(t', \mathsf{next}(t''))),$$
$$w_1 = \mathsf{cons}(\mathsf{cons}(\mathsf{nil}, \mathsf{mnt}(t')), \mathsf{right}(\mathsf{mnt}(t''))) \quad (= \mathsf{cons}(|t'| + 1, |t''| - 1)),$$
$$w_2 = \mathsf{cons}(\mathsf{next}(t'), \mathsf{mnt}(t'')).$$

In what follows, in studying the relation between conjugates of primitive recursive numeric functions and primitive recursive tree functions, we find it is useful to have a reasonable embedding of the class $\mathbf{PR}(\mathbf{N})$ of primitive recursive functions over $\mathbf{N}$ into the class $\mathbf{PR}(\mathbf{T})$ of primitive recursive functions over $\mathbf{T}$.

2.3 Lemma   For each n-ary numeric function $f \in \mathbf{PR}(\mathbf{N})$, there exists an n-ary tree function $\underline{f} \in \mathbf{PR}(\mathbf{T})$ such that for each $m_1, m_2, ..., m_n \in \mathbf{N}$

$$\underline{f(m_1, m_2, ..., m_n)} = \underline{f}(\underline{m_1}, \underline{m_2}, ..., \underline{m_n}).$$

Proof   We define tree functions $\underline{f}$ recursively, as follows:

1. $\underline{\mathsf{zero}_n} = \mathsf{nil}_n$.
   $\underline{\mathsf{suc}}(t) = \mathsf{cons}(\mathsf{nil}, t)$.
   $\underline{p_{n,i} : \mathbf{N}^n \to \mathbf{N}} = p_{n,i} : \mathbf{T}^n \to \mathbf{T}$.
2. $\underline{g \circ (g_1, ..., g_l)} = \underline{g} \circ (\underline{g_1}, ..., \underline{g_l})$.
3. $\underline{h * g} = \underline{h}' * \underline{g}$ where $\underline{h}'(\boldsymbol{t}, t', t'', s', s'') = \underline{h}(\boldsymbol{t}, t'', s'')$.
   Here the notation $h * g$ in the lefthand side stands for the numeric function defined by primitive recursion from g and h; that is,

$$(h * g)(\boldsymbol{x}, 0) = g(\boldsymbol{x}), \quad (h * g)(\boldsymbol{x}, x + 1) = h(\boldsymbol{x}, x, (h * g)(\boldsymbol{x}, x)).$$

Then it is easy to see by induction on $\mathbf{PR}(\mathbf{N})$ that the functions $\underline{f}$ so defined satisfy the required property. $\square$

2.4 Lemma   The conjugates $\mathsf{cons}_\tau : \mathbf{N}^2 \to \mathbf{N}$, and $\mathsf{left}_\tau, \mathsf{right}_\tau : \mathbf{N} \to \mathbf{N}$ are primitive recursive.

Proof   By definition of cons_τ, we have

$$\mathsf{cons}_\tau(m_1, m_2) = \nu(\mathsf{cons}(\tau(m_1), \tau(m_2))) = \nu(\mathsf{cons}(t_1, t_2)) = \nu(t)$$

where $t_i = \tau(m_i)$ $(i = 1, 2)$ and $t = \mathrm{cons}(t_1, t_2)$. Then by applying Lemma 1.6 we get

$$
\begin{aligned}
\mathrm{cons}_\tau(m_1, m_2) = &\sum_{n < f(m_1) + f(m_2) + 1} B(n) \\
&+ \sum_{n < f(m_1)} (B(n) \times B(f(m_1) + f(m_2) \dot{-} n)) \\
&+ (m_1 \dot{-} g(m_1)) \times B(f(m_2)) \\
&+ (m_2 \dot{-} g(m_2))
\end{aligned}
$$

where

$$
\begin{aligned}
B(m) &= (2 \times m)! \div ((m+1)! \times m!), \\
f(m) &= \mu x < m[m \le \textstyle\sum_{n \le x} B(n)] \quad (= |\tau(m)| \,), \\
g(m) &= \textstyle\sum_{n < f(m)} B(n) \quad (= \nu(|\tau(m)|) = \nu(\mathrm{mnt}(\tau(m)))\,).
\end{aligned}
$$

The functions left_τ and right_τ can be expressed as

$$
\begin{aligned}
\mathrm{left}_\tau(m) &= \mu x < m[\exists y < m[\mathrm{cons}_\tau(x, y) = m]], \\
\mathrm{right}_\tau(m) &= \mu y < m[\exists x < m[\mathrm{cons}_\tau(x, y) = m]].
\end{aligned}
$$

Thus the three functions are primitive recursive.   □

2.5 Lemma   For each $t \in \mathbf{T}$, we write $\theta(t) = \underline{\nu(t)}$. Then the function $\theta : \mathbf{T} \to \mathbf{T}$ satisfies the following:

- θ is primitive recursive; that is, $\theta \in \mathbf{PR}(\mathbf{T})$.
- θ gives an isomorphism (i.e., order preserving bijection) between $(\mathbf{T}, \preceq)$ and $(\underline{\mathbf{N}}, \le)$ where $\le$ is the total order in $\underline{\mathbf{N}}$ defined by $\underline{n} \le \underline{m} \Leftrightarrow n \le m$.
- There exists $g : \mathbf{T} \to \mathbf{T}$ in $\mathbf{PR}(\mathbf{T})$ such that

$$
\forall t \in \mathbf{T}, \forall n \in \mathbf{N}[\theta(t) = \underline{n} \iff t = g(\underline{n})].
$$

By abuse of notation, we write θ^{-1} for the function g.

Proof

- $\theta : \mathbf{T} \to \mathbf{T}$ is primitive recursive, because

$$
\begin{aligned}
\theta(\mathrm{cons}(t', t'')) &= \nu(\mathrm{cons}(t', t'')) \\
&= \underline{\mathrm{cons}_\tau(\nu(t'), \nu(t''))} \\
&= \mathrm{cons}_\tau(\underline{\nu(t')}, \underline{\nu(t'')}) \\
&= \mathrm{cons}_\tau(\overline{\theta(t')}, \overline{\theta(t'')}).
\end{aligned}
$$

(For the definition of $\underline{\mathrm{cons}_\tau}$, see 2.3.)
- The function θ, being the compostion of two isomorphisms $\nu : (\mathbf{T}, \preceq) \to (\mathbf{N}, \le)$ and $\_ : (\mathbf{N}, \le) \to (\underline{\mathbf{N}}, \le)$, gives an isomorphism between $(\mathbf{T}, \preceq)$ and $(\underline{\mathbf{N}}, \le)$.

– Define $g : \mathbf{T} \to \mathbf{T}$ by primitive recursion;

$$\begin{cases} g(\mathsf{nil}) = \mathsf{nil}, \\ g(\mathsf{cons}(s, t)) = \mathsf{next}(g(t)). \end{cases}$$

Then $g(\underline{0}) = \mathsf{nil}$, and $g(\underline{n+1}) = g(\mathsf{cons}(\mathsf{nil}, \underline{n})) = \mathsf{next}(g(\underline{n}))$. Therefore by induction $g(\underline{n}) = \mathsf{next}^n(\mathsf{nil}) = \tau(n)$; thus

$$t = g(\underline{n}) = \tau(n) \iff \nu(t) = n \iff \theta(t) = \underline{n}. \qquad \square$$

2.6 Lemma   If $f \in \mathbf{PR}(\mathbf{N})$, then $f_\nu = \theta^{-1} \circ \underline{f} \circ \theta$. That is,

$$f_\nu(t_1, ..., t_n) = \theta^{-1}(\underline{f}(\theta(t_1), ..., \theta(t_1))).$$

Proof   By Lemma 2.3, we have

$$\begin{aligned} f_\nu(\boldsymbol{t}) = s &\iff f(\nu(\boldsymbol{t})) = \nu(s) \\ &\iff \underline{f}(\theta(\boldsymbol{t})) = \underline{f}(\nu(\boldsymbol{t})) = \underline{\nu(s)} = \theta(s) \\ &\iff \theta^{-1}(\underline{f}(\theta(\boldsymbol{t}))) = s. \qquad \square \end{aligned}$$

2.7 Corollary   If $f \in \mathbf{PR}(\mathbf{N})$, then $f_\nu \in \mathbf{PR}(\mathbf{T})$.

Proof   Immediate from Lemmas 2.6, 2.5 and 2.3. $\square$

2.8 Theorem $\{f_\nu | f \in \mathbf{PR}(\mathbf{N})\} = \mathbf{PR}(\mathbf{T})$.

Proof   Since inclusion $\subseteq$ has been proved, we now verify

$$\forall g \in \mathbf{PR}(\mathbf{T}), \exists f \in \mathbf{PR}(\mathbf{N})[g = f_\nu]$$

by induction on $\mathbf{PR}(\mathbf{T})$.

1. $\mathsf{nil}_n = \nu_{-1} \circ \mathsf{zero}_n \circ \nu = (\mathsf{zero}_n)_\nu$.
   $\mathsf{cons} = \nu_{-1} \circ \nu \circ \mathsf{cons} \circ \nu_{-1} \circ \nu = (\mathsf{cons}_\tau)_\nu$ where $\mathsf{cons}_\tau \in \mathbf{PR}(\mathbf{N})$.
   $(p_{n,i} : \mathbf{T}^n \to \mathbf{T}) = \nu_{-1} \circ (p_{n,i} : \mathbf{N}^n \to \mathbf{N}) \circ \nu = (p_{n,i} : \mathbf{N}^n \to \mathbf{N})_\nu$.
2. If $g = g_0 \circ (g_1, ..., g_l)$ and $g_j = (f_j)_\nu$ $(j = 1, ...l)$, then

   $$g = (f_0 \circ (f_1, ..., f_l))_\nu.$$

3. Let $g = g_1 * g_0$ and $g_j = (f_j)_\nu$ where $f_j \in \mathbf{PR}(\mathbf{N})$ $(j = 0, 1)$. It suffies to show that the function $f = g_\tau = \nu \circ g \circ \tau$ belongs to $\mathbf{PR}(\mathbf{N})$, since $g = f_\nu$.

From the definition, we have

$$
\begin{aligned}
f(\boldsymbol{m}, 0) &= (\nu \circ g \circ \tau)(\boldsymbol{m}, 0) \\
&= \nu(g(\tau(\boldsymbol{m}), \mathsf{nil})) \\
&= \nu(g_0(\tau(\boldsymbol{m}))) \\
&= f_0(\boldsymbol{m}), \\
f(\boldsymbol{m}, m+1) &= (\nu \circ g \circ \tau)(\boldsymbol{m}, m+1) \\
&= \nu(g(\tau(\boldsymbol{m}), \mathsf{cons}(t', t''))) \\
&\qquad \text{where we write } \mathsf{cons}(t', t'') = \tau(m+1) \\
&= \nu(g_1(\tau(\boldsymbol{m}), t', t'', g(\tau(\boldsymbol{m}), t'), g(\tau(\boldsymbol{m}), t''))) \\
&= f_1(\boldsymbol{m}, m', m'', f(\boldsymbol{m}, m'), f(\boldsymbol{m}, m''))
\end{aligned}
$$

where
$$
\begin{aligned}
m' &= \nu(t') = \nu(\mathsf{left}(\tau(m+1))) = \mathsf{left}_\tau(m+1), \\
m'' &= \nu(t'') = \nu(\mathsf{right}(\tau(m+1))) = \mathsf{right}_\tau(m+1).
\end{aligned}
$$
Since $\mathsf{left}_\tau(m+1), \mathsf{right}_\tau(m+1) < m+1$, and $\mathsf{left}_\tau, \mathsf{right}_\tau \in \mathbf{PR(N)}$, the description of f implies that f is primitive recursive. (cf. [5])   □

3 Recursive Functions over **T**

In this section, we define two classes of recursive functions over **T** and the class of functions computable by while programs over **T**. Then we study their properties in connection with conjugates of recursive functions over **N**. As in the case of numeric functions, we call a function from a subset of $\mathbf{T}^n$ to **T** a *function over* **T** or a *tree function*.

3.1 Definition   We define the class $\mathbf{R(T)}$ of *recursive functions* over **T** recursively, as follows.

1. (primitive recursive functions) $\mathbf{PR(T)} \subseteq \mathbf{R(T)}$.
2. (minimization)   If $f : \mathbf{T}^{n+1} \to \mathbf{T}$ is primitive recursive, then the (partial) function $\mu_{\mathbf{T}} f : \mathbf{T}^n \rightharpoonup \mathbf{T}$ defined by

$$
(\mu_{\mathbf{T}} f)(\boldsymbol{t}) = t \iff \forall s \preceq t[f(\boldsymbol{t}, s) = \mathsf{nil} \iff s = t]
$$

belongs to $\mathbf{R(T)}$. We call $\mu_{\mathbf{T}} f : \mathbf{T}^n \rightharpoonup \mathbf{T}$ the **T**-*minimization function* of f along the values $\tau(0), \tau(1), \tau(2), \dots$ of $\tau : \mathbf{N} \to \mathbf{T}$.
3. (composition) $\mathbf{R(T)}$ is closed under composition. That is, if partial functions $g : \mathbf{T}^l \rightharpoonup \mathbf{T}$ and $g_1, g_2, \dots, g_l : \mathbf{T}^n \rightharpoonup \mathbf{T}$ belong to $\mathbf{R(T)}$, then so does the partial function $f : \mathbf{T}^n \rightharpoonup \mathbf{T}$ defined by

$$
f(\boldsymbol{t}) = s \iff \exists s_1, \dots, s_l \in \mathbf{T}[g_1(\boldsymbol{t}) = s_1, \dots, g_l(\boldsymbol{t}) = s_l, g(s_1, \dots, s_l) = s].
$$

As before we will write $g \circ (g_1, \dots, g_l)$ for the function f.

One may wonder whether Definition 3.1.2 is the only reasonable way of defining the minimization function. For example, how about the following as an alternative?

3.2 Definition   For a primitive recursive function $f : \mathbf{T}^{n+1} \to \mathbf{T}$, define a partial function $\mu_{\underline{\mathbf{N}}} f : \mathbf{T}^n \rightharpoonup \mathbf{T}$ by

$$(\mu_{\underline{\mathbf{N}}} f)(t) = t \iff \exists m \in \mathbf{N}[t = \underline{m} \,\wedge\, \forall n \le m[f(t, \underline{n}) = \mathsf{nil} \iff n = m]].$$

We call $\mu_{\underline{\mathbf{N}}} f : \mathbf{T}^n \rightharpoonup \mathbf{T}$ the $\underline{\mathbf{N}}$-*minimization* of $f : \mathbf{T}^{n+1} \rightharpoonup \mathbf{T}$ along the values $\underline{0}, \underline{1}, \underline{2}, ...$ of bijection $\_ : \mathbf{N} \to \underline{\mathbf{N}}$. We will write $\mathbf{R}_{\underline{\mathbf{N}}}(\mathbf{T})$ for the class of tree functions defined exactly as $\mathbf{R}(\mathbf{T})$ except that we replace the minimization operator $\mu_{\mathbf{T}}$ with $\mu_{\underline{\mathbf{N}}}$. The (partial) functions in $\mathbf{R}_{\underline{\mathbf{N}}}(\mathbf{T})$ are called $\underline{\mathbf{N}}$-*recursive functions*.

Next, we define the notion of (high-level) while-programs over $\mathbf{T}$.

3.3 Definition   A while-*program* over $\mathbf{T}$ is of the form;

$$\mathsf{input}(\boldsymbol{x}); S_1; S_2; ...; S_k; \mathsf{output}(y)$$

where each S_i is a statement, which is either an assignment statement or a while-statement. An *assignment statement* is of the form

$$x := f(\boldsymbol{y})$$

and a while-*statement* is of the form

$$\mathsf{while}\ f(\boldsymbol{y}) \ne \mathsf{nil}\ \mathsf{do}\ [S_1'; S_2'; ...; S_l'].$$

Here, f is an arbitrary primitive recursive function (in $\mathbf{PR}(\mathbf{T})$), x, y are variables (to store trees in $\mathbf{T}$), $\boldsymbol{x}$ is a sequence of distinct (input) variables, and $\boldsymbol{y}$ is any sequence of variables. S_j''s in the while-statement are (either assignment or while-) statements.

The (partial) function *computed by* a while-program P over $\mathbf{T}$ is defined as usual, assuming that the initial values of all variables other than input variables are set to nil, and it is denoted by $f_P : \mathbf{T}^n \rightharpoonup \mathbf{T}$ where n is the number of input variables of the program P.

First, we study the relation between the three classes; the class of conjugates of recursive functions over $\mathbf{N}$, the class $\mathbf{R}_{\underline{\mathbf{N}}}(\mathbf{T})$ of $\underline{\mathbf{N}}$-recursive functions, and that of functions computable by while-programs over $\mathbf{T}$.

3.4 Lemma   We extend the definition of $\underline{f}$ in lemma 2.3 for $f \in \mathbf{PR}(\mathbf{N})$ (cf. 2.3) to the case where $f \in \mathbf{R}(\mathbf{N})$, as follows.

- The function $\underline{f}$ for $f \in \mathbf{PR}(\mathbf{N})$ is defined as before.
- If $f \in \mathbf{PR}(\mathbf{N})$, we define $\underline{\mu f} = \mu_{\underline{\mathbf{N}}} \underline{f}$; that is,

$$\underline{\mu f}(t) = t \iff t = \underline{\min\{m \in \mathbf{N} | \underline{f}(t, \underline{m}) = \mathsf{nil}\}}.$$

$$- \; g \circ (g_1, ..., g_l) = \underline{g} \circ (\underline{g_1}, ..., \underline{g_l}).$$

Then the functions $\underline{f}$ where $f \in \mathbf{R}(\mathbf{N})$ satisfy the following.

1. $\underline{f} \in \mathbf{R_N}(\mathbf{T})$.
2. $\underline{f}(\underline{m_1}, \underline{m_2}, ..., \underline{m_n}) = \underline{m} \iff f(m_1, m_2, ..., m_n) = m$.
   (In particular, $\underline{f}(\underline{m_1}, ..., \underline{m_n})$ is defined iff $f(m_1, ..., m_n)$ is defined.)
3. $f_\nu = \theta^{-1} \circ \underline{f} \circ \theta$.

Proof   By induction on $\mathbf{R}(\mathbf{N})$. (For details, see [3].)   □

3.5 Corollary $\{f_\nu | f \in \mathbf{R}(\mathbf{N})\} \subseteq \mathbf{R_N}(\mathbf{T})$.

Proof   The inclusion follows immediately from Lemmas 3.4 and 2.5.   □

3.6 Lemma $\mathbf{R_N}(\mathbf{T}) \subseteq \{f_P | P \text{ is a while-program }\}$.

Proof   By induction on $\mathbf{R_N}(\mathbf{T})$. For example, the $\mathbf{N}$-minimization function $\mu_\mathbf{N} f$ of $f \in \mathbf{PR}(\mathbf{T})$ can be computed by the while-program

$$\begin{aligned}
&\mathsf{input}(\boldsymbol{x}); \\
&y := \mathsf{nil}; \\
&\mathsf{while}\; f(\boldsymbol{x}, y) \neq \mathsf{nil}\; \mathsf{do}\; [y := \mathsf{cons}(\mathsf{nil}, y)]; \\
&\mathsf{output}(y)
\end{aligned}$$

□

3.7 Lemma $\{f_P | P \text{ is a while-program }\} \subseteq \{f_\nu | f \in \mathbf{R}(\mathbf{N})\}$; that is, functions computable by while-programs over $\mathbf{T}$ are conjugates via ν of recursive functions over $\mathbf{N}$.

Proof   Given a while-program P over $\mathbf{T}$, we construct a while-program Q over $\mathbf{N}$ which simulate computation of P step by step. The program Q is obtained from P by simply replacing each primitive recursive function g ($\in \mathbf{PR}(\mathbf{T})$) in P with its conjugate $g_\tau = \nu \circ g \circ \tau$ ($\in \mathbf{PR}(\mathbf{N})$) and nil with 0. Thus, for assignment statements

$$x := g(\boldsymbol{y}) \quad \text{becomes} \quad x := g_\tau(\boldsymbol{y}),$$

and for terminating conditions in while statements

$$g(\boldsymbol{y}) \neq \mathsf{nil} \quad \text{becomes} \quad g_\tau(\boldsymbol{y}) \neq 0.$$

Under this construction, we can observe the equivalence

$$f_P(t_1, ..., t_n) = t \iff f_Q(\nu(t_1), ..., \nu(t_n)) = \nu(t)$$

between the function f_P computed by while-program P over $\mathbf{T}$ and the function f_Q computed by while-program Q over $\mathbf{N}$. In other words, we have $f_P =$

$\nu^{-1} \circ f_Q \circ \nu = (f_Q)_\nu$. This completes the proof, since $f_Q \in \mathbf{R}(\mathbf{N})$.   □

3.8 Theorem $\{f_\nu | f \in \mathbf{R}(\mathbf{N})\} = \mathbf{R_{\underline{N}}}(\mathbf{T}) = \{f_P | P$ is a while-program $\}$.

Proof   Immediate from Corollary 3.5 and Lemmas 3.6 and 3.7.   □

Next, we see the relation between the two classes of recursive functions over **T**.

3.9 Theorem $\mathbf{R}(\mathbf{T}) = \mathbf{R_{\underline{N}}}(\mathbf{T})$.

Proof   To see the inclusion $\subseteq$, it suffices to find a while-program to compute the **T**-minimization function $\mu_{\mathbf{T}} g$ of $g \in \mathbf{PR}(\mathbf{T})$, since by definition the class $\mathbf{R_{\underline{N}}}(\mathbf{T})$ includes $\mathbf{PR}(\mathbf{T})$ and closed under composition. But it is easy; the following while-program over **T** clearly computes the function $\mu_{\mathbf{T}} g$.

> input($\boldsymbol{x}$);
> $y :=$ nil;
> while $g(\boldsymbol{x}, y) \neq$ nil do $[y := $ next$(y)]$;
> output(y)

To see $\supseteq$, all we need is to show that for each $g \in \mathbf{PR}(\mathbf{T})$ the **N**-minimization function $\mu_{\underline{\mathbf{N}}} g$ belongs to $\mathbf{R}(\mathbf{T})$. For the purpose, we define a new function

$$g'(\boldsymbol{t}, t) = \begin{cases} g(\boldsymbol{t}, t) & \text{if } t \in \mathbf{N}, \\ g(\boldsymbol{t}, \text{nil}) & \text{otherwise,} \end{cases}$$

and note the equivalence

$$(\mu_{\underline{\mathbf{N}}} g)(\boldsymbol{t}) = t \iff (\mu_{\mathbf{T}} g')(\boldsymbol{t}) = t.$$

This means $\mu_{\underline{\mathbf{N}}} g = \mu_{\mathbf{T}} g' \in \mathbf{R}(\mathbf{T})$, since $g'(\boldsymbol{t}, t) = \text{if}(\underline{\mathbf{N}}?(t), g(\boldsymbol{t}, t), g(\boldsymbol{t}, \text{nil}))$, which belongs to $\mathbf{PR}(\mathbf{T})$ by Examples 2.2.3.   □

It is shown in [3] that a tree function belongs to $\mathbf{R}(\mathbf{T}) = \mathbf{R_{\underline{N}}}(\mathbf{T}) = \{f_\nu | f \in \mathbf{R}(\mathbf{N})\} = \{f_P | P$ is a while-program $\}$ if and only if it is representable by (type-free) λ-calculus. Due to space limitation, we omit the details.

4 Choice of Coding Functions

In this section, we study how the choice of coding function $\nu : \mathbf{T} \to \mathbf{N}$ affects the class $\{f_\nu | f \in \mathbf{PR}(\mathbf{N})\}$ of conjugates of primitive recursive numeric functions, and the class $\{f_\nu | f \in \mathbf{R}(\mathbf{N})\}$ of conjugates of recursive numeric functions. The proof idea in the first half of this section (4.1 - 4.3) is originally due to [2] Chapter III.

4.1 Lemma   Suppose $a : \mathbf{N} \to \mathbf{N}$ and $b : \mathbf{T} \to \mathbf{T}$ are bijections. Then

1. If $\mathsf{suc}_a = a^{-1} \circ \mathsf{suc} \circ a \in \mathbf{PR}(\mathbf{N})$, then $a^{-1} \in \mathbf{PR}(\mathbf{N})$,
2. If $\mathsf{cons}_b = b^{-1} \circ \mathsf{cons} \circ b \in \mathbf{PR}(\mathbf{T})$, then $b^{-1} \in \mathbf{PR}(\mathbf{T})$.

Proof In the second case, the function b^{-1} can be defined by primitive recursion as

$$b^{-1}(\mathsf{cons}(t', t'')) = (b^{-1} \circ \mathsf{cons} \circ b)(b^{-1}(t'), b^{-1}(t'')).$$

The first case is similar. □

4.2 Lemma Suppose $a : \mathbf{N} \to \mathbf{N}$ and $b : \mathbf{T} \to \mathbf{T}$ are bijections. Then

1. $a^{-1} \circ \mathbf{PR}(\mathbf{N}) \circ a = \mathbf{PR}(\mathbf{N}) \iff a, a^{-1} \in \mathbf{PR}(\mathbf{N})$,
2. $b^{-1} \circ \mathbf{PR}(\mathbf{T}) \circ b = \mathbf{PR}(\mathbf{T}) \iff b, b^{-1} \in \mathbf{PR}(\mathbf{T})$.

Here we write $a^{-1} \circ \mathbf{PR}(\mathbf{N}) \circ a$ for the set $\{a^{-1} \circ g \circ a | g \in \mathbf{PR}(\mathbf{N})\}$, and similarly for $b^{-1} \circ \mathbf{PR}(\mathbf{T}) \circ b$.

Proof For the direction $\Rightarrow$ of the second case, since the condition implies $\mathsf{cons}_b = b^{-1} \circ \mathsf{cons} \circ b \in \mathbf{PR}(\mathbf{T})$, we know $b^{-1} \in \mathbf{PR}(\mathbf{T})$ from Lemma 4.1.2. Since the condition can be stated as $b \circ \mathbf{PR}(\mathbf{T}) \circ b^{-1} = \mathbf{PR}(\mathbf{T})$, we also have $b \in \mathbf{PR}(\mathbf{T})$. For the direction $\Leftarrow$, the assumption $b, b^{-1} \in \mathbf{PR}(\mathbf{T})$ implies

$$b \circ \mathbf{PR}(\mathbf{T}) \circ b^{-1} \subseteq \mathbf{PR}(\mathbf{T}) \quad \text{and} \quad b^{-1} \circ \mathbf{PR}(\mathbf{T}) \circ b \subseteq \mathbf{PR}(\mathbf{T}),$$

from which we obtain $\mathbf{PR}(\mathbf{T}) \subseteq b^{-1} \circ \mathbf{PR}(\mathbf{T}) \circ b \subseteq \mathbf{PR}(\mathbf{T})$. The first case is similar. □

Based on these facts, we show a necessary and sufficient condition for a coding function $\nu' : \mathbf{T} \to \mathbf{N}$ to satisfy $\{f_{\nu'} | f \in \mathbf{PR}(\mathbf{N})\} = (\nu')^{-1} \circ \mathbf{PR}(\mathbf{N}) \circ \nu' = \mathbf{PR}(\mathbf{T})$ (cf. Theorem 2.8).

4.3 Theorem For any bijection $\nu' : \mathbf{T} \to \mathbf{N}$, the following conditions are equivalent.

1. $(\nu')^{-1} \circ \mathbf{PR}(\mathbf{N}) \circ \nu' = \mathbf{PR}(\mathbf{T})$.
2. $\mathsf{cons}_{(\nu')^{-1}} = \nu' \circ \mathsf{cons} \circ (\nu')^{-1} \in \mathbf{PR}(\mathbf{N})$, and $\mathsf{suc}_{\nu'} = (\nu')^{-1} \circ \mathsf{suc} \circ \nu' \in \mathbf{PR}(\mathbf{T})$.

Proof The direction $1 \Rightarrow 2$ is obvious. To see the direction $2 \Rightarrow 1$, suppose $\nu' : \mathbf{T} \to \mathbf{N}$ satisfies the condition 2. Then

$$\nu^{-1} \circ \nu' \circ \mathsf{cons} \circ (\nu')^{-1} \circ \nu \in \nu^{-1} \circ \mathbf{PR}(\mathbf{N}) \circ \nu = \mathbf{PR}(\mathbf{T})$$

because the standard coding function $\nu : \mathbf{T} \to \mathbf{N}$ satisfies 1. Now, since $\nu^{-1} \circ \nu' = ((\nu')^{-1} \circ \nu)^{-1}$, we know $\nu^{-1} \circ \nu' \in \mathbf{PR}(\mathbf{T})$ from Lemma 4.1.2. Similarly, since

$$\nu \circ (\nu')^{-1} \circ \mathsf{suc} \circ \nu' \circ \nu^{-1} \in \nu \circ \mathbf{PR}(\mathbf{T}) \circ \nu^{-1} = \mathbf{PR}(\mathbf{N}),$$

we know $\nu \circ (\nu')^{-1} \in \mathbf{PR}(\mathbf{N})$ from Lemma 4.1.1. Then it implies

$$\begin{aligned}
(\nu^{-1} \circ \nu')^{-1} &= (\nu')^{-1} \circ \nu \\
&= \nu^{-1} \circ (\nu \circ (\nu')^{-1}) \circ \nu \\
&\in \nu^{-1} \circ \mathbf{PR}(\mathbf{N}) \circ \nu = \mathbf{PR}(\mathbf{T}).
\end{aligned}$$

Thus we have $(\nu^{-1} \circ \nu')$, $(\nu^{-1} \circ \nu')^{-1} \in \mathbf{PR}(\mathbf{T})$. Hence

$$\begin{aligned}
\mathbf{PR}(\mathbf{T}) &= (\nu^{-1} \circ \nu')^{-1} \circ \mathbf{PR}(\mathbf{T}) \circ (\nu^{-1} \circ \nu') \quad \text{by Lemma 4.2.2} \\
&= (\nu')^{-1} \circ (\nu \circ \mathbf{PR}(\mathbf{T}) \circ \nu^{-1}) \circ \nu' \\
&= (\nu')^{-1} \circ \mathbf{PR}(\mathbf{N}) \circ \nu' \qquad\qquad \text{by Theorem 2.8.}
\end{aligned}$$

This completes the proof.   □

Next we show that under the condition of Theorem 4.3, the choice of coding function does not affect the notion of recursive functions over $\mathbf{T}$. More precisely, $\{f_{\nu'} | f \in \mathbf{PR}(\mathbf{N})\} = \mathbf{PR}(\mathbf{T})$ implies $\{f_{\nu'} | f \in \mathbf{R}(\mathbf{N})\} = \mathbf{R}'(\mathbf{T}) = \mathbf{R}(\mathbf{T})$. Here $\mathbf{R}'(\mathbf{T})$ is defined as $\mathbf{R}(\mathbf{T})$ except that the minimization operator $\mu_{\mathbf{T}}$ in the definition of $\mathbf{R}(\mathbf{T})$ is now replaced with $\mu'_{\mathbf{T}}$, which is defined by

$$(\mu'_{\mathbf{T}} f)(t) = t \iff \forall s \preceq' t[f(t, s) = \mathsf{nil} \iff s = t]$$

where $\preceq'$ is the total order in $\mathbf{T}$ induced by ν'; i.e.,

$$s \preceq' t \iff \nu'(s) \leq \nu'(t).$$

First we note that proofs in previous sections (in particular, those for Lemmas 2.5, 3.4, 3.7 and Theorems 3.8) can be carried out as before even if we replace with any bijection ν' satisfying the condition of Theorem 4.3. Thus for example we obtain

4.4 Lemma   Under the condition of Theorem 4.3, the function $\theta' : \mathbf{T} \to \mathbf{T}$ defined by $\theta'(t) = \underline{\nu'(t)}$ satisfies the following:

- $\theta' \in \mathbf{PR}(\mathbf{T})$.
- θ' gives an isomorphism between $(\mathbf{T}, \preceq')$ and $(\underline{\mathbf{N}}, \leq)$.
- There exists a function $g : \mathbf{T} \to \mathbf{T}$ in $\mathbf{PR}(\mathbf{T})$ such that

$$\forall t \in \mathbf{T}, \forall n \in \mathbf{N}[\theta(t) = \underline{n} \iff t = g(\underline{n})].$$

4.5 Theorem   Under the condition of Theorem 4.3,

$$\{f_{\nu'} | f \in \mathbf{PR}(\mathbf{N})\} = \mathbf{R}_{\underline{\mathbf{N}}}(\mathbf{T}) = \{f_P | P \text{ is a while-program}\}.$$

Based on these facts, we can prove the following counterpart of Theorem 3.9 by slightly modifying the previous reasoning.

4.6 Theorem   Under the condition of Theorem 4.3, $\mathbf{R'(T)} = \mathbf{R_{\underline{N}}(T)}$.

Proof   The inclusion $\subseteq$ can be verified as before except that the while-program to compute $\mu_{\mathbf{T}}g$ is now replaced with the following while-program to compute $\mu'_{\mathbf{T}}g$;

$$
\begin{aligned}
&\text{input}(\boldsymbol{x}); \\
&y := \text{nil}'; \\
&\text{while } g(\boldsymbol{x}, y) \neq \text{nil do } [y := \text{next}'(y)]; \\
&\text{output}(y)
\end{aligned}
$$

Here we define $\text{nil}' = \tau'(0)$ and $\text{next}' = \text{suc}_{\nu'} = \tau' \circ \text{suc} \circ \nu'$ where $\tau' = (\nu')^{-1}$.

To see the converse, as before all we need is to show that for any $g : \mathbf{T}^{n+1} \to \mathbf{T}$ in $\mathbf{PR(T)}$ the minimization function $\mu_{\underline{N}}g : \mathbf{T}^n \rightharpoonup \mathbf{T}$ belongs to $\mathbf{R'(T)}$. For the purpose, define g' by $g'(\boldsymbol{t}, t) = g(\boldsymbol{t}, \theta'(t))$, so that $g'(\boldsymbol{t}, \tau'(n)) = g(\boldsymbol{t}, \underline{n})$. Then

$$
\begin{aligned}
(\mu_{\underline{N}}g)(\boldsymbol{t}) = s &\iff s = \min\{n | g(\boldsymbol{t}, \underline{n}) = \text{nil}\} \\
&\iff s = \overline{\nu'(\min\{s' \in (\mathbf{T}, \preceq') \mid g'(\boldsymbol{t}, s') = \text{nil}\})} \\
&= \overline{\theta'((\mu'_{\mathbf{T}}g')(\boldsymbol{t}))}.
\end{aligned}
$$

Thus we have $\mu_{\underline{N}}g = \theta' \circ (\mu'_{\mathbf{T}}g') \in \mathbf{R'(T)}$ since $\theta', g' \in \mathbf{PR(T)}$.   □

4.7 Corollary   For a bijection $\nu' : \mathbf{T} \to \mathbf{N}$ and its inverse $\tau' : \mathbf{N} \to \mathbf{T}$, the following conditions are equivalent.

1. $\text{cons}_{\tau'} \in \mathbf{PR(N)}$ and $\text{suc}_{\nu'} \in \mathbf{PR(T)}$.
2. $\{f_{\nu'} | f \in \mathbf{PR(N)}\} = \mathbf{PR(T)}$.
3. $\{f_{\nu'} | f \in \mathbf{PR(N)}\} = \mathbf{PR(T)}$, and
   $\{f_{\nu'} | f \in \mathbf{R(N)}\} = \mathbf{R'(T)} = \mathbf{R(T)} = \mathbf{R_{\underline{N}}(T)} = \{f_P | P \text{ is a while-program}\}$.

Proof   Immediate from Theorems 4.3, 4.5 and 4.6,   □

References

[1] W. S. Brainerd and L. H. Landweber (1974). *Theory of Computation*, John Wiley & Sons.

[2] S. Eilenberg and C. C. Elgot (1970). *Recursiveness*, Academic Press.

[3] M. Kimoto (2000). *On Computability of Functions over Binary Trees*, Master Thesis, Department of Mathematical and Computing Sciences, Tokyo Institute of Technology.

[4] D. E. Knuth (1973). *The Art of Computer Programming*, Vol.1 – Fundamental Algorithms, Addison Wesley.

[5] H. E. Rose (1984). *Subrecursion – Functions and Hierarchies*, Clarendon Press, Oxford.

[6] M. Takahashi (1998). A primer on proofs and types, *Theories of Types and Proofs*, MSJ-Memoirs Vol.2 (M.Takahashi, M.Okada, and M.Dezani, eds., Mathematical Society of Japan), pp.1 - 44.

[7] M. Takahashi (to appear). Lambda-representable functions over term algebras, *International Journal of Foundations of Computer Science*.

[8] J.V.Tucker and J.I.Zucker (to appear). Computable functions and semicomputable sets on many-sorted algebras, *Handbook of Logic in Computer Science*, Vol.5 (S.Abramsky, D.M.Gabbay and T.S.E.Maibaum, eds., Oxford University Press).

Sharpening the Undecidability of
Interval Temporal Logic

Kamal Lodaya

Institute of Mathematical Sciences,
C.I.T. Campus, Taramani, Chennai 600 113, India
Email: *kamal@imsc.ernet.in*

1 Motivation and results

Interval temporal logics (ITLs) were introduced in the philosophy of time (see [Ben95] for a survey) but have proved useful in artificial intelligence and computer science [All83, HMM83, HS91, ZHR91]. They provide a rich specification language for systems working with dense time (for example, [RRM93]). By now, there is a whole menagerie of ITLs. In this paper, we work with the simplest (propositional) ITLs and discuss their decidability.

Let T be a set linearly ordered by $\geq$. An interval $[a, b]$ is defined as usual for $a, b \in T$, $b \geq a$.

Formulas of the basic propositional Interval Temporal Logic C build on a countable collection of propositions by closing under the logical connectives $\neg$, $\vee$ and $\frown$ ("chop"). The other Boolean connectives are defined as usual. We identify a special proposition ℓ_0 which we will use to mark intervals $[a, a]$ consisting of one point [Ven91]. To be more precise, the logic can be called C_0 [LR00] but in this paper we use the simpler notation.

Given a proposition p, a valuation $\mathcal{V}$ assigns intervals on which it is true, subject to the condition that the special proposition ℓ_0 is made true exactly on point intervals of the form $[a, a]$. A model is a pair $\mathcal{M} = ((T, \geq), \mathcal{V})$.

A formula is assigned truth value inductively, the only nontrivial case being for the "chop" operator:

- $\mathcal{M}, [a, b] \models p$ iff $[a, b] \in \mathcal{V}(p)$,

J. He and M. Sato (Eds.): ASIAN 2000, LNCS 1961, pp. 290–298, 2000.

- $\mathcal{M}, [a, b] \models \phi \vee \psi$ iff $\mathcal{M}, [a, b] \models \phi$ or $\mathcal{M}, [a, b] \models \psi$,
- $\mathcal{M}, [a, b] \models \phi^\frown\psi$ iff $\mathcal{M}, [a, m] \models \phi$ and $\mathcal{M}, [m, b] \models \psi$, for some m such that $b \geq m \geq a$.

An example formula is $\neg\ell_0{}^\frown\phi^\frown\neg\ell_0$, which we denote <D>$\phi$. It says that ϕ holds somewhere within an interval. Its dual [D]ϕ is $\neg$<D>$\neg\phi$. Similarly <B>ϕ and <E>ϕ are defined to be $\phi^\frown\neg\ell_0$ and $\neg\ell_0{}^\frown\phi$ respectively, and they specify assertions holding in a "beginning" or "ending" interval. As an aside, note that the proposition ℓ_0 can be defined as [B]false.

As an example of a formula not definable in C, we mention <A>ϕ, which holds in an interval $[a, b]$ if ϕ holds in a "neighbouring" interval $[b, c]$ for some c.

These formulas come from a pioneering paper by Halpern and Shoham [HS91] which studied decidability questions of ITLs. This paper sharpens their results.

Instead of the binary "chop" modality, Halpern and Shoham consider the logic HS with the three unary modalities <B>, <E> and <A>. Observe that <D>ϕ is definable in HS as <B><E>ϕ. Venema's paper [Ven90] shows that chop is not definable in HS. The logic having the chop modality as well as the three unary modalities is called CDT [Ven91].

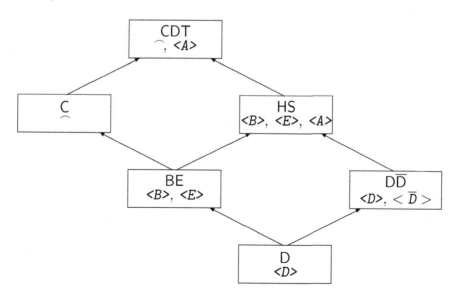

We will also be interested in two sublogics BE and $D\overline{D}$ of HS. BE only has the modalities <B> and <E> and is also a sublogic of C. $D\overline{D}$ has the two modalities <D> and $< \overline{D} >$, where $< \overline{D} > \phi$ holds if ϕ is true in an interval *of which* the current interval is a subinterval (a kind of "mirror image" of <D>). We also define D to have the single modality <D>.

Halpern and Shoham [HS91] showed that the logic HS (and therefore CDT) is undecidable on many reasonable kinds of ordered structures (including the natural numbers and the reals), and raised the question of decidability of BE and $D\overline{D}$. The decidability of the logic C has also remained open.

In this paper, we show that BE (and therefore C) is undecidable. Specifically, validity is r.e.-hard. We expect that $D\overline{D}$ can also be shown undecidable by a refinement of the Halpern-Shoham argument, similar to the one below. On the other hand, the logic D should be decidable.

We do not claim a great deal of originality for our proof, which closely follows Halpern and Shoham [HS91]. They reduce the non-halting problem of a Turing machine on a blank tape to the satisfiability problem of HS. Looking at their proof, we see that most of it is carried out in the BE sublogic. Our aim is to convert the remaining part to BE.

Our proof shows that satisfiability is undecidable over the ordinal $\omega + 1$ — equivalently, over the natural numbers when intervals of the form $[a, \infty)$ are allowed. This is in contrast to monadic second-order logic MSO[<], which Büchi showed to be decidable (in fact, over all countable ordinals). Our results show that a translation of formulas from the logic into MSO *à la* [Pan95, Rab98] will not work for the entire class of valuations.

The logic HS was shown to have a complete axiomatization by Venema [Ven90]. In [Ven91], Venema showed that CDT is also complete. In a forthcoming paper, we report on the axiomatization of BE and C [LR00].

Related work

Many papers provide decidability results for ITL and Duration Calculus (or DC, an extension of ITL). The reason they are able to do this is because they work with models where the valuation function is restricted from being so wild as to assign an arbitrary set of intervals for a proposition.

For instance, much of the DC literature [ZHR91, ZHS93] interprets a proposition's being true in an interval as holding *almost everywhere* [Bur82], that is, "most" subintervals of this interval must also make it true. We call models with such valuations **ae-models**. Zhou, Hansen and Sestoft encoded a proposition as a string of formulas and then used regular language techniques to prove decidability of DC on ae-models [ZHS93].

Pandya [Pan95] works with an interesting variation where the valuation for propositions only needs to be provided for point intervals. We call these **pi-models**. Pandya shows decidability of DC (and extensions of it) on pi-models [Pan95] by embedding the logic into the monadic second-order logic of order MSO[<].

Another class considered is that of *finitely varying* models, where a proposition can only change value finitely many times during any finite interval [ZHR91]. We call these **fv-models**. (For instance, all models over a discrete time line fall into this class.) Rabinovich shows decidability on fv-models [Rab98], again by translation into MSO[<].

Like Halpern and Shoham, we are working on models where the valuation is unrestricted, hence none of these decidability results apply.

Acknowledgements

Paritosh Pandya suggested to us that the logic C may be undecidable over dense time. Suman Roy worked on some of the ideas in this paper. I thank both of them for discussion.

2   The undecidability proof

Idea

Halpern and Shoham represent a Turing machine computation as an infinite sequence of IDs (instantaneous descriptions, which are sometimes also called configurations of the machine). In specifying this sequence, they use the <A> modality.

Each ID is a finite sequence of tape cells containing a unique tape symbol, and one of the cells has additional information representing the head position and state of the machine.

The most ingenious part of Halpern and Shoham's construction lies in using a proposition *corr* ("corresponds") which makes it possible to talk about consecutive IDs. For instance, *corr* would be true of an interval which begins with the 1936th tape cell of an ID and ends with the 1936th tape cell of the next ID. Again, this requires using an <A> modality.

Once this is done, the transition function δ of the Turing machine can be respected by examining a group of three cells in an ID and determining the value of the same three cells in the next ID.

Our aim is to do the coding within BE, i.e. to eliminate the use of the <A> modality. We achieve this by treating the entire infinite computation as being inside a dense interval $[a, b]$. Now the <D> modality can be used to talk about consecutive IDs, sequences, etc.

Details

Our claim is that the formula *computation* $\land$ *comp-properties* below, parameterized by a Turing machine, is satisfiable if and only if it does not halt on a blank tape. We closely follow the proof in [HS91, 8.2]. In particular, analogues of Lemmas 8.9, 8.12 and 8.14 of that paper hold for our reduction.

We assume the TM only writes the symbols 0 and 1. Let Q be its set of states. The propositions of our language include $L = \{0, 1, (q, 0), (q, 1), (q, B) \mid q \in Q\}$. There are also other propositions like *cell*, *ID* etc, which we describe below.

The formula *comp-properties* enforces properties that an interval $[a, b]$ where the proposition *computation* holds must satisfy. Assume such an $[a, b] \models computation$.

comp-properties = computation ⊃
    not-contains(computation) ∧
    seq(ID) ∧ seq(ID)-properties ∧
    <B>init-ID ∧ ID-properties ∧
    cell-properties ∧ seq(cell)-properties ∧
    corr-properties ∧ obeys-δ

First, we have a generic specification that an interval does not contain a subinterval satisfying a particular proposition. For the formula above, this will show that no proper subinterval of $[a, b]$ will have *computation* true.

not-contains(x) = ¬<B>x ∧ ¬<D>x ∧ ¬<E>x

Now we encode generic sequences using the chop operator. Hence we are outside **BE**, but we will show how to eliminate the chops later.

seq(x)-properties = [D] (seq(x) ⊃ x ⌢ seq(x)) ∧
    [D] (x ⊃ ¬ seq(x))

comp-properties now shows that $[a, b] \models ID\frown seq(ID)$, and by repeated application, $[a, b] \models ID\frown ID\frown \ldots$ (that is, an infinite sequence of IDs). The same trick works for IDs, showing it to be an infinite sequence of cells, additionally requiring that it contains a unique cell containing a state.

ID-properties = [D] (ID ⊃ not-contains(ID) ∧ seq(cell) ∧ one-state)
one-state = <D>state ∧ ¬ <D>(<B>state ∧ <E>state)

Some special IDs are abbreviated:

init-ID = ID ∧ [D] ((cell ⊃ blank) ∧ (state ⊃ init-state))

The properties of a cell are described below. We also abbreviate some special cells.

cell-properties = [D] (cell ⊃ not-contains(cell) ∧ unique-val)
unique-val = $\bigvee_{l \in L} l \land \bigwedge_{l \neq m} (l \supset \neg m)$
cell(l) = cell ∧l
state = $\bigvee_{l=(q,i)\in L}$ cell(l)

$$\text{init-state} = \bigvee_{l=(q_0,i)\in L} \text{cell}(l)$$

$$\text{blank} = \text{cell}(B) \vee \bigvee_{l=(q,B)\in L} \text{cell}(l)$$

Now we come to Halpern and Shoham's ingenious *corr* proposition. It is true of an interval if and only if it starts and ends with a cell, and these cells are corresponding cells in consecutive IDs.

corr-properties = [D](cell-rule ∧ ID-rule ∧ corr-starts ∧ corr-ends
$$\wedge \ (\text{corr} \supset \text{not-contains}(\text{corr})))$$
cell-rule = corr ⊃ (<B>cell ∧ <E>cell)
corr-starts = (<B>cell ∧ <E>corr) ⊃ <B>corr
corr-ends = (<E>cell ∧ <B>corr) ⊃ <E>corr
ID-rule = ID ⌢ cell ⊃ corr

The last two formulas above are simpler than in [HS91] because we are only concerned with an infinite computation.

Finally, the transition function is respected by examining a group of three cells and determining the value of the middle state in the next ID. Here is our formulation of Halpern and Shoham:

3-cell(x,y,z) = cell(x) ⌢ cell(y) ⌢ cell(z)
$$\text{obeys-}\delta = \bigwedge_{i,j,k\in L} \text{[D]}(\ \text{<B>corr} \wedge \text{<B>3-cell(i,j,k)} \supset$$
$$\text{<B>}(\text{corr} \ \frown \ \text{cell}(\delta(i,j,k))))$$

As stated earlier, the formula *computation*∧*comp-properties* will encode a Turing machine.

Undecidability of BE

Now we have undecidability of C, but to prove that of BE we have to replace occurrences of chop by operators definable within BE. First of all, we can rewrite our sequencing operation:

seq(x)-properties = [D] (seq(x) ⊃ <B>x ∧ [E] (x ⊃ seq(x)) ∧
$$\text{[D]} (x \supset \neg \ \text{seq(x)})$$

The 3-*cell* formula was already written by Halpern and Shoham in BE, as also a 2-*cell* formula which we will require later:

$$3\text{-cell}(x,y,z) = \texttt{<B>}\text{cell}(x) \wedge \texttt{<D>}\text{cell}(y) \wedge \texttt{<E>}\text{cell}(z)$$
$$\wedge \ \texttt{[D]}(\text{cell} \supset \text{cell}(y))$$
$$3\text{-cell} = \bigvee_{x,y,z} 3\text{-cell}(x,y,z)$$
$$2\text{-cell} = \texttt{<B>}\text{cell} \wedge \texttt{<E>}\text{cell} \wedge \texttt{[D]} \neg \text{cell}$$

We modify the interpretation of *corr* slightly: it holds if and only if it starts and ends with a cell, and the ending cell is the successor of the cell corresponding to the starting cell in the next ID. Now we can define the transition relation within BE. Our trick requires a modification of *ID-rule* as well:

$$\text{ID-rule} = (\texttt{<B>}\text{ID} \wedge \texttt{<E>}2\text{-cell} \wedge \texttt{[E]} \neg \ 3\text{-cell}) \supset \text{corr}$$
$$\text{obeys-}\delta = \bigwedge_{i,j,k \in L} \texttt{[D]}(\ \texttt{<B>}\text{corr} \wedge \texttt{<B>}3\text{-cell}(i,j,k) \supset$$
$$\texttt{<E>}(\text{cell}(\delta(i,j,k))))$$

Undecidability over $\omega + 1$

We have used a simpler argument than Halpern and Shoham's, representing each ID as an interval containing an infinite sequence of tape cells, and the computation as an infinite sequence of IDs. So our proof shows that satisfiability is undecidable over the ordinal ω^2.

On the other hand, Halpern and Shoham use *markers* of two kinds: cell-markers separating consecutive cells and ID-markers separating consecutive IDs. This means that the entire computation can be represented as a single infinite sequence with each cell/ID delimited by the appropriate kind of marker.

It is not difficult to add this level of detail to our proof. Notice that our initial interval $[a, b]$, which satisfies the proposition *computation*, has to have inside it the entire computation, hence the point b must be *after* the computation. Hence we obtain undecidability of BE over $\omega + 1$. The same effect may be achieved if we work over the natural numbers by allowing intervals of the form $[a, \infty)$.

References

[All83]   J.F. Allen. Maintaining knowledge about temporal intervals, *Commun. ACM* 26,11 (Nov 1983) 832–843.

[Ben95]   J. van Benthem. Temporal logic, in D.M. Gabbay, C. Hogger and J.A. Robinson (eds), *Handbook of logic in artificial intelligence and logic programming* IV (Oxford, 1995) 241–350.

[Bur82]   J.P. Burgess. Axioms for tense logic II: time periods, *Notre Dame J.FL* 23,4 (Oct 1982) 375–383.

[Dut95]   B. Dutertre. On first order interval temporal logic, Tech Report, Royal Holloway College, University of London (1995), `http://www.csl.sri.com/~bruno/publis/TR-CSD-94-3.ps.gz`. [Also in *Proc. 10th LICS* (1995).]

[HMM83]   J.Y. Halpern, Z. Manna and B. Moszkowski. A hardware semantics based on temporal intervals, *Proc. ICALP, LNCS* 154 (1983) 278–291.

[HS91]   J.Y. Halpern and Y. Shoham. A propositional modal logic of time intervals, *J. ACM* 38,4 (Oct 1991) 935–962.

[LR00]   K. Lodaya and S. Roy. Lines, a while and intervals, presented at the *Workshop on Many-dimensional logical systems, ESSLLI '00*, Birmingham (2000).

[Pan95]   P.K. Pandya. Some extensions to propositional mean-value calculus: expressiveness and decidability, *Proc. CSL, LNCS* 1092 (1995) 434–451.

[Rab98]   A. Rabinovich. On the decidability of continuous time specification formalisms, *J. Logic Comput.* 8,5 (1998) 669–678.

[RP86]   R. Rosner and A. Pnueli. A choppy logic, *Proc. 1st LICS* (1986) 306–313.

[RRM93]   A.P. Ravn, H. Rischel and K.M. Hansen. Specifying and verifying requirements of real-time systems, *IEEE Trans. Softw. Engg.* 19,1 (Jan 1993) 41–55.

[Ven90]   Y. Venema. Expressiveness and completeness of an interval tense logic, *Notre Dame J.FL* 31,4 (1990) 529–547.

[Ven91]   Y. Venema. A modal logic for chopping intervals, *J. Logic Comput.* 1,4 (1991) 453–476.

[ZHR91]   Zhou C., C.A.R. Hoare and A. Ravn. A calculus of durations, *IPL* 40,5 (Dec 1991) 269–276.

[ZHS93]   Zhou C., M.R. Hansen and P. Sestoft. Decidability and undecidability results for duration calculus, *Proc. STACS, LNCS* 665 (1993) 58–68.

Author Index

Lecture Notes in Computer Science

For information about Vols. 1–1893
please contact your bookseller or Springer-Verlag

Vol. 1927: P. Thomas, H.W. Gellersen, (Eds.), Handheld and Ubiquitous Computing. Proceedings, 2000. X, 249 pages. 2000.

Vol. 1928: U. Brandes, D. Wagner (Eds.), Graph-Theoretic Concepts in Computer Science. Proceedings, 2000. X, 315 pages. 2000.

Vol. 1929: R. Laurini (Ed.), Advances in Visual Information Systems. Proceedings, 2000. XII, 542 pages. 2000.

Vol. 1931: E. Horlait (Ed.), Mobile Agents for Telecommunication Applications. Proceedings, 2000. IX, 271 pages. 2000.

Vol. 1658: J. Baumann, Mobile Agents: Control Algorithms. XIX, 161 pages. 2000.

Vol. 1756: G. Ruhe, F. Bomarius (Eds.), Learning Software Organization. Proceedings, 1999. VIII, 226 pages. 2000.

Vol. 1766: M. Jazayeri, R.G.K. Loos, D.R. Musser (Eds.), Generic Programming. Proceedings, 1998. X, 269 pages. 2000.

Vol. 1791: D. Fensel, Problem-Solving Methods. XII, 153 pages. 2000. (Subseries LNAI).

Vol. 1799: K. Czarnecki, U.W. Eisenecker, Generative and Component-Based Software Engineering. Proceedings, 1999. VIII, 225 pages. 2000.

Vol. 1812: J. Wyatt, J. Demiris (Eds.), Advances in Robot Learning. Proceedings, 1999. VII, 165 pages. 2000. (Subseries LNAI).

Vol. 1932: Z.W. Raś, S. Ohsuga (Eds.), Foundations of Intelligent Systems. Proceedings, 2000. XII, 646 pages. (Subseries LNAI).

Vol. 1933: R.W. Brause, E. Hanisch (Eds.), Medical Data Analysis. Proceedings, 2000. XI, 316 pages. 2000.

Vol. 1934: J.S. White (Ed.), Envisioning Machine Translation in the Information Future. Proceedings, 2000. XV, 254 pages. 2000. (Subseries LNAI).

Vol. 1935: S.L. Delp, A.M. DiGioia, B. Jaramaz (Eds.), Medical Image Computing and Computer-Assisted Intervention – MICCAI 2000. Proceedings, 2000. XXV, 1250 pages. 2000.

Vol. 1937: R. Dieng, O. Corby (Eds.), Knowledge Engineering and Knowledge Management. Proceedings, 2000. XIII, 457 pages. 2000. (Subseries LNAI).

Vol. 1938: S. Rao, K.I. Sletta (Eds.), Next Generation Networks. Proceedings, 2000. XI, 392 pages. 2000.

Vol. 1939: A. Evans, S. Kent, B. Selic (Eds.), «UML» – The Unified Modeling Language. Proceedings, 2000. XIV, 572 pages. 2000.

Vol. 1940: M. Valero, K. Joe, M. Kitsuregawa, H. Tanaka (Eds.), High Performance Computing. Proceedings, 2000. XV, 595 pages. 2000.

Vol. 1941: A.K. Chhabra, D. Dori (Eds.), Graphics Recognition. Proceedings, 1999. XI, 346 pages. 2000.

Vol. 1942: H. Yasuda (Ed.), Active Networks. Proceedings, 2000. XI, 424 pages. 2000.

Vol. 1943: F. Koornneef, M. van der Meulen (Eds.), Computer Safety, Reliability and Security. Proceedings, 2000. X, 432 pages. 2000.

Vol. 1945: W. Grieskamp, T. Santen, B. Stoddart (Eds.), Integrated Formal Methods. Proceedings, 2000. X, 441 pages. 2000.

Vol. 1948: T. Tan, Y. Shi, W. Gao (Eds.), Advances in Multimodal Interfaces – ICMI 2000. Proceedings, 2000. XVI, 678 pages. 2000.

Vol. 1952: M.C. Monard, J. Simão Sichman (Eds.), Advances in Artificial Intelligence. Proceedings, 2000. XV, 498 pages. 2000. (Subseries LNAI).

Vol. 1953: G. Borgefors, I. Nyström, G. Sanniti di Baja (Eds.), Discrete Geometry for Computer Imagery. Proceedings, 2000. XI, 544 pages. 2000.

Vol. 1954: W.A. Hunt, Jr., S.D. Johnson (Eds.), Formal Methods in Computer-Aided Design. Proceedings, 2000. XI, 539 pages. 2000.

Vol. 1955: M. Parigot, A. Voronkov (Eds.), Logic for Programming and Automated Reasoning. Proceedings, 2000. XIII, 487 pages. 2000. (Subseries LNAI).

Vol. 1960: A. Ambler, S.B. Calo, G. Kar (Eds.), Services Management in Intelligent Networks. Proceedings, 2000. X, 259 pages. 2000.

Vol. 1961: J. He, M. Sato (Eds.), Advances in Computing Science – ASIAN 2000. Proceedings, 2000. X, 299 pages. 2000.

Vol. 1963: V. Hlaváč, K.G. Jeffery, J. Wiedermann (Eds.), SOFSEM 2000: Theory and Practice of Informatics. Proceedings, 2000. XI, 460 pages. 2000.

Vol. 1966: S. Bhalla (Ed.), Databases in Networked Information Systems. Proceedings, 2000. VIII, 247 pages. 2000.

Vol. 1967: S. Arikawa, S. Morishita (Eds.), Discovery Science. Proceedings, 2000. XII, 332 pages. 2000. (Subseries LNAI).

Vol. 1968: H. Arimura, S. Jain, A. Sharma (Eds.), Algorithmic Learning Theory. Proceedings, 2000. XI, 335 pages. 2000. (Subseries LNAI).

Vol. 1969: D.T. Lee, S.-H. Teng (Eds.), Algorithms and Computation. Proceedings, 2000. XIV, 578 pages. 2000.

Vol. 1970: M. Valero, V.K. Prasanna, S. Vajapeyam (Eds.), High Performance Computing – HiPC 2000. Proceedings, 2000. XVIII, 568 pages. 2000.

Vol. 1971: R. Buyya, M. Baker (Eds.), Grid Computing – GRID 2000. Proceedings, 2000. XIV, 229 pages. 2000.

Vol. 1974: S. Kapoor, S. Prasad (Eds.), FST TCS 2000: Foundations of Software Technology and Theoretical Computer Science. Proceedings, 2000. XIII, 532 pages. 2000.

Vol. 1975: J. Pieprzyk, E. Okamoto, J. Seberry (Eds.), Information Security. Proceedings, 2000. X, 323 pages. 2000.

Vol. 1976: T. Okamoto (Ed.), Advances in Cryptology – ASIACRYPT 2000. Proceedings, 2000. XII, 630 pages. 2000.

Vol. 1977: B. Roy, E. Okamoto (Eds.), Progress in Cryptology – INDOCRYPT 2000. Proceedings, 2000. X, 295 pages. 2000.

Vol. 1983: K.S. Leung, L.-w. Chan, H. Meng (Eds.), Intelligent Data Engineering and Automated Learning – IDEAL 2000. Proceedings, 2000. XVI, 573 pages. 2000.

Vol. 1987: K.-L. Tan, M.J. Franklin, J. C.-S. Lui (Eds.), Mobile Data Management. Proceedings, 2001. XIII, 290 pages. 2001.